FRUSTRATE THEIR

Ben Pimlott is the author of *Labour and the Left in the 1930s* (1977), *Hugh Dalton* (winner of the 1985 Whitbread Biography Prize) and of the best-selling *Harold Wilson*. He teaches politics at Birkbeck College, London. He has been a columnist for several newspapers, and writes frequently for the *Guardian* and *Independent on Sunday*.

FRUSTRATE THEIR KNAVISH TRICKS

Writings on biography, history and politics

Ben Pimlott

HarperCollinsPublishers

HarperCollins*Publishers*
77–85 Fulham Palace Road,
Hammersmith, London W6 8JB

This paperback edition 1995
1 3 5 7 9 8 6 4 2

First published in Great Britain by
HarperCollins*Publishers* 1994

ISBN 0 00 638320 3

Printed in Great Britain by
HarperCollinsManufacturing Glasgow

TO
Joan and Sam

Contents

PART THREE: GHOSTS

PART FOUR: THE LAST PARTY OF KARL MARX

Preface

This book covers nearly twenty years of writing, and amounts to a personal and political notebook of the period. Many of the items relate to my own changing preoccupations. Portugal, unemployment in the North-East, the 'popular front of the mind', political biography, all reflect phases and hobby-horses.

I have resisted the temptation to apply the wisdom of hindsight: it seemed to me that to re-cook pieces for this kind of collection would be confusing, and take away much of the point. However, in a few places I have restored unused passages that had been cut. The Portugal diary (previously unpublished) has been edited down, titles of pieces have been amended, and there are other minor alterations, generally to remove overlap and repetition.

A lot of people have helped. I am especially grateful to Tony Gould, Blake Morrison, John Rentoul and Richard Gott for suggesting books for review and ideas for articles, and for their example, tolerance and friendship. I have appreciated the interest and encouragement of my publisher, Stuart Proffitt, and of my literary agent, Giles Gordon. Once again I would like to thank my immensely capable editor, Rebecca Wilson.

The biggest debt I owe is to my wife, Jean Seaton – ever my fiercest critic, and my inspiration.

BEN PIMLOTT
June 1994

Preface to the Paperback Edition

The publication of a paperback edition has given me a chance to correct a few misprints and errors of fact. I have left everything else alone, despite obvious places where, in the light of recent events, amendments might have been made.

Some of the political points seem more pressing after a few months, others less. The mid-term election disaster for the Democrats in the United States certainly takes the shine off any naïve optimism about the Clinton administration. Yet it also seems to me to reinforce the argument that the Left can only lose by echoing the Right's contempt for the state; and that state power (for all its dangers and limitations) remains the most vital means to protect, not just the poor and helpless from the oppressions of the well off, but also those J. K. Galbraith has called the 'contented majority' from the folly of their own social indifference.

In Northern Ireland, conditions have improved, in East Europe they have got worse. Meanwhile, the chances of a change of government in Westminster have grown. A couple of pieces in the book touch on this opportunity – and on the risk that it may not be seized. One essay, from the 1980s, dismisses the notion of a post-war 'consensus'. Here the temptation to add to what I wrote is especially strong, partly because of the historical debate that has taken place around this particular piece of revisionism; and partly because of an uneasy feeling that, in the mid-1990s, a consensus of a largely negative kind has developed. Indeed, it looks as if our twentieth century – an 'age of extremes' as Eric Hobsbawm has called it – may end with a whimper of agreement over market and technological panaceas, as the only escape from an otherwise terrifying bewilderment about where to go and what to do next.

BEN PIMLOTT
February 1995

PART I

Premiers and Presidents

DOMESTIC MR CHURCHILL

IN THE INSOUCIANT 1990s, caddishness is à la mode. More than twenty-one thousand people apparently telephoned the switchboard of the *Sun*, demanding to read the Camillagate tapes in full; and Alan Clark – a former Tory MP of indisputably blimpish proportions – has written a book review backing a suggestion that Winston Churchill ruined the country!

There was little surprise, and not much outrage, when the tabloids yielded to public pressure on the subject of royal sex. By contrast, the attack on Winston Churchill's reputation, triggered by John Charmley's *Churchill: The end of glory*, sparked a right royal uproar. It was as if – in this post-Cold War, Maastrichtian epoch – Churchill had become more necessary to us, not less, as a national symbol.

While Britain shrinks, the world's memory of Churchill remains big. He may, indeed, be more admired abroad than at home. Yet it is not just foreigners who almost universally think of him as the greatest Britisher of all (as well as the only one many of them have ever heard of), so do we. Churchill – 'half-American, half-drunk, pro-Soviet, pro-Zionist, pro-Liberal, pro-Labour,' as Paul Addison aptly sums him up – is in our bones. He is Britishness personified, Britishness boiled down, distilled and bottled for the heritage industry and for us Britons to toast ourselves with when we are feeling glum, as after a lost football match, or when our trade figures are so much worse than everybody else's.

But is it true, as John Betjeman once pondered, on the subject of the mystical beauty of the Virgin Birth – is it true? There is no ultimate answer to the question of whether Churchill was a hero or a knave. Nevertheless, the central place he continues to hold in our culture gives the examination of his life much more than a purely academic importance, which is why it happens so often. Martin Gilbert, the

Churchill on the Home Front 1900–1955, Paul Addison (Jonathan Cape, 1993)

official biographer, has devoted most of his career to the topic, producing thirteen huge volumes (including editions of Churchill's papers). Of many other biographical studies, Henry Pelling's single-volume life stands out for its clarity and historical grasp; meanwhile, William Manchester is two-thirds of the way through a major trilogy. Before Charmley, there had certainly been no lack of information available for anybody who wished to consider it.

If much of it has been presented in a reverential way, this is not simply because of Churchill's position in the nation's iconography. It is also because of a well-founded sense of his importance. It cannot be proved, of course, that Hitler would have defeated Britain but for Churchill, but it is undoubtedly true that many people who lived through the Second World War believed this to be the case at the time. It is with such a view, vividly recalled by veterans still living, and reflected in the newspapers, diaries, novels and poems of the period, that revisionist historians have to contend. The period of intense danger was undoubtedly brief: nineteen months at most, between May 1940 and December 1941, when America came into the war. Even before then, Churchill's popularity had waned, because of a series of setbacks and disappointments. It did not fully recover. By the time of the first Gallup Polls since the start of hostilities, conducted early in 1945, Labour was 20 per cent ahead. By-election results suggest that Churchill might not have survived any national poll fought on normal party lines from 1942 onwards.

By then, however, his place in history was assured, and even those who opposed his politics acknowledged his greatness. Ever since, it has been as if there were two, quite distinct, Churchills. One was the People's Winston – the colossus, the world statesman, the warrior, the father of his nation. This Churchill had warned about Germany in the 1930s, but did not properly come into existence until, at the age of sixty-five, he was made Prime Minister. This was the Churchill of the Battle of Britain, the Blitz and the Atlantic Charter, of boiler suits, V signs and cigars. After the war, the outline once again became hazy, because it had been defined by a negative: an enemy repelled, and a fate averted. This Churchill, however – commemorated (or caricatured) in a statue in Parliament Square – stood above the inter-party fracas. Friend and political foe alike thanked, admired and loved him.

The other Churchill has largely passed out of public memory. The second one was as easy to hate and distrust as to love, and for more than half a century was an intensely political, frequently mischievous player in the Westminster scrum. Long before Charmley, there had been a tendency for historians to treat this non-heroic politician as a failure. Churchill was in his element in the war, ran the argument, but out of his depth, even eccentric, in peacetime.

It is the important achievement of Paul Addison's outstanding and judicious study that it goes far to redress the balance, underlining the continuing role Churchill played in British affairs, and stressing that it is impossible to understand the warfaring Churchill except against such a background. Addison avoids histrionics, opting for subtle impressions rather than simple explanations. He is positively delighted when the evidence points in contradictory directions; his greatest pleasure lies in the wry paradox. Yet he is not afraid to challenge orthodox interpretations. Indeed, if Charmley's book tried to cut Churchill down to size as a war leader, Addison is no less revisionist in seeking to elevate him as a maker of domestic policy.

Churchill on the Home Front 1900–1955 is not exactly a biography. Discussion of defence and foreign affairs is reduced to a minimum, so that there is sometimes a sense of Hamlet without the Prince. The virtue of Addison's specialization, however, is that it permits a close and detailed examination, making connections across the whole of Churchill's career. A key question is whether this was no more than a picaresque adventure, with little theme. Addison emphasizes the element of pattern, tempered by an instinct for survival, a thirst for self-advancement and a desire to be in fashion. He argues that in home affairs Churchill remained all his life a somewhat self-cancelling Liberal – on the one hand, a Gladstonian believer in Free Trade, capitalism and an unfettered economy, but on the other, an uninhibited interventionist who, in accordance with pre-1914 'New Liberalism', believed that the state should ensure minimum standards for the poor. In all this, there was a large dash of aristocratic paternalism (or 'Tory Democracy' in the Churchills' family phrase). Addison shares Michael Foot's view that the man whose radio oratory moved millions 'never had the foggiest notion of how British people lived, how they earned their bread, how society functioned', and that his warmth 'rarely embraced the people except in his rhetoric'.

So was Winston ever a Thatcherite? Claiming the mantle of Churchill has been standard practice among politicians of many persuasions ever since he left the stage, if not before. For the currently fractured Conservative Party, however, the question of Churchill's true beliefs has a special piquancy. As Prime Minister in the early 1980s, Lady

Thatcher consciously (if blush-makingly) linked her Lilliputian victories in the South Atlantic to the great war leader's finest hour. Addison shows how right she was not to draw too much attention to Churchill's record at other times. He provides evidence that Churchill – fully *compos mentis* and in control of events at least until his stroke in 1953 – was 'soaking wet' (apparently the term was already in use), leading an administration made up of fellow aquatics 'for whom social harmony was a higher priority than economic efficiency'. He argues, moreover, that post-1951 policy douches were not merely a pragmatic response to social change, but harked back to ideas which Churchill had acquired before the First World War and never fully discarded. Tory apologists have tended to dismiss the early phase as youthful exuberance, the later one as soft-headed senility. Addison argues that, on the contrary, the period of aberration was what came in between.

The author shows that, even between the two World Wars, when Churchill was widely attacked as an incorrigible reactionary, much of his right-wingery was merely bluster, and that he was generally much more open-minded and conciliatory in the Cabinet Room, or in private gatherings, than on the public platform. Addison also demonstrates – and this is one of the most interesting things to come out of the book – that Churchill was at almost all times an ardent supporter of political alliances and coalitions, was happiest when more than one party was in government, and sought persistently – against the centripetal pressures of the two-party system – to bring such a state of affairs about.

If Churchill gained a reputation for extremism, this was partly because he was apt to campaign for any cause he adopted with relentless determination; and partly because his frequent changes of party (from Tory to Liberal to Constitutionalist and back to Tory) made it necessary to convince suspicious colleagues of his partisanship. 'At 35 he was more Liberal than the Liberals,' suggests Addison. 'At 55 he was on his best behaviour as a Tory.' However, the formative stage of his career was as the terrible twin to David Lloyd George in the Campbell-Bannerman/Asquith administration. It is salutary to be reminded just how left-wing Churchill was at this stage in his career. Echoing the Fabian socialists, he threw his political weight behind the concept of a safety-net welfare state, and its 'progressive elevation as the increasing energies of production permit'. Anthony Crosland was to say much the same in *The Future of Socialism* forty years later. Although Churchill denounced the socialist doctrine as 'a monstrous and imbecile conception' (this was to be an oft-repeated theme for public consumption), as Liberal President of the Board of Trade he set William Beveridge to work on a comprehensive scheme for unemployment insurance; and as Home Secretary he proposed a plan (which still looks good today) for a much-reduced House of Lords, composed of 150 members, two-thirds elected and one-third appointed.

This of course was not the whole story. If Churchill continued in some respects to look more socialist than Labour's rather stodgy MPs, he also earned the undying hatred of Welsh miners for his role in crushing the Tonypandy riots. Addison argues that his reputation as a hammer of the trade unions (reinforced during the 1926 General Strike) was not entirely fair. The important point, however, about Churchill during the last years before 1914 is that war clouds were turning his attention away from domestic affairs. As soon as war broke out, the western front took over from the home front altogether as his first concern. Here the author's approach comes a bit unstuck, because Churchill's foreign and domestic thoughts are inextricably entangled. Thus, his post-war activism against industrial militancy in Britain is inseparable from his madcap 'war of intervention' in 1919–20 against the Bolsheviks in Russia.

Addison does show, however, the extent to which the impact of Labour, and destruction of the Liberals as an electoral force, buffeted Churchill's opinions in the 1920s. After losing his seat in 1922, the former Liberal minister was faced with a stark choice: political oblivion, or joining the Tories. Naturally he opted for the second. No further explanation of his change of allegiance is needed and – argues Addison – if the rhetorical noises he began to make reflected the change of party label, who could blame him? New Liberalism went out the window; old Liberalism returned. At the Treasury from 1924, Churchill was a pre-deluge Gladstonian, 'the last orthodox Chancellor', as he himself admitted, 'of the Victorian epoch', who devastated the British economy by returning to the Gold Standard. It was scarcely a creditable episode. Meanwhile, he expressed a fervent admiration for Mussolini, informing the Duce that if he had been Italian, 'I am sure I should have been wholeheartedly with you from the start to finish in your triumphant struggle against the bestial appetites and passions of communism.'

In some ways, the 1930s were even worse. In New York during the 1929 Crash, Churchill happened to witness an auto-destructing financier flying past his fifteenth-storey window. The experience did not soften his economic approach. Addison acknowledges that Churchill during the Slump was no Roosevelt, and showed little interest in the expansionary proposals of Keynes and Lloyd George. Cold-shouldered by Baldwin and Chamberlain, and ranting on about India, to the delight of the squires and the despair of the Left, he entered his years of outsiderdom.

However, though backward-looking in some respects, Churchill was ahead of his time in others. His warnings about Hitler are well known. Less familiar, but deserving of emphasis – perhaps even more than Addison gives it in his book – is the revival of his dormant interest in cross-party arrangements and alliances. This came to nothing in the short run. But a series of feelers which began at the time of Munich, aimed at building an anti-Chamberlain coalition in the House of Commons, eventually bore fruit in wartime. Churchill's success at leading a government that included Labour ministers owed much to this pre-war episode when, on foreign matters at least, it had been possible for him to do business with the Opposition.

In Addison's best-known book, *The Road to 1945* (first published in 1975), the author made brilliant use of recently available state papers to show how political thinking evolved in the wake of the 1942 Beveridge Report, and how the report itself became a Frankenstein's monster as far as Tory ministers were concerned, increasing popular support for the pro-Beveridge, Labour wing of the coalition. In this new study, Addison shows the extent to which Churchill was himself responsible for a missed opportunity. It is hard to blame the wartime leader for refusing to be distracted from the job of beating Hitler. Nevertheless, his rearguard action against controls and rationing ('fair shares for all', as the public saw it) did him undoubted political harm.

So was he a Tory reactionary after all? Addison sees his attitude, rather, as a reassertion of the old Gladstone in him, wickedly incited by his press-baron cronies, Lord Beaverbrook and Brendan Bracken. He considers Churchill not so much as ideologically Conservative as out of touch, and quite willing to return to benign paternalism if knocked about enough by his Labour colleagues, with whom he got on remarkably well. A coalitionist to the end, he would willingly have continued the arrangement into peacetime (as would the Labour leadership), had circumstances permitted.

Churchill's infamous 'Gestapo' speech (apparently written under the influence of Hayek's *Road to Serfdom*, Lady Thatcher's favourite bedtime read), delivered during the 1945 election campaign, helped put paid to the happy fantasy of a re-formed National Government under his own leadership. To the public, the wartime hero now looked like a domestic dinosaur, and was widely talked about in the past tense. He was seventy; many expected him to retire, and it is extraordinary that his colleagues did not insist that he should do so. In fact, he showed a remarkable resilience. His post-defeat misery quickly passed: as Addison says, such bouts of depression were 'invariably the prelude to a revival of ambition'. During the next few years, he presided over, or at any rate allowed to happen, a rapid revolution in Conservative social and economic thinking which enabled his party to combine, in a heady cocktail, the popular appeals of welfarism and consumerism.

As Addison indicates, a man who wins a general election at the age of seventy-six cannot be dismissed as a wash-out. Neither can his second administration be dismissed as a failure. Undoubtedly, it shirked difficult economic decisions. Politically, however, it was triumphant, marginalizing Labour, and bequeathing to its successor a contented nation. In 1951, Churchill would have liked to include Liberals in his Government. When this proved impossible, he adopted Liberal policies instead.

In sum, it is Addison's assessment that Churchill was a non-party man, a political humanist, a Con–Lib–Labist, a consensus politician for most of his life. This, he suggests, was the real secret of Churchill's wartime success as leader of the nation. The thesis is convincing. What comes across most strongly, however, from Addison's far from hagiographical book is Churchill's unique versatility; his exceptional psychic stamina; the Himalayan vastness of his ego; and his incontestable superiority over every other twentieth-century occupant of his office.

Times Literary Supplement, 19 February 1993

CLEMENT ATTLEE

WHAT MADE CLEMENT ATTLEE TICK? The best clue to the workings of the mind of Britain's most socialist prime minister ever is contained in a few lines of doggerel verse from his own pen:

> Few thought he was even a starter
> There were many who thought themselves smarter
> But he ended PM
> CH and OM
> An earl and a knight of the garter.

The Attlee story, as Kenneth Harris shows in this fascinating and well-judged biography, was one of mediocrity transformed into unpretentious greatness. The unsolved mystery behind it is whether the ascent was mainly the product of sterling qualities and amazing luck, or of a very large dose of discreetly directed ambition.

Attlee's point of departure was not poverty or disadvantage, but failure. Contrary to myth, there was nothing ordinary about his background. His father was an extremely successful solicitor who became President of the Law Society and left £70,000 in 1908, so that none of his eight children had to worry much about making a living. This was lucky, because making a living was not something to which Clement – runt of the brood, smaller, weaker, shyer than the rest – seemed naturally suited. After Haileybury and Oxford, he read for the Bar partly for family reasons, partly because of a secret, slightly ridiculous dream of entering politics, 'for which I had a sneaking affection'. But despite good chambers and excellent connections, he earned only £50 in three years, and appeared in court on just four occasions. In this unremunerative period, Harris records, 'he lived the life of a gentleman, and a

Attlee, Kenneth Harris (Weidenfeld & Nicolson, 1982)

gentleman, in his view, was what he was and should continue to be.'

What changed his life was a casual contact with Haileybury boys' club in Stepney, a paternalistic foundation set up on muscular Christian lines to bring religion and discipline to the deserving poor. Regular visits turned into a full-scale commitment, and Attlee became general manager, giving up his unpromising legal career. What motivated him? He enjoyed the boy-scout parody of military life and the sense of communal endeavour. Though he took a humane interest in social problems, this stemmed mainly from his devotion to the club. Perhaps his main satisfaction lay in discovering his own talent for organization and leadership.

Meanwhile he had joined the Fabian Society of Sidney Webb and Bernard Shaw ('Have we got to grow a beard to join this show?') and then the Independent Labour Party. Loyalty was a key aspect of his personality. Having once chosen his team, he stuck to it. Within a couple of years, he had become a socialist enthusiast. For seven years, he was a rank-and-file activist at a time of social ferment – a middle-class, left-wing member of the bed-sit brigade.

He cut up loaves to feed dockers' children during the strike of 1911, collected money for the Irish transport workers in 1913, led parties from Stepney to gatherings of international socialists, knew 'what it is to carry a banner from Mile End Waste across central London to Hyde Park.' If there had been a Rank-and-File Co-ordinating Committee or a Campaign for Labour Party Democracy, he would certainly have been a supporter. He was a grass rootser, not a leader. This mattered later: other middle- and upper-class Labour recruits came in near the top, having made their mark outside, and without having shared on equal terms the tedious jobs involved in street corner propaganda and door-to-door agitation. Where others were prima donnas, Attlee had a worm's eye view which gave him an instinct for attitudes and reactions on the Movement's lowest rung.

But there was more to it than experience and training. There was geography, too. Attlee had a character-forming and heroic war (twice wounded, rising to major). After it, Labour began to take over from the Liberals in one working-class district after another. Attlee's political career took off on his home ground. In no time, he was LCC councillor, mayor of Stepney and then MP for Limehouse, a seat which he held even in 1931 when all but the poorest and most homogeneous of working-class constituencies were lost to the National alliance.

What might Attlee have achieved without Labour's massive 1931 defeat? He did well as a new MP – Prime Minister's PPS, then junior minister, Chancellor of the Duchy, Postmaster-General. He was a work-horse. Reliable, efficient, scrupulous, punctual, he had a combination of qualities that was rare in politics, and would probably have been enough to guarantee him, after ten or twenty years, a place in a Labour Cabinet.

But it was 1931 that made him – thrusting him to the forefront as the only possible deputy leader of the shrunken PLP, much to the anger and envy of the seatless party barons. He was forty-eight. From now on, he must have seen that 'though there were many who thought themselves smarter' there was none with a better opportunity. Four years later, the deference Labour always gives to office-holders *in situ*, plus lack of agreement among his opponents about an alternative, gave him the party leadership, a position which he was to hold for the next two decades.

No Leader of the Opposition has been more abused, nor with more justice, than Attlee in the late 1930s. In a time of massive social, economic and international problems, when vigorous attacks on a complacent Establishment were desperately needed, Attlee offered sleep-inducing speeches, dull homilies and an appearance of nervous inadequacy. 'I was interested to see Teddy Hall go head of the river,' he wrote to his brother just after the Polish guarantee in 1939. His public utterances scarcely gave a greater sense of the urgency of the times, and it was left to others in the Labour Party – Cripps, Dalton, Greenwood – to give expression to the great concerns aroused by the crisis.

Yet, as in the past, Attlee revealed a remarkable capacity for growth. The First World War had given him the confidence to become a politician. The Second developed in him the capacity to be Prime Minister. The formation of Churchill's coalition in May 1940 hoisted him into the War Cabinet, and in 1942 he became deputy premier. To the public, he remained largely unknown. The present Opposition leader should take comfort from some of Attlee's wartime ratings: in 1942, when his party was already ahead in the opinion polls, only 2 per cent of the electorate mentioned his name as their preferred candidate for Prime Minister, should something happen to Churchill.

Yet behind the scenes he was a surprisingly effective political force, rapidly learning the trade. Harris quotes an interesting letter to Churchill, written in January 1945, in which Attlee vigorously complained of 'the method or rather lack of method in dealing with matters requiring

Cabinet decisions'. The Prime Minister, he protested, often did not even bother to read notes provided for his guidance. Churchill replied huffily, 'You may be sure I shall always endeavour to profit by your counsels,' and did so.

Between 1945 and 1951 Attlee presided over the most rapid period of peacetime change this country, and perhaps the world, has ever seen. Basic industries were nationalized, the welfare state was founded, India became independent, a Jewish state was set up, and Britain began to manufacture atomic weapons. Much that happened in the direction, or acceptance, of these developments has been criticized. But could anybody have managed things better? Harris thinks not, and he is probably right.

Some aspects of Attlee's style did not change. Civil servants might praise him for making quick decisions, but (except over India) he seldom initiated. He led from behind. 'He did not interfere: he appointed and he sacked.' He ran his Government as he had run the Haileybury club, 'a few expulsions having a salutary effect'.

His secret – and here Kenneth Harris's argument is particularly convincing – was a close relationship with the Foreign Secretary, Ernest Bevin, who was also head of the Transport and General Workers' Union and the most powerful union boss in the land. 'I was very fond of him,' Attlee said simply, 'and I understand he was very fond of me.' The moral for all Labour Party leaders remains clear: with a firm union base, your position is secure. If Attlee was the most conspired against Leader of the Opposition there has ever been, he was also the subject of more plots than any other prime minister. He survived because he kept his head, judged his challengers coolly and looked to Bevin for support.

Kenneth Harris gives Attlee good marks on everything except the atom bomb and Palestine – over which, he feels, Attlee took insufficient note of Israeli passions. According to the author, Attlee was pro-Arab though 'not in the least anti-Semitic'. This particular judgement, however, is open to question. On one occasion, not recorded here, the Prime Minister excluded two promising young backbenchers from his Government partly on the grounds, as he explained to a colleague, that they belonged to 'the Chosen People'.

Harris's biography can be criticized on a number of more substantial counts. The author refers little to unpublished sources other than Attlee's own papers, his use of secondary works is not as wide-ranging as it might have been, and he relies a bit too heavily for background

material on Hugh Dalton's memoirs. On the other hand, he makes
masterly use of interviews with Attlee's family, friends and colleagues,
and of his own meetings with his subject. Some of the best chapters
describe Attlee's style of government and his family life, and there is
an extremely sensitive account of a loving marriage to a devoted, but
problematic wife:

> 'Most of our friends are Conservatives,' Vi said to the author
> once in the late 1950s. 'Clem was never really a socialist, were
> you, darling?' Attlee, sitting next to her reading *The Times*, pipe
> in mouth, made a mildly dissenting noise. 'Well, not a rabid one,'
> she said.

And that, as Kenneth Harris rightly says, was that.

New Society, 23 September 1982

CHARLES DE GAULLE

'POWERFUL PERSONALITIES, organized for conflict, crises, great events ... are usually blunt and uncompromising, without social graces. Although deep down the masses may obscurely do them justice, recognizing their superiority, they are rarely loved and in consequence rarely find an easy way to the top.'

No, the above quotation is not a self-justificatory passage from Lady Thatcher's recent memoirs. It appears in a lecture delivered by Captain Charles de Gaulle to the *École Supérieure de Guerre* in 1927 on the subject of military leadership, something of which he had no personal experience. Yet there is no doubt that he was talking about himself.

Some are born to greatness, and others are unflinchingly certain that sooner or later it will be thrust upon them. One of the themes of Charles Williams' excellent and vigorously written biography is that de Gaulle was very much in the second category. He had a sense of his own great destiny which, to any mere spectator, appeared both arrogant and ridiculous, but which – because of the certainty of the conviction – was one of his most priceless assets. 'There was never a time in my life', he told an associate after the Second World War, 'when I had any doubt that I would one day be at the head of France.' Such a belief, as Williams shows, was an absolute necessity in 1940 and the critical years thereafter, when de Gaulle effectively announced his headship to an incredulous world. Yet what is extraordinary about de Gaulle, and marks him out from others similarly called, is that he seems to have taken scarcely any interest in civilian politics as a young or even middle-aged man, and until his fiftieth year barely stepped outside the narrow – and stuffy – limits of French military life.

Digging around for childhood causes is always difficult. Williams comes up with nothing specific, though de Gaulle does seem to have

The Last Great Frenchman: A Life of General de Gaulle, Charles Williams (Little Brown, 1993)

grown up with a sense of being an outsider that married uneasily with
the fierce patriotism and conventional pieties of his background. Part
of it had to do with his startling appearance. The borderline between
grandeur – a lonely stag, on a mountain outreach – and physical ludi-
crousness (pear-shape, pixie ears, elongated hooter) was one upon
which his personality seemed to tremble dangerously throughout his
life. As a boy he was ungainly, shy, aloof, repressed – he hated to be
seen naked by others of his sex – and remained so. According to his
son, he 'did not have an amusing childhood', but it was not an unhappy
one either and (like other famous men) he was particularly close to his
mother. If he had an expectation of eventual triumph, he also had –
as he confided at the end of his life – 'the conviction that Mama would
have been behind me always and in everything'. But the harsh routines
of the Jesuits also played a part in his training, both in the inculcation
of a spartan devotion to duty and also, perhaps, of a belief in ends
justifying means.

Although there was little early distinction (de Gaulle was 119th out
of 221 entrants to the military academy of St Cyr), there were some
powerful formative experiences. Williams makes much of de Gaulle's
lucky combination in the First World War of action on the western
front, and capture (at Verdun in 1916) in time to save him for posterity.
Two frustrating years in German POW camps not only steeled and
matured him: they also provided a period of reflection (later to be
paralleled during his political exile at Colombey after the Second
World War) which helped him to get his thoughts in order. 'Prison
was his university,' suggests the author, and de Gaulle emerged from
the war with ideas about military theory which he was determined to
bring to the attention of his superiors.

The man most prepared to take on new ideas was one of France's
most celebrated, as well as unorthodox, soldiers, who also happened
to have been de Gaulle's commanding officer: Marshal Philippe Pétain.
De Gaulle became a member of Pétain's personal staff, often dined
with him, and may even have named his son Philippe after him.
(Allegedly, before the war, the two had chased the same women at
Arras.) One of the most interesting chapters describes this historically
important relationship and Williams rightly stresses the significance
(as well as the irony) of Pétain's influence.

Eventually, the relationship soured. ('Pétain was a great man,' de
Gaulle said later of his rival for the title of saviour of France. 'He died
in 1925.') De Gaulle was too much of an individualist to be loyal to

any other human being for long, and was determined to strike out on his own. As Williams reminds us, de Gaulle's historic protest in 1940 had a background in military controversy for much of the preceding decade. De Gaulle believed, and publicly argued to the fury of many colleagues, that the next war would be one of blitzkrieg and movement. When events proved him right, his bitterness was directed as much against the failure of his superiors to listen, as against those who had lost the heart to fight.

Among politicians, a rare supporter of de Gaulle was Paul Reynaud, who eventually brought him into the Government as Under-Secretary of State for War – a few days before the French defeat became absolute. Here Williams makes valuable use of some British accounts, which reveal the mixed reception, at first cautiously welcoming, that de Gaulle received in Britain as he hammered on the doors of the War Cabinet, seeking military assistance to his beleaguered country. A week after de Gaulle's appointment, Jock Colville wrote in his diary: 'There is, apparently, a young French general called de Gaulle, of whom Winston thinks a great deal.'

But de Gaulle was also, as Desmond Morton put it, 'a magnificent crook, another Max Beaverbrook', or becoming one fast: although his political experience was zero, he was picking up the tricks. According to Williams, the famous BBC broadcast that launched the Fighting French – 'l'Appel du 18 Juin' – was 'full of Jesuitical subtlety and cunning', a magnificent exercise in the art of the possible. There was also a mad vision about it that was much in the French tradition, though more that of Robespierre than of Joan of Arc. Indeed it is an aspect of de Gaulle properly stressed in this book (and often neglected by British politicians who cast him as a French Churchill) that his whole political career was based on a revolutionary concept: that an individual's sense of patriotic duty may be allowed to transcend legality.

After the Second World War, de Gaulle's claim to leadership was based less on democracy than on the semi-mystical authority he had acquired in his moment of treasonable defiance. If he was (as he has been described) the 'father and the mother' of the largely successful Fifth Republic, that owed more to his suspicion of parliamentary democracy, and his belief in the need to keep politicians in their place, than of any love for it.

He remained, as Charles Williams says, a soldier first and foremost, yet one whose political sensitivities were second to none and who succeeded (as Churchill never did) as both a wartime and a peacetime leader. This book does not seek to be the last word on the subject, and is largely based on secondary sources. However, it synthesizes known evidence with great skill, and with a sensitive treatment of de Gaulle's private life (especially his gentle, affectionate relationship with his Down's Syndrome daughter), as well as of his public personality. It conveys the sense of a man of great intellect, stiffness, conceit, guile, fire and judgement – in a narrative that is difficult to put down.

Independent on Sunday, 31 October 1993

JOHN KENNEDY

SELDOM HAS A ROMANCE so gripped a nation's imagination as the legend of Jack Kennedy. No outreach of the Babel's Tower of the American Dream is more bewitching, and none less solid. Yet, as with many myths, the core of reality is almost mundane.

John F. Kennedy was a wealthy young American politician of little distinction who (like Bill Clinton in 1992) got to the White House largely by default after a long period of Republican occupancy. His brief administration was notable mainly for an ill-advised invasion at the Bay of Pigs and a scary gamble with nuclear weapons during the Cuba missile crisis. There were no major domestic achievements. The blurb to Nigel Hamilton's book calls Kennedy 'this century's most popular and charismatic American president'. In fact, in terms of votes obtained at an election, he was one of the least popular. If he had been older and uglier and had died of a heart attack, he might also be one of the least known – a sort of American Andrew Bonar Law.

The 'charisma' has been largely posthumous. It was the glamour of the Kennedy court, the style, the money, but above all the theatrical public killing that turned the name of Kennedy into that of a godhead, a deified Caesar immune from the depredations of mere historians, or of witnesses who wanted to put the record straight. Varieties of mud have been flung at the living Kennedy, in an attempt to show him up as a fickle, philandering scoundrel. So far from such revelations tarnishing the image, they have given it added shine, reminding us that on Olympus, mortal standards do not apply. They have done nothing to discourage political hopefuls from seeking to be regarded as the new Kennedy. Dan Quayle was memorably ticked off for his hubris in comparing himself to the late President. Last year Clinton coolly blasphemed his way to office, invoking not just the name but the

JFK: The Life and Death of an American President, Nigel Hamilton (Century, 1993)

mannerisms and rhetoric (perhaps even the coiffure) to brilliant effect.

But the question remains, as Hamilton puts it: 'Who really *was* John F. Kennedy behind the winsome orthodontically perfect smile?' and begins to provide an answer in the first volume of his carefully researched biography. Gods and icons are illusive: it helps that Hamilton is British, not American, and hence less susceptible to the mystique. The result is a work which deftly analyses the seamiest aspects of Kennedy's background. At the same time the author builds the impression of a man driven both by a demon of ambition, and by an exceptional vitality.

Out of a mass of material, much of it new, the author weaves together a fascinating story, as valuable for the backcloth as for the account of the central character. Its description of the grubby world of Bostonian political fixing, in particular, is a telling reminder of the scaly underbelly to the romance of Camelot.

An important part of the Kennedy legend was the notion of the clan as a happy family infused with, and united by, bog Irish warmth. Hamilton deals with that one ruthlessly. Making use of a cache of previously undiscovered letters from Jack to a boyhood friend, Lem Billings, he sketches out a bleak picture of private horror and pretence. Joe Kennedy – Jack's father, and founder of the family fortunes – appears as part crook, part political fantasist and part old goat, who when not ludicrously plotting to displace Roosevelt as US President was trying to bribe his sons' girlfriends to sleep with him. Jack's mother Rose has been presented as the saintly earth mother and dedicated materfamilias of a purposeful brood: here she appears as a repressed social climber who imposed an icily impersonal discipline upon her children, retreated from her husband's maltreatment into the rituals of her faith, and tacitly condoned the dreadful decision to lobotomize their retarded daughter Rosemary, as a means of curbing her rebellious behaviour.

Thus – in Hamilton's interpretation – it was not an abundance of love but the precise opposite that provided the motor to Kennedy aspiration. But there were also other elements. One was social exclusion. Having acquired money by dubious means, Joe attempted to buy his way into smart Boston society. He encountered, however, a brick wall of anti-Irish ethnic prejudice, which his own reputation as a shady operator did not help, and which placed his children in 'social quarantine'. Hence, Hamilton speculates, they had a specially strong urge to prove themselves, one way or another, in the adult world.

In Jack's case, there was yet another factor: physical illness. Hamilton meticulously unravels the details of a series of ailments that dogged the future President from his childhood, casting a shadow over his future. Photos of him show a delicate, emaciated teenager, with wide eyes, protruding nose and nervous smile. Many months were spent recovering, as much from quackish courses of medical treatment as from the conditions they were supposed to cure. On one occasion, leukemia was incorrectly diagnosed. There followed a bout of pokings and scrapings by expensive doctors, whose lugubrious attention was drawn to the misbehaviour of his bowels. 'They give me enemas till it all comes out like drinking water which they all take a sip of,' Jack told a friend. As soon as he regained his strength, he took his revenge by trying to seduce the nurses. 'The girls are few and far between,' he wrote from a convalescent home in Palm Beach, 'but speaking of between, I expect I shall get laid shortly.'

Getting laid became a major preoccupation. 'What he wanted was fun,' says Hamilton, and despite his illnesses (or because of them) he usually got it. Sex was one ingredient. There was also a bookish, even intellectual, streak. Jack's elder brother Joe – killed on a flying mission in the Second World War – had it too, and studied under Harold Laski at the London School of Economics. Jack was less earnest, and roamed restlessly around Europe, though liking England best, partly because of the débutantes. He also made use of his father's base as American ambassador in London to go to bed with as many as he could and to write a book, aptly called *Why England Slept*, which turned him into a minor celebrity.

Hamilton shows that despite FBI suspicions that his Danish mistress was a German agent, he had a good war. The author gives an interesting account of the naval operation in the Pacific that turned Jack into a national hero. Following a ramming by a Japanese destroyer, young Kennedy – in a kind of Chappaquiddick in reverse – swam for help, saving the lives of his men at great risk to himself. The episode had the incidental advantage of equipping him, in the eyes of would-be backers, for a political career.

By far the most important of his backers was his own rich and unscrupulous father, who – frustrated in his own ambitions – was largely responsible for bribing and bullying his son's way into Congress at the unusually young age of twenty-nine, with some help from Jack's maternal grandfather, 'Honey Fizz' Fitzgerald. Hamilton concludes this volume with the observation that, in spite of everything, the budding politician had escaped Joe's 'narrow, selfish, Boston-Irish bigotry and found a pluralist, idealistic, and yet internationally committed liberalism'. There is little evidence of self-sufficiency here, however, and we must await volume two for proof of so remarkable a severance from his roots.

Independent on Sunday, 3 January 1993

HAROLD MACMILLAN I

HERE IS A BIT OF ADVICE for political leaders who wish to be well regarded by posterity: put off dying for as long as possible. The late Lord Stockton is a case in point. In extreme old age the former prime minister – once regarded by every progressive as an incorrigible rogue – enjoyed an extraordinary Indian summer as the thinking socialist's Tory.

It was partly the climate of the times. At any rate, Stockton's quavering attacks on Mrs Thatcher for her neglect of the unemployed and selling off of the family had an astonishing effect. Suddenly, there was an upsurge of nostalgia for a supposed lost age of chivalry when – in contrast to the grasping Gradgrind present – the rich man in his castle took a paternalistic interest in the poor man at his gate, and a myth was born, cultivated by the old illusionist himself, about the period in between. Approaching death, the nonagenarian earl was transformed into a great elder statesman – the ex-premier who had held the national consensus in his palm, and gently guided post-imperial Britain towards its modest destiny.

As usual with legends, this one contained a grain of truth, but also a lot of rubbish. In the Tory prime minister stakes, Harold Macmillan was not the worst. His record compares favourably with Baldwin's inertia, Chamberlain's obstinacy, Churchill's peacetime senility, Eden's bellicosity, Home's genial ignorance, Heath's tunnel vision and Thatcher's shallow fanaticism. He was also a skilful party leader. In style an archetypal grandee, he teased and flirted with the Tory blue rinse brigade, which he cordially despised, while the superficial calmness of his public performances soothed a flustered electorate and brought off the unexpected 1959 Conservative victory. But by other standards, his tenure of office was an undistinguished, wasted

Macmillan: Volume 1, 1894–1956, Alistair Horne (Macmillan, 1988)

opportunity. His seven years at No. 10 were mainly characterized by stumbling economics and a frivolous consumerism.

Yet politicians are not only interesting for what they do. They are sometimes worth considering for what they are. It is a tribute to the author's skill that Macmillan emerges from this first volume of biography a very human, though still mysterious, individual. Macmillan's character was so flawed and his life so scarred that Horne's account of it – which might have been the story of a cheery rise up the greasy pole – is a tale as much of tragedy as of success. There are still some historians who maintain that in recording the careers of the famous, it is better to stick strictly to 'political' biography, with murky secrets left out. There has seldom been a more telling demonstration of the narrowness of such a view than in this work. As the author shows, domestic misery of one kind or another was one of the main engines pushing the hero forward.

There was also class. Born to a yuppy family (his father was an industrious and prospering publisher), the young Harold was dominated by the steely aspirations of his Indiana-born mother, Nellie ('No one who has not experienced it,' he wrote later, 'can realize the determination of an American mother defending her children'). The vehicle for preferment, naturally, was education: Summer Fields (a posh prep. school), Eton and Balliol.

It was a training which equipped the future premier with appropriate manners, but also with a depressive and fatalistic temperament. He only enjoyed the last phase, at Oxford: an idyll traumatically ended in 1914. The war shattered him emotionally as much as physically. Several times wounded, he emerged with lasting injuries and a lifetime of pain. More serious, however, was the mental damage: the loss of friends and the sense of guilt and foreboding.

In 1920 he married Lady Dorothy, daughter of the Duke of Devonshire, who was Governor-General of Canada. Why? Horne says they were in love, and Harold seems to have stayed faithful in mind and body until her death. Yet it was a surprising match, and a socially elevating one: despite Eton, a chasm separated the Bloomsbury Macmillans from the languid aristocratic Cavendishes. It was, in any event, catastrophic. Dorothy was evidently a selfish monster: domineering, cruel and humiliatingly (because quite openly, within the confines of society) unfaithful. Her lifelong affair with the Tory MP Robert Boothby wrecked Harold's happiness, condemning him to sexual abstinence. The Macmillans' home life was ruined. All four of his putative children – one of whom, Sarah, was fathered by Boothby – eventually turned to drink. Harold himself suffered a massive nervous breakdown, which nearly caused him to leave politics.

It was against this backcloth of loneliness and domestic tension, that Macmillan strove for success. It was a fairly tumultuous passage. Elected MP for Stockton-on-Tees in 1924, he lost the seat in 1929, regained it in 1931 and lost it again in 1945. The uncertainty of his base turned him into something of a dilettante; the poverty of his North-Eastern constituency made him a maverick. He came close to joining Sir Oswald Mosley's New Party (before Mosley went completely off the rails) and might even have joined Labour, if the pre-war Labour Party had not seemed so cautious. His book, *The Middle Way*, bravely and thoughtfully attempted to inject Keynesianism into the body politic. Horne covers this period adequately, though without adding much that is new, and there are some surprising errors (he states, wrongly, that Sir Stafford Cripps was a pacifist and that G. D. H. Cole was editor of the *New Statesman*).

An ally of Churchill in the late thirties, Macmillan first gained office with the formation of the 1940 coalition as a junior minister. Later, he was given the key post of Minister Resident in North Africa and eventually 'Viceroy of the Mediterranean'. One of Macmillan's personal credos ('take it as it comes, it never turns out as you expect') was now overtaken by another ('when you get a chance, take it').

By the end of the war, Macmillan had moved from the margins to the centre of the Tory stage – though not without acquiring some bloodstains in the process. Horne works valiantly to exonerate him over the ghastly 'Victims of Yalta' affair – involving the handing back of thousands of White Russians to the Soviets to face summary execution. The question of moral culpability remains complex. However, Macmillan's partial responsibility (and also his subsequent remorse) is clear.

As a post-war minister, Macmillan is mainly remembered for his pledge to build 300,000 houses if the Tories returned to office, and his fulfilment of it. This certainly brought him to public attention. But it was not until Eden's premiership that he became a contender for the top job.

At the outset of the Suez operation in 1956, Macmillan was on the side of the warmongers; before the end, he had become (in Brendan Bracken's scornful phrase) 'Leader of the Bolters'. It was believed at the time, and has continued to be believed since, that he suddenly became aware of his own mistake (as Chancellor of the Exchequer) when the Americans pulled out the financial rug. His own rationaliz-ation, that the invasion had achieved its military objective and therefore hostilities should cease on that ground alone, was certainly disin-genuous and mainly for Tory Party consumption. Horne ends with the succession of Macmillan as Prime Minister – which surprised every-body, though apparently the Cabinet voted overwhelmingly for him.

Part of the implicit understanding in 'official' biography is that the author should be counsel for the defence. Because such an approach is expected it is particularly hard for the author to be convincing: over-eager advocacy can easily backfire. In this case, a sensitive yet admiring approach succeeds, at the personal level, if not at the political. Despite the constraints, the impression is of an attractive, intelligent, acutely nervous, reflective, humorous, emotionally driven political ani-mal who became an increasingly obsessive hunter in the jungle game. Yet the reader's sympathy may be easier to maintain because, for a large part of this book, Macmillan was as much quizzical observer as central participant. Volume two – covering the premiership – will be the tougher challenge. It will be fascinating to see what Horne makes of it.

New Statesman and Society, 14 October 1988

HAROLD MACMILLAN II

WHAT CAN BIOGRAPHY DO that narrative history cannot? In one sense, the second volume of Alistair Horne's study of Harold Macmillan provides an answer, fully justifying the form. Yet it also demonstrates some unsolved (perhaps insoluble) problems, and shows how difficult it is to bring this kind of study off.

The first part of a notable life is always the easiest, if the sources are available. In volume one, Horne took his hero from comparatively modest bourgeois origins through the playing fields of Eton and Balliol and the killing fields of France, and up the stepping-stones of social and political advancement. We saw the raw, unknown Macmillan: the gifted, sardonic, semi-intellectual, semi-rebel, who found escape from the humiliations of cuckoldry in the maelstrom of Westminster. Much of it belonged to the world of *Brideshead Revisited* and *A Handful of Dust*: the bizarre triangle involving doughty Lady Dorothy and raffish Robert Boothby in particular. From the intertwining of private and public emotions, the author was able to tease out the developing political personality, leaving it at the point where – to a modern generation – it became recognizable. Yet until 1957 Macmillan was not much more than an above-average Tory politician. It is this second volume that gives point to the whole enterprise.

It was also by far the tougher assignment. The difficulty is that, though almost every minute of a Downing Street day is copiously documented, little can be discovered about prime ministers as individuals because their personalities merge into the organic life of the office, and their stories become hard to distinguish from the history of the nation itself. How is achievement to be judged? One man or woman may effectively defuse a crisis with a shrug, or by delegating it; another may vigorously and ineffectively intervene. It is not easy for

Macmillan: Volume 2, 1957–1986, Alistair Horne (Macmillan, 1989)

the biographer to convey the superiority of the former, as conductor of the political orchestra.

Not only did the pressures of office exclude private life, Macmillan himself seems consciously to have eschewed it, and to have retreated in his later years into a conscious reticence about family matters. Though Horne had access to his diary, personal details seem to have been almost entirely absent. It is thus with the public Macmillan, only occasionally leavened by cries of despair during bouts of melancholia, that we must rest content.

That is a limitation, for which the author cannot be blamed. A more culpable fault is that Horne comes perilously close to going native on his subject, and sometimes fails to distance himself sufficiently from the latter's values and assumptions. Macmillan's snobbery spills on to the author, who seems to share his subject's view of the 'entrepreneurial classes' as composed exclusively of people who graduate from Oxbridge; and who describes Hugh Gaitskell – an effective and high-ranking wartime official – as a mere 'clerk' in Whitehall during the Second World War.

The fault, however, is more than offset by the biographer's success in synthesizing diary, interviews and other sources. One test of this kind of biography is that it should make the reader feel sympathy for the subject, despite political disagreement. In this respect, Horne's portrait is a *tour de force*. For all his grievous flaws, Macmillan comes across as a thoroughly engaging, even lovable, old rogue.

Whether he was any good as Prime Minister is another matter. Today, it is fashionable – on the left, even more than on the right – to recall the era of the so-called 'consensus' of which he was supposedly high priest. At his death, he was feted by leaders of all parties as a lost statesman. Yet (as Horne points out) it was not so at the time of his departure from office. Only briefly was he admired, and then largely as a performer.

Yet he had his measure of success. Never in peacetime has a new prime minister taken over a more ill-starred government, and to have survived at all was a political achievement. In the shaming aftermath of Suez, the widespread assumption was that any Tory administration would be a caretaker pending the return of Labour to office, with Gaitskell at the helm. Instead, Macmillan was able to ride the tide and win a resounding election victory in 1959. However, except in the brief period of the Labour Party's disarray over unilateralism and Clause Four, his entire period of office was characterized by its fragility.

Macmillan was a premier who could not believe his luck. Not only had he never expected to take the top job: he was perpetually aware of his good fortune in keeping it. He was also sufficiently sensitive to the nation's plight to appreciate the gap between his own unflappable rhetoric, and the long-term reality. Politicians have to live with their own phrases, often quoted out of context. Macmillan's association with the 'you've never had it so good' tag is unfair: the remark was a warning, rather than a complacent boast. Part of Macmillan's tragedy was that his premiership coincided both with the most rapid period of economic growth in history, and with the most calamitous episode of relative national decline. Superficially prosperous, these were desperately uneasy, troubled times.

Labour saw Macmillan as the symbol of what was wrong. But of all the Tories, he was the most sympathetic to their aims. He acknowledged the growing fashion for economic planning, and his Etonian-dominated Cabinet heralded Labour's post-1964 corporatism. 'I intended to run [the government] as a *centre* party,' he later reasonably claimed. It was Macmillan, too, who calmly accepted the wind of change in Africa, and presided over the dismantling of empire.

Yet if he admitted to feeling 'a certain atmosphere of unreality and even absurdity' about his office that is in some ways refreshing (does Mrs Thatcher ever feel the same?), there was always more than a little absurdity about his occupancy of it, as though the whole thing was a rather unfortunate practical joke. As Harold Wilson (whom Macmillan feared much more than he feared Gaitskell) shrewdly put it: the Prime Minister's 'role as a poseur was itself a pose'. The idea that the country could for long be governed like an old-fashioned merchant bank, with the Prime Minister as affable chairman, mistook the mood. As relative economic performance relentlessly sank, Bertie Woosterdom seemed increasingly out of place.

The Profumo scandal was an appropriately farcical climax, well described by Alistair Horne, who shows how blameless was the unfortunate premier, and also how catastrophically nonplussed. 'The old "Cliveden" set was disastrous politically,' Macmillan mused, 'the new "Cliveden" set is said to be equally disastrous morally.' For him it was an issue, not so much of morals, but of social ethics. 'Profumo does not seem to have realized,' he noted, 'that we have – in public life – to observe different standards from those prevalent today in many circles . . .' (It is an irony, nevertheless, that Macmillan should earlier have rewarded

Boothby's long adultery with Lady Dorothy by giving him a life peerage.)

As we all remember, 1963 was the year that sexual intercourse was invented – too late for Philip Larkin and, alas, too late for Macmillan even to begin to understand. Many aspects of society were beginning to change, and not just in sexual *mores*: there was a stirring of attitudes that eventually produced a new social order out of the ruins of the 1964–70 Labour Government. The Profumo hysteria marked the beginning of the revolution, and Macmillan was one of its victims.

Could he have survived politically, not just Profumo, but also the prostate operation which was the ostensible reason for his departure? And if he had, would Labour have been defeated yet again in 1964? Horne, fondly, gives affirmative answers. Yet it is by no means clear, if Macmillan had staggered on, that his tattered reputation and the gathering sense of an inept, elderly, music-hall turn way past his best, would have fared any better than Sir Alec's untainted amateurism.

Douglas-Home lingered, enjoying a political afterlife. So, in a way, did Macmillan, castigating Mrs Thatcher, long after many people had imagined him well dead. Yet his departure as Prime Minister came at the right historic moment – marking the effective end of *noblesse oblige* in British politics. Horne's elegant volume captures the strangely distant feeling of that sunset age.

New Statesman and Society, 23 June 1989

THE FALL AND RISE OF
HAROLD WILSON

CAN IT BE that Lord Wilson of Rievaulx – Britain's most despised Prime Minister before John Major – is starting to emerge as a model for future leaders to emulate? If so, it would be a fine irony, and also a telling judgement on the seventeen ragged years since his departure. That revisionism is under way is underlined by Philip Ziegler's skilful and highly enjoyable official biography, and by a new collection of pithy sketches of Labour leaders by Peter Shore. Neither commentator is uncritical. But both reinforce a growing sense that, in the search for remedies for Britain's malaise, the lessons of the 1960s and 1970s should not be neglected.

Until recently, the 'Wilson era' was regarded (as much on the left as on the right) as a time of missed opportunity. Yet if Wilson was disliked by rich, clever or highly educated people, he also commanded great popular affection. This was partly because he was seen as a quintessentially British figure, sentimentally attached to the dominions, English summer holidays, high tea, the monarchy, Oxford University, Nonconformist values and a belief in our national greatness. At the same time, he had a Pooterish aspect that caused irritation to the sophisticated: where Winston Churchill personified how the British liked to see themselves, Wilson was disconcertingly closer to what we had become.

Harold Wilson first came to public attention in 1947 when he was made President of the Board of Trade – then an enormous, sprawling department with immense powers over the daily lives and purchases of every household in the kingdom. He has remained in the nation's consciousness ever since, in one guise or another. While he was

Wilson: The Authorized Biography, Philip Ziegler (Weidenfeld & Nicolson, 1993); *Leading the Left*, Peter Shore (Weidenfeld & Nicolson, 1993); *Harold Wilson*, Austen Morgan (Pluto Press, 1992)

an active politician, his public image passed through a series of chameleon-like phases, each startlingly different from the one before.

As the youngest member of the Attlee Cabinet by a decade, he was colourless almost to the point of anonymity. In fact, he was scarcely a politician at all – a dapper little fellow with a ridiculous moustache which he grew to make himself look older, but which actually had the opposite effect. John Freeman describes him at this time as 'like an unusually able motor-car salesman – very bright and very superficial', and that is how he appears in the newsreels. But he was also the essence of suffocating puritanical bureaucracy, the man who decided how much the ration-book would withhold and, patronizingly, how much it would bestow.

In 1951, the image changed dramatically when he resigned with Aneurin Bevan over NHS charges and the rearmament programme. This unexpected act of rebellion transformed him (in the eyes of press and public, if never in those of sceptical colleagues) into a 'left-wing intellectual' – a type then associated with bohemian pre-war poets. This was how many people continued to see him for the next dozen years although, in truth, he was always a judicious Bevanite, centre-left rather than extremist.

After Hugh Gaitskell's death in 1963, Wilson became Leader of the Labour Party, and immediately embarked on a new phase: the scourge of privilege, the evangelist of modernization, the herald of a new age. This episode was the most remarkable of his life and – arguably – one of the key moments in post-war history. As Ziegler reminds us, Wilson's famous speech in which he described a Britain that was to be 'forged in the white heat of the technological revolution' struck a nerve in the public's consciousness and identified Wilson in their eyes with all that was hopeful and adventurous. The point is put even more strongly by Peter Shore, at the time one of Wilson's closest advisers. 'Without doubt', he writes, 'no Leader of the Opposition, before or since, has equalled in sustained brilliance and effectiveness Wilson's campaign that started in February 1963 and which continued to its successful conclusion on polling day, October 1964.'

The phase continued through the period of a knife-edge Labour majority in 1964–6. During it, Wilson seemed to bring together – uniquely – Labour idealism, state-of-the-art economics and popular enthusiasm. This was a time when 'charismatic' seemed an appropriate adjective to describe his personality and leadership. Sparkling at impromptu gatherings, master of the big audience, skilled in the new medium of television, rapier-like in Parliament, he built a formidable alliance of manual workers, technicians and what would nowadays be called the chattering classes, who were briefly persuaded by his vision of a streamlined, meritocratic future.

The mid-1960s was a time of hope shared by economists, editors, even businessmen, many of whom gave their support to George Brown's 1965 National Plan. The hope, painstakingly cultivated, vanished in the deflation that followed from the Prime Minister's refusal to countenance the devaluation of sterling in July 1966. Within days, Wilson the saviour became Wilson the ostrich, betrayer and frightened paranoiac. If the mid-1960s were his best years, the late 1960s and early 1970s were his worst, as one by one his bright promises – over Rhodesia, Vietnam, trade union reform – turned to dust. The nadir was reached during the Heath Government of 1974. Wilson, as Opposition Leader, battled for survival against increasingly hysterical pro- and anti-marketeers – each side hating and scapegoating him with equal venom. 'Mr Wilson has now sunk to a position where his very presence in Labour's leadership pollutes the atmosphere of politics,' wrote one left-wing editor, reflecting what had become conventional wisdom among the progressive intelligentsia.

But this was not the end. When Wilson took everybody by surprise by winning in February 1974 and confirmed his victory at a second election in October, there was a temporary recovery in the press perception of him – especially after he brought the European ship to port in the carefully calculated referendum of 1975.

For a few months, he ceased to be a cynical opportunist and became a wise old bird. Then, at a moment of his own choosing, Wilson resigned. In his memoirs, he makes clear that by this time he was happy to be remembered as a Labour Baldwin. Briefly, indeed, he seemed to fit G. M. Trevelyan's description of the pre-war Prime Minister: 'an Englishman indeed; in whom was much guile, never used for low or selfish purposes. In a world of voluble hates, he plotted to make men like, or at least tolerate one another.' However, the ex-premier was no sooner on the backbenches than a whole cattery of damaging rumours began to circulate, denying him the role of venerated elder statesman.

It was partly his own fault. A frivolous resignation Honours List, and a mystifying series of taped interviews with two journalists (sensationally published as *The Pencourt File*), seemed to indicate a man with dubious friends and poor judgement. In addition, there was the acidic contribution of Wilson's No. 10 press officer, Joe Haines, whose Downing Street memoir, *The Politics of Power*, presented the prime minister's office in Wilson's final days as a kind of sadomasochistic dungeon in which the Prime Minister cowered beneath the whip of his dominatrix secretary. Andrew Roth's *Harold Wilson: A Yorkshire Walter Mitty*, published in 1978, captured in its title the post-resignation view of Wilson – a provincial dreamer, a car salesman promoted above his station.

This became the settled opinion. After 1979, the Wilson–Callaghan years were lumped together by both the Thatcherite Right and the Bennite Left as an age of never-to-be-repeated failure. Labour's social-democratic tendency, meanwhile, reserved its nostalgia for Gaitskell. The defection of the SDP at first made Wilson even more anathema to his own party: for several years, Labour's prospectus – pro-unilateralism, anti-Europe, isolationist, nationalizing – was a million miles from his own. Wilson himself, entering a twilight zone of old age, could not respond to the ritual denunciations of what he had stood for. Yet even now, the view of Wilson did not remain static. In 1987 the revelations of the former MI5 officer, Peter Wright, provided evidence that some of his accusations against the British security services, made just after he left office, might not have been the wild delusions most observers had assumed. Yet the ex-premier remained a deeply unfashionable figure, seldom mentioned, except in the context of an unfavourable comparison with Mrs Thatcher.

When, in 1988, I undertook to write an unauthorized biography of Harold Wilson, I had no prescience about future attitudes towards him. I was curious about Wilson, who had won elections, had presided – for good or ill – over a large chunk of our history, and had stood for so much in my youth. My own attitude to him was neutral, though I was conscious of my own perverse enjoyment of projects that make people at parties look puzzled and pitying. As soon as I had accepted the commission, I quickly discovered that this one fell into such a category: friends and acquaintances took some interest in the supposed mystery of Wilson's resignation, but regarded the idea of a serious examination of his career with blank incomprehension.

Once I had embarked, my attitude inevitably evolved. Biography is part clinical, part aesthetic. As a clinician, I tried to see the world as Wilson must have done: 'empathy' is not quite the appropriate word for this process, but it is close. In Wilson's case it was peculiarly difficult, partly because of his own lack of introspection. Once, however, I had begun to break the code, it was impossible not to be intrigued: both by his quicksilver intelligence and by his strange aloofness – often politically useful, frequently the reverse – in personal relations. It was not my aim to be revisionist, except in the sense that I did not want to repeat the old clichés. Nor was I particularly bothered about being 'fair': fairness is for courts of law. (You don't say to Lucian Freud: 'But she's actually better looking than that.') My goal was an accurate, convincing, and original portrait, that would make people think, not just about Wilson, but about politics in general. As I began to research the book, I became intrigued by his ability to outsmart rivals, marvelled at his energy and brilliance, and was stunned, at times, by his crass stupidity.

Meanwhile, opinion on Wilson had been on the move. In 1988, David Leigh's *The Wilson Plot* succeeded in showing that Wilson had, indeed, been maligned by people in the intelligence world. In 1990, Paul Foot's *Who Framed Colin Wallace?* provided even stronger evidence, while *Smear! Harold Wilson and the Secret State*, by Stephen Dorril and Robin Ramsay (1991), assembled a dossier to show that many in the Establishment had it in for Wilson. Significantly, all these books came from the Left: a decade earlier, no self-respecting left-wing journalist would have been seen dead trying to get Wilson off the hook.

After the partial accounts, the door-stopper biographies. Austen Morgan's *Harold Wilson*, published in March 1992, contained new research but more or less backed up the already outmoded leftish conclusion: that Wilson was to be dismissed as a no-account sell-out and traitor to socialism. My own biography, published last October, was mystifyingly described in some quarters as a 'rehabilitation'. Perhaps some commentators were still so unused to hearing *anything* positive about Wilson that a book which attempted to take his premiership seriously seemed a novelty. More important, the book coincided with a sharp change in the political temperature: it was published within weeks of 'Black Wednesday', a date as devastating to the Thatcher–Major scheme of things as the collapse of sterling in July 1966 had been to Wilson's.

It was a moment for Roy Jenkins, Wilson's less-than-admiring rival, to comment wryly that if he were a dealer in prime ministerial shares he 'would at present buy Wilsons as eagerly as I would sell Majors, although there is room for a very sharp recovery in Wilsons before they begin to approach par'. The ex-chancellor would certainly not have lost money: as Major's reputation has plummeted almost to the point of receivership, Wilson's has floated gently upwards. Not long ago, 'Wilsonian' was an adjective applied to a piece of sharp practice. Yet the other day, Peter Mandelson, never far from the heart-beat of the Labour Party, wrote in the *Sunday Express* of how, at the TUC, 'Mr Smith showed Wilsonian skill in outmanoeuvring the cliques which had been trying to sabotage his proposals.' The leader John Smith most reminded him of, he declared, was Harold Wilson, the party unifier. Mandelson's opinion is powerfully backed by Philip Ziegler, who emphasizes Wilson's strong belief in social justice, and by Peter Shore (a Euro-sceptic), who points to Wilson's success in keeping pro- and anti- ministers together in the same government.

Arguably, such opinions are predictable: official biographers do not usually savage their subject, and Shore was a friend and protégé. My hunch, however, is that their assessment will enjoy wide support. The reason is not so much the past as the present: versions of Wilsonism are due for disinterment because, on both sides of the Atlantic, the ideology of the unbridled market is a busted flush. In the 1960s, the economy performed no worse than in the 1980s, and much better than in the 1990s. We may soon expect new attention to be paid to modest forms of collectivism and state planning: it is noticeable that the 'white heat' approach, with its stress on training and government-led investment, is not treated by economic commentators with the same ribaldry as in the days of Thatcherite tribalism.

Will Wilson ever become a people's hero, a member of the socialist pantheon? I doubt it. He was much too complex a character, and a good deal too fallible. We may agree with Ziegler that, although possibly on the side of the angels, it is hard to see him as 'a champion in the angelic hosts'. We may expect his name to be invoked on anti-Tory platforms more and more, as bitter memories fade. The difficult thing, in these less credulous times, will be to recapture the campaigning Wilsonian magic. Yet to remember that (in the former premier's words, for which he later paid dearly) 'the Labour Party is a moral crusade or it is nothing' may offer Labour's best, and only, means of survival.

Independent on Sunday, 26 September 1993

EDWARD HEATH

THERE HAS PROBABLY never been an occupant of Number 10 Downing Street quite so lamentably unsuccessful as Edward Heath. John Major, of course, offers hot competition: but even he has not yet equalled Heath's record for making enemies and getting into avoidable scrapes. Do we need an 876-page biography of such a man? It is a mark of John Campbell's achievement in this finely written and judicious study that – by the end – the reader is deeply engaged in the purposes and ideals of this unlovable, unlucky yet perversely admirable man. Biography, if it is to work, has to make the reader have sympathy for the subject, however unattractive. Heath is in many ways a very unattractive man – rude, stubborn and selfish. Yet Campbell's well-balanced portrait also presents him convincingly as a decent and honourable leader, fatally flawed by bad judgement.

What makes Heath of special interest, regardless of what he did, is his background: apart from Bonar Law (briefly premier in the 1920s) he was the first modern Tory leader not of conventional upper-class or aristocratic birth. His progress was that of an inter-war species that no longer exists: the scholarship boy (or girl) who – through talent, grit, parental encouragement or inspired teaching – cuts a path through a hostile education system into the Establishment. The cost, in those days, was a social and psychic isolation which in Heath's case took a particularly acute form. He was not unclubbable (allegedly in private he has 'a sense of fun'); but many people found him unapproachable, and he was apt 'to give the impression of regarding women as by definition frivolous'. Attempting to get through the rhinoceros hide that surrounds Heath's emotions, Campbell admits defeat. 'It is not impossible that he is a latent or repressed homosexual,' he suggests with legal-minded prudence. 'The alternatives are that he is a repressed heterosexual or that he is simply asexual.'

Edward Heath: A Biography, John Campbell (Jonathan Cape, 1993)

A model (but lonely) pupil in the sixth form, a model undergraduate at Balliol, and a model officer in the war, Heath had all the qualifications to become a model Permanent Secretary. In fact, he had set his mind on politics as a career from an early age and by careful planning won a marginal but promising seat in 1950, at the age of thirty-four. In Parliament, he was part of a remarkable generation of non-top-drawer Tories that included Macleod, Maudling and Powell – none of whom, however, he much resembled. He was the tortoise of the group: whose steady ascent was nevertheless assured. In the whips' office his skills as a natural school prefect were quickly recognized and within five years of entering the House he was Chief Whip.

As a teenager, according to the author, Heath 'thought that breaking a school rule amounted to disloyalty to the school'. The same ethic infused his term as an 'implacable and unforgiving' whip – an episode contemporaries did not forget: habits of obedience and fear, as well as of resentment, were not easily shed. Meanwhile Heath's policy attitudes – consistently paternalist, pro-Keynesian and pro-intervention – were closely in tune with those of Harold Macmillan, whose devoted lieutenant he became. The Macmillan era of tinsel prosperity was his launch pad, and he was shifted from one high-profile economic portfolio to another. Until the débâcle of Home's 'fourteenth earl' premiership, he was not seen as a potential leader. It was Harold Wilson who effectively acted as kingmaker: convincing the Conservative elders that if Labour's secret weapon was a clever grammar school boy they needed one too. Yet in Parliament, Heath was easy prey: seldom have Conservatives squirmed more than in the mid-sixties when Wilson was able time and again to make merciless sport of an Opposition leader who seemed ploddingly incapable of humour.

If Heath had lost for a second time in 1970, he would have been replaced by somebody more glamorous. Having won unexpectedly, he was given an exceptional opportunity – far greater than that of either Wilson in 1964 or Mrs Thatcher in 1979, both of whom took over at times of crisis. In 1970, the economy was in surplus, and offered a rare chance for restructuring and imaginative reform. Heath, moreover, had a strong team, including men who respected his abilities, and admired his attitudes. Yet somehow he managed to trap himself between his own economic beliefs (which differed little from those of the outgoing government) and the 'Selsdon Man' rhetoric which he had uneasily, and uncharacteristically, employed some time before the election. The outcome was a few half-hearted gestures in a rightward direction, swiftly abandoned in a series of 'U-turns' quite as spectacular as any of Wilson's.

Campbell fairly gives Heath credit for the successful conclusion of the Common Market negotiations, leading to formal entry in 1973 (though it is virtually certain that Wilson, who was preparing another Euro-assault at the time of the election, would have done the same). Otherwise, it was a case of tossing away advantages and making rods for his own back. It was a singular feat for a former Minister of Labour, whom many trade union leaders continued to like and trust more than they ever did Wilson, both to antagonize the unions with an unenforceable Industrial Relations Act and to take on the miners (who were more moderate, as well as stronger, than they later became) twice, and lose on each occasion. As a result, the abiding memory of the Heath premiership is, as Campbell rightly says, 'a conflated recollection of power cuts and flickering candlelight, and the hoarding of candles and the rediscovery of oil lamps'. Meanwhile, Heath had permitted an ill-starred economic gamble by Anthony Barber, Britain's worst post-war Chancellor before Norman Lamont.

'Who governs Britain?' was Heath's question in the February 1974 election. By holding the unnecessary poll at all, Heath was giving one kind of answer: he had shown that he could no longer do so. 'An opportunist election ... timed to catch the Opposition off balance and exploit the national emergency for party ends, was exactly what Heath did not want.' Really? If so, the contest – which the antennae of a Wilson or a Thatcher would have warned against – is even more mystifying.

Campbell gives a vivid if terrifying account of Downing Street life at this moment of national near-collapse, far more serious than Labour's winter of discontent five years later, with Heath's far from impartial civil service chief, William Armstrong, raving about a battle between good and evil before being packed off to Barbados to recuperate. The picture is nicely rounded off with a description of Heath glumly swallowing oysters from Prunier's ('his favourite') as the election results came through.

After that, it was downhill all the way. Tory leaders are supposed to win elections: uniquely, Heath lost three out of the four he fought. In the circumstances, his sense of betrayal when Mrs Thatcher took the crown seems misplaced. Such feelings, however, are seldom rational, and for the past eighteen years the enmity between the two superficially similar former leaders has been one of the best known feuds in politics. When Mrs Thatcher's own nemesis came, Mr Heath apparently 'made no secret of his delight'. As Father of the House in the present Parliament, his former usurper blissfully absent, he has visibly flowered like a dehydrated cactus serendipitously rescued by an unexpected shower of rain.

During the Thatcher era, Heath gained a reputation, as Campbell says, as 'a political Cassandra – very largely right but not believed'. But his supporters dwindled, and his clarion calls – so far from rallying the dissidents – sent nervous backbenchers running for cover. Today, Heath is always worth listening to and often more left-wing than the Labour leadership. He is seen as brave, principled, austere, a true Roman senator, in a party increasingly composed of time-serving plebs. He is probably regarded with more sympathy than at any previous time in his career. Yet – after reading this judicious and generous book – one is still left with the unanswerable question (to adapt a remark Attlee made about Stafford Cripps): 'what made him such a political goose?'

Independent on Sunday, 4 July 1993

MARGARET THATCHER

'WAS MARGARET THATCHER GREAT?' It won't be many years before luckless undergraduates face this exam poser, alongside similar imponderables about Alfred, Napoleon and Attila the Hun. Students will have no shortage of contemporary accounts to draw on: there are already a dozen books, according to Hugo Young's bibliography, with 'Thatcher' in the title. As a scientific analysis of the woman and her politics, this one caps them all, and may be destined to become the set text.

What it won't be is a crib. Young, most Olympian of newspaper columnists, offers no easy solution to the conundrum of the Prime Minister's true worth. Neither (alas) does he give us any shocking revelations. There is little here that isn't already publicly available. Instead of much new information, what he provides is a potent combination of political sensitivity and careful reflection, communicated in a style that is both elegant and highly readable. His portrait is critical, quizzical, neither admiring nor unimpressed. He does not love his subject or sympathize with her outlook, but soberly acknowledges her formidable qualities and dissects them with dispassionate rigour. In short, he does her justice – perhaps more than she deserves.

Effort, luck and a suitable family background are commonly the ingredients of political success. Mrs Thatcher seems to have become Prime Minister, according to this account, by combining all three. Her appetite and endeavour have never been in dispute, and there is indeed a sense in which the Tory leadership was offered on a plate.

Less obvious has been her privileged birth. Young makes a good case for it. 'Margaret Thatcher was born to be a politician,' he observes. 'Her lineage and formation allowed of few other possibilities.' His argument is that, though socially humble by normal Tory standards, the Roberts' grocery throbbed with public life and political aspiration.

One of Us: a Biography of Margaret Thatcher, Hugo Young (Macmillan, 1989)

Her father – mayor, school governor and magistrate – proudly rubbed shoulders with local gentry and even members of the peerage.

Young contrasts these well-directed origins – spartan, yet neither poor nor low in local status – with those of the genuinely working-class Edward Heath. He might have made a comparison with those of another near-contemporary – Harold Wilson, also the product of a northern, lower middle class, Nonconformist, two-child, father-dominated family, similarly infused with the Samuel Smiles ethic of self-improvement (with grammar-school-plus-Oxford as the ladder) and with an admiration for the political caste, which seemed to epitomize worthwhile achievement.

The child is mother to the woman. There are tantalizing questions, on which the author can't shed much light. We want to know more about the shadowy Mrs Roberts, inexplicably excluded from the Prime Minister's *Who's Who* entries; and about Margaret's sister Muriel, who 'trained as a physiotherapist and never featured importantly in Margaret's life again', or indeed at all in the book. (Are there Grantham family reunions – and if not, why not?) We learn nothing of girlhood escapades, sibling battles, teenage flirtations.

Seeking to penetrate the darkness, Young finds little except gloom. What fired the furnace of such desperate ambition? She came, he suggests, 'from a contented but pretty joyless home'. A childhood friend confides: 'I don't think she had much of a sense of humour. I don't think her father had and I certainly don't think her mother had.' Was she noisy, generous, greedy, loving, rivalrous? Did she punch her sister on the nose, or stop the ladders in her stockings with chewing gum? She does not seem to have made enough of an impression for anybody to remember.

In one important respect she differed from the boy Harold, another model schoolchild: he was brainy, she was not. For Wilson, it was scholarships all the way; for Margaret Roberts, the upwardly mobile path was a hard slog. She wasn't stupid. Getting to university at all was a notable achievement for a woman of her class. There was no suggestion, however, of brilliance. She squeaked into Somerville by the skin of her teeth in a year of weak competition, and did not shine once she was there ('a beta chemist', according to her tutor).

Instead, she used Oxford as a political springboard, becoming president of the University Conservative Association in the notably unfashionable year, for Tories, of 1945. There followed marriage to the stalwart and helpfully prosperous Denis, a fleeting industrial career, a candidature at twenty-four, motherhood, and a safe seat at thirty-four.

It was, by many standards, a promising start; by others (Gladstone, Disraeli, Lloyd George, Churchill – even Wilson and Heath) a singularly dull one. As a woman in a man's world she had done well. But for inspiration and originality, she deserved about as many marks as a middling bureaucrat in the Ministry of Works.

And so she continued. Despite a junior post in the Macmillan Government, followed by six years in Opposition, few people had heard of her until she became Secretary of State for Education and Science under Edward Heath. As such, she was a loyal, efficient and profoundly orthodox member of an administration whose whole direction she was later to denounce. It is a nice irony that the education minister who approved more schemes for the abolition of grammar schools than any other was Margaret Thatcher.

It was not until after Heath's defeat in February 1974, and a leadership contest had become a probability, that she put down her marker. Involvement in the Keith Josephite Centre for Policy Studies made her available as a possible candidate of the Tory right.

It was not this, however, so much as her availability – or courage, or ambition – that gave her the prize. 'The defenestration of Heath was essentially a personal, not an ideological event,' Young points out. Mrs Thatcher was a dark horse who won largely because Tory MPs had decided that they wanted Heath to lose, and none of the dithering grandees had the guts to enter the race. It was, as Young says, the first moment of real distinction in her life. But it was also a symptom of two serviceable qualities: decisiveness and a sense of timing.

Since that happy day she has, of course, frequently been in debt to Mistress Luck. Oppositions do not win elections, governments lose them. Where might she be now, if Callaghan had called an election before the winter of discontent, instead of being forced precipitously into one after it?

Some remember her, in rosy retrospect, as a good Leader of the Opposition. It did not seem so to the public at the time. Ineffective against a confident and contemptuous Prime Minister in the Commons, she trailed behind him in the personal popularity ratings even when her party stood far ahead of Labour. The likely truth about the watershed election of 1979 is that Labour was destined to be routed whoever the Conservatives had at the helm.

Few governments have had as disastrous an opening phase as her first administration, when British manufacturing industry collapsed, aided by her own policies, and opinion polls pointed to the most decisive defeat for any prime minister since the war. Then, in 1981, Mars took up her cause. Her biggest – and most paradoxical – stroke of luck was the Falklands War into which the Government incompetently stumbled.

It was here that the two qualities which Young identifies – her sense of rectitude (we may say, self-righteousness) and her pragmatism – came most effectively into use. It was also her biggest, maddest gamble. To have lost the war would have been a national catastrophe, as well as a political and personal one. She played recklessly with other people's lives and futures, but coolly and well, and she won. She has been reaping the rewards ever since.

Arguably British politics has continued to be dominated by the memory of the conflict of eight years ago: that silly, trivial adventure which should never have been risked and which revealed so much about our tattered national psyche. The episode also shaped the way the public would see Mrs Thatcher and the way she sees herself. The image of bulldog patriotism, resolute leadership, instinctive populism derives largely from this bizarre credential – reinforced by the Brighton bomb, a trauma which added to her sense of walking with destiny.

There have been other factors – such as the changing nature of the voters and Labour's autonomous slump – to explain her longevity in power. Young's major case, however, is that it has not been the abstraction 'Thatcherism', still less an inexorable movement of social forces of the kind that left-wing determinists so frequently put forward, but the lady herself who has altered the flow of British history. She has been, he suggests, neither an intellectual, nor an ideologue, but a highly expedient operator. One thing that she certainly has not lacked is dominance.

Surveying the ruins of the welfare state and education system, and the number of legislative acts that bear her mark, it is hard to disagree. Yet the personal steel involved can be exaggerated: not individual, so much as single-party, dominance may be the most critical element. What might a Callaghan or a Kinnock have done with the enviable political tool of three election victories in a row? Arguably, almost any prime minister, equipped for so long a period with the colossal powers inherent in the office of elective dictator, would gain a reputation for strength, and acquire a taste for using it.

This does not diminish the quality, even the greatness of Mrs Thatcher's *finesse* at staying at the top. Neither does it reduce the greatness of her scorn for the poor, sick, young and excluded – or the greatness of what the author aptly calls her 'cold indifference to the misery of unemployment'. Future students will have to decide how to weigh the various types of greatness on the scales – and to consider whether her effective attacks on bureaucratic inertia should, in fairness, be added to the calculus. When they do, they will find this an indispensable guide to a bleak decade – and one of the best interim biographies of any politician to have been written.

New Statesman & Society, 14 April 1989

BILL CLINTON
AND THE NEW DEMOCRATS

A YEAR AFTER his election win, America and the world are beginning
to get used to Bill Clinton. They are still puzzled and exasperated by
the new President, and they still don't quite trust him. But they have
grown accustomed to a more affable style in Washington, to blue-
stocking young women and bearded young men in government, to a
genial First Family that isn't gerontocratic, and to remarks, both from
the First Lady and the First Gentleman, that do not come off an
autocue but which seem – at least on domestic policy – to reflect a
degree of independent thinking. The Clintons, people are saying, may
not yet have learnt to avoid tripping over their own shoe-laces. But
they are an interesting couple, which is an exciting development in
itself.

At the beginning of his presidency, it was hard to take Clinton
seriously at all. In his first few months, he seemed not so much a chief
executive as a kind of Sergeant Bilko figure, issuing commands that
automatically splattered back in his face, causing universal hilarity.
There was his would-be Attorney-General's Peruvian servant, and then
the mishandled gays-in-the-military business, that seemed to parody
conservative stereotypes of liberal angst. There was a chapter of
stumbles over the deficit, the budget and the economy. There was the
uncertainty over Bosnia that infuriated America's European allies.
After Clinton's first hundred days, his public approval rating dipped
to a humiliating 37 per cent; at the end of his second, Professor James
MacGregor Burns wrote in the *American Prospect* that the President
reminded him of 'a spirited but errant deer, chased by hounds,
struggling through thickets and bogs and headed for quagmires'.

Eventually, however, things began to pick up. Foreign policy has
continued to be pretty chaotic, as Clinton – burdened by the seemingly
misanthropic Warren Christopher as Secretary of State – struggles to
find something resembling coherence. But domestic policy has been a

little better. There have been notable minor victories: the National Service Bill, for instance, which introduces a kind of domestic peace corps linked to the provision of college grants. Most important, however, has been the fanfare surrounding the Clinton health care plan, and Hillary's dazzling performance as her husband's envoy on Capitol Hill. In September, the presidential approval rating slipped back over the 50 per cent mark.

If ever there was a quagmire, the health care issue certainly provides one – and the sheer complexity of a field of activity that accounts for a staggering 14 per cent of national income is pretty well bound to bog down everybody involved, long before the 1996 election. But for the moment, President Clinton, antlers nobly tossing, is getting credit for making the attempt.

That is fair, because health care is much more than just a topical problem that has landed on the plate of a new administration. Not only is it of fundamental importance to the United States. The question addressed by Clinton's enormous document lies at the heart of the crisis facing left-of-centre parties everywhere: is it possible for a progressive government in the modern world to link the fate of those who are seriously deprived to that of ordinary citizens, without committing electoral suicide?

In one sense, of course, the problem of what to do with the marginal poor has been an embarrassment to the Left since the invention of social democracy. The masses have never been homogeneous: the notion of a single 'working class' (as distinct from the 'working classes', an earlier usage) was a nineteenth-century invention that owed more to ideology than to observation. Even Marxists acknowledged the reality of division, when they pointed to the existence of a 'lumpen' proletariat, whose condition was so wretched that it could not be seen as the natural ally of the majority of workers. Bourgeois hostility towards this stratum (of the kind vividly expressed by Ebenezer Scrooge in *A Christmas Carol*) has always found ample support from those just above the breadline. Neither Dickens nor any other Victorian writer, however, made the mistake of confusing the concerns of ordinary working men with those of unfortunates whose destiny lay in the poorhouse.

For whom was the socialist enterprise intended? You do not have to read books to find the answer. Look at any social realist painting. Socialism was not charity. The aim, in the words of the British Labour Party's 1918 Constitution, was to benefit the producers, 'to secure for the workers by hand or by brain the full fruits of their industry'. Socialist art depicted muscular men and healthy women in appropriate settings – the coal mine, the factory, the farm, the family hearth. It seldom represented unpopular fringe groups: gypsies, new immigrants, single mothers, alcoholics. Socialists – and liberal reformers, like the Roosevelt Democrats – might have sympathy for such outsiders, but they were also wary of them, and did not regard their rescue as a high priority.

Yet for a long time, the layered nature of the masses did not cause too many difficulties for public policy, because – although there were differences – there were also plenty of needs that were shared. To put the point at its most basic, until quite recently most people – in work or not, healthy or sick – were poor, or in constant danger of becoming so. Consequently there was an electoral coalition: popular demands for rights at work, housing, pensions, social security, helped to provide the basis for the social democratic majorities of the early post-war years. It was always a precarious combination, and the domestic policy theme of the last generation has been its gradual erosion. Indeed its very achievements (in terms of reducing the numerical strength of the poor) have made it possible to drive a wedge between the better off and adequately secure groups, and those for whom fundamental requirements had not yet been met.

Margaret Thatcher was the first western leader to seize the new political opportunity, as her recently published memoirs remind us. It is becoming hard to remember that as recently as the 1970s unemployment was regarded as a political killer, which no government could survive above a certain level, because of its effect on the voting behaviour of those who had jobs, as well as those without them. Her discovery was that this principle no longer held. It was a breakthrough that changed the electoral game across the democratic world. In one country after another, right-wing leaders found that they could plunder the traditional constituency of the Left by simply abandoning the former 'consensual' commitment to the welfare state, and isolating those who made the biggest demands on it. Lady Thatcher draws the comparison between her own strategy and that of the Republicans in the United States, when she writes that, in the early 1980s,

the more numerous and dissatisfied Labour supporters were in the rising working and lower-middle class – the same group that in America Ronald Reagan was winning over and who were known as 'Reagan Democrats'. They were benefiting from the opportunities we had made available, especially the sale of council houses; more important, they shared our values, including a strong belief in family life and an intense patriotism. We now had an opportunity to bring them into the Conservative fold.

The process of peeling off formerly left-wing voters who decided that they preferred higher disposable incomes to public investment helped to fuel the yuppie fashions of the Thatcher–Reagan decade. Earlier in the century, the plague of unemployment had been so unsparing in its ravages that electors had reacted against the do-nothing governments they held responsible. Now it was possible both for voters and the governments they elected to shelter behind the tautology that 'successful' people did not fall out of work. Much more than in the 1930s, joblessness was concentrated in the ghetto of the poorly educated, the less skilled, members of ethnic minorities, older workers in antiquated industries, and young people without the means to express their grievance except in the occasional urban riot.

In the new climate, the Right was able to draw the lucky majority under its protective banner, while blaming the disaster either on the fecklessness of those afflicted by it (an approach symbolized in Britain by Norman Tebbit's famous recommendation to the unemployed that they should follow the example of his father, who 'got on his bike' in search of work) or on the Sodom and Gomorrah of spendthrift welfarism. Previous governments, Conservative and Labour, Republican and Democrat, had believed that cuts in social spending would cause a general resentment, even among people not directly affected. It was another discovery of the Thatcher–Reagan era that prejudice against those at the bottom of the heap – and, along with it, approval of measures to reduce spending on them from the public purse – actually increased, as the least fortunate got pushed further to the margins.

The effect has been colossal. That the so-called 'underclass' (a label that gained currency during the Reagan years) is becoming worse and worse off both in absolute terms and by comparison with average people, with whom it has less and less in common, is officially acknowledged on both sides of the Atlantic – although oddly (or significantly) it is not something either the Democrats or the Labour Party have chosen to make too much fuss about. In Britain, the DSS's survey on 'Households Below Average Income', published in June 1993, showed that in the period 1979 to 1991, average incomes rose by a real 35 per cent, but that the incomes of the worst-off tenth of all households had actually fallen by a real 14 per cent. Figures released in October show a strikingly similar picture in the United States. According to Daniel H. Weinburg, chief of the Census Bureau's Housing and Household Economic Statistics Division, the number of poor in that country ('poor' is defined in fixed terms, linked to subsistence costs) has increased by 5.4 million since 1989, from 12.8 per cent of the population to 14.5 per cent. As a result, the number of Americans living in poverty in 1992 was greater than at any time in the preceding thirty years.

For a long time, these realities were either treated by conservative leaders in both Britain and the United States as a necessary feature of a lean economy, or they were ignored. The word 'poverty' occurs only twice in Lady Thatcher's voluminous account of the period that spanned its greatest post-war growth: once to congratulate herself on reinventing the Victorian distinction between the 'deserving' and 'undeserving' poor, and once to denounce Labour councils for spending money to alleviate hardship. The strategy of redistribution in favour of the better off caused neither her, nor her successor, any political difficulty; indeed, Labour's commitment to taxing high earners in order to pay for social projects was widely felt to have scared many ordinary voters – not just those in the top bracket – into the Tory camp.

George Bush was less fortunate. 'If unemployment had been 5.5 per cent in the United States instead of 7.5 per cent', says Jeff Faux of the Economic Policy Institute in Washington, 'Bush would still be President.' The key difference between the American and British elections was not the relative slickness of the Clinton campaign, or a 'New Democrat' manifesto, or that the Democrat leader had more charisma than the Labour one. It was timing. The American election took place seven months later than the British one in a year of deepening economic troubles. If Major's poll had coincided with Bush's (after Britain's 'Black Wednesday', instead of before it), Neil Kinnock might be Prime Minister.

There may, however, have been more to Clinton's victory than a high degree of economic pessimism. If it was 'the economy, stupid' that lost Bush the election, the reason was not just the mounting statistics of unemployment, but the people they were affecting: increasing numbers of what Americans call 'the middle class' – which means ordinary citizens, blue and white collar alike. For the first time in half a century, decent, God-fearing middle America felt a chill of fear, as friends and neighbours lost their jobs and real-estate values plummeted. Even so, not many Republicans or 'Reagan Democrats' voted for Clinton who – at 43 per cent – polled lower than Michael Dukakis in 1988. That Clinton won was partly because of the *poujadiste* intervention of Ross Perot, whose maverick candidature 'departisanized the critique of Bush', as the Democrat strategist Paul Tully put it, and picked up 19 per cent of the vote.

So the moral to be drawn from Bill Clinton's election success remains tantalizingly uncertain. Does it mean that Americans have rejected neo-liberalism – or just an unpopular President who had let the deficit rise *and* had broken his word on taxation? More important, can it be taken as a vindication of the elegant thesis put forward in John Kenneth Galbraith's essay *The Culture of Contentment* – or as a destruction of it?

Galbraith, veteran economist and presidential adviser who helped Roosevelt with his speeches and was a friend of Kennedy, wrote his book from the point of view of the weary and disheartened traditional liberal. Contemplating a nation in which the poor seem even more politically listless and excluded than in other industrial countries, Galbraith claims that the American system has corrupted liberalism: instead of a free people governing itself, there is now a country in which the 'Contented Electoral Majority', made up of the economically and socially fortunate, 'rule under the rich cloak of democracy' – but a democracy in which the less fortunate take no part. As a result, they become less fortunate still, more listless, and even less likely to be on the voting register, or to cast their votes if they are.

Galbraith is in no doubt about what the situation in rapidly polarizing America requires: the acceptance of federal responsibility. The language he uses is uncompromising and old-fashioned. 'In no economically advanced country – a sadly neglected matter –', he points out, 'does the market system build houses the poor can afford.' Furthermore,

> Life in the great cities in general would be improved, and only will be improved, by public action – by better schools with better-paid teachers, by strong, well-financed welfare services, by counselling on drug addiction, by employment training, by public investment

in housing that in no industrial country is provided for the poor by private enterprise, by adequately supported health care, recreational facilities, libraries and police. The question once again, much accommodating rhetoric to the contrary, is not what can be done, but what will be paid.

In short, the author calls for a New Deal or Great Society programme, of which, however, he sees little prospect from either American political party. Galbraith completed his book shortly before the emergence of Clinton as Democratic standard-bearer, and does not mention any contemporary Democrat by name. However, it isn't hard to imagine the kind of people he has in mind when he writes, with heavy irony, that the principal talent now needed in a Democratic presidential candidate is a mastery of electoral arithmetic:

From this modest mathematical competence comes the conclusion: to win, one must subtract voters from the other side. Accordingly, a Democratic presidential candidate must be no less acquiescent to the contented majority than a Republican. This requires that he makes no serious bow to the non-participating, non-voting minority, that would arrest all recruitment from the opposition with the further chance of losing comfortable Democratic voters. In consequence of the foregoing, all recent presidential elections have been fought between twin exponents of the broad position of the contented majority.

This was an attack on Carter, Mondale and Dukakis, not Clinton. Nevertheless, there are ways in which it applies even more to the present Democratic leader than to his predecessors. It was as a proponent of the revisionist teachings of the Democratic Leadership Council, and his espousal of a 'New Covenant' between governing and governed, that the young governor of Arkansas came to the fore as a national possibility. Clinton's policy stances in 1992 did not differ sharply from those of Dukakis in 1988; but where Dukakis seemed hesitant, Clinton stated his case with boldness. Backed by fellow 'New Democrats', he made fewer gestures towards old liberals in his party, and wooed middle-class America almost wantonly. Nobody who heard Bill Clinton's speech as presidential candidate to the Democratic Convention in New York City on 16 July 1992, came away thinking he was a socialist, or even a New Dealer:

We need a new approach to government – a government that offers more empowerment and less entitlement, more choices for young people in the schools they attend . . . A government that expands opportunity, not bureaucracy – a government that understands that jobs must come from growth in a vibrant and vital system of free enterprise . . .

We offer opportunity. We demand responsibility. We will build an American community again. The choice we offer is not conservative or liberal. In many ways it's not even Republican or Democrat. It's different. It's new. And it will work.

Actually, much of it was old, though artfully designed both to reach out to the people Thatcher called 'Reagan Democrats', who had voted Republican in the 1980s, and to lose as few as possible of the poorer Democratic voters who, however, had nowhere else to go (except to the populist Perot). Yet Clinton's message was not mere marketing cosmetics. Against a background of bad economic news, it punched home because it spoke directly to voters Clinton identified as 'all the people who do the work, pay the taxes, raise the kids, and play by the rules . . . the hardworking Americans who make up our forgotten middle class' – the same middle class, indeed, that had been contented enough in the past, but now – recession-hit – was feeling angry.

Clinton promised not to raise taxes for the middle class (a promise, by the way, he welshed on almost as soon as he took office). He promised to fight crime, and make college kids work for their grants and the poor work for their benefits. But he also made a commitment of a classic, welfarist kind which touched an area of growing 'contented majority' concern, and one where the interests of majoritarians and minoritarians were unusually aligned. He promised – in a country where few pledges could be more revolutionary – 'An America in which health care is a right, not a privilege. In which we say to all of our people: your government has the courage – finally – to take on the health care profiteers and make health care affordable for every family.'

Health care, of course, has long been an item in the concerned or altruistic Democrat's baggage. Some 37.4 million Americans lack the health insurance that provides access to private (i.e. mainstream) medicine. Inevitably, the biggest concentration is among the poor. If, however, health care was exclusively a problem for the non-participating badly off, it would scarcely have had so prominent a place in Clinton's campaign. What raised its political status was partly the spiralling cost; partly alarms caused to ordinary citizens by insurers failing to meet their obligations in expensive cases; and partly the abandonment of a 'community rating' system of fixing premiums, in favour of the 'cherry-picking' of low-risk customers by aggressive insurance companies and a consequent rise in premiums for those assessed as high risk. At a time of job insecurity, a kind of panic swept a country in which employment and insurance are commonly linked. What if I should have to move, or change job? An estimated 60 million Americans go through periods of lacking any health insurance. The fear that age, or a medical defect in a family member, might cause major insurance difficulties has become widespread, not confined to the marginal or those on low incomes.

Health care became a major national issue in 1990, as unemployment rose and the numbers able to afford insurance fell. It took off in the following year, in the campaign to elect a little-known liberal, Harris Wofford, as Senator for Pennsylvania in a 'special' (i.e. by-election) contest. Wofford fought on health. 'If criminals have the right to a lawyer', he said, 'I think working Americans should have the right to a doctor.' Wofford started two-to-one behind the Republican: he finished 10 per cent in front. After that, health was a topic nobody could ignore. In the Democratic primary race, Senator Bob Kerrey of Nebraska highlighted the issue, and Clinton picked up the baton. Among Clinton's campaign pledges were promises to ban underwriting practices that tried to discover which patients were bad risks, to prohibit companies from denying coverage to individuals with 'pre-existing' medical conditions, and to guarantee every citizen a 'core benefit package', so that, in the candidate's words, 'No one will be cut off, cancelled, denied or forced to accept inferior care.'

That is the background to President Clinton's keen interest in the subject, and the launching of what the *Washington Post* has called 'the most complex and far-reaching legislative package since the New Deal' – which would provide guaranteed coverage for all citizens, largely paid for by employers. Much remains to be worked out (and much, no doubt, to be shot down). However, from the mass of horrendously intricate detail in the plan, a number of things stand out. First, although the health care plan is being presented as modern, regulated capitalism, it is actually a Robin Hood scheme in the best social democratic tradition. It will take from the better-off, healthy, securely employed and young and give to the less well-off, medically high-risk, insecure and middle-aged; it may also cream something off cowboy insurance companies, exploitative hospitals and greedy physicians. Second, as Hillary made clear in her testimony on the Hill, its introduction signals the abject failure in a major field of service provision of the Reagan–Bush free-for-all. ('In order to choose among everyone sitting in this room who is and who is not a good risk', the First Lady sweetly explained to hardbitten Congressmen, some of whom looked as if they were due for bypass surgery, 'that takes a lot of time and a lot of manpower, and a lot of personal cost. And so I think that, if you look at the ways the current private sector operates, you will find an enormous amount of inefficiency.') Third, the plan is much more than a tidying-up operation. If it does what it says, it will provide America with what the country has hitherto lacked: the core ingredient of a welfare state.

Finally, for the first time since the 1960s, a major liberal proposal has jerked the national consensus in the United States sharply to the left. Nobody is starry-eyed about the Clinton Plan, which has many critics, not just among the financial, medical and pharmaceutical lobbyists who will spend tens of millions of dollars on alarming people about its implications. But even the most sceptical accept, shamefacedly, that something must be done about a system which, as Mickey Kaus, author of *The End of Equality* puts it, is extremely efficient about just one thing: transferring the maximum share of GNP to doctors and hospitals. When Republican Senator Phil Gramm of Texas recently unveiled his own 'conservative' plan, involving large-scale new regulation of the insurance and health care industries, new burdens on employers, a tax increase and a big new government-funded entitlement programme, *Post* columnist Michael Kinsley marvelled at how far the Senator had moved since before the election. Yet Gramm's proposal, he observed, 'now represents the far-right flank of the opposition to Clinton on health care'.

In short, all is not yet lost to 'Culture of Contentment' politics in America. Many of Professor Galbraith's arguments undoubtedly ring true and must be heeded. Special note needs to be taken, in particular, of his warning that neglect of the inner cities will almost inevitably lead to explosions of violent unrest. But it would be absurd to conclude that because of the political dominance of the Right in the Thatcher and Reagan years, voters have been permanently and irrevocably beguiled by their slogans, and the Left must mutate accordingly. It will be months, or even years, before the Clinton experience can be judged: for the moment, however, the lesson seems to be that when the participating majority bids content farewell, it is not the market, but the state, it turns to for succour – to the possible advantage of everybody.

Times Literary Supplement, 19 November 1993

HOW TO DE-SELECT YOUR PM

HOW DO YOU DISPOSE of a prime minister whom practically nobody wants? Chris Mullin – who once wrote a pamphlet called *How to De-Select Your MP* – ought to turn his pen to this one. It would surely be a bestseller.

In a sense, of course, the answer is simple, as Margaret Thatcher discovered: you put up a plausible challenger. Or there is the 'men in grey suits' scenario, the glass of whisky, the loaded revolver. But the first method depends on the hoped-for successor being able to stand, which might be difficult in Kenneth Clarke's case unless (as happened in 1975) a head of steam builds up behind someone else; and the second depends to some extent on the Prime Minister playing the game like, well, a gentleman.

Historically, the business of getting rid of a premier other than at a general election has seldom, if ever, gone like clockwork. Although prime ministers have invariably suffered from paranoia, in practice they have enjoyed much greater security of tenure than the ministers they have appointed and sacked at whim. When a leader has been pushed, the successor has sometimes been unexpected, or unexpectedly bad, or (as with John Major) both. But premature obituaries have outnumbered actual assassinations ten to one; and actual conspiracies have been rare and generally botched.

For Major's enemies, history offers little encouragement. It was a Cabinet plot that got rid of Asquith in 1916, but that was under the special conditions of a wartime coalition. Conservative MPs were responsible for the abrupt departure of Lloyd George in 1922, but there is no analogy with the present because Lloyd George was a Liberal, and his Tory supporters were simply terminating his contract.

Andrew Bonar Law, the 'unknown' Prime Minister who held office for only seven months in 1922–3, was also a sick one, and departed of his own volition. The next two premiers, Stanley Baldwin and Ramsay MacDonald, who alternated in office for fourteen years, were never in danger from their parties. In 1931 MacDonald sacked his government, rather than the other way round, staying in office at the head of a 'national' administration. Both men carried on in office until their fading mental and physical powers made it obvious, even to themselves, that they could no longer do so.

Although the inter-war years were marked by industrial turmoil, mass unemployment and the rise of fascism, no prime minister apart from Lloyd George lost office except by choice or electoral defeat. Since 1939 the political pressures on premiers have been greater and there have been several sudden departures: yet none of them suggests that the process is easy, or its outcome predictable.

Apart from Thatcher, the most clear-cut case was that of James Callaghan, who failed to hold the House on a confidence vote by a margin of one in 1979, called an election, and lost it. However, Labour had been a minority government for three years and an election was due anyway within months. Callaghan's plight does not compare with Major's. It is much more like MacDonald's at the end of 1924, when the first minority Labour government had the rug pulled out from under it by the Liberals.

Three post-war premiers have gone at elections, stepping down or being forced out as party leader while in Opposition (Attlee, Douglas-Home, Heath). Three others have gone because of old age (Churchill) or ill-health (Eden, Macmillan), though in each of these cases the decision was taken against the background of a clamour for their departure. Uniquely, Harold Wilson retired in 1976 at a moment of his own choosing, when neither ill nor old, and under no pressure.

Yet even with Eden and Macmillan, the departures were not forced, and a 'men in grey suits' dismissal, often described as the Tory way, has in reality never happened to a serving prime minister.

There is, however, one resignation of which Major should take note, and that is Neville Chamberlain's in May 1940. On that occasion, Tory rebels combined with the Opposition to turn a debate on a failed operation (Norway) into an indictment of the Prime Minister's war leadership. In the subsequent division, the Government won by a large majority, but with forty-one of its normal supporters voting against, and some sixty-five abstaining. There is no doubt that Chamberlain was constitutionally entitled to carry on; it is clear, moreover, that he wanted to do so, and hung on until the last moment ('like a very sticky piece of chewing gum', as one opponent put it). But within a couple of days he had gone and Churchill was kissing hands as his successor.

In some ways, Major's position today is weaker than Chamberlain's. Not only was Major defeated in the Commons on a key element in his policy, which never happened to the architect of appeasement; Chamberlain, unlike Major, was highly regarded in the House and the country. When Chamberlain appealed to his 'friends' in Parliament to support him, he had in mind the country squires on the back benches who had followed him through the pre-war battles over foreign affairs and who remembered him as an estimable health minister and Chancellor of the Exchequer. Major, by contrast, has little personal following, and few MPs would sacrifice themselves to save him.

What Major does have on his side, paradoxically, is the democratic method of picking a leader. 'Look, you elected me,' he can say, as Chamberlain never could, 'and I remain the legitimate office holder until you reverse that decision.' Meanwhile, MPs go on holiday, tempers cool, the economy picks up. Would Churchill ever have been Prime Minister if the decision had been postponed until after the summer recess?

So Major may be around for longer than it is currently fashionable to think. Wilson, after all, survived innumerable attacks on his leadership in 1968–9, when things looked almost as bleak. And Thatcher before the Falklands was the most unpopular Prime Minister ever. But neither Wilson nor Thatcher suffered the humiliation inflicted on the Prime Minister last week. If Major does remain, he will certainly chalk up another prime ministerial record – as the bounciest rubber ball in political history.

Independent on Sunday, 25 July 1993

PART II

Rogues and Radicals

WAS ANYONE AFRAID OF
LEONARD WOOLF?

LEONARD WOOLF IS BEST KNOWN as a 'man of letters' – critic, essayist, editor, journalist, publisher, husband of Virginia, friend of Lytton and Maynard: one of the mythic figures at the heart of the Bloomsbury firmament. Few think of him now as a politician. Yet for several decades he led, and often dominated, Labour Party international and imperial advisory committees; he published more than thirty political books and pamphlets; and, by his own claim, spent most of his working hours for more than half a century on politically related activities.

Labour politics held few obvious attractions for a man of Woolf's tastes and sensibilities: he was not born into the Labour Movement, he was never more than 'a socialist of a sort' and his closest friendships were among folk who were, in general, snobbishly disdainful of the working class. Why then this record of loyalty and service, of thankless devotion to committees depressingly stocked with fools who, as he himself affirmed, he never suffered gladly? Sir Duncan Wilson's penetrating study of Woolf's political work and ideas raises this question, but leaves it unresolved.

Youthful enthusiasm? Woolf showed little active interest in politics until he was in his thirties and then kept up his involvement for a lifetime. Ambition? According to Wilson, Woolf may have been briefly attracted by the idea of 'The Rt. Hon. Leonard Woolf PC, MP,' but if so this was a passing fancy; he stood only once for Parliament, in 1922 for a hopeless seat, refused to be nominated again and generally expressed a distaste for what he regarded as the monotonous drudgery of House of Commons life. Alienation? The author rejects – perhaps too readily – an explanation based on Woolf's own background as a Jew. Culture and caste may have worked together. It is at any rate

Leonard Woolf: A Political Biography, Duncan Wilson (Hogarth Press, 1978)

interesting to note Woolf's roots in that strange substratum of the English social system which George Orwell called the 'lower upper middle class': the shabby genteel whose concern to maintain standards in the face of economic circumstances exposes the values they seek to uphold.

There are some striking parallels with the early life of Orwell: an adolescence of social discomfort as a poor scholar at a public school; a failure to live up to early academic promise; an improbable and isolating career as a colonial official in the Far East. But Woolf, unlike Orwell, went to university between school and Empire, and the experience was formative. Entering Trinity in 1899, Woolf (like the Cambridge Fabians, Rupert Brooke, Hugh Dalton and Clifford Allen a few years later) came under the spell of G. E. Moore, whose *Principia Ethica* completed Woolf's conversion to a religion of rationalist idealism, and set him on an iconoclastic road.

Moore's ethics had no direct political message. What they provided, in Woolf's words, was 'the fresh air and pure light of plain common sense' in morals, that led easily to a practical, political and irreverent 'ought'. At the end of his life Woolf remembered Moore as the only 'great man' he had ever met, a secular prophet whose ideals and behaviour guided his own. His decision to become an administrator in Ceylon was dictated more by examination failure and a lack of alternatives than conviction. Nevertheless, 'if it had not been for *Principia Ethica*', he wrote, 'I believe I should have become an usher.'

Seven years in Ceylon, including three in the role of what Wilson calls a 'selfless dictator' in charge of a district, were interesting, fulfilling, successful. Rapid promotion gave hope of a distinguished career, and when Woolf left the service in 1912 to marry Virginia Stephen the decision had little directly to do with politics. Yet he had become conscious, if not yet of the exploitative nature of colonialism, at least of its hypocrisies.

Again, the interesting comparison is with Orwell. For example, Woolf's account of his discomfiture when seeking to impose measures to counteract cattle disease brings to mind the incident described in Orwell's famous essay, 'Shooting an elephant'. 'I was issuing from on high orders to their village which seemed to them arbitrary and resulted in the shooting of their cows,' Woolf recalled. 'I drove away in dejection, for I have no more desire to be God than one of his victims.' Orwell, describing a real or imaginary event in Burma a generation later, tells how he felt compelled to shoot a perfectly healthy elephant in order to satisfy a native crowd: 'It was at this moment, as I stood there with the rifle in my hands, that I first grasped the hollowness, the futility of the white man's dominion in the East.' In each story, with its suggestion of symbolic sacrifice to maintain a morally bankrupt authority, the writer is repelled by what he finds himself doing as an agent of the system, and reacts against an illusion of power masking the reality of constraint. There is also a resemblance in the sequel: both writers escaped into the literary life, yet were held in the grip of their experiences, marked as opponents of the Establishment they had both served.

Here, however, the similarity ends. Orwell suffered real poverty. Woolf's lifestyle, based on the bedrock of Virginia's £400 a year, was never in serious jeopardy. Orwell was always an outsider, the champion of underdogs and losers. Woolf, rejecting one establishment, rapidly embraced another: the London literary coterie of which, as a former Cambridge 'Apostle', he was already an honorary member. Orwell's early writings were rough, undigested, politically naïve but sharply original. Those of Leonard Woolf, viewed down the decades, spring unmistakably and sometimes a trifle arrogantly from a readily identifiable *milieu*. Woolf's sincerity, and his independence, are never in doubt. But his failure to take many steps away from the avant-garde of his day limits the significance of his work.

In 1912 Woolf was 'a liberal but not a Liberal, and half way to socialism'. In March 1913 he visited Leeds, Glasgow, Bristol and Bolton, studying the co-operative movement. 'He was profoundly impressed by the drabness of life in the great provincial cities,' writes Wilson (perhaps he would have been even more impressed if he had ever lived in one). For a time, co-operatives continued to engage his attention. His main interest, however, was soon taken up (at the Webbs' instigation) by the comparative abstraction of international affairs. Wilson considers that Woolf's *International Government*, published in 1916, was his most influential work – helping to shape the text of the League of Nations Covenant and an important if less direct ancestor of later international organizations including the UN.

Defending himself against the charge of political inactivity in his youth, Woolf wrote in 1965: 'Things were improving – therefore we did not think so much about them. It was the 1914 war that made people think as they do today.' The war gave Woolf a clear direction: to ensure that the cataclysm should never happen again. Deriving his analysis from J. A. Hobson and H. N. Brailsford, he saw European rivalries and imperialism as inseparable evils and sought through Labour committees 'to get the party and its leaders to understand the complications and urgency of what was happening in remote places and among strange peoples about whom they were profoundly and complacently ignorant.' It was a worthwhile aim, and Labour's modest record of support for colonial movements owes much to the work of Woolf and others like him. Despite the impact of the Union for Democratic Control, of which Woolf was a leading member, and of *International Government*, his personal influence on foreign policy was smaller. Labour's reluctant acceptance in the 1930s of the need for collective security and rearmament owed less to Woolf's patient deskwork than to Dalton, Bevin and the rugged instincts of the TUC.

'The world today and the history of the human anthill during the last 57 years', wrote Woolf in the last volume of his memoirs, appropriately entitled *The Journey Not the Arrival Matters*, 'would be exactly the same as it is if I had played ping pong instead of sitting on committees and writing books and memoranda.' This was too modest. Labour's approach to foreign affairs would have been less confident, less practical, less open-minded without him. Yet he was never more than a minor figure. Intellectually he was a clarifier more than an innovator. Politically he was remote. There was a reluctance to descend from the pedestal and dirty his hands. As Wilson acknowledges, his faith in rational argument 'seemed even to reflect a certain naïvety about how power is exercised'. Absent from this book, and presumably from Woolf's life, is any sense of the rough and the tumble, the hustling and the compromise, of effective political action.

'He wrote well, talked better, and led an outstandingly full life,' Wilson concludes. 'A man of some political achievement, of much political influence, of great personal quality.' This shrewd and professional study is more important as an analysis of a phenomenon (the high intellectual in politics) and of a tradition (what A. J. P. Taylor called 'the trouble makers' of British foreign policy) than as the examination of the ideas and impact of a man.

New Society, 5 October 1978

BEATRICE AND SIDNEY WEBB

MUCH HAS BEEN WRITTEN about the Webbs. Beatrice herself published two volumes of autobiography, and Margaret Cole supplemented these with diary selections which take the account up to 1932. But the Webbs' voluminous correspondence (much of it deposited at what Beatrice used to call 'Sidney's child' – the London School of Economics) has hitherto only been available to researchers, if at all. These superbly edited volumes add greatly to our knowledge of the Webbs' political activities, and of their many spheres of influence. The letters also provide, half submerged beneath the blue books and committees, a detailed account of a romance which helped determine the course of British socialism: the bizarre, productive love affair which Beatrice always deceived herself was merely a 'partnership'.

Norman MacKenzie's introductions and linking passages give the selection continuity, as well as providing some thoughtful assessments. His account of the 1931 political crisis (in which Sidney played a passive and undistinguished part) is a splendidly lucid compression, though arguably a shade too favourable to the currently fashionable pro-MacDonald interpretation of this episode. He quotes liberally from hitherto unpublished sections of Beatrice's diary, which often reveal her at her most tart and vivid: it is a pity that the diary in its entirety is to be published only in microfiche, and not book form.

All the letters printed are by Beatrice and Sidney Webb. Some are of marginal interest, except to the researcher, and the editorial decision to include no letters *to* the Webbs may be questioned. The best sections (which form a major part of each volume) are the exchanges between husband and wife. Elsewhere, the material seems frustratingly incomplete, and the replacement of some of the more technical items with

The Letters of Sidney and Beatrice Webb: Volume I, Apprenticeships 1873–1892; Volume II, Partnership 1892–1912, Volume III, Pilgrimage 1912–1947, ed. Norman MacKenzie (CUP, 1978)

letters from recipients, especially Bernard Shaw, Graham Wallas and H. G. Wells, would have added to the interest at little sacrifice. But these are minor quarrels. A measure of MacKenzie's success is the ease with which the reader is carried along.

From the start, Beatrice Potter appears precocious, nosey, precise. 'Dear Kate,' she wrote in 1862, aged four, 'do you know that poor, Miss Macmichael is very ill for she had a paraletic stroke and I am afraid she is not expected to recover is it not a great pity for she was such a nice person.' With only a scratchy, largely informal education, but with a handsome appearance and the prospect of an ample dowry, Beatrice seemed destined for a successful marriage. What saved her from high social status and historical oblivion was a combination of deep neurosis and indomitable will, both inherited, or acquired, from a depressive mother who dolefully longed for a career, wished for a son and despised her feminine role.

The few letters which survive from Beatrice's Joseph Chamberlain phase (she believed herself to be passionately in love with the Liberal statesman for six years, from 1883 to 1889) do not dispel the mystery surrounding this mythic connection. They indicate Chamberlain's courteous restraint, and the extent of Beatrice's obsession and turmoil. They show that Beatrice continued to regard the ending of their relationship as solely the product of her own principled determination to avoid an intellectually and spiritually cramping match. But they provide no evidence of an actual proposal.

Beatrice met Sidney Webb after the last of several breaks in the Chamberlain affair, in 1890, when she was thirty-two and Sidney a year younger, both by now minor, but notable, figures in overlapping circles. There began what Sidney called 'a pretty piece of intellectual communism' and a courtship characterized by Sidney's declarations of love and self-abasement, and Beatrice's brutal and increasingly frantic rejections of anything other than a companionship of the mind. As their work together prospered, so Beatrice's refusal to accept the reality of her emotional dependence on the ugly, lower class Webb became more obstinate. 'This is not merely a close friendship between a woman and a man,' wrote Sidney, 'but one between a woman and a man deeply in love with her.' When Sidney proposed, 'you were personally unattractive to me,' she informed him, 'and I doubted whether I *could* bring myself to submit to a close relationship.' Yet, 'Dear Sidney – I will try to love you – but do not be impatient; do not think the world faithless because I fail to do so. What can I do more – I am doing more than I would for any other man – simply because you are a socialist and I am a socialist.'

Part of Beatrice's ambivalence towards Chamberlain (which may also have been a defence against his ambivalent attitude towards her) was the fear of repeating her mother's subordination and frustration. Sidney presented no such dilemma. Nevertheless, at the end of 1890 Beatrice and Sidney agreed to end the romantic aspect which was interfering with their working relationship, and Beatrice drew up a contract of friendship which included the clause: 'That all the letters written by either to the other up to the end of this year should be returned to the writer thereof in a sealed packet; and that the sender should declare that none have been retained.' In the spring of that year she had written, 'Personal happiness to me is an utterly remote thing'; in the autumn that she felt 'very very miserable'. The following May they became secretly engaged, and in 1892 they married. On their Dublin honeymoon, spent gathering facts about the Irish labour movement, Beatrice wrote a footnote to a letter from Sidney to Graham Wallas: 'We are very very happy – far too happy to be reasonable.'

Much more reticent than his wife, Sidney yet appears in these letters as an emotional and romantic man, very different from the placid and imperturbable image he presented to the world. When Beatrice was displeased, as happened often enough during their strange courtship, he would spend 'a sleepless night of pain'. (When Sidney annoyed *her* she was 'thoroughly upset and unable to eat any breakfast'.) While Beatrice continued to dramatize her *grand amour* with the great and famous Chamberlain, Sidney repeatedly asserted his present love and admiration.

There is much material here for a sexual interpretation of Beatrice. Indeed, the creative power of her repressions is hard to mistake. 'When you have studied women', she lectured Sidney shortly before their engagement, 'I think you will find this desire to be helpful, to watch over "the manners that maketh man", to round off the corners of life – is the secret of their influence. It is, I suppose, part of the mother's instinct, and joined with their intellectual dependence (a curious trait in even the most intellectual women) it lends a friendship between men and women that subtle usefulness which will always make such friendships one of the great factors of life – so long as it is not blurred by the predominance of lower feeling – when I think it becomes the source of pure evil – whatever the relationship may be.' After eight years of marriage and a strengthening bond of affection, she confided in her diary that she had married Sidney from a combination of pity and 'altruistic utilitarianism'. She wrote that 'neither my physical passion nor my social ambition' were stimulated by him.

Beatrice Webb's contempt for sexual indulgence, her own or that of others, was matched by her disdain for people in general who displayed 'a very low standard of effort and a very high standard of comfort'. It is certainly difficult for a modern reader not to see links between Beatrice's prudery (her condemnation of Wells as 'a Goethe-like libertine', of Shaw for his 'philanderings with all kinds of odd female', or of Bertrand Russell for his lack of 'mental hygiene'), her faddish dietary habits inflicted on a reluctant Sidney, her recurrent depressions and her hypochondriacal ailments – and her obsessive appetite for work. While Sidney's exertions reflected a serene love for the business of problem-solving, Beatrice's bursts of energy punctuated by collapse appear as catharsis, a frantic search for escape from guilt and despair.

Sidney's mind was essentially administrative. Beatrice provided the missionary zeal. Yet her objection to poverty derived more from an abstract social conscience and distaste for the irrational than from sympathy for the oppressed. Neither had much belief in the power of the masses to manage their own affairs. Beatrice's socialism combined the Tory paternalism of her background with an earlier, evangelical strain; Sidney's socialism was based in Comtian positivism and the British civil service. Together they provided an extremely persuasive advocacy in favour of benevolent élites. The Fabian tactic of permeation was based on a belief in the power of existing rulers to make major changes: 'The more cliques you have access to, the broader the foundations of your power to get things done.' The Webbs merely envisaged a different kind of clique: 'An élite of unassuming experts, who would appear to be no different in status from the common man.'

It is notable how easily, without any flash of sudden conversion, the Webbs slipped, in the early 1930s, into their final campaign – in support of Soviet communism. The attraction was the appearance of a 'puritanical religious order'. There was no inconsistency. 'I am to that extent "heartless",' Beatrice had written in 1890, 'that I regard everything from the point of view of making my own or another's life serve the community more effectively.' To Beatrice, stalinist Russia appeared as the apotheosis of the ruthless utilitarian ethic whose discipline she had voluntarily embraced throughout her life.

'One never knows into whose hands letters fall,' she once warned

Sidney, 'and a close relationship is a sacred thing not to be looked into by another.' Poor Beatrice. How furious she, at least, would be at the publication of these volumes. But how lucky we are to have them.

New Society, 11 May 1978

BERTRAND RUSSELL

THERE WERE TWO Bertrand Russells. The most important was the philosopher of genius whose analytical approach has dominated his field for eighty years. This Russell was one of the intellectual giants of the age. Yet in the British popular imagination a second image continues to dominate: that of a political saint or (more commonly) an 'old fool'. The second Russell was an indefatigable campaigner, a defender of minority causes, an Establishment outsider, a professional Jeremiah. Clearly the two Russells are linked, and although the first might have existed without the second, the second is, to a degree, dependent on the first. In this clever, lucid and witty book, Alan Ryan employs his own wide understanding of political philosophy in order to explore the nature of the relationship.

It is the connections between pure and applied thought that mainly interest him. He dislikes the concentration in Ronald Clark's enormous study of Russell on the philosopher's emotional odyssey, and he is contemptuous of the view that Russell 'engaged in intellectual and political work only to take refuge from his private ecstasies and miseries'. Yet it remains an open question whether it is possible to divide up a human experience in order to explain it. Ryan denies that he is writing a biography; yet the structure and method of his book is traditionally biographical, and he is sufficiently conscious of the interplay of cerebral and emotional in Russell's life to refer quite frequently to personal events within it.

Explaining Russell's politics in philosophical terms is made especially hard both by the fickleness of his beliefs and by the casualness with which they were acquired. Politically, Russell remained a loner: his ideas existed on a private egocentric plane, and owed allegiance to no individual, group or class.

Yet, as Ryan points out, class helped to form him. His was the

Bertrand Russell: A Political Life, Alan Ryan (Allen Lane, 1988)

arrogance of the aristocrat. He also owed something to his female emancipationist mother ('I wish I could *whip* her', Queen Victoria reputedly declared). What part did his own isolated childhood, or the sexual puritanism of his upbringing, have to play in the creation of an advocate of the brotherhood of man, and an exponent of free love? Ryan concludes that such early influences 'coloured his character more than his intellect'. Intellect and character, however, seem to have had an intimate liaison, as Russell's remarkable *Marriage and Morals* makes clear. Ryan himself points to the link between Russell's personal loneliness and his quest for a human universe based on passion and the absence of barriers between individuals.

The link between rationality, tolerance and freedom in Russell's thought is best summed up by the famous tale (which Ryan sadly tells us is apocryphal) about the vicar who, on visiting Bertie and Dora's experimental school at Beacon Hill and encountering a naked child, declares: 'My God!' 'There is no God,' replies the child. The story also encapsulates another aspect: what Ryan calls Russell's delight in 'teasing the righteous', a consistent and most engaging predilection, which lasted a lifetime. Perhaps there was also a snobbish element. From 1907, when he stood for Parliament in a by-election as a female suffragist candidate, until the doughty anti-Vietnam-war campaigning of his dotage, the desire to outrage the Grundyish political and sexual sensibilities of the middle class seems to have been a driving force. To be denounced, pilloried, blackballed provided the vindication for his successively liberal reformist, anti-war and crypto-socialist views.

The latter reflected an empiricist's belief in the necessity of applying reason to politics, while also taking due account of the irrationality of man. Unpersuaded by Marxian economics, Russell stressed the importance in advanced societies of the power of opinion, which he saw as treacherous and impulsive. In his major political work, *The Principles of Social Reconstruction*, he presented a civic universe that was anything but utopian, relating social and political events to individual psychology. Yet there was a paradox: while acknowledging the absurdity of human behaviour, he frequently allowed his own intellectually watertight but politically naïve solutions to harm his own reputation and negate his influence for good. There were contrasts. Nothing did him greater credit than his courageous opposition to the insane slaughter of the First World War. But his credibility as a prophet of peace was shaken by his advocacy, after the Second World War, of a preventive war against the Soviet Union. Critics could be forgiven for seeing, in the latter position, intellectual logic, but a complete lack of political (or moral) sense.

'The wonderful briskness and flair with which Russell writes', comments Ryan, 'and the entertaining invective with which he laces his work, perhaps disguised from both his audience and himself a curious thinness in his argument.' There was also a hollowness to his political persona, for all the energy of his campaigning, generally for fine causes. This may partly be because, though a member of the powerful class, he never exercised the slightest power himself. But it also had to do with passion, his own pet subject. He believed – but did he feel? If his friend in the peace movement, Fenner Brockway, had said of his own work, 'I wrote on these matters as someone who saw the sufferings of mankind and suffered with them', the remark would be taken as a simple statement of fact. Coming from Russell, there is just a whiff of cant.

Russell's political influence – especially over attitudes to the family, and to disarmament – has been significant, and almost wholly positive. He was bold, persistent, and often ahead of his time. Russell No. 2, however, pales beside Russell No. 1, and in the long-run is unlikely to be remembered except as an adjunct to him. Ryan's book helps to illuminate the versatile temperament of a great philosopher. It also shows how great is the gulf an abstract thinker has to cross if he is to understand and affect the concrete world.

The Listener, 30 June 1988

MAYNARD KEYNES

WHAT SHOULD A POLITICAL biography contain? No literary form
has evolved as rapidly in the last generation, yet the change has been
little discussed, and few people – least of all the biographers themselves
– have considered what they are, or what they should be, up to. In
some ways, of course, that is what gives the form its glory.

I was reminded of this fluidity while reading the second volume of
Professor Skidelsky's monumental, and absorbing, life of Keynes. It is
interesting to compare Skidelsky's new study with that of Roy Harrod,
which first appeared in 1951. Both are, in their different ways, deeply
devotional works. Harrod was a Keynesian economist, a disciple and
evangelist, and even an acolyte of the Bloomsbury Circle of which
Keynes was a leading member. Skidelsky is an historian of Keynesianism, a second-generation apostle, whose major works have all been
infused by an admiration for the master, and whose reverence for his
present subject has taken him to the point of inhabiting Keynes's
country residence at Tilton.

Skidelsky made his reputation with the now classic *Politicians and
the Slump*, which argued that if Ramsay MacDonald had listened more
to the great economist the second Labour Government might not have
come a cropper. He jeopardized it with a biography of Sir Oswald
Mosley, which argued provocatively that the important thing about
the founder of the British Union of Fascists was his early espousal of
Keynes, not his later totalitarianism. Since then, Skidelsky has appeased
his critics with the excellent first volume of the present work, about a
man whom he here describes as a world saviour. Volume one ended
with the publication of *The Economic Consequences of the Peace* in 1919,
as a result of which Keynes became well known. This volume takes
the story up to the appearance of *The General Theory of Employment*,

John Maynard Keynes: The Economist as Saviour, Volume 2, 1928–1937, Robert Skidelsky
(Macmillan, 1992)

Interest and Money in 1936, upon which Keynes's claim to world status largely rests.

Skidelsky's study is more detailed than Harrod's, and also more scholarly. There are occasional lapses: for example, the account of Keynes's relationship with his secretary, Naomi Bentwich, which quotes extensively from letters and from her diary, is mysteriously not referenced at all. In general, however, the author cites a wide range of sources, while taking into account Keynes's many analysts and critics. It is one of Skidelsky's strengths as an historian that he is above all an arguer rather than a chronicler, and some of the most stimulating passages are, in effect, discursive essays about aspects of the Keynesian theory in which, with an Olympian sweep that is almost the equal of the great economist, he takes on all comers.

These include Peter Clarke, whose insightful *The Keynesian Revolution in the Making 1924–1936* covers much of the same ground: but whereas Clarke to a large extent modifies, and even depersonalizes, the notion of a specifically 'Keynesian' revolution, pointing both to the pool of ideas from which *The General Theory* emerged, and the partial nature of Keynes's own contribution, Skidelsky reasserts the supremacy of Keynes himself. Unfortunately, a rival biography of Keynes by the Cambridge economist D. E. Moggridge was published too recently for Skidelsky to take its critique of his first volume into account.

In addition to the theory, Skidelsky has an enduring interest in the Bloomsbury Circle. According to his account, Bloomsbury 'died in 1914', partly because of the war, but also because, by then, the translation of many Bloomsberries from Cambridge to London 'had started to break down the homosexuality of the pre-war Cambridge Apostles'. Nevertheless, the G. E. Moore-derived ethic lived on, influencing – as Skidelsky shows well – Keynes's own comfortable mix of recklessness, hedonism and moral purpose, which was predicated on an assumption of the absolute superiority of himself and his friends over almost everybody. When Lytton Strachey was asked during the war why he was not fighting for civilization, he is supposed to have replied: 'Madam, I *am* the civilization for which they are fighting.' Skidelsky reasonably comments: 'Lytton's joke was Maynard's belief: his life was spent fighting for the civilization which his friends at least partially represented.' This point, brought out even more clearly (and without irony) in Harrod's life, is a key to understanding Keynes, who had little concept of working-class people, except as a potential threat to 'civilization', if the political élite was foolish enough to impoverish or mismanage them.

Skidelsky is good at weaving together Bloomsburian political ideas and Keynesian economic philosophy – making clear that Keynes was not so much a logician of economics as a brilliantly intuitive visionary. He quotes him tellingly on the subject of Sigmund Freud, whom Keynes regarded with both scepticism and interest, on one occasion pointing out that Freud's ideas would still have an appeal if he had made all his evidence up. Critics of the Keynesian theory (as later of the Friedmanite one) levelled much the same charge.

The author gives an entertaining and sometimes moving account of Keynes's courtship and marriage to the Russian ballerina Lydia Lopokova, complementing Moggridge's account. He charmingly describes a dance performed by Maynard and Lydia before select Bloomsbury gatherings called the 'Keynes-Keynes', a parody of the can-can. He is less interesting (at any rate to this reader) when he describes the social-cum-sexual relationships of the Bloomsberries – with a few exceptions a tediously self-regarding assemblage of the second-rate. Fortunately, there is less about Keynes's own sexual habits than in volume one, partly because by the 1920s the hero seems to have traded in a promiscuously homosexual lifestyle for a monogamously heterosexual one.

Far more important is Skidelsky's account of Keynes's intellectual growth, and here the author argues with confidence. Indeed, this intelligent and ambitious book is not one study but several: of Keynes's economics, of his political and cultural ideas, as well as of his private persona. The quicksilver character of Keynes remains strangely elusive, separate from his intellect and achievements. For all that, Skidelsky's second volume is an immensely valuable work.

Independent on Sunday, 8 November 1992

HAROLD LASKI

WHO READS HAROLD LASKI TODAY? Possibly a few conscientious undergraduates who find *The Grammar of Politics* on their recommended list. Yet there was a time when everyone read him – so much so that the inter-war period could be called the Age of Laski. He was unavoidable. Rabid revolutionaries, liberal prime ministers, reactionary professors, all avidly or angrily devoured his latest article, essay or book. Laski was not just the socialist intellectual incarnate. He was also a central figure in the wider world of ideas.

Three years after Laski's death in 1950, Kingsley Martin wrote an affectionate memoir about him. For forty years there was nothing more – a silence that reflected Laski's posthumous fall from grace. Biographies are like London buses: now, just as socialism of any kind, let alone Laski's pretty rich variety, is in deep recession, we have two.

Both have been a long time in preparation, and are careful, scholarly works. The more ambitious is the joint study by the American political scientist Professor Kramnick (who did the writing) and the Labour MP, Barry Sheerman – it is a sensitive, highly readable and well-rounded account which breathes life into the driest corners of Laski's personality, while retaining a critical distance. Professor Newman's book focuses on Laski's political thought. Though marred by a few lapses of expression, this is a closely argued study which offers an intelligent and spirited defence. Perhaps it is merely coincidence that these two books should appear together. Alternatively, Laski is due for a revival.

Partly because of his name, Laski was often attacked by Tory blimps as a foreign Jew. In fact, he came from a family long established in Manchester. As a young man at the turn of the century, he enjoyed a conventional middle-class education at Manchester Grammar School

Harold Laski: A Life On The Left, Isaac Kramnick and Barry Sheerman (Hamish Hamilton, 1993); *Harold Laski: A Political Biography*, Michael Newman (Macmillan, 1993)

and New College, Oxford. Only two things marked him out from contemporaries – poor health and a love affair with a free-thinking woman eight years his senior, 'the first non-Jewish girl of his acquaintance', whom he married even before entering university. The marriage became the anchor of his life, but it also bitterly alienated his parents, and thereby contributed to his politics. When Laski later wrote that political beliefs were often shaped in reaction to a 'bad psychological atmosphere' at home, he had this rupture in mind.

After leaving Oxford, Laski became a prototype of the modern go-getting academic, zig-zagging across the Atlantic, with an eager-beaver obsession about getting into print as often as he could. Yet he was concerned to do much more than climb to the top of the educational ladder, or even to influence abstract political theory; and his frenetic university life was combined with an equally busy career as agitator, campaigner and party politician.

Together with his wife, he became closely involved in the suffragette movement, an interest which led him, bizarrely, into terrorism. Kramnick and Sheerman have done some brilliant detective work to show that Laski was responsible for placing a time-bomb (which detonated without causing injury) in the gentleman's lavatory at Oxted Station. Laski fled to France incognito and was never caught. If he had been, he would presumably have languished in jail, and we might never have heard of him. Instead, he lectured at Harvard, where he first acquired serious notoriety for alleged rabble-rousing during the 1919 Boston police strike. One American opponent wrote that Laski 'should be deported and consider himself fortunate in not being shot'.

In 1920, Laski returned to England and a job at the London School of Economics, with which his name was hereafter closely associated. He was twenty-seven and his mission was just beginning: his aim now, he wrote, was to bring 'some very real political influence within my grasp'. How far he succeeded is a moot point. His proximity to men of power – in journalism, in the Labour Party, in the White House and among colonial students who had a habit of ending up as heads of state – is beyond dispute. The extent to which those who were stimulated by him ever tried to put his ideas into practice is more doubtful. He remained intellectually and politically isolate. He was often cordially disliked by fellow thinkers. Many within his own circle considered him a braggart who, as Beatrice Webb put it, 'knows, or says he knows, everyone of importance'. In an age when socialists altered their opinions with even greater promiscuity than the present,

Laski had an exceptional propensity to be dogmatic in one direction one day, and in a contrary direction the next.

He was a showman and, partly for that reason, a successful teacher. He had, according to Newman, 'a particular conception of a university', which today seems sadly dated, 'in which the relationship between academic staff and students was the central element.' His pupils worshipped him. The 1920s LSE must have been a splendid place, with William Beveridge ruling the roost, Hugh Dalton booming on public finance, R. H. Tawney reflecting on social history, and Laski 'frail, sickly, bookish, bespectacled, dark, verbal' filling his students with ideals. Meanwhile he was placing himself close to the centre of power in the Labour Movement – driving a car for union officials in the 1926 General Strike, and in 1931, writing Labour's most doomed election manifesto ever.

When Labour was reduced to fifty seats by the 1931 poll, left-wing intellectuals outside Parliament came into their own. If the 1930s was the 'red decade', Laski was one of the reddest. He blamed the King for setting up the National Government, and called on the next Labour administration 'whenever that might be' to take Emergency Powers in order to carry out rapid nationalization. This was elective dictatorship with a vengeance: but Laski was never a communist or even a fellow-traveller. In fact, he was unusual for his time in treating Marx's writings as a curate's egg – good, but only in part. His heyday as a propagandist came in 1936, when Victor Gollancz launched the hugely successful Left Book Club, with Laski as a member of the ruling directorate.

Laski was active in the Second World War on Labour's committees, often causing irritation among Labour ministers who feared that his leftish stirrings would bring about the break-up of the Coalition Government. When the war ended, he suffered a rapid eclipse, marginalized partly by a new international mood. Newman argues persuasively that a British version of McCarthyism cast Laski as a subversive. Yet Laski's own political ineptitude may also have been a factor. As Chairman of the Labour Party just before the 1945 election, he persistently attempted to undermine the leadership of Clement Attlee, thereby giving the Tories ammunition: Winston Churchill's 'Gestapo' speech was targeted at Laski. When the election result was known, a New York newspaper proclaimed: 'Clement R. Attlee Made Prime Minister Of England But The Boss Is Harold Laski A Pro-Russian Figure.' Shortly before the poll, Laski had written privately to Attlee telling him to resign. Just after it, he wrote again, pointing out his own qualifications to be ambassador in Washington. It is not surprising that the new premier declined the offer.

Laski died at the age of fifty-six, when Attlee was still in office. By then, the trouble had become – as Richard Crossman put it – that no leading member of the Labour Party believed more than two per cent of what he said. However, this was Laski the meddler, Laski the inveterate talker with an instant opinion on everything under the sun. There had also been a more challenging Laski, who had been prepared to set aside the orthodox doctrines of the Left, yet who had never been cowed by the conventional wisdoms of the Establishment.

The second Laski stands the test of time far better than Strachey, or even G. D. H. Cole, rival inter-war thinkers. The scale of Laski's, mainly forgettable, writing tends to distract attention from the elements that deserve to be remembered – for example, his work on the Constitution, and on America. These two new books admirably sort out the good from the bad – and serve as a reminder of an era when ideas from the Left could be both radical and fashionable.

Guardian, 6 July 1993

VICTOR GOLLANCZ

SUCCESSFUL PUBLISHING and left-wing politics are unlikely bed-fellows. Hence a biography of Victor Gollancz is of special interest, as much for the phenomenon as for the man. How did he manage to break the rules, pursuing idealism and profit at the same time? How did a single egotistical individual, in a country whose politics have always been overwhelmingly dominated by exclusive parties, become a separate political force in his own right?

One answer seems to be that, like the best newspapers and journals, Gollancz's publishing enterprises were always an expression of the personality of the man at the centre – in his case, a peculiarly extravagant and naïvely enthusiastic one, which at various times struck a chord among thousands of people who would not normally have supported radical causes.

'The first thing to realize about Victor is that he was absurdly young,' a colleague wrote about him in his pre-publishing days. 'He was also absurdly clever, absurdly amusing, absurdly childish in many ways, absurdly affectionate.' Absurdity stalked the Gollancz booklists – but so, too, in the heyday of the firm, did some of the other attributes as well.

Gollancz's aspirations were partly the product of the social and intellectual ambitions of the highly-Anglicized north London Jewish family into which he was born. His father was a shrewd and prosperous jeweller, primarily interested in diamonds till the end. Victor was sent to St Paul's, to become an English gentleman.

Here his main interests, apparently in common with most of his peers, were in passing exams, God and masturbation – on the last of which he was later to write extensively. The first took him to New College, Oxford, as a classics scholar – and to a late Edwardian world of elegant friendships and effortless superiority which provided the

Victor Gollancz: A Biography, Ruth Dudley Edwards (Gollancz, 1987)

parameters of his intensely competitive spirit for the rest of his life.

Aged twenty-one in 1914, he belonged to the generation (and, by now, the class) that died on the Somme. Gollancz was fortunate. Commissioned in the Northumberland Fusileers, he was dispatched to the remote, and peaceable, outpost of Blyth, where his most exciting military adventure was a court martial for the unlikely offence of 'obtaining a horse under false pretences, representing that he could ride a horse with spirit and allowing the horse to lie down endangering the King's Highway'.

Unluckily, or luckily, the horse was the colonel's. Shortly afterwards (and what other nation would have thought of such a civilized solution?) he was seconded to Repton, the public school, as classics master with special responsibility for the OTC. It was a strange assignment, fattening up officer-caste geese for the slaughter of the western front, but he proved more than equal to it, and stayed on when the war ended.

In addition to his absurd youth and idealism, he was absurdly popular with the boys, a point which came to the attention of the headmaster, the Revd Fisher, later Archbishop of Canterbury, who determined to put a stop to it. According to Fisher, the school contained two classes: the teachers and the taught. 'The "popular" master was suspect, and rightly so, by his colleagues and the more thoughtful among the boys.'

This was Victor's first real experience of a divided world, and it affected him. He loved Repton: the boarding-school ethos, romanticized from the perspective of a master, was part of the reverie that stayed with him. For some of his near-contemporaries, university life was the model: the easy, equal camaraderie of college life offering the promise of a future socialist society. For Gollancz, Repton had most of the necessary qualities. His socialist utopia was always hierarchical, paternalist, even totalitarian, as well as rather hearty, with remarkably little tolerance of alternative points of view.

Yet there was an aspect of public school life (as of the army) that did not appeal. Authority figures (other than himself) were Gollancz's problem. When Fisher's reprimands failed to tame him, he left under a cloud – having tried to publish subversive literature using the school's imprint. Gollancz Ltd was the outcome, but not immediately. First came a meteoric career with Ernest Benn, an encourager of talent who gave the young man his head, promoting him and backing him until the inevitable break.

Gollancz left Benn in 1927, borrowing money through the Jewish network to set up his own firm. He was thirty-four. Within five years ('thirty-nine but looking forty-nine') he had become a major publishing force in the land, with a huge and increasingly profitable confidence that 'interest in books is more widely diffused than ever', and a populist instinct for titles to meet the new demand. In these early days, he was never far from scandal or the law courts, and his brushes with the censor were frequent. 'You may say bloody but may not say bugger,' he and his friends would chant in protest: 'You may say bottom but may not say balls.'

Though novels long remained the mainstay of the company, it was politics and political books that drew him. At the outset, he had intended to enter politics himself at the age of forty-five. Personal success and the rise of the Labour Party brought this plan forward, and in May 1931 he wrote to the Prime Minister, Ramsay MacDonald, asking to be made a parliamentary candidate and declaring a wish 'to devote as much time and energy as possible to working for the party'. The message was ill-timed; within two months MacDonald had formed the National Government, and within six Labour had suffered the worst setback in its history. Gollancz's road into politics was destined to follow a non-parliamentary route.

Gollancz had always been a fierce, if somewhat undefined, radical. It was the rise of Hitler that pushed him, like many of his contemporaries, towards Soviet communism. It was a disposition which his standing as a leading publisher gave wide public significance. For if the 1930s may be seen as the 'red decade', this was, to a large extent, Gollancz's doing.

It was Gollancz who discovered among insurance clerks, civil servants and teachers, a quite remarkable willingness to buy cheap popularized books which, increasingly, followed the Moscow line of the moment. As always, Gollancz was plain-speaking about his own approach. 'On topics which I believe to be of vital importance', he declared as early as 1932, 'I am anxious to publish nothing with which I am not myself in agreement.' This remained his credo when he notoriously refused to publish Orwell's *Homage to Catalonia* because of its expected hostility to the International Brigade in Spain.

By then, Gollancz had established himself as something much more than a publisher: rather, as a kind of political patriarch, able to exercise a very direct influence and patronage in left-wing affairs. This was because of the most important event in his career: the launching of the Left Book Club in 1936, in response to the Comintern call for a

Popular Front against fascism and, in particular, against Franco's military rebellion in Spain. The idea was simple: for a small sum, members received monthly book 'choices' (personally selected by Gollancz, in conjunction with Harold Laski and the communist, John Strachey), thus enabling Gollancz, because of a guaranteed sale, to publish large quantities at a low price.

The LBC succeeded beyond anybody's wildest dreams, and became a political movement: the radicalized lower middle class on the march. Briefly, not only the Communist Party, but the Labour Party itself, was overshadowed. What other politician, let alone publisher, could pack 7,000 of his cheering supporters into the Albert Hall?

This was his zenith. The Nazi–Soviet pact brought disillusion, and Gollancz moved sharply away from Communism, devoting much of his attention, previously directed towards peddling its propaganda, to unmasking its pretensions. His crusading days were not over: for the next quarter of a century, he campaigned for a range of worthwhile liberal, socialist and Christian causes. But his claim to historical importance must rest on this unique and heady phase, which helped to educate a generation in readiness for the 1945 Labour landslide. Despite sporadic attempts, the LBC experience has never since been replicated or even approached.

In this large and carefully researched book, Ruth Dudley Edwards explores Gollancz's many worlds, his public enthusiasms and his private tumults, with imaginative thoroughness. Highly readable, if also occasionally prolix, it is a book that succeeds admirably in presenting a man of vast energy, simple vision, inspiring courage and an obsessive concern to create a better world.

New Society, 23 January 1987

ARTHUR KOESTLER

DOES KOESTLER BELONG TO ART – or to politics, science, even religion? It has been partly the refusal to be categorized, the impatient hopping from one mental plane to another, that has made it hard to take the creator of Rubashov and Ivanov ('sympathy, conscience, disgust, despair, repentance and atonement are for us repellent debauchery') as seriously as he deserves.

The rational eccentricity of his death – the careful self-execution, the apparently calculated selfishness – seemed to parody Koestler's scientific utopianism; while the chair in parapsychology insults what we imagine to be our intelligence. Koestler's literary legacy was certainly mixed – at its worst hectoring, shallow, bizarre. There should, however, be no dispute about the limpid brilliance of his best. As a novel about the insane logic of total ideology, *Darkness at Noon* stands, clinically, alone.

Like other critics, Levene compares Koestler to Orwell, opposites in personality, yet closely related and interdependent in many of their preoccupations. Perhaps surprisingly, they admired each other's work, though Orwell remarked that 'the chink in Koestler's armour is his hedonism.'

More significant, however, was Koestler's rootlessness, the source both of imaginative leaps and of a limiting instability. Where much of Orwell's writing remains parochially national, Koestler's work has no settled attachment. His religions were intense, intellectual, transitory. Zionism was followed by liberalism, liberalism by communism. 'I became a socialist because I hated the poor,' says one of his characters, 'and I became a Hebrew because I hated the Yid.' Unlike Orwell, Koestler identified – sometimes fiercely – with ideas, never with unideological classes of ordinary people.

After a training in science, engineering and modern languages, he began his career at twenty-two as Middle Eastern correspondent of

Arthur Koestler, Mark Levene (Oswald Wolff, 1985)

the House of Ullstein, 'the embodiment of everything progressive and cosmopolitan in the Weimar Republic'. There followed journeys, and journalism, in Palestine, Paris, Berlin, chasing cerebral and sexual stimuli with the same restless inconstancy.

An interest in communism, acquired in reaction to the rise of anti-Semitic German fascism, took him to stalinist Russia, and thence to Spain as a party investigator and propagandist. Arrested as a spy and sentenced to death, he spent three months in prison, an experience that induced a 'spiritual transformation'. A year later he left the Communist Party, a decision that 'filled me with the wild elation that I had experienced every time that I had burned my bridges'.

'It seems to be a general law in politics', he wrote later, 'that hatred increases in proportion to the amount of shared convictions and interests.' Koestler's Spanish gaol was a fascist, not a communist, one, and after he left the Party he retained a vestigial sympathy for its aims and sense of purpose. Nevertheless, the finest of his writings were in reaction to his communist phase, when for a time he accepted the authority for which, he believed, the Old Bolsheviks indicted in the Moscow Trials confessed and died 'to do the Party a last service'. Orwell, too, turned against communism, but without the self-rebuke of having been a member.

Ambivalence towards absolute moral logic – horror and yearning combined – became a hallmark. Did Koestler ever scale his own, private, totalitarian walls? According to Levene, in *The Age of Longing* (1951) he 'amasses a quantity of evidence to prove the futility of any action that does not have its origins in absolute belief'. Ends continued to justify means – as in Palestine, during the Jewish resistance to the British – even if only 'within very narrow limits'. 'Rubashov's unyielding belief in reason emerges in all his actions,' Levene writes of the hero of *Darkness at Noon*, 'and by the time of the last interrogations, we come to expect nothing from him but the most rigid self-justifying logicality.' Rubashov is a savage caricature (so we are told) of Radek and Bukharin. Yet there remained much of Rubashov in Koestler.

What saves Koestler is the perplexity that accompanies his search for meaning, and a substratum of political realism. Politically, Orwell remained quizzically naïve. Koestler had been, and thought of himself as, a man of action – with much more ground than Orwell for despising those (Sartre, de Beauvoir, Camus) whom he called 'voyeurs' of history, who 'masturbate' with ideas and commitment.

For Koestler, political motivation as it actually existed was quite as mysterious as sex, with which (as a somewhat crude Freudian) he invariably associated it. In later life, Koestler was apt to see the world as medically mad, literally schizophrenic: the only cure, an 'adaptive mutation'. One outcome of his perplexity was the obsession with parapsychology, *reductio ad absurdum* of Victorian scientism. But another was a disquieting readiness to point to contradictions, and to pose questions that others were too prudent or cowardly to ask.

This little book is a minor mystery in itself – first published in America last year, paperbacked here without blurb, preface or briefest comment on the author. Whoever or whatever he may be, Levene has written as briskly elegant a collection of critical essays as one could hope for so soon after his subject's death. His study succeeds both as a concise guide to Koestler's major writings, and as a sharp commentary on a writer who (in the words of one admirer) belongs in the front rank of those who have saved our century from disgrace.

New Society, 23 August 1985

EDGAR HOOVER

J. EDGAR HOOVER – squat, piggy-eyed and pug-ugly – symbolized, during the Cold War years, the American way of bigotry. For almost half a century, he ruled the FBI in Washington – terrorizing politicians as much as criminals; treating actors, journalists and professors of liberal tendency as if they were headlice; and backing rich, racist and reactionary leaders with ghoulish enthusiasm. When Hoover died in 1972, vice-president Spiro Agnew spoke of his 'dedication to principle' and 'complete incorruptibility'. But draft-dodgers, intellectuals and people who simply believed in freedom rejoiced to see him go.

A biography which merely reminds us that Hoover was a fearful brute is therefore less than shocking. True, there are probably still some subscribers to *Reader's Digest* living in the remoter parts of small-town America who remember Hoover as a patriotic hero. But their number is surely small. For a more sophisticated public there is a need for a carefully analytic study of Hoover and his place in the American system and psyche. That need is not met by this book.

In the preface, Anthony Summers claims to have spoken to 850 people – an average of nearly two per page. This Kitty Kelley-type thoroughness fails to inspire confidence, however, partly because many of the witnesses to such a murky career are themselves murky; partly because the un-numbered references make it difficult to work out the source of any particular bit of information; but mainly because all the evidence points in one direction – towards the sordid, the sensational and the conspiratorial. When so much mud is thrown, and no point ever made in mitigation or even reasoned explanation, credibility is lost.

Indeed, the author achieves the singular feat, long before the end, of arousing in the reader a furtive sympathy for Hoover. Notably

Official and Confidential: The Secret Life of J. Edgar Hoover, Anthony Summers (Gollancz, 1993)

missing from the account is any proper description of what made him a charismatic figure to so many people, and what made him (skulduggery apart) such a formidable bureaucratic operator. The book is perhaps best treated as a kind of Damon Runyon picaresque adventure: its story is at least readable and entertaining.

Edgar Hoover was born in 1895, the son of a minor government employee who went mad and died in an asylum. As a child, and perhaps later on as well, he was a Mama's boy who had to act tough to compensate. As a young student with notably right-wing views, he drifted into the then infant Federal Bureau, and before the age of thirty was heading it. Having gained his spurs as a scourge of Bolshevists and anarchists during the Red Scare of the Twenties, he dug himself in – and acquired a public reputation chasing such gangsters as John Dillinger and Machine Gun Kelly in the 1930s. Meanwhile, he built the Bureau into a legendary force, with a dangerously élitist and even fascistic *esprit de corps*: raw recruits were indoctrinated with a quotation from Emerson – 'An institution is the lengthened shadow of one man.'

The FBI was much expanded during the Second World War, despite the poor relations that existed between Hoover and Roosevelt, whom the director regarded as suspiciously left-wing. It was in the late 1940s and early 1950s, however, that the Bureau really came into its own. Much more than Senator McCarthy himself, whom Hoover dourly and loyally supported through thick and thin, the FBI director was the sinister force behind the wire-tapping, dossier-collecting and blackmailing we call McCarthyism. According to the author, Hoover would stop at nothing to get his way, and criticism in the press was silenced by the simple expedient of smearing journalists who dared to voice it. Within the Bureau itself, it was an axiom that the director was never wrong: when Hoover announced his grief at the killing of an agent who had in reality only been wounded, fellow agents jokingly drew lots for who would finish him off. Hoover had a way with words: opponents were suffering from 'mental halitosis' or were 'cocksuckers'.

The latter insult was one levelled at Hoover himself, and if this book has a central theme it is that the FBI director – who affected a public Grundyism, and ruthlessly exploited his privileged knowledge of the sexual peccadilloes of Washington personalities – was himself secretly a practising homosexual, at a time when such activity was illegal. It is also the author's case that the otherwise inexplicably easy time given to the Mafia by the Bureau was because the Mob knew about this proclivity and threatened to expose it. Summers quotes a certain Carmine ('the Doctor') Lombardozze: 'J. Edgar was in our pocket. He was no one we needed to fear.'

Hoover's homosexuality is perfectly plausible, as is the allegation of Mafia pressure on the basis of it. Neither claim, however, is demonstrated by this book. True, there is scarcely a chapter that does not quote a series of informants who maintain that Hoover's tendency was common knowledge. Hoover was unmarried, and had a lifelong friendship with a colleague, Clyde Tolson, which was affectionate and close. But the nearest to evidence is an account of a photograph, allegedly in the possession of a leading CIA officer, James Angleton, showing Hoover and Tolson supposedly in a compromising position. Angleton of all people! Summers fails to mention that Angleton was himself a dangerous paranoiac, whose allegations of sex'n'spying against people as varied as Harold Wilson, Olaf Palme and Henry Kissinger caused a mixture of bewilderment and hilarity throughout the western intelligence community. Otherwise, Summers has to resort to the unreliable comments of such people as Hoover's psychiatrist's widow and an obviously *parti pris* West Coast mafioso, Frank 'Bomp' Bompensiero, who once remarked at the races in Hoover's hearing that the director was 'a punk, a fuckin' degenerate queen'. Hoover apparently took it meekly. But that is scarcely proof.

The evidence for cross-dressing is flimsier still. An elderly divorcée called Susan Rosenstiel is reported as saying that she encountered the director at a transvestite orgy in a Plaza Hotel suite in New York in 1958; he was in full drag, wearing 'a fluffy black dress, very fluffy, with flounces and lace stockings and high heels, and a black curly wig. He had makeup on, and false eyelashes ... It was obvious he wasn't a woman, you could see where he shaved. It was Hoover.' But was it? Mrs Rosenstiel attended the party with her then husband, a notorious ex-bootlegger, and by her own account she met Hoover only once afterwards, three years later. Her uncorroborated testimony is scarcely worth printing. The story is typical of the book, and of its flaw. What might have been scandalizing isn't, because you don't know when a tale or a recollection is accurate. In this subject area, the reader has to be especially wary: the twilight, semi-lunatic secret zone of undercover operations is walled with distorting mirrors.

There is also a wider aspect. Summers quotes one of Hoover's own colleagues, instructing a junior agent about the boss: 'You must understand that you're working for a crazy maniac, and that our duty is to find out what he wants and to create the world that he believes in, and to show him that's the way things are . . .' It is this which Anthony Summers's book insufficiently explores. For the world that Hoover believed in was not unique to him. It was also believed in by millions of decent, freedom-loving Americans. In the end, what is so scary about the notorious FBI chief is not his villainy itself but the national neurosis about enemies within, which allowed it to flourish.

Independent on Sunday, 7 March 1993

HUGH GAITSKELL

WHEN HUGH GAITSKELL DIED in 1963 there was a sense of an opportunity tragically missed. Yet today, except among the dwindling number who knew him well, his memory is more revered outside the Labour Party than within it. His name is seldom invoked on political platforms. The mantle of Nye is far more acceptable than the mantle of Hugh. That this should be so reflects the colossal shift in mood and temperament of the Labour Party in the seventeen years since Gaitskell's death: a change which Philip Williams's masterly study brings sharply into view.

This is biography on the grand scale: in some ways uncompromisingly old-fashioned, in others strikingly modern. It is a political, not a psychological study, and in the preface the author hints at a private life he has chosen not to explore. More than half of the 1,000-page text is devoted to the seven years of Gaitskell's leadership. In marked contrast to Michael Foot in his eloquent but under-researched life of Aneurin Bevan, Williams never offers a speculation without providing evidence, never attempts to read his subject's mind, and seldom gives a fact or observation without a reference – sometimes two or three times over. He also makes extensive and systematic use of an extremely wide range of personal interviews.

The result is a fascinating book of awesome scope and skill, which makes no pretence at impartiality. Williams is a Morley to Gaitskell's Gladstone, sharing many of his subject's passions and commitments, and presenting a powerful, though not uncritical, plea for the defence.

What went into the making of the Labour Party's third major leader, who got the job after only a decade in Parliament and one year as a senior minister? His father was an Indian civil servant, and family traditions were Tory, paternalist and administrative. His youth at Winchester and New College was unremarkable and apolitical. At Oxford

Hugh Gaitskell: A Political Biography, Philip Williams (Jonathan Cape, 1979)

he moved among the aesthetes, joined the socially exclusive Gridiron Club and played golf. The General Strike, which took place when he was twenty, deeply affected him and changed his life. 'Henceforth', he wrote to an astonished aunt, 'my future is with the working class.' The reason for this conversion is not clear. Gaitskell was always a pragmatist, never a theorizer. His egalitarianism had no profound philosophical base, but it was strongly felt. An element of genteel poverty may have helped. 'How I loathe the conceited ineffective snobbish rich!' he wrote. 'I suppose I have been insulted by them so often, and to be insulted by people one despises is intolerable.'

After Oxford, he taught adult education classes in Nottingham before taking a more congenial job at University College, London. His experience of Nottingham miners was not wasted. 'They taught me what economic feudalism was,' he recalled. 'They taught me what the natural exercise of arbitrary power meant. They taught me what it was to be victimized.' They also reinforced his desire for a political career.

He was always candid about his intentions. 'I think life would be more amusing if one were ambitious,' he wrote at the age of twenty-five, and the following year he declared: 'I have decided that I really do want to be a great man. By great I simply mean powerful, in the public eye, important,' adding, 'My motives may be mostly egotistical but because of a controlling altruism, my actions may lead to excellent results.' After one hopeless contest he was adopted as candidate for the safe seat of South Leeds in 1937, and his future was assured – as one of the first generation of young men in the Labour Party who were able coolly and with a minimum of risk to fix on politics as their profession.

Yet it was the war that formed him: plucked from the ranks of the Ministry of Economic Warfare by his friend and mentor, Hugh Dalton, in 1940 and put into the private office as *chef de cabinet*. Gaitskell moved with Dalton to the Board of Trade in 1942 and disappeared 'into a tunnel of steady, efficient, laborious administration', at which he excelled. When he entered Parliament in 1945, aged thirty-nine, he had spent five years as a ministerial adviser or administrator. Perhaps such an experience should be compulsory for potential party leaders. Perhaps it should be forbidden. At any rate, Gaitskell's political outlook was shaped by it for the rest of his life.

He returned to policy-making and government after less than a year on the back benches, and quickly gained promotion to Minister of

Fuel and Power. Like most successful politicians, he combined talent with luck: his major good fortune was to be appointed to a Treasury post just in time to be natural successor when Sir Stafford Cripps resigned as Chancellor because of ill-health. Bevan was furious, and Gaitskell felt that Harold Wilson was 'inordinately jealous, though in view of his age there is really no reason for it'. In fact, there was every reason for it: the Chancellorship was a passport to the top from which, but for Gaitskell's early death, Wilson might have been excluded for ever.

Gaitskell's tenure of the Chancellorship was short, partly for reasons of his own making. Should he have conceded more to Bevan over health charges? No doubt Gaitskell was right on the issue, but an early disastrous election might have been avoided had he done so. In fact, the struggles between Bevan and Gaitskell had little to do with principle. According to Crossman in 1952, there were 'only differences of emphasis, temperament and will as regards domestic policy between Nye and Hugh Gaitskell', and this was largely true of foreign policy as well. Nationalization was not an issue until Gaitskell raised it; most Bevanite revolts concerned defence. 'It was a battle between us for power,' Gaitskell said of the 1951 dispute. Yet it is too crude to attribute the bitter guerrilla warfare that lasted a decade to arrogance, megalomania or unscrupulousness on the part of one or other protagonist. Behind each was arraigned a major political force, and both sides cared about much more than personalities.

It was a question of style: and style reflected class. 'How can you support a public school boy from Winchester against a man born in the back streets of Tredegar?' Bevan asked the miners' leader, Sam Watson. But most Bevanites were not miners, and the trade union MPs were allied to the public school Gaitskellites. The great tribal divide in the Labour Party was (and to some extent still is) determined less by ideology than by social attitude. The *New Statesman* was passing a social as well as a political judgement when it called Gaitskell 'the Gentleman from Whitehall'. To the Left, Gaitskell's insufferable sense of responsibility was a reflection of a class position. They agreed with Harold Macmillan when he taunted the Labour leader for missing all the fun of Opposition: 'The trouble about Mr Gaitskell is that he is going through all the motions of being a government when he isn't a government.'

Gaitskell, for his part, dismissed the left-wing challenge as an 'attempt at mob rule by a group of frustrated journalists'. Harold

Wilson was the most appropriate standard bearer the pre-1964 Left ever had. Superficially, his background was identical to that of the party leader: Oxford PPE, university senior common room, wartime temporary civil service. But Wilson came from a different layer of the middle class, liberal, northern and lower, not Tory, southern and upper, and typified the aspirant Labour Party *petite bourgeoisie* who really hated the public-school-for-generations, public-spirited class of which Gaitskell was an equally typical representative.

According to Williams, Gaitskell was 'constitutionally incapable of a snobbish thought, word or deed' but that is a matter of definition. He did not kiss duchesses, like MacDonald, but nearly all his intimate friends, within the party and outside it, came from his own milieu. He was more often to be seen at Belgravia lunch parties and at the celebrations of café society than at trade union socials. That he should have sought to disprove the adage, 'no friends at the top', and have determined 'not to subordinate personal friendships to the pursuit of political advantage' was an attractive personal trait. But it was hardly surprising that in a party so deeply based on class feeling and so sensitive to class behaviour the preference of the Leader for the company of a 'Hampstead set' should have caused resentment or given rise to accusations of cronyism.

Like other Labour Wykehamists (especially Cripps) there was a strain of political masochism in his make-up, a desire for a martyr's crown. Crossman accused him of deliberately picking a quarrel with Frank Cousins, 'as if you felt you would be lacking in duty if you failed to have a row at Conference', and of feeling himself 'a hero and a St Sebastian' for standing up to Bevan. He was immensely stubborn and an appalling tactician. He was a teacher 'passionate about getting the argument right'. When Monnet said to him about Britain's entry into the EEC, 'You must have faith,' he replied: 'I don't believe in faith. I believe in reason and you have not shown me any.' This unusual characteristic was widely and rightly admired. But, like Cripps before him, his super-moral rationalism sometimes failed to take major political obstacles into account. Few leaders have given such hostages to fortune as the pledge not to increase income tax in the 1959 election campaign, or the wholly unnecessary battle over Clause Four, his 'ghastliest mistake', according to Denis Healey who supported him.

Unlike Wilson, he lacked the politician's vital armour of self-deceit: the ability to equate expediency with right. 'More than ever he prized courage and loyalty,' and nobody could accuse him of lacking either.

He was Ramsay MacDonald in reverse. MacDonald was a propagandist and a fixer charged with running an administration, who had a fine political touch. Gaitskell was a policy-maker with a ramrod administrative backbone and no political antennae. Is it likely, as Williams suggests, that Gaitskell 'might have been the great peacetime leader that twentieth-century Britain has badly needed, and sadly failed to find'?

Gaitskell would certainly have tried to make his government a crusade. But nobody has yet successfully led the Labour Party from in front. Whether a modern, irreverent rank and file, or a politically independent trade union movement, would have fallen in behind a passionate, inflexible, high-minded, self-righteous, super civil servant in Downing Street – whether indeed a Labour prime minister can be effective without the skills of Houdini – remains open to doubt.

New Society, 18 October 1979

EVAN DURBIN

SOMETIMES A SINGLE, PRIVATE EVENT diverts the course of history. In the late summer of 1948, a young MP called Evan Durbin was drowned saving the lives of two little girls off a beach in Cornwall. Today, only a handful of historians remember him or his influence. Had he lived, it is likely that, as the intellectual leader of a group that was to take control of the Labour Party, he would have become a dominating force in British politics.

In this book Durbin's elder daughter, aged twelve when she witnessed the tragedy and now a professor of economics at New York University, travels in search of her father and of her own roots. It is no ordinary or sentimental journey. What began ten years ago as an attempt at exorcism, became a rigorous analysis of a group of British economists who, in the 1930s, provided the theoretical framework for what today is known as Gaitskellism but which the author shows, without need of special pleading, might more accurately be called Durbinism. In so doing, she shows the other side of the 'Red Decade'. While Cambridge Apostles dreamed of revolution and joined Stalin's secret service, their Oxford equivalents planned to transform capitalism, and helped to bring about a revolution in socialist thought.

Evan Durbin was born in 1906, the son of a Baptist minister, and remained a preacher all his life. At New College in the 1920s, his church became the rising Labour Party, and his theology economics. Taught by the formidable (and far from socialist) Lionel Robbins, he formed close friendships with Hugh Gaitskell and Douglas Jay, and helped to build a team of clever, highminded, ambitious and worldly-innocent young men who sought, with some success, to give socialist aspirations an intellectual underpinning. Others joined the Communist Party, went on marches, fought in Spain. Durbin and his companions,

New Jerusalems: The Labour Party and the Economics of Democratic Socialism, Elizabeth Durbin (Routledge & Kegan Paul, 1985)

unglamorously, rewrote Labour's domestic policy, using organizations like the New Fabian Research Bureau (set up by G. D. H. Cole) and the City-orientated, clandestine XYZ Club (patronized by Hugh Dalton) as their base.

Their activities were important for two reasons: first, the vacuum that existed in Labour thinking (Beatrice Webb denounced 'abstract' economics as 'a sheer waste of time'); second, the rapid development of expansionist ideas in Cambridge and elsewhere in response to unemployment. It was the achievement of the Durbin–Gaitskell–Jay group to produce a Labour policy which made sense in economic and not just ethical terms. This, indeed, was the intention: according to Elizabeth Durbin, their hope was to combine 'the influence of Cole's stimulating mind, of Dalton's political drive without his "fierce intolerance", of Keynes's economics without his social philosophy and of Tawney's moral teaching with less of its emotionalism and puritanism.'

The key breakthrough (and here, implicitly, there is a message for today) was in creating a socialist approach to economics that was part of, and not marginal to, the intellectual mainstream: one which uncommitted economists would take seriously, and even find persuasive. Like the Institute of Economic Affairs in our own time, the New Fabians boldly set out to create a new consensus. If much of the Fabian message was echoed in the writings of such Tory reformers as Harold Macmillan, this showed, in part, the success of the socialists in capturing the advance ground.

Political and economic arguments were consolidated in *The Politics of Democratic Socialism* (1940), Durbin's major work. The fruits of New Fabian industry are also to be found in Labour's 1937 programme, substantially implemented eight years later. By the time of Durbin's death, Labour had become fully committed to a Keynesian-socialist economic policy, for which Gaitskell and Jay, as Treasury ministers, were to have direct political responsibility.

The later phase should provide excellent material for a second volume, about the relationship between theory and practice. As it is, Professor Durbin has produced a fascinating study, enhanced by deeply affectionate interest, of an important and uncharted episode in the history of ideas. She also points (sometimes unintentionally) to the seeds of later divisions: not just the philosophical differences between mixed economy statists and workers-control class strugglers, but also the cool élitism of the pre-war vanguard, productively yet vulnerably insulated from those for whom they wished to build a New Jerusalem.

What if . . . ? This review happens to be written within sight of Atlantic waves beating against Cornish cliffs. What if the waves had not claimed their victim? Where would Evan Durbin have wished the Labour Party to go? Wisely, his daughter offers no suggestions. Her conclusions, however, may be readily endorsed. 'British democratic socialist thought has a rich tradition of designing realistic programmes,' she writes. Her stimulating book is a reminder both of the strength of the tradition and of the work to be done.

Financial Times, 27 April 1985

WOODROW WYATT

'THE MAIDS HAVE BEEN COMPLAINING to me that your sheets always have a horrible wet mess on them,' the matron of Eastbourne College told Master Wyatt. 'You are abusing yourself. It's a disgusting habit. You must stop it or I'll report you.' Today, Sir Woodrow pleads innocence: how could he prevent himself dreaming? We shall never know the answer. The episode, however, is symbolic: his has been a fancy-filled, pleasure loving life.

Woodrow Wyatt was always a bounder and a cad. The reason, or excuse, was his father, a bullying prep school headmaster, who thought young Woodrow bad at games, a coward, a liar and a cheat – all of which was true. From the start there was a lazy, flabby, Bunterish quality, that made you itch to boot his behind, and at Eastbourne there were plenty of Harry Whartons and Bob Cherrys to oblige. Not that they succeeded in improving him. Many of his later years seem to have been spent eating tuck, waiting for a postal order, or wasting time with *girls*.

Billy Bunter was a crashing snob. So is Wyatt. 'Snobbishness can be a virtue,' he bleats, 'the creative aspiration to be among the best and to be the best yourself, the most obvious manifestation of which is the general regard for the upper reaches of society and power.' It was Bunterish snobbery that propelled him into the Labour Party. Wyatt's family lived in middle-class Esher. 'Esher determined me to seek fame and the famous in a wider, more exciting world where people made witty remarks and great decisions.' And who had ever heard of Eastbourne College?

Almost flung out of school, almost ducked in the college pond at Oxford, undistinguished (semi-mutinous) military service: it was not a propitious beginning. But every GMC delegate, at the end of an anti-fascist struggle, loves a soldier. At twenty-seven Wyatt became a

Confessions of an Optimist, Woodrow Wyatt (Collins, 1985)

Labour MP, justifying all the worst prognoses. He got about; there was a delegation to India, and meetings with Gandhi. Discovering that the half-naked fakir was really just a liberal-minded Englishman in disguise, young Wyatt turned the conversation, naturally, to tuck. 'Oh, there was never any risk of my dying,' said the Mahatma, in reply to a sympathetic inquiry about fasts-unto-death. 'I always drink fruit juice when I am fasting. I can keep going for months. Fasting is very good for the health. Hee, hee, hee, you look as though you could do with a fast.'

At home, Wyatt went to posh parties, and joined the extremist 'Keep Left' group, thorn in the side of the Attlee Government. ('It was the forerunner of the dissident cliques which were to plague the Labour Party and still do.') There was a brief spell as a junior minister at the War Office, during the dying months of the administration. Wyatt contemplated sending a general who had disciplined him in 1944 on a posting to somewhere like Tristan da Cunha, but refrained.

These were happy days: acolyte of Nye Bevan, then of Hugh Gait-skell; close friend of Driberg, Crosland, Jenkins; member of the Reform. In 1955, he lost his seat to the Boundary Commissioners, and became a household name as host on a pioneering television chat show. In 1959 he was back, with Gaitskell's support, as MP for Bosworth. Office beckoned: but Gaitskell died before Labour returned to power, and this 'closed my prospects in the Labour Party'. He and Wilson disliked each other, and he backed Brown for the leadership. There remained a career as maverick: Wyatt and Desmond Donnelly used Labour's thin majority in 1964 and the consequent importance of their own votes, to force a postponement of steel nationalization.

In the 1970 election, Wyatt lost his seat unexpectedly, and the Bosworth constituency party deselected him. There was little hope of finding another. Like old soldiers, most ex-MPs simply fade away. Wyatt stayed obstinately corporeal, best known as a splenetically read-able pro-Thatcher columnist.

I once interviewed him. The great, iron garden gate of the ex-left-winger's fortified mansion swung open electronically, and a manservant guided me from the front door to the ancestor-lined dining-room. Perched at the end of a huge table a baby-faced man who dressed and spoke like Winston Churchill or, as I now appreciate, the Owl of the Remove, blinked at me. He waved a long cigar. 'Have some cham-pagne.' It was an entertaining hour or so, full of odd insights, but it was not particularly informative. Neither is his autobiography – unless you count stories like the one about Tom Driberg holding Jim Callaghan's penis and saying, 'You've got a very pretty one there.'

Why has he been serialized by the *Sunday Times*? One possible answer is on pages 336–37: 'I first began to know Rupert Murdoch after I rang him up ... Rupert was at Worcester College, the same college as mine ... If I were not myself I should most like to be Rupert.' Along with his other vices, Woodrow Wyatt is an outrageous toady.

He is also a very clever writer, and this is a deliciously, wickedly funny book. I expect it will make him huge sums of money. He will like that. Yaroo!

New Society, 21 June 1985

BARBARA CASTLE

DURING THE LAST ELECTION CAMPAIGN, Baroness Castle enjoyed an Indian summer as a star turn. At sanitized public meetings she would be wheeled out, just as the carefully screened audience of well groomed C2 Labour supporters was nodding off, in order to screech socialism. The effect was electric. The audience woke up with a jolt and, invariably, responded with tumultuous applause. People liked to be reminded that, once upon a time, their party had stood for something more than chasing the latest opinion poll up its own decimal point. Meanwhile, the party management felt privately relieved that Madam Nostalgia was safely in retirement.

Of course (as she herself makes clear in this readable and robust autobiography), Barbara Castle built a highly successful political career out of being principled. In an arena largely composed of cynical self-serving males, it was her trade mark. Anti-fascism, a free health service, Cyprus, Rhodesia, Vietnam: if there was a good cause, Barbara would be there as champion, gathering (as ungallant chauvinists like Jim Callaghan would wrily observe) a headline or two, plus the odd vote for the NEC, in the process. For her – and it is interesting that a woman can admit it more freely than a man – political crusading and position-seeking were one and the same. An aim of her book, she tells us in the introduction, is to disclose 'what it is like for a woman to fight her way through the political jungle into the Cabinet'.

No female politician in modern Britain before Margaret Thatcher has been such a determined wielder of the machete. What is it about Nonconformist lower-middle-class communities in small-town provincial middle England that produces ambitious political women? It can scarcely be coincidence that the gender trail-blazers of Britain's two main political parties came from virtually identical backgrounds, both making their way from grammar school to an Oxford women's college,

Fighting All the Way, Barbara Castle (Macmillan, 1993)

and both keenly aware of the hopes of a powerful, adored, and politically minded father.

There were differences. The Roberts household seems to have been a pretty humourless affair, and one of chilling philistinism; by contrast, Barbara Castle convincingly portrays her parents as people of literary culture as well as of intelligence. Barbara's mother was a 'William Morris socialist', who believed that the world should be a place of beauty for everyone. Her father, Frank Betts, was a tax inspector who had several secret lives: as a socialist and partisan of the evangelical Independent Labour Party, as a poet and classical scholar befriended by Gilbert Murray, and as a discreet adulterer.

Barbara's taste in men was set by Frank, 'tall, black-haired and big-boned', who believed it was the 'duty of every free spirit to challenge convention'. Her first and possibly greatest love was William Mellor, a marxist propagandist and leader of the 1930s Socialist League ('Physically he was my kind of man: tall, black-haired, erect, with a commanding presence and strong, handsome features'). Later, her political hero, Aneurin Bevan, was in a similar mould, and it is interesting that she writes of Denis Healey that he was 'an instinctive bully, but bullies always bring out the best in me'. However, while she enjoyed pugilism she did not want to be ruled by anyone and it is notable that she never allowed the men in her life to eclipse her or usurp her limelight. Mellor and her eventual husband, the journalist Ted Castle, were MPs *manqués*: neither ever won a seat.

Trained and steeled in the pre-war Labour Left, she entered Parliament as Member for Blackburn in 1945 and took her place in a then almost entirely male world. She already knew Sir Stafford Cripps, Bevan and the young Michael Foot. Harold Wilson entered her consciousness when he succeeded Cripps as President of the Board of Trade in 1947, and she became his parliamentary private secretary. It was the start of an affectionate, though often wary, alliance that lasted for three decades and was of benefit to both of them. Like Castle, Wilson belonged to the same exclusive club of Nonconformist provincial grammar school products, and they spoke the same language. Her relations with him were a bit like that of two rival swots in the upper sixth. 'When he used to rattle off statistics at me', she recalls, 'I retorted by quoting reams of poetry at him.'

In others, lack of poetry was a besetting sin. Both Castle and Wilson sided with Aneurin Bevan in his row with Hugh Gaitskell in 1951, and moved together into the group of left-wingers that pinned their hopes on Bevan's eventual succession as party leader. The Right regarded her with a special venom, and she responded in kind. She admits to having 'disliked Gaitskell intensely' for his caution and 'lack of poetry'. She saw him as prim, in Bevan's famous phrase a 'desiccated calculating machine'. He was, however, a surprisingly twinkle-toed one. On one occasion he invited her on to the floor at a Blackpool Conference grand ball. She was startled both by the Labour Party leader's skill and by his athletic enthusiasm as a ballroom dancer.

Unlike Margaret Thatcher, who was little-known until she became a Cabinet minister, Barbara Castle was well established as a 'fiery' (her own favourite self-description) campaigner in Opposition, though not necessarily destined for high office. It was her closeness to Wilson that put her on the accelerator after Labour's victory of 1964. Hitherto, female ministers had been minor players, or merely token ones. Barbara Castle quickly made plain her intention to be neither. She was helped by a prime minister who not only listened to her privately, as one of the few members of his government he felt he could trust, but declined to shut her up in Cabinet. He also declined to act on her advice on international issues, shifting her from her first post at Overseas Development to the Ministry of Transport and then, in 1968, making her Secretary of State for Employment and Productivity.

By now, Labour was in the doldrums, seats were falling like ninepins in by-elections, and the government was in a state of post-devaluation trauma. The key question in British politics was how long the Prime Minister could survive – he was, it was said, on probation. When Wilson took up the issue of industrial relations, and gave Castle the task of introducing reforms, many saw it as a desperate last throw to placate the electors and save his own bacon. Yet if that was how it began, it soon became much more, as this book points out. The story is a curious one with elements of tragedy and farce.

At the time, it seemed puzzling that a minister associated with the Left should find herself on the same side as the employers' organizations. In retrospect, however, it is hard not to agree that the trade unions would have done well to have put their house in order before a less friendly government was able to impose punitive shackles on them. The account of the *In Place of Strife* fiasco given here reinforces the impression, first, of the Employment Secrtary's disregard for diplomatic skill, when she became convinced she was in the right; second, of the enduring dinosaur (or lemming) tendency within the trades union movement; and third, of the almost feckless courage of both

Castle and Wilson in sticking to their guns when many who agreed with them in Cabinet were running for cover.

After that, as she ruefully admits, her chance of holding the highest offices was never the same. In earlier days, she had been one of the Government's most confident members, a scourge of Whitehall and a darling of the normally anti-Labour press. From 1969 she became, in Labour terms, a politician with the mark of Cain – a leader who had been seen off by the trade unions. When Labour returned in 1974, she was given another major post as Social Services minister, and she fought doggedly against the Right on Europe. But she lasted in office only as long as her patron. When Wilson resigned in 1976, Jim Callaghan – an arch-opponent who had prudently taken the trade unions' side over *In Place of Strife* – summarily dismissed her.

There was an after-life. She stood successfully as an MEP and served as an energetic leader of Labour's European group, before becoming her party's most marbleful reminder of its once glorious past.

Barbara Castle's memoirs do not add much detail to the account of the Wilson Governments in her published diaries. But they make instructive reading, nonetheless. They contain evocative descriptions of passionate days when socialism was a secular religion, and they are shrewd and wittily forensic about people. They encapsulate the almost forgotten era when Labour either saw itself as the natural party of government or peddled a distinctive alternative.

They reveal a woman of vigour, tenacity and warmth, who must have been exhausting to work with yet had a heart as large as her ego. She was the first woman to hold an important post in a British government, but also, perhaps, the last of a species. Who is there today to screech as effectively in her place?

Guardian, 15 June 1993

GEORGE BROWN

INCREASINGLY, HISTORIANS ARE re-defining the 1960s, once seen as a decade of disillusion, betrayal and failed promise. With the passage of time, and especially since the collapse of the Thatcherite panacea, it is possible to see some good features alongside the bad: that it was a period of rapidly changing values, and also of bold (if sometimes over-optimistic) experimentation. One of the boldest political figures of the mid-1960s was George Brown, and a biography of him – particularly as it is the first to have been written – is therefore of great potential interest.

Brown is better remembered than many colleagues who survived him politically, partly because he was always a creature of myth, much of which he carefully cultivated. He enjoyed the reputation of being a 'character', a man of warmth and human colour, in contrast to the supposedly ice-cold Wilson. Although, for a time, powerful within the Labour hierarchy, he was familiar to strap-hangers, gossip-writers and foreign dignitaries mainly as a Falstaffian figure of fun: a boorish loud-mouth, a lachrymose boozer who never used a two-syllable word if a vernacular expletive would do, yet who endeared himself to his public by sometimes saying, in his cups, the truths that needed to be uttered.

His biographer has collected many anecdotes about him, and indeed there were enough in circulation in his heyday to fill the Apocrypha. There was always a tragi-comic, or perhaps tragi-embarrassing, aspect to such tales; the listener was left wondering whether to laugh, or be disgusted. Paterson quotes one near the end of the book, that is typical of the genre: after Len Williams, ex-general secretary of the Labour Party, had accepted the somewhat ludicrous post of Governor-General of Mauritius from Harold Wilson, Brown (an enemy) asked him if his duties would involve wearing a plumed hat. Williams admitted that

Tired and Emotional: the Life of Lord George-Brown, Peter Paterson (Chatto, 1993)

they would. 'Well', said the former Foreign Secretary, 'I hope your fucking feathers fall out.'

It is curious to reflect that Brown almost became Leader of the Labour Party at a time when it stood poised to win a general election, and might therefore have been the first prime minister to have addressed the British people, regardless of gender, as 'Brothers'. If this had happened, he might have drunk less and been a better statesman than Wilson. Perhaps Britain would have devalued earlier and in good order (as Brown advocated), abandoned East of Suez sooner, and entered what was then known as the Common Market at a propitious moment: such are the counter-factual speculations such hypotheses give rise to. On the other hand – as this biography shows – Brown's drinking was already well advanced by the time of Hugh Gaitskell's death in 1963, and there is no reason to believe that the rigours of party leadership (let alone of the premiership if Labour had still won) would have offered much in the way of therapy – indeed, given the ruthlessness of the media towards Labour leaders, it is a fair bet that Brown would have fallen or destroyed himself sooner than he did. So on balance, it is hard to see Brown (as many still see Gaitskell) as a 'lost leader', the saviour who might have been.

Yet he had a remarkable life, and it is wrong to present him (as this book sometimes appears to) as a Labour politician who accidentally drifted to the top. His rise was marked, rather, by a degree of energy and imagination that often left better-educated colleagues panting to keep up.

Brown belonged to the tiny club of genuine proletarians who held some of the highest offices in the land, and the even smaller number which regarded its lowly origins as a badge of honour. The son of a Lambeth lorry driver, he moved from the basement of John Lewis's in Oxford Street, where he earned his living beating furs, to the sales room, and thence to the offices of his trade union, the Transport Workers, dominated in the 1930s by the massive personality of Ernest Bevin – on whom he seems to have modelled himself, although temperamentally they were quite different.

Unlike Bevin, Brown pinned his hopes on Parliament early on. He burst into the consciousness of his party nationally with a mood-capturing speech at the 1939 Labour conference, when he denounced the upper-class Sir Stafford Cripps for wasting the Movement's time over the Popular Front. Brown was taken up by Hugh Dalton and Harold Laski, and was elected an MP in 1945. Rising fast from the ranks (though not as fast as Wilson), he was briefly Minister of Works in 1951. During the subsequent period of Opposition he was associated with the Labour Right, although too egotistical – and too class-conscious – to be a member of Gaitskell's Hampstead Set.

In a party that still took its roots seriously, Brown was able to play the horny-handed card: he was much more acceptable to middle-ground MPs than intellectual right-wingers like Douglas Jay or Patrick Gordon Walker. But there was more to it than that. It was often said, patronizingly, that he had 'the best untrained mind in politics': although (according to Paterson) he seldom read a book, his mind was continually and restlessly active, and he had an instinctive ability to see the core of a problem when colleagues were fussing over the periphery.

The tragedy in Brown's career occurred at the moment of his ascendancy. When Gaitskell died, Brown was deputy leader, and heir apparent. Many MPs, however, when faced with Tony Crosland's dilemma between 'a drunk and a crook', deserted the Right and reluctantly opted for the crook. Brown never forgot or forgave. Many of the teething problems of the 1964 administration can be put down to the deep mistrust that existed between the Prime Minister and his most brilliant and troublesome senior colleague.

Brown was given the key post of Secretary of State for Economic Affairs, or Minister of 'Planning' – now a dated concept, but then the heart and soul of Labour's white-heat ideology. No minister was better suited to launching the ambitious venture of the 1965 National Plan, or, probably, less suited to the arduous task of following it through: the whole scheme collapsed like a pack of cards in the sterling crisis of 1966, and with it Labour's self-esteem for the next quarter century.

Brown was made Foreign Secretary and became famous for the exuberant kissing of ambassadors' wives. After leading an unsuccessful bid for Britain to enter Europe, he lost his temper with the Prime Minister once too often and made what was (according to the author) his seventeenth offer of resignation, which this time was wearily but gratefully accepted. He lasted in Parliament only until the 1970 election, and – as Lord George-Brown – became a tabloid figure of fun, best known for splenetic outbursts against former colleagues and for falling flat on his face in the gutter. He died in 1985, before his seventieth birthday, of cirrhosis of the liver.

Thus stated, it was not a glorious career, and it is hard to pinpoint achievements. His period as a Cabinet minister, from October 1964 to March 1968, was shorter than that of many of his well-known contemporaries. Nevertheless, he deserves a more substantial biography than this one, if only to explain the high regard in which he was held by many of his colleagues even when they were most exasperated by him (after one resignation threat, a hundred MPs quickly signed a petition demanding that he remain in the Government); and a widespread view, not just amongst the tribal Labour Right, that George drunk was better than Harold sober.

Paterson writes fluently and often amusingly. His account of Brown's private life is sensitive and illuminating: he dispels the legend of Brown as the robust family man who occasionally enjoyed a drop too much, and presents him as an alcoholic for whom the twin obsessions of drink and politics were two attempts to escape some inner grief. But apart from family members, he makes little use of interviews; there is a plethora of factual errors; and the key policy debates are either oversimplified or ignored.

The author successfully fleshes out the George Brown of the caricaturists: the man 'one would not invite to cucumber sandwiches with one's maiden aunt' who 'probably wrote more letters of apology than any politician in history'. The need, however, is for a book that explains and revises, rather than one that merely reinforces the stereotype.

Guardian, 18 May 1993

ANTHONY CROSLAND

QUESTION: WHAT DID ANTHONY CROSLAND, inheritor and developer of the Webb–Dalton–Gaitskell school in British progressive politics, have in common with Tony Benn, reviver of an equally distinctive tradition of messianic evangelism? One possible answer: both married beautiful, talented, determined, upper-class alumnae of Vassar College, USA.

A frivolous observation, perhaps. A statistically freakish coincidence. Or possibly one small symptom of the social incestuousness which, for more than a generation, lay at the heart of British Labour politics. For those who believe that ideological divisions in major political parties reflect broad socio-economic fissures, it may also seem irrelevant that Crosland was Benn's undergraduate tutor at Oxford; and that Roy Jenkins was treasurer of the Oxford Democratic Socialist Club when Crosland was chairman. On the other hand, for those whose history comes in kings and queens, such early intimacies may help to explain middle-aged rivalries that affected the policies of governments, and the nature of the Labour Party, many decades later.

Susan Crosland's brilliant memoir-cum-biography is about kings, queens and courtiers. Above all, it concerns the intensely self-regarding group of Labour politicians known in the press (and resented in some sections of the Labour Movement) as the Hampstead Set, which revolved around the personality of Hugh Gaitskell and his Camelot at Frognal Gardens, NW3; and which later became the most talented and, on the whole, least socialist element within the Wilson–Callaghan Cabinets of the 1960s and 1970s.

Much of the book is devoted to the unfolding fortunes of this group, and their interrelations. There are also important chapters of political and administrative history, dealing with Crosland's periods of office successively at Economic Affairs, Education and Science, Board of

Tony Crosland, Susan Crosland (Jonathan Cape, 1982)

Trade, Environment and Foreign Office. To these are added a tender and unsentimental account of a relationship – a deeply affecting love story that is hard to read without shedding tears of laughter and sadness.

The author blends techniques: she combines personal memories, the use of her own and her husband's diaries and papers, and the fruits of a wide range of interviews with former colleagues and friends. To these sources she brings a professional ear for dialogue, and a novelist's skill in planting clues: the text is paced with symbols of disaster and premonitions of death, so that when the tragic climax is reached, we are prepared. 'Tony's and my luck held,' she writes simply at the end; 'six nights and five days at the Radcliffe Infirmary gave us time for a long farewell.'

Crosland remains for many, not of his generation, a uniquely attractive political figure. This book helps to explain why. He was one of very few Labour politicians for whom the much-abused term 'intellectual' was an apt description. *The Future of Socialism* stands in a class by itself among modern political writings – its virtues of elegance, honesty, lucidity, paradoxically growing the more evident as its short-run message loses relevance. Crosland eschewed political cant and humbug, and – so it always seemed – could not be bothered to tell lies in public statements. In a world of hard-faced men, all antennae and no soul, there was something baroque about Crosland: an eighteenth-century aristocrat whose air of casual superiority belied a generous imagination and a will of steel.

Yet there was a fierce ambition there as well – perhaps more than Susan Crosland, for all her candour, is prepared to acknowledge. That her husband was a man of principle is clear. So is the evidence of his political courage. Yet at every turn we also find the hero of this tale making decisions, with studied nonchalance, which push him up another notch in the ratchet of success. 'Don't give the bloody Tories the pleasure of knowing you're nervous,' he instructed his new wife during the count at the 1964 election. That was the secret. *Don't let them know you care.* But he did, all the same.

At the core of Crosland (his other secret) was the expectation of being loved – the result of an adoring family, buttressed by a powerful physical presence and extraordinary good looks. This produced an ability to charm which left beautiful women and powerful men glazed with servile adoration. Susan Crosland, who eventually tamed him, takes a touching pride in his earlier compulsive promiscuity. During his first, unsuccessful, marriage, 'he behaved badly,' she asserts, much as one might describe a small boy who persists in climbing trees and stealing apples, having promised not to.

But it was Crosland's success with older men that counted politically. Was there, perhaps, an emotional ambivalence in his make-up? Certainly, he does not seem to have been reluctant to make use of the vulnerability of others of his own sex. One such friendship – with Hugh Dalton, a former Labour Chancellor – led directly to Crosland's first parliamentary seat. Susan Crosland illustrates the strong element of platonic love on Dalton's side by quoting an extraordinary letter from the elder statesman to the young MP, written in 1950:

> I have told you last summer how I feel towards you – that I believe tremendously in you and your future, and admire immensely your wonderful diversity of gifts, and am *very* fond of you (but with no disturbing carnal thoughts about you) and get great stimulus from your company and from what you say and write, and would do anything anytime, if you asked me, to help you.

Crosland's other major conquest was Hugh Gaitskell, Leader of the Labour Party from 1955 until his death seven years later, and himself a Daltonian protégé. 'The two men admired, loved, maddened one another,' the author recalls.

Crosland had much in common with Gaitskell: both were public school and Oxford educated economists, with civil servant fathers. However, there were key differences as well. Gaitskell's background was Anglican and Establishment. Crosland's parents were Exclusive Plymouth Brethren – a heritage which goes far towards explaining the odd combination in the son of puritan work ethic, rebellious hedonism and the need to construct a blueprint for a better life. It also helps to account for one of Crosland's most pleasing features: a lifelong refusal to run with the pack. Even (or especially) after *The Future of Socialism* had made him the philosopher of the Gaitskellites and their Jenkinsite successors, he kept his distance, taking his own decisions. Former allies called it opportunism when he declared himself lukewarm over the Common Market. Susan Crosland regards it as stubborn independence of mind. Possibly both were right.

The Croslands met during the Suez crisis in 1956 and married in 1964 – both for the second time. Eight months later Tony entered the first Wilson Government and began his spiral ascent. Often in biographies, interest flags once the hero achieves importance: there is a sameness about public lives which dehumanizes and reduces authors to sterile narrative. Susan Crosland's account is unusual in this respect for two reasons: first because of an interlacing of chapters of personal recollection – domesticity and family crises in Holland Park. Second, because of her lightness of touch in dealing with political events – a product of her own fascination with what was going on.

'Thank God I do not have a political wife,' she quotes him as saying. He was right – he didn't. When he was Secretary of State for Education and Science, presiding over the comprehensive revolution ('If it's the last thing I do,' he told her, 'I'm going to destroy every fucking grammar school in England'), she admitted that she didn't even know what a comprehensive school was. There are drawbacks to her own lack of politics: it means that there is an incomplete understanding either of the passions or the nuances of Labour Movement affairs. Yet on the whole it is an asset, enabling her to appraise people and events with far more detachment than is common among those close to the political coal-face.

One of the most interesting sections of the book describes the growing breach between Crosland and the Jenkinsites during the period of the Heath Government – and here there is a strong implicit theme: whatever else, Tony most certainly would not have joined the SDP. One of the author's most delightful, and significant, stories describes an alleged attempt in 1971 by Bill Rodgers (of whom they were both apparently quite fond) to blackmail her husband into backing the Jenkinsite ticket in the Shadow Cabinet, with the threat of withdrawal of support for Crosland's own candidature:

... during this bizarre scene my mind was occupied with [the following] reflections. These were: (1) Is Bill Rodgers deranged? (2) If he's not deranged, what has happened to his judgement for him to think this a fruitful approach to someone of Tony's personality? (3) Did a long-ago American B-film, possibly about gangsters, have a subliminal effect on Bill's mind?

Crosland, indeed, had a way with those who threatened not to back him. Roy Hattersley dropped in during the 1976 leadership contest and asked: 'Would you like to know why I'm not voting for you?' The Secretary of State for the Environment's reply was a version of Queen Victoria's remark about not being amused, but shorter. 'No. Fuck off.'

Most of Tony's political friendships, though much battered by rivalries and manoeuvrings, were nevertheless on the Right of the Party: Jenkins, Rodgers, Callaghan, Hattersley. But there was also Tony Benn, 'Jimmy' to his intimates, who had the peculiar habit of ringing up with a phoney working-class accent, inviting the Croslands to guess who was on the line. Crosland wrote that Benn was a 'hopeless neurotic' and later that he 'creates endless crises'. But he would defend Jimmy to strangers: 'I'm devoted to Tony Benn. Nothing the matter with him, except that he's a bit cracked.'

Crosland was the opposite to Benn in major respects – a cavalier to Benn's roundhead, a loner in politics rather than a leader. Susan writes shrewdly of her husband's early failure to make headway in the leadership stakes: 'The ball was at his feet – and they expected him to pick it up ... They wanted to rally round, but he didn't present himself to be rallied round.' He could make enemies by not suffering fools gladly and, as Dalton remarked, he sometime aroused in opponents 'a pent-up hatred, spitefulness and jealousy which is almost unbelievable'.

But perhaps George Brown (under whom Crosland served at the ill-fated DEA) should be allowed the last word. 'He could irritate every part of me,' the former deputy leader recalls, '– drape his hand on the mantelpiece, look at me in that patronizing way – but he couldn't make me dislike him.' Arrogant, languid, self-indulgent, narcissistic – and, in later years, far more of a stylish and professional administrator than a radical – Tony Crosland had many faults. But British politics is desperately impoverished without him.

New Society, 3 June 1982

PAUL NITZE

IT IS AN ODD but indisputable aspect of public life that dedicated officials (especially ones who spend a lot of time in the company of foreigners) frequently turn into caricatures of their own national stereotype. While mandarin Brits naturally assume a self-deprecating air of genteel poverty, their American equivalents present themselves as patrician, genial, hunky and insurmountable.

This memoir of a leading policy-maker who helped run the Cold War for four decades certainly fits the mould. Paul Nitze calls himself 'an assertive, hard-nosed pragmatist' and his splendid autobiography is as American as apple pie. Part fly-on-the-wall observation of Washington decision-taking from Roosevelt to Reagan, part description of his own active involvement, part shrewd evaluation, it is inspired throughout by a top-nation ethic, which, with an almost naïve sincerity, equates the advantage of his compatriots with the welfare of humanity in general. It is written, moreover, in such a beguilingly confident style – full of unconscious literary vanities – that it is hard not to believe he is right.

Sometimes he is Fitzgerald ('My two years at Hotchkiss were full of camaraderie, athletics, girls and studies – pretty much in that order'); sometimes he is Hemingway ('I have travelled, climbed mountains, caught fish, shot quail, played bridge, danced, loved, been loved in return, laughed and cried'); occasionally he is Mark Twain or perhaps Damon Runyon (age seven, he was picking up valuable political experience as a mobster in a Chicago protection gang). Yet if, in a way, it is an innocent book, it is also intelligent, and compulsively readable.

Nitze was not born to the Washington purple, but political aspirations began to intrude early on. His first memories include a European trip just after Sarajevo, and nostalgia for imagined pre-First World War values became (he tells us) a guiding star – with the prospect of

From Hiroshima to Glasnost: At the Centre of Decision: A Memoir, Paul Nitze (Weidenfeld & Nicolson, 1990)

a restoration of the *status quo ante bellum* as his personal utopia.

It was the Second World War that took him to the American capital, where he learned about modern weaponry in an outfit called the Strategic Bombing Survey. One discovery during this apprenticeship was that dropping bombs on key industrial targets had little effect (a lesson which might have been applied later in Vietnam, but wasn't). Nitze also produced a plan to beat the Japanese by November 1945 (a year sooner than most people expected) using conventional weapons and without invading the Japanese home islands. Unfortunately, the military were sceptical, and Nitze found himself inspecting the damage in Hiroshima and Nagasaki instead.

It was an experience which gave him a measure both of the horror and the limitations of nuclear weapons, and launched him on a career in which the possibility of total war was never far from his thoughts. In the late 1940s he was drawn into long-term strategic planning and was responsible, in the aftermath of the 1948 Berlin airlift, for NSC 68 – an influential report which helped shape American thinking for a generation. In this study, Nitze unblinkingly records, 'We drew a clear distinction between the aims of the United States, which were to protect and preserve the institutions of a free society, and those of the Soviet Union, which centred on preserving the Soviet Communist Party and its base, the USSR, but also on extending the Kremlin's domination outward as far as possible.'

So simple a dichotomy required an equally simple remedy: massive western re-armament and 'a firm policy intended to check and roll back the Kremlin's drive for world domination'. Here was the essence of American Cold War dogma, and Nitze (though by no means an uncompromising hawk) shows little sign of having abandoned it after Stalin's death – or of having seriously considered that one side's 'extending domination outward' might be the other's 'rolling back the drive for world domination', and vice versa. Indeed, the basic, 1940s morality play seems to have accompanied him through all his nation's vicissitudes.

In the 1950s Nitze backed losers: Stevenson against Eisenhower and (for the 1960 Democrat nomination) Humphrey against Kennedy. When Kennedy was elected, he had to settle for a job under Defence Secretary Robert MacNamara, which at first looked like bottle-washing but, in practice, brought him into intimate contact with the President and his key advisers during the administration's developing paranoia over Cuba. Nitze shared the prevailing fears. He opposed the American-sponsored invasion at the Bay of Pigs but not on principle:

'The Soviet Union had inserted itself in our backyard by stealth and deception ... Like a spreading cancer it should, if possible, be excised from the Americas.' He merely considered the operation impractical. Later, after the Russians had yielded over missile shipments, he thought Kennedy should have pushed home his advantage and refrained from the 'no invasion' pledge which allowed Cuba to remain as a Marxist fifth column in the western hemisphere.

Nevertheless, Nitze's incisive account of the Kennedy–Khrushchev confrontation over Cuba – when American warlords calmly discussed whether the risk of a few H-bomb explosions in Italy or Turkey was worth taking – is one of the best firsthand analyses to have been written. Of almost equal interest is his description of Washington machinations during the war in Indo-China. It was a time when Nitze had to keep a particularly cool head. For the first four years of the Johnson administration, while American involvement was rapidly increasing, Nitze was Secretary of the US Navy. Yet he remained a consistent opponent of committing American ground troops to Vietnam because, as he puts it, 'there was no such thing as being a little bit pregnant': once the step had been taken, it would be impossible to set limits. He gives a vivid account of the misery of a beleaguered president and government, unable to win yet rich enough not to have to lose. He tells how Johnson railed against an unhappy general: 'Kill the goddam bastards, kill 'em, kill 'em, kill 'em!'

In the last section of the book, the author describes in detail his final, and possibly most influential, role as chief arms control negotiator in successive Salt talks. He portrays the surreal nature of the calculations – though shows little intimation of the impending upheaval. He concludes: 'We, together with Gorbachev, have changed the nature of the game.' Yet the real cause of progress during Reagan's presidency was the Russians' determination to make the negotiations work: precious little generosity was visible on the western side.

Still, there is an obvious sense in which Nitze and his colleagues can claim to have won: the East–West struggle is effectively over, and largely on western terms. The question raised by this revealing work is whether the taken-for-granted principles of American foreign policy which it portrays can evolve with the rapidity and sensitivity which the challenge of a post-imperial Soviet Union and a fragmented, cacophonous, East Europe urgently requires.

Sunday Times, 15 April 1990

NICHOLAS RIDLEY

NOW THAT THE TORY PARTY is starting to crack up, instant memoirs from the pens or tape recorders of grumpy yesterday's men have become quite the thing. Sir Bernard Ingham was the first to tumble into print with his splenetic autobiography, a few weeks ahead of Nicholas Ridley. Effusions of a different order are to be expected from the likes of Nigel Lawson and Sir Geoffrey Howe. All will have in common the refighting of the Government's internal battles. How happy Neil Kinnock must feel.

Nicholas Ridley has little in common with Bernard Ingham in background and interest. Ridley is patrician with a lot of blue chip money and education and a proud career of arrogant Left-baiting. Ingham is a working-class ex-socialist who served Labour ministers as a civil service information officer before moving to No. 10. Yet the books of both men have a strikingly similar tone. This partly consists of a kind of right-wing macho – a positive enjoyment of a public role *contra mundum*, and of doing and saying things they believe to be shocking. Its most remarkable feature, however, is a form of heroine worship that is almost as interesting a phenomenon as Thatcherism itself. Both works display a devotion that goes far beyond normal loyalty, and takes the form of an exalted courtly love.

Thus Ridley describes his last lunch with Mrs Thatcher as Prime Minister as 'one of the saddest, most moving occasions of my life'. His thoughts, he says, were personal ones: 'How dignified she was in the face of rejection, how loyal to those who were loyal to her, how brave in adversity,' and so on. Her sense of humour was special, her industry prodigious, her integrity absolute and her judgement almost infallible. Her few mistakes were themselves the product of virtues, which included kindness even towards those who didn't deserve it. Thus,

My Style of Government: The Thatcher Years, Nicholas Ridley (Hutchinson, 1991)

Westland would never have happened if she had sacked Michael Heseltine as soon as he began to be difficult.

Those who attacked her are beneath contempt. 'The *Guardian*, in particular, seemed to pursue a relentless vendetta against her and all her works,' Mr Ridley informs us. '. . . Bernard Ingham protected her from the full horror of these onslaughts by letting her have only a summary sheet of the day's press each morning . . . to have exposed her fully to this uncaring hate campaign might have been more than she could have borne.' Elizabeth I's courtiers, who included some of Mr Ridley's ancestors, wrote in similarly chivalrous tones. In the sixteenth century, traitorous scribblers had their hands chopped off. Luckily in the twentieth, the faithful Bernard was available, to stand between the Prime Minister and the 'sour and turgid hostility of frustrated intellectuals'.

But perhaps we should not scoff at Mr Ridley's angry protectiveness, despite the ridiculous side to it. Dedication to an individual is in some ways more attractive than dedication to a cause. Personally, indeed, Mr Ridley is rather appealing. In opposition (and effectively he is now in opposition) as in office, Ridley's indifference to conventional attitudes, and his refusal to play the politician's game of pussyfooting around with language, make him seem refreshingly like a member of the human race, in contrast to some of his creepier former colleagues.

The author denies ever having said, on the subject of local taxation, that there was no good reason why a duke and a dustman should not pay the same for the same service. That is a pity, because the apocryphal quote nicely encapsulated an approach which is quite unlike that of 'the professional men, the Tory fixers, the accountants and lawyers and merchant bankers' for whom 'the important things were to be loved, to be popular, to be re-elected', a species of political animal which Ridley deplores, and which he implies now dominates the parliamentary Conservative Party.

Yet the other side of bloody-mindedness is a stubbornness which was the main cause not only of his own downfall, but that of his leader as well. Mr Ridley's mistake was increasingly to regard the unpopularity of a policy as proof of its correctness, and to believe that sticking to your guns is a virtue regardless of the issue.

Ridley blames Lawson *père* for the unpardonable sin of refusing to obey orders. He blames Lawson *fils*, the editor of the *Spectator*, for a 'disgraceful piece of sensational journalism' in publishing remarks made during a taped interview. He does not consider the possibility that it was his own careless offensiveness that helped to spark the Conservative civil war, and which damaged his own side irreparably.

A politician who can write that the advocates of a single European currency were merely 'the usual groups of wets, Thatcher-haters and malcontents', rather than people who had come to a different conclusion from his own; a former Environment Secretary who can describe the inhabitants of cardboard city as 'dropouts, people making a protest against society'; and a man who is passionately vociferous on the shaky loyalty of Mrs Thatcher's colleagues in her last hours – yet says nothing about the brazen disloyalty to Ted Heath which got her there in the first place – is dangerously out of touch with reality.

Indeed Ridley's book, like Ingham's, reveals a bunker mentality which effectively disposes of the theory both writers seek to put forward, that the *putsch* which got rid of her was a result of betrayal and faintheartedness. 'Life at the top is a never-ending vigil for the leader to safeguard himself from leaks and plots and conspiracies and attempts to destabilize,' says Mr Ridley. 'It was ever thus.' Yet history shows that ministers and premiers who start to see the world in these terms are usually on the way out.

Mr Ridley fondly believes that but for his own resignation Mrs Thatcher would have survived, and might even have won the coming election, if the economy somehow came right. As he says, we shall never know. Yet the atmosphere conveyed by this book, as by that of Mrs Thatcher's former press secretary, is not merely of the passing of a notable reign, but of the ending of an epoch.

Guardian, 11 July 1991

NORMAN TEBBIT

WHY DO WE FEEL SO FOND of Mr Tebbit nowadays, and even regard him as rather cuddly? One reason is that he no longer matters. The pit-bull of the distant 1980s has become the chihuahua of the nondescript 1990s, able to growl naughtily but not seriously to bite. Thus, the interest of this ruminative essay on contemporary problems lies not so much in its prescriptions, which – God willing – pose no imminent threat, but in what they reveal about the present crisis in Tory philosophy.

The 'unfinished business' of the title is the project Margaret Thatcher began with the author's help, and which Mr Tebbit thinks is in need of completion. Proudly declaring himself a Thatcherite, Mr Tebbit gives his own encapsulation of a religion which he believes has a continuing relevance. 'Thatcherism', he tells us, in a sentence which also reveals the essence of Tebbitism, 'was about recreating an economic and social structure in which carrots and sticks would be applied once again to the appropriate ends of the donkey.'

The lucky (or unlucky) jackass in question is you and me and the neighbourhood wino – in short, the British people. On such matters, Mr Tebbit eschews compromise. He scorns the late Earl of Stockton's 'middle way between Manchester and Moscow' as unConservative. It is Mrs Thatcher, having 'achieved more change for good than any of her predecessors', who is the true inheritor of the traditions of Edmund Burke and Robert Peel. This is a bit hard on Mrs Thatcher's successor, and it is meant to be. Implicitly, the whole book reeks of the ultra-Right's bitter sense of betrayal. If Mr Tebbit has become a chihuahua, John Major is the dog that significantly fails to bark. The words 'Thatcher', 'Thatcherite', 'Thatcherism' appear on almost every page. The name of our present Prime Minister is mentioned only twice, once in a patronizing swipe at Mr Major's now forgotten Citizen's

Unfinished Business, Norman Tebbit (Weidenfeld & Nicolson, 1991)

Charter. The author writes reverentially of the 'three Thatcher admin-istrations', while passing in stony silence over the current adminis-tration, whose virtues he will (presumably) be extolling in the coming election.

Mr Tebbit is dismissive of 'Eurofanatics' who want to consign our national rights to a 'polyglot' European parliament, and accuses his former Cabinet colleague Sir Leon Brittan of being 'infantile' on the subject. To Mr Tebbit, the issue is one of sovereignty, with money as the crux. 'If there is to be drawn a line in the sand,' he says, and one can visualize a squad of Tory MPs trying to draw lines on Dover beach, 'over which the United Kingdom could not pass without setting out along the path to the status of a province, not nation, it is the creation of a single currency.'

In the old days, such fervent little-Englandism was usually combined with sentimentality about the Commonwealth, or at any rate the white bits of it. It is a sign of the changing times that, for all his views on Europe, Mr Tebbit has little patience even with the old dominions, and believes that the club of which the Queen is honorary head should be retained only as long as it costs Britain nothing. Yet what is contra-dictory about Mr Tebbit's stance on the Community (he suggests that we explore the option of coming out) and the Commonwealth (he deplores the issuing of British passports to Hong Kong Chinese) is that it combines external protectionism with the dogma of Victorian liberalism for internal affairs.

Thus, Mr Tebbit wishes to exclude competition from abroad on the grounds that the nation isn't up to it. He even manages a xenophobic dig at the constitutional pressure group, Charter 88, whose signatories are allegedly 'foreigners seemingly obsessed with the desire to make Britain more like the countries from which they have fled'. Yet he views with equanimity the effects of home-grown competition on the weakest citizens.

It is a canard of Tebbitism that we will all take 'soft options' unless bribed or beaten into doing otherwise. What is needed is a system 'which leaves individuals free to succeed – or just as important, to fail'. Failure (having your children taken into care, sleeping rough and so on) is a necessary part of the calculus. Mr Tebbit apparently thinks there would be fewer single-parent families if there were no extra benefits for single mothers, and fewer inhabitants of cardboard cities if local authorities were not required to accommodate the homeless.

Such sentiments, deplored by the Government as the election

approaches, need not be taken very seriously. Still, there is one bit of the book which, frivolous or not, threatens to cause outrage among parents of children in under-funded state schools. Teachers of quality, Mr Tebbit tells us, have been 'steadily replaced by ill-disciplined, intellectually lazy if not lacking, third-raters'. Gee, thanks. But if quality isn't what it might be, could that be because of a lack of financial incentive to enter the profession? Of course not. Extra money for salaries and small classes 'is only likely to increase costs without affecting standards or the volume of production'.

So much for carrots, sticks and the market mechanism.

Independent on Sunday, 13 October 1991

KENNETH BAKER

LIKE OTHER BREEDS of politician, Tories come in different shapes and sizes – the operator, the squire, the bother boy and so on. Kenneth Baker has always belonged to one familiar and easily recognizable type: the card. This sub-species is generally a bit overweight, and frequently wears hair oil and horn-rimmed glasses. It has a very bluff manner, smiles a lot, and has eyes that dart around the room. Cards are regarded as clever because they are extremely good at evading difficult questions. It is also a key feature of the card that he delights simple, orthodox members of his own party – especially the women, whom he reminds of their own over-indulged sons – while making everybody else feel queasy. Reginald Maudling was the prototype Tory card, Michael Howard is the current model, but there was never a Conservative more cardlike than Kenneth Baker. *Spitting Image* had him to a tee: as an exceptionally slimy snail, oozing sycophancy and self-satisfaction out of every orifice.

The card is seldom dangerous to fellow politicians, amongst whom he is regarded as clubbable and even companionable – this is the secret of his frequent success. The general public is more wary – though in Baker's case there is a sort of perverse, posthumous affection for him, possibly helped by his departure from office in 1992 and consequent avoidance of blame for the Jacques Tati-like mishaps of the last sixteen months. Those, however, who might have been inclined to forgive and forget will find more than enough in this volume to reimpose old prejudices.

In his social origins, Baker was fairly typical of the Heath–Thatcher generation of Tories: neither *noblesse oblige* nor rags-to-riches but somewhere in between, with a frugally aspirant family already moving up. His grandfather was an active trade unionist in the Dock, Wharf, Riverside and General Workers' Union and an associate of Ben Tillett,

The Turbulent Years: My Life in Politics, Kenneth Baker (Faber & Faber, 1993)

his father a civil servant and then an accountant who was able to pay public school fees at St Paul's. His youth was almost as uneventful as the Prime Minister's: unlike Major, however, he went to university (Magdalen, Oxford, where he was friendly with Dudley Moore). A few years of modest success in business preceded his entry to Parliament at a by-election in 1968 at the age of thirty-four.

From the start of his career, Baker was a machine man – first as Heath's PPS and junior minister, and then as a rising star under Mrs Thatcher. Despite his close identification with the *ancien régime*, the transition caused him no problems, and from the moment he became Minister of Information Technology in 1981 – and embarked on the privatization of BT – he was in the vanguard of the Thatcher revolution, and an enthusiast for its most doctrinaire ideas. He was also close to the throne throughout Mrs Thatcher's years of office. When Major took over, it was never the same. Baker became Home Secretary, but the old intimacy with No. 10 had gone and with it (as the author openly admits) any hope of the succession.

Kenneth Baker is probably best known for his spell as Education minister between 1986 and 1989 – at any rate by schoolchildren, who cherish the mid-term holidays known as 'Baker days'. The author is himself particularly proud of this episode and devotes several chapters to it – which should, however, carry a health warning. People with high blood pressure – especially if they happen to be parents, teachers or educational administrators – would do well to avoid material that is a shocking revelation for what it fails to reveal, namely any appetite for tackling the problem by means other than blaming advisers and attacking ideological opponents. Having taken over from the Jeremiah-like Sir Keith Joseph, who put up the backs of the teaching profession but nevertheless commanded its respect, Mr Baker set out to upset practically everybody, except the Prime Minister and the party faithful.

True, he did at least acknowledge that British education was in a mess and had been getting worse since Mrs Thatcher came to power in 1979 (the challenge was one which, he says, 'seven years of Conservative government had not readily addressed'). But instead of trying to find out what was actually going on in classrooms, he chose to bully and insult. The result has been an approach to reform that has triggered a stampede out of teaching – and has reduced morale in many schools to its lowest level in living memory. The author scapegoats 'left-wing' teachers (a tiny minority) and civil servants: and singularly fails to talk about resources. He also has the cheek to write of the 'expansion' of higher education – in reality a conjuring trick based on increased student intake, but no comparable growth in funding or staff – as if it were a miracle of government-induced productivity.

One of Baker's themes is the importance of good English. He was disappointed by the 1988 Kingman Report which he had hoped would recommend 'a model of English which would serve as a basis for teachers to be trained to teach it and for pupils to learn how to use language fluently and correctly' and which failed (mercifully, some may think) to come up with anything so deadeningly rigid. The former Education minister's own command of the mother tongue is beta query minus: he expresses himself competently but flatly, in a tone that is a cross between party conference and Keesing's Contemporary Archives – part high-flown rhetoric, part staccato chronicle. Occasionally there is a telling portrait, and the author is at his most sensitive on the topic of Lady Thatcher's doings and motivations. Even here, however, he often resorts to saloon bar cliché ('Like her or loathe her, people knew what she stood for and where she was going').

Elsewhere, there are some barbs at ex-colleagues, but mainly a high degree of caution, and a good deal of banality. It is not wildly exciting to be told that Nicholas Ridley used to doodle naked ladies, or that after his death the fishmonger whose stall he frequented said: 'It's very sad about Mr Ridley. He was a wonderful person.' And although there are a few flashes of wit, the standard of humour in the higher reaches of the Conservative Party seems to require its own national curriculum:

> Margaret was very tired and almost dropped off to sleep during the dinner. Jeffrey Archer, at our end of the table, decided to liven things up, by joking, 'Hello, hello, hello, why doesn't a Sloane Ranger like a gang bang?' I responded, 'Jeffrey, tell us why doesn't a Sloane Ranger like a gang bang?' Jeffrey replied, 'Because afterwards there are too many thank-you letters.' This produced a burst of laughter . . .

Get it? Answers, please, on a postcard.

Independent on Sunday, 12 September 1993

NEIL KINNOCK

THERE IS A DIFFICULTY in writing 'anticipatory' biography of the kind under review. The problem is not just that the history of a man without a past is dominated by present impressions. It is also that these impressions are in a state of flux. During the new Opposition Leader's first year – in which the mood of the Party has shifted from post-electoral shell-shock at Brighton to besieged defiance at Blackpool – perceptions of him have significantly altered.

Both these books are diligent, fair and interesting. Both, however, suffer from the difficulty that so far there is not a great deal to be said. As the titles imply, they cover much the same ground. Of the two, Harris wins decisively on points. He is the better writer, his characterization is more subtle, and he gives to his account the shape, and something of the pace, of a thriller. Much of what he says is based on conversations with Kinnock's colleagues and enemies, and he has spent valuable time in South Wales digging at the Party Leader's grass roots. Drower relies mainly on newspaper clippings, and as a result gives too much importance to routine statements to the press of a kind that politicians shove out every night before brushing their teeth. Neither book is 'authorized', and both seek to show their subject warts and all. Both writers, however, obtained interviews with Kinnock himself, and Harris in particular makes extensive use of material gained thereby. This is understandable, but a mistake. The portraits might have been sharper, with fewer punches pulled, if there had been no sense of obligation. Politically, both books are rather blandly uncommitted.

There is little disagreement about the facts or their interpretation. Central to each account, as to the Labour leader's own self-image, is his ordinariness. The theme is well-established: likely lad from a Welsh mining village – bad at work, good at games – shows no special aptitude

The Making of Neil Kinnock, Robert Harris (Faber & Faber, 1984); *Neil Kinnock*, G. M. F. Drower (Weidenfeld & Nicolson, 1984)

until his early twenties. Then a mixture of talent, guts and fate raises him aloft. Both agree that it was Cardiff University and the rough-house of the students' union that set him up. Meetings were held at lunch-time: it was here that, with his future wife Glenys as his ally, he learnt to raise his voice above the din of the canteen. He campaigned for left-wing causes, became student president, and flunked his exams. He got a pass degree at his second attempt. 'I just permitted myself to be distracted', he admits, 'by sport or debates or politics or going to the cinema in the afternoon.'

What turned a B-stream 'lazy sod' (a friend's description) at grammar school into a high flyer? Both writers mention Kinnock's youthful enthusiasm for Aneurin Bevan, and the history of unemployment and industrial injury in his own family. Frivolity rather than seriousness, however, characterized Kinnock's roustabout undergraduate career. 'I've been fortunate', Kinnock claims, 'in that I've never suffered from personal ambition.' His biographers rightly disbelieve him. Yet the lift-off of the 'average student at an average university' (as Drower calls him) is not closely examined, and the mystery of his motivations remains unsolved.

The spur to succeed was certainly sharp. Having left university, Kinnock moved fast. He took his first and only pre-parliamentary job, at twenty-four, as a tutor for the WEA. Three years later, he was selected as Labour candidate for one of the safest seats in the United Kingdom, and a year after that he was in Parliament. Future party leaders usually start young. Several – Churchill, Eden, Home and Wilson – have, like Kinnock, become MPs before the age of thirty. No leader in this century, however, has had so brief an experience of the world of work outside Westminster. Nor has any politician, once elected, travelled so quickly to the top of his party. What was Kinnock's secret? Both authors stress his speaking ability and his charm. Then, somewhat at a loss, they turn to luck. Kinnock, they say, was born lucky. Even when his car somersaulted off the motorway with him inside, divine intervention was at hand to save him. 'Someone up there likes me,' said Kinnock at the time. Harris agrees. This remark, he suggests, not only summed up a miraculous escape, 'it also . . . seemed to sum up Kinnock's entire career.'

To say that Kinnock's career has been lucky, however, is a way of avoiding the need for explanation. If Kinnock has had a habit of being in the right place at the right time, this has been because he has put himself there. Indeed in his first years in Parliament he showed a formidable ability to create his own opportunities. Thus, principle and self-advancement were judiciously combined during the 1974–9 Parliament when Kinnock opted for backbench independence, and refused offers of a junior ministerial post. It was in these years that he made his name with a series of well-targeted attacks on the Government's managerial drift, and – in particular – with a brilliantly effective assault on plans for Welsh devolution. Courage or far-sightedness? Arguably, both. There were many other Labour MPs, easily tempted by office, who have since vanished without trace. Staying his ground, and accepting the disapproval of the Cabinet hierarchy, Kinnock was also building himself a Labour Party base.

According to Harris, a witty speech at a Tribune rally during the 1975 Party Conference was the turning-point of his career. 'He went a bomb,' says Joe Ashton, a fellow MP. 'He was the star of the show. And there were 500 constituency votes in that audience.' Standing for the Party Executive the following year, he picked up more than 150 of them. In 1978 he was elected, second only to Benn in the constituency parties section. The reason? 'There were few MPs attacking the Government as vociferously as he was,' suggests Harris. It was Kinnock's perception of the widening gap between the Government and its active supporters, and his energy in capitalizing on the split, that turned him into a leading politician. Though he criticized ministers in Parliament, Parliament was by no means the main focus of his interest. Harris has done a count. In his first year as an MP, Kinnock voted in nine divisions out of ten: by 1982 he had one of the worst attendance records of any Member. 'I've always considered that speaking around the country is an important part of being a Labour MP,' he says, disarmingly. 'You're a full-time, paid political activist.'

Before the 1979 general election, Kinnock may have had long-distance hopes, but he cannot have anticipated the speed of his elevation. Callaghan was still in charge, Healey the heir apparent. After Labour's defeat, three developments put Kinnock in the centre of the stage: first, his own determination, having accepted the shadow education portfolio, to resist the demands of former allies on the left; second, the surprise election of Foot as leader, making another contest in the near future likely, with a good chance that the Party would go for a younger man; and third, the constitutional upheaval which gave the PLP a mere 30 per cent of the total vote in the new electoral college, and ensured that MPs would live in terror of their (usually left-wing) general management committees.

Like three predecessors (Attlee, Wilson, Foot), Kinnock gained the leadership while moving from the Left toward the middle ground. In 1978, the press had called Kinnock an extremist and a fanatic. After 1979, he appeared, in media terms, a member of the 'sensible' Left. There was his refusal, despite strong pressure, to pledge Labour to restore Tory education cuts in full. There were his views on Arthur Scargill ('He's destroying the coal industry single-handed') and on Militants ('They once stuck a dead rat and a used sanitary towel through my door'). There was his opposition to Benn in the deputy leadership contest ('I thought we needed a contest like we needed bubonic plague'). By 1982, some of his former friends were calling him 'Judas'.

At the time it was tough for Kinnock, and he risked losing his NEC seat as a reprisal. In the long term – as his detractors point out – he had much to gain. If there was bitterness against the Right after the 1979 poll for betrayals in government, there were likely to be recriminations against the far Left after the subsequent election, once it had been soundly lost. The party leadership, moreover, would once more be on the market. So it proved. Even before the election had taken place, the fight for Foot's succession had begun. At one of Kinnock's meetings a heckler shouted: 'Mrs Thatcher's got guts.' Kinnock replied, in the best one-liner of the whole miserable, humbug-ridden campaign: 'And it's a pity that other people had to leave theirs on the ground at Goose Green in order to prove it.' Far from being a 'major political blunder', as Drower suggests, this remark helped to make Kinnock front runner when a few weeks later, Foot resigned as leader. Two factors determined the outcome: Benn's general election defeat in Bristol, which pushed him out of the race; and the trade unions. In the event, the trade unions went quickly and massively for Kinnock. Deprived of a serious left-wing alternative, the constituency parties followed suit. Battered MPs, relieved not to be offered anybody more frightening, fell into line. There was no bandwagon. The battle was no sooner joined than won.

What, from these two books, can we learn about Kinnock as a man? That he is emotional, impulsive, voluble, funny, informal. That he is gregarious, naturally egalitarian and hates privilege. That – at his best – he is an outstanding stump orator. That he is likeable and straightforward, acute without being devious. That he is a middle-brow, closer to Attlee and Callaghan than to Gaitskell, Wilson or Foot. Drower calls him a meritocrat. The term is inappropriate. Kinnock is untested.

He has no area of expertise, and no experience of administration. He has climbed no promotional ladder. He has made his way, instead, on the basis of a sixth sense for the Labour Movement's sensibilities, an instinct for its values and a keen judgement of its byzantine procedures. He is good with middle-class socialists, to whom he speaks the language of the student debating chamber. He is even better with trade unionists, who feel that he is one of them. He is best of all in working men's clubs. Pretty wife, rugby fanaticism, frequent use of 'bloody' in off-the-cuff exchanges, give him a rank-and-file macho with which no other post-war leader has been equipped.

In style and rhetoric, like his hero Aneurin Bevan, he is a product of Methodist halls and an ancient tradition of Celtic Independent Labour Party evangelism. Yet he is also a break with the past. Gaitskell, Wilson, Callaghan, Foot – all four of his immediate predecessors – entered the Commons in 1945. First elected a quarter of a century later, Kinnock skips not one political generation but two. As an MP, he knows nothing of Crippsian austerity or Wilsonian pursuit of growth, or of the years of so-called 'consensus'. Michael Foot spent his youth attacking Neville Chamberlain; for Kinnock, the enemy was Lyndon Johnson. In spirit, like many of his entourage, he still belongs to the anti-Vietnam war, anti-authority, campus power 1960s. Already he has presided, with considerable assurance though not without criticism, over a restoration of balance and unity in the Labour Party.

Times Literary Supplement, 12 October 1984

KEN LIVINGSTONE

IS THERE SUBSTANCE TO 'municipal socialism'? Is Ken Livingstone the shape of things to come? This excellent short biography of the council leader known to *Sun* readers as 'the most odious man in Britain', suggests that town-hall radicalism is a force which legislative magic wands will not easily wave away. Tracing the contours of what has become a remarkable career, the local government correspondent of the *Guardian* presents his subject, not as the mahdi of a new movement, but as a representative – even archetypal – figure within it.

Like many Labour politicians, Livingstone came from the aspirant, house-buying, Tory-voting, upper end of the working class. Though there was show business in the family (his mother was a circus performer), young Kenneth showed little early interest in public display. Eleven-plus failure and alienation in a big comprehensive led him instead into a private world of dumb fauna, from which – he claims – his later view of human organization is derived. It was his first job as a lab technician, taking him across the crucial divide between respectable working- and straitened lower-middle class, that introduced him to politics. Learning about Wilsonian socialism from work-mates, the nineteen-year-old Livingstone was 'trembling with excitement' when Labour won the 1964 election. Four years later, unlike his student contemporaries who were leaving it, he joined the Labour Party.

With Labour in power at Westminster, the Party was at its nadir in the constituencies. It was a time of octogenarian general management committees, of local executives that could not raise a quorum. It was also a time when any determined newcomer could have a local council seat for the asking. Within months Livingstone was on the ladder. In 1973, somewhat to his surprise, he found himself a member of the Greater London Council.

John Carvel tries to make something of Livingstone's manoeuvrings

Citizen Ken, John Carvel (Hogarth Press, 1984)

during the early 1970s in and around Camden and Norwood, and of the training he received from 'Red Ted' Knight of Lambeth. In fact, the young councillor's early political experiences were little different from those of dozens of others, picked up in committee or on the doorstep in London's poorer areas, and passed through the filter of Labour bar-room fad and fancy. There was never much in the way of theory. Livingstone's table-talk, extensively quoted in this book, reveals firmly held prejudices – in favour of justice for the underdog and other equally unpopular causes – but apart from Stuart Holland-derived references to the power of capital and some crude social darwinism ('a vision of a hunter-gatherer society with microchips' as Carvel puts it), there is little that comes from book-learning and almost nothing from Marx.

As a politician, Livingstone's success came from *not* joining left-wing groups. His tactic was to mobilize the Left, organize the Left, run with the Left, yet always to stand somewhat apart and aloof from the Left. At first, he was a centrist. In the early 1970s, the real division in local Labour politics was social and generational, not ideological. The battle was between the dinosaur old guard, rooted in communities that had ceased to exist, and better-educated upstarts, filling gaps on councils after Labour's crushing municipal defeats of 1968 and 1969. This injection of youth and ambition began a process of revitalization that was well advanced before most outsiders noticed the decline that had earlier occurred.

What has Livingstone's GLC actually achieved? With central government whittling away local responsibilities at every opportunity the answer in policy terms is not much. 'Fares Fair' was effectively crushed. The Council's other most publicized and controversial policy – funding what journalists call 'minority groups' – accounts for a tiny percentage of its discretionary budget. Nevertheless, in public relations terms the new régime has been a triumph. Here is an interesting paradox. Seldom has a local authority received such a bad press; never has a London leader been subject to such calumny. Yet it has been precisely because of Livingstone-induced notoriety that the new gas-and-water socialists have been able to achieve the astonishing feat of making council work appear glamorous. The adage about all publicity being good publicity is particularly apt. Citizen Ken's present status as cockney folk hero, and the Government's embarrassment as it tries to destroy him, owe much to the prurient headlines in the *Sun* and *Mail* which have given him his fame. British local government was conceived as a means of defusing opposition by letting local notables take the decisions that did not matter. Livingstone and his colleagues have forced a Cabinet that can treat the parliamentary Opposition with contempt to bring out its biggest guns against resistance in the localities.

There is another paradox. The Livingstone régime has made its name by raising two fingers, not just at Michael Heseltine and Mrs Thatcher, but also at the London electorate. Where previous LCC and GLC leaders worried about the electoral effects of a penny-in-the-pound increase in rates, the new, psephologically informed generation has been aware that only an earthquake can shift municipal voters from their indifference to local issues. Livingstone's relaxed – and in the end, vote-winning – candour has been one consequence. What national politician, greeting reporters after seeing the Transport Secretary, would venture to remark: 'He asked to see me again. I think he must want me for my body'?

To be pilloried by the media is to be exalted by the faithful. For Livingstone, the only electorate that really matters is an intra-party one. That is the real meaning of Labour Party democracy. Part of Livingstone's success has been in turning the GLC into a personal platform. *Per ardua ad astra.* Livingstone is a professional who does his homework, a twenty-four-hour operator living for the thrills and spills of his obsession. He understands the currency of political principle, and unlike the legatees of Herbert Morrison, he enjoys smashing eggs. He speaks for a harsher, nastier, more resilient, less deferential and more effective breed of socialist, than existed in the past. John Carvel's readable, intelligent and unillusioned book does not eulogize its subject. It encourages a belief, however, that Livingstonians will be around, fixing meetings, counting heads and making rude noises, when Social Democrats of blessed memory are breaking moulds in the sky.

Times Literary Supplement, 22 June 1984

DEGSY

WHEN YOUNG 'DEGSY' HATTON was in the fire service, he happened to be cleaning up the road one day after a lorry had squashed a girl student's head. 'Aye, aye – another one joining the brain drain,' said his mate, swilling the gutter with a hose. Degsy found the remark helpful: 'It taught me that sometimes you have to be absolutely ruthless in order to take other people with you.'

Degsy likes to think of absolute ruthlessness as his trade mark. Take, for example, an incident from his footballing days. The referee made a decision Degsy did not like, so Degsy punched him in the face, earning a lifetime's ban from the county league. You might think he would be a bit shy about it. Not Degsy: 'It illustrates one of my failings,' he writes. 'I do have a very short fuse, and if somebody really gets in my way without good reason I'm likely to react violently without even thinking.' Moral: don't get in Degsy's way, even if it's only to blow a whistle.

The truth is that Degsy never got the point about referees, fair play, democracy. He prefers the pragmatic approach. There are plenty of protests in this book about the Labour Party leadership's 'mobilizing against Militant', but listen to how Degsy describes his own and his pals' Old Salem for official or Labour critics when 'The Tendency' took control of Liverpool in 1983:

> Some moaned and whined to the Press. So what! I've never cared what people thought about me, but I cared that we should find the moles and move them, that we should find the leaks and stop them. Our campaign was more important than the careers of a few whingeing armchair radicals who hadn't the guts to stand up and be counted.

Inside Left: The Story So Far, Derek Hatton (Bloomsbury, 1988)

Yet this is not the blueprint of a fanatic, or even the confessions of a mafioso. It is the (heavily ghosted) money-spinner of an adventurer – significant for what created him.

Degsy belonged to the other 1968: not hippies and libertarianism, but the dank fag-end of a consumers' decade. Frequent references to (and self-comparisons with) idols of the Brian Epstein era provide the clue to this sad, cocky tale. The 1960s were about affluence, freedom, opportunity. Degsy came of age when it was all ending. The natty suits, the fast cars, the night-clubbing, above all the delight in public display reflect an old, desperate, displaced, Liverpudlian fantasy. At grammar school, Degsy wanted to be an actor. Instead he became an insurance clerk, then a fireman. There followed a period of drifting and eventual absorption, Moonie-style, into the conspiratorial beer-hall world of Militant.

This book tells little new about Militant's techniques, or its tenure of power. It does show, however, that procedural cunning was combined with block-headed innocence on policy. The Militant councillors seem to have believed, like the courtiers of King Canute, in the power of title-holders to govern the waves. Those who pointed out the difficulties were traitors. The revolution had begun: 'The plan was quite straightforward,' says Degsy. 'We had taken office. Now we would bring the train to a standstill. Everything had to stop. Then we would re-route the engine and the whole council train onto our own track.' Heady, nihilistic stuff, and Degsy – deputy leader in name, front man in practice – built his fame on its inevitable collapse.

Television played a key role. Degsy's sub-Marxian polysyllables became the ludicrous, yet also faintly disturbing, symbol of alienation, the lurking threat of the unemployed and the concrete estates. The tabloids recognized a winner: swiftly they gobbled up Degsy and disgorged him on to the nation's breakfast tables, providing the stardom he craved. 'They can exile me to the political wilderness,' he boasts today, '. . . but when the history books are written for the 1980s, the name of Militant and Derek Hatton will be right there, alongside those of Kinnock and Thatcher.'

Is this – as the title implies – Degsy's *Mein Kampf*, written at a moment of temporary setback in a life of destiny? I doubt it. Off the council, out of the Party, estranged even from the former Militant comrades, and not – actually – angry about anything except those who have thwarted him, Degsy may have a future in show business, but scarcely in politics. Nevertheless, Mr Kinnock should not believe that by stamping on Militant he has destroyed the Degsy phenomenon. Unless the Party Leader's 'listening' campaign tunes in – not just to the yuppies of the marginals but to the needs of the urban junkyards where Labour, and Militant, find strongest support – there will be plenty of Degsy clones to fill the gap.

Observer, 21 February 1988

DAVID MARQUAND

WHY CAN'T THE LEADERS of the Labour Party 'face the fact that they are not sectaries of an outworn creed, mumbling moss-grown demi-semi Fabian marxism,' wrote Maynard Keynes in 1939, 'but the heirs of eternal Liberalism?' As the author of this sparkling collection of essays and sketches of left-of-Right politicians points out, Keynes's frustration has been shared by generations of advanced, efficient, straight-talking, modern thinkers. The result has been not so much a progressive dilemma as a progressive angst. Labour's maddening ability to survive despite its stubborn adherence to a peculiar form of ancestor worship has ensured the exclusion of non-mumblers from the degree of influence which they believe they deserve.

David Marquand – son of a Labour minister, distinguished biographer, ex-Labour MP, unrepentant Gaitskellite, SDP pioneer, Social and Liberal Democrat programme writer, constitutional reformer – is perhaps the quintessential non-mumbler. There is certainly nothing remotely mumbling about this book, which is enviably limpid, incisive, readable and even, in places, quite cruelly funny. Compared with many of the very dull people who have held office in past Labour governments or hope to hold office in future ones, Marquand shines like a star: as, indeed, do some of the other renegades whose political careers, through choice or miscalculation, came to a full stop. His book, which seeks to examine what went wrong for Labour, may also be helpful in diagnosing the errors of those who wished to put it right.

One of his sharpest attacks is upon his former friend and colleague David Owen who, as he reminds us, was never remotely Liberal at all. Nor does Marquand trivialize by laying the main blame for mistakes at the door of individuals – though the vacillations of Harold Wilson and the ambitions of Owen tried him sorely. His indictment is of the

The Progressive Dilemma: from Lloyd George to Kinnock, David Marquand (Heinemann, 1991)

Party, the movement and the culture into which he was born and towards which he continues to feel (and this is part of the interest of his book) a passionate or obsessive fascination. One does not want to get too Freudian but it is as though the author is an angrily rebellious child who, while rejecting the values of its old-fashioned parents, yearns for a way to retie the umbilical.

In this respect, of course, Marquand is quite different from Keynes, a liberal capitalist for whom the Labour Party was a faintly hilarious beast in the political menagerie. Marquand, by contrast, views it with emotion as a continuing tragedy. Marquand's argument is that Labour has failed in two critical ways. Unlike its predecessor in the two-party quadrille – the Gladstonian Liberal Party, which managed to hold office about half the time – Labour has generally been in the wilderness. There have only been Labour administrations for twenty out of seventy-two years since universal male suffrage was introduced. Only twice (in 1945 and 1966) has Labour obtained a House of Commons majority in double figures. Marquand attributes this failure to the inability of Labour leaders to lead electors, as distinct from the party faithful. 'One reason why the death of Liberal England was not followed by the birth of a comparable Labour England', he maintains, 'is that Labour politicians have been less good at "shaping" values than have their rivals.'

The second failure is even more culpable: on the rare occasions when Labour has held office, it has done precious little with it – with the notable exception of the Attlee administration which stands as a reproachful reminder of what might have been achieved. The explanation for this second failure lies deeper, considers the author, than Labour's outworn creed of woolly socialism. Rather 'it was a kind of woodenness, a lack of political imagination, a hardness of the intellectual arteries, which prevented Labour ministers from creating new opportunities and turning the flanks of their opponents in the way that Roosevelt and Lloyd George so often did.' Thus the political persona of Harold Wilson should be seen as a symptom rather than a cause of the Party's mediocrity. Wilson's conservatism, 'his corrupting mixture of left-wing talk and right-wing deeds', was also that of the parliamentary party which supported him.

Of Wilson it was once remarked (possibly with a touch of admiration for such a remarkable talent) that 'if he swallowed a sixpence he'd shit a corkscrew'. But behind Wilsonian doubletalk and doublethink, Marquand claims, lay the trade union and working-class ethos of the

Labour Movement, which characterizes present-day Kinnockite revisionism, in contrast to its forward-looking Gaitskellite predecessor. While Hugh Gaitskell 'remains an inspiration for all who believe that representative democracy depends on trust ... and that trust is built on telling the truth', Neil Kinnock's pragmatic patching up operation 'fitted the essential defensiveness of the Labour ethos like a glove'.

It is an analysis which combines brilliant insights and a deep seam of historical fallacy. For Marquand is a very dangerous kind of historian – a chronicler with a mission. Despite his intimacy with the facts of Labour's past, he writes in tones of exhortation and exasperation as if he were describing a wayward but alterable personality.

The logic of what he says – namely that Labour's heritage constrains the Party to behave and talk in ways which members of the liberal-minded professional classes find incomprehensible – ought to incline him to a greater tolerance. His conclusion is wisely accommodating. His prescription of a rainbow coalition of progressive parties (which have many policies in common) makes obvious sense. Yet Marquand accepts, ruefully, the durability of Labour without fully embracing what flows from it: namely the need for the loftier heirs to eternal Liberalism to accept that moss-grown Labour rhetoric provides both the vehicle and the necessary vernacular, for any serious attempt at radical social change.

Guardian, 7 February 1991

CHRISTOPHER HITCHENS

A GOOD WAY TO JUDGE a book is by its cover, and this one tells you a lot. On the front is a snapshot of the author smoking at a table in a café or pub, empty glasses strewn around him. A lighter bulges in his top pocket, his hair needs a wash and so does his shirt. His blank defiant stare and folded arms say: 'I am a rebel and I don't give a shit.' They also say (for an author who picks a photo of himself looking dissolute exercises a choice): 'I am stuck in a 1960s art-movie fantasy about being a rebellious writer who doesn't give a shit.'

Hitchens is an English journalist who lives in the United States, where he is a cult figure in progressive circles and writes for the radical periodical the *Nation* and for *Vanity Fair*. This is a collection of reviews and essays written since the mid-1980s, though mainly in the last five years. There are more than seventy items, some of them very short, on everything from trotskyism in New York, to booze and fags, and *Daniel Deronda*. Most are in one way or another about politics, especially about politics in America. There is something about the puritan conscience of the liberal establishment in the United States that makes it relish flagellation, especially from a foreigner, and nobody wields a scourge with more exquisite enjoyment of the pain inflicted on his flabby-minded victims than Mr Hitchens.

The test of this kind of book is for the reader to be able to open it anywhere and be drawn into the argument: it's a test Hitchens passes time and again. There is some overlap and repetition, though. He accuses Norman Mailer of self-plagiarism, but is guilty of it himself: on page 168 he tells us that 'another defeat would expose Labour as the party that had tried everything – *everything* – to please, and still not got the mix quite right'; six pages later he asks: 'And what does a party do when it has tried everything – *everything* – and nothing works?' But his prose is full of well-honed surprises, and he has a special gift

For the Sake of Argument, Christopher Hitchens (Verso, 1993)

for the lip-curling one-liner. On West Coast culture, he writes of the 'decaffeinated hedonism' of Los Angeles. The British Labour Government of 1976–9 under James Callaghan is memorably described as 'a sort of Weimar without the sex'.

His method is to move between a kind of grubby demotic accessibility, scholarly erudition that stops just short of showing off, and venomous invective. He can be devilishly funny, but he is also capable of writing with acid seriousness. There are particularly good essays on the wriggles of the British Government over the Salman Rushdie affair, on the banalities of Reagan and Bush, and on the horror of Bosnia.

He is best value when the subject is squalid ('Nobody likes a bit of filth more than the present author,' he tells us). Of Tom Driberg he remarks: 'He just liked to administer free blow-jobs to the masses. How many modern Members of Parliament can claim as much?' Pretension, hypocrisy and sentimentality are Hitchens's enemies: his sport is to bite through to the rottenness beneath.

'Swiftian' might be an appropriate tag for some of his writing. But the essayist with whom he would most like to be compared is, I suspect, George Orwell. There is a similarity in interest and range, and Hitchens, like Orwell, is a non-affiliated supporter of unpopular causes, a quizzical camera, a ragger of the pompous who likes to deconstruct as well as to observe. However, there is an important difference. Where Orwell is deceptively clever at embracing his readers, and making you feel that you and he, though fallible mortals, are on the same side, Hitchens can be excluding. At his best he makes you applaud in envious admiration, or laugh wickedly out loud, but he does not make you want to side with him. This is partly because of an element of snobbery that lies oddly with his radicalism. He is keen to tell us that he knew Bill Clinton at Oxford, that the Princess of Wales's stepbrother is 'my old chum', even (by including their surnames on the dedication page) that his godchildren belong to famous literary dynasties.

This is innocent enough, but there is also an uncomfortable edge. When Hitchens jokes that Norman Mailer once complained of being 'the victim of a London faggot literary coterie, consisting of Martin Amis, Ian Hamilton and myself', it is only half a joke: this is boastworthy company, and you are conscious of being in the presence of a name-drop. As a reader, you have an unnerving sensation that you probably fall into one of a large number of categories of people who don't measure up.

Many of these categories merit the derisive treatment they receive from Hitchens. What diminishes his impact, however, is an inability to see human beings in the round. Politicians, for instance, don't always deserve to be regarded as the lowest form of life. If it is true that there is no profession in the world, not even the oldest, that is so full of cant and moral corruption, it is equally true that somebody has to do their job. Hitchens's impatient failure to consider this aspect, or even to attempt to understand the predicaments politicians find themselves in, is one reason why he can leave you with an increased sympathy for the person he is savaging.

It is as if there is a not-quite-grown-up element to some of his writing. Possibly he still owes too much to a 1960s nihilism which treated everybody in authority with even-handed contempt for the single reason that they were in charge. There is a sense in which he is a kind of journalistic Emma Goldman: an incendiary bomber, an anarchic and mesmerizing but destructive and sometimes undiscriminating force. You do not feel after reading him (as you often do, for instance, after reading essays by Orwell) morally the cleaner.

Nevertheless, we should certainly celebrate a writer who compels us to press our noses against the glass. 'In the non-debate over non-issues that goes on here', Hitchens writes on the political correctness fad in the United States, 'the hands-down winner is the culture of euphemism.' As a zapper of euphemisms he has no par, and that is a good enough reason, or excuse, for finding his byline irresistible.

Independent on Sunday, 20 June 1993

JOHN SMITH

WHAT WERE YOU DOING when you heard the news about John Smith? Most people this weekend can answer that question. Many will be able to for the rest of their lives – much as an earlier generation still recalls the shock of Kennedy's assassination. That the death of a political leader out of office should have been such an event is a symptom of the unhappy state of British politics. It is also a tribute to a leader whom people of all opinions and classes warmed to, had confidence in, and felt they could trust.

The tragedy of John Smith's death is partly to do with what he might have achieved, rather than what he did. There is a sense of being cheated: a feeling that here was a man with the intelligence, integrity, steel but also – vitally – the psychological balance to have made a great prime minister, who would have restored the office to its proper dignity and shown that it is not necessary to be megalomaniac or shallow to hold supreme power.

Smith was leader of his party for just twenty-two months – a shorter period than any predecessor apart from Arthur Henderson, who took over from Ramsay MacDonald in 1931 and then lost his seat in the ensuing general election. He is the sixth Labour Leader never to have become Prime Minister. But he is the only one apart from George Lansbury, who led the miniscule PLP in the early 1930s and resigned just before the 1935 poll, never to have taken his party into a general election. Given such a short period at the helm, it is not surprising that his concrete achievements should be few.

Chosen as leader after the election, he distinguished himself in his handling of Maastricht. His most important success was over One Member One Vote – an issue that had dogged, depressed and debilitated the Labour Party for fifteen years or more, and on which his predecessor had been forced to accept an unhappy compromise. Smith was attacked both for allowing himself to rush headlong into a confrontation with the unions on a matter that needed tactful diplomacy, and for allowing navel-gazing to dominate Labour Party business to the exclusion of everything else.

It was a gamble: his hair's breadth victory at last year's party conference vindicated his stand, and marked the symbolic end of Labour's long road back to respectability. Yet his achievement lay in consolidating the work of his predecessor, rather than in striking out in a new direction. Credit for the basic work of restoring the Party to sanity still belongs to Neil Kinnock.

Judged by immediate results, Smith's record is not a remarkable one. What he achieved was intangible: he made Labour seem, for the first time since the 1970s, a party most people would trust in government. That remains his legacy.

Since his death, Smith has been compared with Hugh Gaitskell – who died suddenly at an almost identical age, and at a comparable moment in his party's history. In fact, they were quite different political personalities. Both were men of principle and courage. In Gaitskell's case, however, there were contrasting pictures. To his friends, Gaitskell seemed a man of ideas and a visionary leader. To his enemies, and there were many, he seemed an élitist prig. Smith was more of a piece. His image was indistinguishable from the reality, and his cleverness – and self-confidence – were of a homespun variety. For all his lawyer's skills, nobody could accuse him of being an intellectual.

What he offered was a combination of shrewd management and a generous political and personal style. Unlike Gaitskell, he was not arrogant or cliquish. He was comfortable enough with himself, and his own opinions, to be able to listen to those of others and to appreciate different points of view. He was the least paranoid leader the Labour Party – or any party – has had in modern times. He could combine intimacy with friends and an olive branch to those who had previously caused trouble. There was no 'Hampstead Set', or exclusive club of cronies, similar to those who kept Gaitskell company. Grumpier leaders, like John Prescott, were brought in from the cold.

Smith created space to think and talk and air grievances. 'It was wonderful not to have the Thought Police,' as one Walworth Road official puts it. When Gaitskell died, Bevanites expressed sympathy through gritted teeth. By contrast, some of the most moving tributes for John Smith have come from left-wingers. Smith was equally relaxed with those outside the Party, and he did much to reduce the instinctive horror of a Labour government that existed in the City.

There were also gaps. It is tempting to look back through rose-tinted spectacles at a man struck down in his prime – as happened both with Gaitskell and, for a time, with Kennedy. Smith was certainly not beyond criticism. The most frequent point made against him – oddly, for the leader of a party that had lost four elections in a row – was complacency. He was content to allow the Government to dig its own grave, and he saw too little value in offering a radical alternative.

Scarred by his experience as Shadow Chancellor during the 1992 election, he showed a deep reluctance to make any policy suggestions that might involve increases in public expenditure. At this moment of mid-term Government disarray, his methods seemed to reap electoral results. But there have been no great policy innovations associated with his leadership, and commentators generally agreed that the politician Labour had most to thank for its local election gains was Mr Major. Gaitskell left a Labour Party that was a cauldron of policy debate. By comparison (though it would be unfair to blame Smith too much for this) today's party has seemed ideologically uncertain.

Yet – and it is on this that his place in history rests – he turned Labour from a party on the margins of British political life to one that is now firmly back in the mainstream, and one which can claim to have recaptured the consensus. 'Neil wanted to win,' as one member of the Shadow Cabinet puts it. 'John knew he was going to.'

If not Gaitskell, who in Labour's history does he most resemble? Conceivably the past leader he was most like was Clement Attlee, a man of prosaic opinions, imperviousness to fashion, private virtue, concern for the unprivileged, love of the Labour Movement and – as his six years as premier demonstrated – outstanding judgement, who travelled great distances by never looking too far ahead.

Independent on Sunday, 15 May 1994

THE FUTURE OF
POLITICAL BIOGRAPHY

WHAT IS WRONG with British political biography? The obvious answer is very little. 'Read no history, nothing but biography', wrote Benjamin Disraeli, 'for that is life without theory.'[1] In a nation traditionally suspicious of theory, many people seem to agree, and the most popular kind of non-fiction – not only among politicians and journalists, but also among scholarly authors, heavy-weight reviewers, the general public and, hence, publishers – has long been biography. Political biographies, moreover, have in some respects been getting better. In the early 1970s, Roy Jenkins – himself a distinguished contributor to the *genre* – commented on the rise of a generation of young academic biographers, who investigated in greater depth than their predecessors. He added that their work had yet to bear fruit.[2] Since that time, there has been a remarkable outpouring of twentieth-century British biography – characterized by close attention to unpublished papers, the more or less systematic use of interviews and a large number of reference notes.

Political biographers might, therefore, consider themselves entitled to a sense of achievement. Yet biography is both the most flourishing and – in intellectual and cultural terms – the least confident form of political writing. Here is a curiosity, and also perhaps a responsibility. Many people with a deep interest in politics, including quite a few practitioners, look to biography for knowledge and insight. But what is on offer frequently disappoints.

Part of the reason may be that, while readers take biography seriously, nobody else does. Biography is at once the most avidly consumed, and the least analysed, form of political writing. A glance at the subject index in any university library reveals the lowly status of

The original version of this essay was delivered as an inaugural lecture at Birkbeck College on 2 March 1989.

the political biographer's art. Literary biography has an honourable, if meagre, place: political biography, apart from a handful of essays, almost none at all. Thriller writers, film-makers, wood-carvers receive a great deal more attention than the unfortunate political biographer whose aims, style, methods and ethics are almost never examined. Reviews of biography generally do little more than summarize the life in question, with a pat or a kick for the author. How seldom do critics pause to wonder why so many people, with such eager patience, wish to discover the often unimportant and usually forgettable details of subject after subject, as each one makes his or her repetitive progress from cradle, via career, to grave. And how seldom do biographers themselves – political or any other kind – think about their craft, or take risks with it. All but the very best titles of the last decade give a sense, less of creative adventure, than of conservatism and stagnation. What is notable about most recent biographers is their impeccable authority; but also the strait-jacket of unspoken, unwritten convention within which they operate. Indeed – for all its popularity and rising standards – biography in our own generation has been the *least* adventurous of the arts. That is a pity and in need of remedy. Here I should like to offer, if not a political biographer's manifesto, then at least a call to action.

One reason why biography is so often dismissed is that it is a hybrid. Though firmly based in the historical method, it frequently involves the use of psychology, sociology and much else. More than the specialist historian, the biographer needs to be a jack of all trades, and hence is liable to be considered the master of none. Unlike, say, a medievalist or a post-structuralist, the jobbing biographer is not an expert. Yet this should scarcely be grounds for an inferiority complex. For biography's most important relationship – central to its claim to separateness – is with another literary form that is no less dilettante, yet escapes the charge: the novel.

'Biography is fiction,' Aneurin Bevan is alleged to have said. It is possible strenuously to deny the accusation, and yet to celebrate the actual link of biography with what is, undoubtedly, its first cousin. In biography as, typically, in the novel, there is narrative, characterization, birth, love, death and moral dilemma. In biography, as in the novel, the author often succeeds by providing a central figure with whom the reader can identify. Many novels – from *Jane Eyre* to *Ulysses* to *The Satanic Verses* – are fictionalized biographies or, very often, only lightly fictionalized autobiographies. If biography combines academic disciplines, its authors often straddle cultural ones. It is a symptom of the intimacy of biography and fiction that biographies are as often written by novelists as by historians. Do biographers make good novelists, or novelists good biographers? Evelyn Waugh's life of Gabriel Rossetti, his first book, is better than several of his novels. Among contemporary writers, Peter Ackroyd has won awards for both biography and fiction, and last year's Whitbread biography prize-winner was the novelist, A. N. Wilson, for his life of Tolstoy.

Of course, there are also important biographers – though less frequently readable ones – who consider themselves scientists, pursuing knowledge about an individual with the kind of rigour that a microbiologist devotes to the study of a cell. Such biographers are not to be disregarded, and in their insistent demand for evidence they set standards for the rest of us. My own view, however, is that even the most ascetic of these truth-seekers deceive themselves. For all their belief that biography is about telling the truth and nothing but the truth, their actual dependence on the novel is greater than they appreciate. Bernard Crick, whose biography of George Orwell does *not* fall into this trap, nevertheless castigates Wyndham Lewis for declaring that good biographies are like novels. 'Lewis did not intend', remarks Crick, 'to let the cat out of the bag.' Perhaps we should not be afraid to let the cat right out of the bag, and permit it to roam around the biographer's study. Crick's point was to criticize an older type of mellifluously written biography in which evidence was a minor extra. But that battle is won. Whatever else, serious biography does not suffer from inadequate research. Biographers need now to show their independence, by holding firm to the rules of historiography, yet seeking to emulate the novelist's imagination.

There is a chasm that separates biography from the novel: it is the gap between fact and invention. It is deep, it is logical, and no biographer can ever cross it. When one speaks of biography as having an affinity to the novel, that does not mean, of course, that biography should be taken away from a vigilant adherence to sources. It is certainly possible to agree with Crick when he writes that 'a biographer has a duty to show how he reaches his conclusions, not to pretend to omniscience; and he should share things that are moot, problematic and uncertain with the reader.'[3] Scholarly biographers clearly have no interest in the type of book known as 'faction', in which the author uses a true story as the basis for his own imaginative theme, deliberately rearranging or inventing minor facts. Such a book is always a novel, albeit a curious and sometimes confusing one, and has nothing to do with historical biography. It is *truth* that gives biography its poignancy – what Virginia Woolf called 'the creative fact; the fertile fact; the fact that suggests and engenders'. In the novel, the author builds castles in the air; in biography, the author is limited to the building blocks of reality. 'The novelist is free,' as Virginia Woolf puts it, 'the biographer is tied.'

Yet, and this is a dangerous but important point, that is the only difference. Everything else is mere convention, and convention exists to be broken. It is convention that seems to compel so many biographers to regard a life as a race-track, to be followed in a straight line from birth to death. It is convention to regard a biography as an encyclopaedia or school report. It is convention which labels some matters as 'public' and others as 'private' and frequently builds chapter walls between them. It has recently become a convention to see the biographer as a kind of super-sleuth, with a duty, by fair means or foul, to ferret out the 'whole truth' about a character. It is a convention that requires the biographer, somewhere along the line, to make moral judgements. It is convention that seems to make so many biographers take on the role of literary nannies, alternately clucking at their charges for minor transgressions, and stoutly defending them against nasty critics in the outside world for major ones.

The biographer is tied by the truth, and has a duty to seek it out and not suppress it. But that does not make him primarily an investigative reporter. Newspapers, publishers, and possibly the public, have an appetite for the new: but biographers should not confuse this with their own artistic duty. With many public figures, indeed, shortage of material is not the problem: there is often quite enough already in the public domain. The main job of the biographer is to tell a story that will make the reader happier, sadder, even a bit wiser. Here his purpose is no different from that of the novelist, and this is the only convention that matters.

Story-telling is the one consistent convention of biography – and it may be as old as language itself. We cannot consider the future of biography without a glance at a history that preceded the *parvenu* novel by millennia. If modern biography now plays second fiddle to the novel, historically the influence was the other way round. Originally, all biography was propaganda. The first western biographies are to be found on Hittite and Egyptian tombs. Biography provides the core of Homer, as of the Nordic legends. The Christian religion itself is based on four, sometimes complementary, sometimes competing, biographies. In the middle ages, the lives of saints and kings provided the bread and butter of historical scholarship, and the tradition of uplifting, or exhortatory, biography long survived the Reformation. If Foxe's *Book of Martyrs* in the seventeenth century constitutes the vulgarization of hagiography, the biographical writings of Isaak Walton provide its apotheosis.

Samuel Johnson was the first in the British tradition to suggest that biography should explore, and not necessarily praise. Johnson's definition of the profession serves, indeed, as a model for our own time. 'The business of the biographer', he wrote, 'is often to pass slightly over those performances and incidents which produce vulgar greatness, to lead the thoughts to domestick privacies, to display the minute details of private life.'[4] Yet, despite Johnson and despite Boswell, in the following century biography seemed to return to an older, reverential mode. The Victorian era was a time when the popularity of the massive, multi-volume biography threatened to suffocate the art with complacency. 'How delicate, how decent is English biography,' wrote Thomas Carlyle, 'bless its mealy mouth.'[5] How much does modern biography derive from the eighteenth century, and how much from the nineteenth? We are taught that Johnson is the father of modern biography, but contemporary biography may owe more to the decent and delicate Victorians than we commonly allow.

The twentieth-century anarchist was Lytton Strachey, whose *Eminent Victorians*[6] and life of Queen Victoria[7] exploded a large bomb beneath the decorous architecture of the elegant apologists of great statesmen, the Morleys, Moneypennys and Buckles. Yet Strachey's lesson has only been half-learned. The point about Strachey is not, or not just, that he took the lid off the old hypocrisies, exposing the ambitions of a Cardinal Newman and the pederasty of a General Gordon; still less that he was a crusader for the 'whole truth', which – emphatically – he was not. The point of Strachey's work is that it belongs to the author, not to the subject. Strachey's portraits are aesthetically confident, in a way that other biographies seldom are. They are 'true' because they are wickedly pleasing. Strachey's camped-up Victoria with her middle-class habits and Highland passions is obviously not the whole truth. A sombre historian, armed with the same facts, could produce an alternative Queen Victoria, and several have. Strachey's *Victoria* succeeds and survives because it uses the facts as he knew them, to present a personality at once engaging and intolerable, who is both believable and symbolic of attitudes that needed to be challenged. Like the markings on the pyramids, it is propaganda, but propaganda of the best kind: it persuades us. The result, as Virginia Woolf puts it, 'is a life which, very possibly, will do for the old Queen what Boswell did for the old dictionary maker. In time to come, Lytton Strachey's *Queen Victoria* will *be* Queen Victoria, just as Boswell's Johnson is now Dr Johnson. The other versions will fade and disappear.'[8] In my opinion, *that*, and not a proliferation of footnotes, is the mark of biographical achievement.

Strachey was a political and social iconoclast – whether he was a successful revolutionary is more doubtful. Certainly, there has been no equivalent innovator, and modern biographies – in weight and implicit flattery – seem to belong to the age he denounced. An important name in post-war biography is Michael Holroyd, whose own biography of Lytton Strachey[9] broke down some of the final barriers of reticence which Strachey had undermined, making not merely the facts of 'domestick privacies' but also the 'minute details of private life' virtually a requirement. Where Strachey had hinted, Holroyd laid bare. Holroyd's achievement was to introduce private details, including hitherto well-hidden sexual ones, in order to explain, without diminishing, his subject. It was a major breakthrough but not one which has changed the direction of biography.

Holroyd's *Lytton Strachey* is likely to be, and remain, Strachey, just as Strachey's *Queen Victoria* is Victoria. But it does not make one feel critical of the Bloomsbury Circle in the way that Strachey makes us critical of the Victorians. If anything, it leads us to romanticize them. If the effect of Strachey's *Eminent Victorians* was to knock a whole mausoleum of Establishment idols off their pedestals, the effect of Holroyd's *Strachey* has been to inspire a succession of biographies of ever more minor actors in the Bloomsbury soap opera, not to mention a colour supplement industry in Bloomsburyana. What we have today is a new species: the warts-and-all hagiography, in which the warts are redefined as engaging quirks or even as beauty spots. Most modern biographies, for all their revelations of promiscuity and personal disorder, have barely departed from the Victorian, and medieval, tradition of praising famous men. Though Strachey may have exploded a bomb, much of the old masonry remains intact. Nowhere is this more true than in the comparative backwater of political biography.

Many political biographies, indeed, are still stuck in the pre-Holroydian age. This is partly because they encounter obstacles which, on the whole, impede literary biographies less. The concern of political figures about every aspect of their reputations extends beyond the grave, often with the help of dragon-like executors. Virginia Woolf makes something of this point. 'The widow and the friend are hard taskmasters,' she wrote. 'Suppose, for example, that the man of genius was immoral, ill-tempered and threw the boots at the maid's head. The widow would say, "Still I loved him – he was the father of my children; and the public must on no account be disillusioned. Cover up; omit".'[10] Robert Skidelsky, who is definitely post-Holroydian, makes entertaining use of Virginia Woolf's comment in the introduction to his own splendid life of Maynard Keynes. Keynes, he points out, had many widows – including a whole school of disciples, who had a collective interest in preserving his reputation and presenting him to the world in unsullied, heroic clothing.[11] These guardians determined the choice of the official biographer, Roy Harrod, who conceived his role as that of an evangelist of the faith and of its messiah. In Harrod's book any reference to Keynes's homosexuality is avoided, and the hero is deftly rescued from his various financial and political scrapes.[12]

Harrod was himself not only a Keynesian, but also a sub-Bloomsburyan, and his biography is marked by elegant style and a lack of footnotes – a literary work indeed, though not in the sense that is here recommended. A more recent example, which takes the principles of the academic school of biography to its limit and possibly beyond it, is that of Philip Williams's enormous, invaluable, and in some ways magnificent biography of Hugh Gaitskell.[13] Williams found himself in a dilemma of a kind that well illustrates the impossible difficulty facing the biographer who believes himself to be an objective truth-seeker. Williams was a passionate Gaitskellite, who had spent many years actively fighting the Bevanite heresy; he was also a dedicated and meticulous scholar, who deplored what he saw as the casual use of evidence in Michael Foot's life of Aneurin Bevan.[14] Williams, therefore, produced a book of great detail and erudition, in which the source for virtually every sentence is carefully recorded, and which contains a novel scholarly device – the two-tiered endnote.

It is impossible to fault Williams's scholarship, and researchers will be using his book as a work of reference for as long as history is written. Yet it is, in the outcome, quite as prejudiced as Foot on Bevan, and it casts a discreet veil over Gaitskell's private life. Curtly, in the preface, Williams explains that he is writing a 'political' biography – thereby absolving himself, Pontius Pilate fashion, from any need to ask about his private world. 'I think', he writes, 'I have omitted no important influences on his intellectual and political development.'[15] Well, that is a matter of opinion. But, as Crick said, such problems and uncertainties need to be shared with the reader. We cannot automatically regard Gaitskell's relationship with a leading aristocratic lady, who mixed in high Tory circles, as irrelevant to Gaitskell's thinking; especially as the Labour leader was, at the time, involved in bitter controversies within his working-class party.[16]

Williams's motives and principles were always of the highest, and it is likely that family pressure was involved. The case is worth mentioning, however, partly because it is arguable that the public–private division is impossible to make (if close companions and dancing partners are irrelevant, what of wives? Should the biographer of Macbeth miss out his queen?) And partly because it illustrates once again how pointless is the search, in biography, for the whole truth. Williams's *Gaitskell* runs to over a thousand pages of which two hundred are devoted to reference notes: yet a dimension of the subject's life which may have been immensely important to his happiness, his feelings about the world, and his intellectual and political development, is treated with euphemism and coyness when it is touched at all. This may not diminish it as a chronicle, but it certainly limits it as art.

But to press, with Holroyd, for lack of censorship, is not the same as equating revelations with good biography. Nor should we think that the unreserved biographer automatically escapes the clammy grip of the Victorians. If Williams may be guilty of *suppressio veri* there is also another, post-Holroydian school which considers – no less culpably – that its duty of criticism is discharged as soon as exposure is complete. Once the 'domestick privacies' have been unearthed, the biographer feels free – perhaps even more free – to return to the serious business of doling out praise and explaining away faults. Thus Richard Ellman's recent life of Oscar Wilde does not spare his reader's blushes.[17] Yet the book, paradoxically, is nonetheless a work of devotion – the author persistently batting on his subject's side. Like Williams, Ellman seems to take it for granted that his role is to defend his subject against attackers. In this he is out of time. Gaitskell and Wilde can stand up on their own, without help from their friends. We live in an anti-heroic age: characters are more interesting, and hence actually more admired, if the author shows less anxiety to convince us.

Williams and Ellman are cited, not because they are worse than other biographers, but because they are better – master craftsmen whose work stands way above the generality. They are sensible, sensitive, meticulous and fair. What they illustrate, however, is the limitation of the tradition from which they stem: a tradition in which, partly out of admiration, partly because of familial pressure or authorial gratitude, but mainly out of an ingrained centuries-old habit of mind, biographers take it for granted that their task is to portray their subject as more worthy than he or she might otherwise be thought to be. Whether a modern biographer hides relevant facts, like Williams, or exposes them, like Ellman, he almost always sees it as his role to do as well for his subject as the facts allow.

It may be protested, isn't that the gentlemanly way? Why else write a biography? To denigrate? There is seldom much point in that. If the object of biography is not to reveal the whole truth, and not to glorify, what is it?

One answer is that the best biography – like the best play, novel or poem – must be the egotistical creation of its author. It is significant that 'portrait' should be the common metaphor. We have compared biography to fiction: let us now consider painting. The aim of the biographer is not to build an exact photographic likeness – that is logically absurd. It is to build an impression, using evidence as the paint. The impression should be recognizable and revealing, and the portrait is of particular interest if the sitter is well known. Yet sitters, however grand, are in the end merely models, more or less idiosyncratic representatives of the human race. Focusing on the subject, the author attempts to build, not a distillation of important facts, still less a logical argument, but a verbal image, using a *pointillisme* of detail and comment. The aim is to create a picture, not to display the paint: the choice of colours and their arrangement will be highly selective. In the process of creating the image, public and private details will be mingled according to need and the artist's fancy. You do not leave out one colour altogether, because it might cause offence; nor do you feel a crusading urge to splash the canvas with scarlet, just because that colour is available.

In biography, as in portraiture, and as in the novel, the aim is not the abstraction truth, except in the artistic sense, but *understanding*. The aim should be to understand an individual life, the forces that shape it and the motives that drive it, in the context in which it is placed. If the quest is for truth, the biographer is liable to become diverted into an obsessive pursuit of sources – and biographies will get longer and longer, *ad infinitum*. But if the search is for understanding, then the biographer's and novelist's eye have much in common. Here what matter are not just the events in the life under scrutiny; also important are facts about friends, enemies and society in general, and the wider stock of ideas and debate. As in the novel, so in the biography, the hero's life should be the focus of intensive study: yet also the vehicle for a wider observation of human nature and the human condition.

If the quest is for understanding, then public and private facts clearly cannot be put in separate boxes. Real life accepts no such partition. It is apparent that every publicly expressed passion – of patriotism, class sentiment, concern for the poor or whatever, has a private dimension; and that 'political character' is always a package in which public and private traits are intertwined. If it is relevant to a biographer of Churchill that he was a failure at Harrow, it is relevant to a biographer of Bevin that he was illegitimate and to a biographer of Lloyd George that he kept a mistress. If the quest is for 'truth' the biographer may decide to examine one category of truth, and separate it from another, and may feel a compulsion either to conceal or to reveal; if the aim is understanding, everything goes into the pot.

If biography is about 'understanding', it is both part of the discipline of history, yet distinct from it. If biography is about scientific truth, what matters is the historical school to which the biographer may be attached. If, in the words of Carlyle, 'history is the essence of innumerable Biographies,'[18] and individuals are to be counted as significant for the influence they exert, then the interest of biography may be ranked according to the status of the subject. If, on the other hand, the Marxist view of history as the product of vast impersonal forces is accepted, then the truth-seeking chronicler of the individual has little to offer. But if biography is about understanding, then it matters little whether the subject is a prime minister or a labourer – provided the material for a story is there – any more than it matters in a novel.

It is interesting here to note a revival of biography across the Continent of Europe associated more with the lives of the ordinary than of the great, or at any rate of adjutants rather than of generals. Biography has become the fertile means of reappraising former enemies and collaborators – in short, of understanding. In the West – in France, Germany, Italy – the movement is linked to a growing historical curiosity about the Second World War. In the East, a fashion for modern biography is part of a conscious rejection of the old determinism. A new school of Russian biography – carefully researched, anecdotal and consciously departing from marxist tradition – is seeking to reinterpret the era of Stalin and Brezhnev.

It would be nice to imagine that, in place of the traditional 'workplace to War Cabinet' biography, future biographers might be permitted to tackle mundane lives, and make them interesting. Alas, there are restrictions. The first is a lack of sources: a biographer needs his paint. A great man leaves a trail behind him – press reports, letters, official records, and a wide circle of acquaintances who also have letters and the rest, in which he is mentioned. One golden rule, if you want to be remembered, is to keep a diary: increasing numbers of politicians obey it, scribbling in shorthand during Cabinet meetings, or talking into tape-recorders late at night. In the age of the video-recorder it may not be long before compulsive diarists speak their thoughts direct to camera: an intriguing, or nightmarish, possibility for the biographer. Among the ungreat, however, record-keeping of any kind is rare.

The second restriction is the marketplace. The public differentiates sharply between novels, which can as easily be about dustmen or stockbrokers as about princes, and biographies. People who read biographies are drawn to the lives of the celebrated or the notorious. This pressure helps to make political biographers valets to the famous, and – because the number of suitable subjects is finite – gives widows the advantage. But the limitation of subjects does not inevitably limit the imagination; and widows, to their credit, are becoming less prudish.

So what does the future hold? At present the life of the biographer is a relatively cushioned one, in which the pressure for innovation is slight. Publishers, reflecting public taste, continue to want orthodox lives spiced with colourful details, of orthodoxly famous people: the best contracts go to those who provide them. Meanwhile in universities, where many political biographers earn their living as teachers, academic pressure encourages humility, the thesis approach, an acceptance of the status of a disciplinary poor relation. Neither in the ivory tower, nor in the garret, is there much sign of a will to experiment. Neither in the universities, nor outside them, does anybody bother much about composition, structure, shape, dramatic effect, sub-plot – kindergarten stuff for any fiction writer. There are exceptions: Hugh Trevor-Roper on Sir Edmund Backhouse,[19] Tony Gould on Colin MacInnes[20] are two examples of biographers who, whether deliberately or not, gave their well-researched books the shape and feel of fiction. In the field of high politics, however, such cases are extremely rare.

Pick up any political biography, and you will find it built like a Wimpey house, with almost identical segments and proportions – as if, somehow, the Great Biographer in the Sky had ordained them.

If it is a cosy arrangement, it is also a risky one: biographers, I believe, are in danger of becoming complacent about their audience, public and academic, as our Victorian forebears were before us. We are in danger of regarding our activity as a minor, respectable branch of the public service. And our work, unless we do something urgently about it, is in danger of ending high on the shelves of second-hand bookshops – magisterial, dusty and forgotten. Yet biography can and will change, and may do so drastically. A single book could make the difference: what is needed now is a radical with the arrogance of a Picasso or a Joyce to smash our encrusted expectations. Such an innovator, and such a deliverance, may yet be produced by the present restless marketplace, in which the urgency of demand is met commercially, but not aesthetically, by the hectic expansion of supply. When the moment does come, the revolution will be rapid. It is possible that biography may then once again become the most advanced, instead of the most conservative, of the literary arts.

Political Quarterly, vol. 61, no. 2, April–June 1990

NOTES

1. Benjamin Disraeli, *Contarini Fleming: A Psychological Autobiography* (John Murray, 1832).
2. Roy Jenkins, 'Modern political biography, 1945–1970,' reprinted in *Gallery of Twentieth Century Portraits* (David and Charles, 1988), p. 197.
3. Bernard Crick, *George Orwell: A Life* (Secker & Warburg, 1980), p. x.
4. *The Works of Samuel Johnson* (1787), Vol. 5, p. 385.
5. Cited in *Chambers Encyclopaedia* (George Newnes, 1970), Vol. II, p. 323.
6. Lytton Strachey, *Eminent Victorians* (Chatto & Windus, 1920).
7. Lytton Strachey, *Queen Victoria* (Chatto & Windus, 1921).
8. Virginia Woolf, *Essays* (Hogarth Press, 1966–7).
9. Michael Holroyd, *Lytton Strachey: A Critical Biography* (Heinemann, 1967–8).
10. Woolf, *Essays*.
11. Robert Skidelsky, *John Maynard Keynes: Hopes Betrayed, 1883–1920* (Macmillan, 1983), p. xx.
12. Roy Harrod, *John Maynard Keynes* (Macmillan, 1981).
13. Philip Williams, *Hugh Gaitskell: A Political Biography* (Jonathan Cape, 1979).
14. Michael Foot, *Aneurin Bevan*, Vol. 1 (Four-Square, 1966); Vol. 2 (Denis Poynton, 1973).
15. Williams, *Gaitskell*, p. xiii.
16. See Mark Amory (ed.), *The Letters of Ann Fleming* (Collins, 1985), for evidence of Williams's missing ingredient.

17. Richard Ellmann, *Oscar Wilde* (Hamish Hamilton, 1987).
18. Thomas Carlyle, 'Essay on History', in (ed. 'G.H.P.'), *Prose Masterpieces from Modern Essayists* (Becker & Sons, 1884).
19. Hugh Trevor-Roper, *Hermit of Peking. The Hidden Life of Sir Edmund Backhouse* (Macmillan, 1979).
20. Tony Gould, *Insider Outsider. The Life and Times of Colin MacInnes* (Chatto, 1983).

THE NAMES
THE WORLD FORGOT

FOR THE MORBIDLY ASPIRANT, there can surely be no higher goal (apart from a slab in the Abbey) than an obituary sketch in the *Dictionary of National Biography* – revered, ever-accreting mausoleum of high achievers, the Establishment's patriotic monument to itself. Think, therefore, of the posthumous fury of those who don't quite get there. To be stuck on a cloud after a lifetime of endeavour, contemplating for eternity the horrible truth: that the editor forgot you! The publication of the suitably titled *Missing Persons*, the *DNB*'s first-ever volume of also-rans, will therefore be welcomed, on both sides of the divide, by those who believe that everyone – even the dead – deserves a second chance.

The *DNB* has a venerable history. Originally compiled in sixty-three volumes between 1885 and 1900, it has been replenished decennially until 1985, when supplementary volumes started to appear five-yearly. Up to now, however, people judged unfit at the time of death were simply excluded. This volume comprises the collective verdict of a long-delayed court of appeal. Taking account of changing fashion and taste (as well as mere error), it adds 1,086 well-crafted and generally expert essays to the 29,120 that had already been published. Obviously, such a book is only useful as a work of reference in the context of all the others: it makes no sense to look somebody up in *Missing Persons* until you have established that they are, indeed, missing. Nevertheless, the book is independently interesting, not least because of the fun to be had in seeing who was formerly disregarded, and wondering why.

Many names will be as unfamiliar now as they were at the time of their original non-appearance. Others are startlingly well known. Was it carelessness, or sexism, that resulted in the earlier exclusion of Mrs

The Dictionary of National Biography: Missing Persons, ed. C. S. Nicholls (Oxford University Press, 1993)

Beaton, Bessie Braddock, Gwen John and Sylvia Pankhurst? Was it philistine or humourless censorship that caused Gerard Manley Hopkins, Wilfred Owen, Charles Laughton and Stan Laurel to be passed over? In some cases, the explanation is simply a time-lag in the building of a reputation (the Bedlam painter Richard Dadd, for instance); in others (engineers, left-wingers), it has been a past snobbery or prejudice that has since eroded. Often, it was simply editorial ignorance. Christine Nicholls, the enterprising editor of *Missing Persons*, tackled the last problem by appealing through the press for nominations. An astonishing 100,000 flooded in, of whom ninety-nine per cent failed the *DNB*'s rigorous vetting procedure, at least until the next trawl.

This one extends from the seventh century to the twentieth, from unjustly overlooked King Ecgfrith whose lustrous reign 'suffered historically by comparison with Edwin, Oswald and Oswiu', his predecessors as rulers of Northumbria, to Alexander Thom, aerodynamicist and archaeologist, who died in 1985 in his ninety-second year. (Ecgfrith was killed in battle near Forfar, exactly thirteen hundred years before the demise of Mr Thom who 'spent every summer accurately surveying megalithic sites on the west coast of Scotland'. So there is a sort of poetic link.) The business community and science do better than in the past, theologians less well. Although the gender gap is cut (12 per cent of entries are female, compared to 3 per cent hitherto), the addition of some 120 women to the tens of thousands of blokes doesn't do a great deal to remedy this particular imbalance.

So who *ought* to be judged heroic, and awarded a niche in the *DNB*? Ought the pantheon to contain shy violets as well as effective self-publicists? And is fame in itself enough? The editor does not answer this question, but she and her advisers have quite rightly made some highly subjective decisions, confirming the sense of quaintness about the notion of a 'national biography'.

To begin with, there is the problem of 'national', which here seems to incorporate not only the UK, but also Southern Ireland before Partition and the colonies up to independence, provided the 'national' in question is of British rather than local origin: this volume, like its predecessors, is rather thin on members of subject races. But when is a Britisher properly British? According to Nicholls, 'the rule was that entrants must have spent a considerable proportion of their working lives in the British Isles, whether or not they took British nationality.' Card-carrying Americans like Jennie Churchill and Sylvia Plath get in, on grounds of residency (and marriage). So, less explicably, does Alfred Sisley – who was born, educated, and lived in France, but happened to have an Anglo-French father.

Don't let's carp: Britain is short on painters, so we're happy to welcome him aboard, along with that well-known British ballerina, Anna Pavlova. In this more open-minded epoch, it is also good to see a few members of the criminal classes, another hitherto discriminated-against group. Robin Hood, unfortunately, is not to be found; but there is a spirited item on Guy Burgess, Soviet spy, while John Christie is splendidly profiled by Ludovic Kennedy.

You have to be guilty: Timothy Evans, hanged for Christie's crimes, seems to have drawn the short straw once again. You also have to be caught. Charles Peace (1832–79), for instance, who was to cat burgling what Christie was to wife-topping, gets here because of his incompetence. Peace 'showed no early aptitude, and was frequently arrested'. He subsequently learnt how to make a dishonest living, but was eventually taken into custody for murdering his lover's husband. Dispatched by train for trial at the Leeds Assizes, he slipped his manacles, and – though a guard held onto his shoe – struggled free, leaping from the carriage window. Later he was found unconscious in the snow.

Peace was not an educated man. Awaiting the gallows, he composed his own memorial card, ending with the words: 'For that I don [sic] but never intended.' The things people will get up to, just to earn an entry in the *DNB*. But then again, perhaps he would have rather stayed a missing person.

Independent on Sunday, 7 February 1993

PART III

Ghosts

UNEMPLOYMENT

I · THE GHOST OF
THE DOLE QUEUE

A PROBLEM IN POLITICS is that the world moves faster than the
stock of terms available to describe it. Quite innocent-sounding words
create a dangerous illusion of continuity. The language of unemployment is a case in point.

Take 'unemployment' itself. The 'unemployed' have long been with
us. 'Other creatures all day long rove idle, unemployed,' wrote Milton
in 1667, and a decade later A. Yarranton noted in *England's Improvement by Sea and Land* that 'there be in England and Wales a hundred
thousand poor people unemployed.' The abstract noun 'unemployment', by contrast, is a nineteenth-century invention: as such, the
product of an age very different from our own, yet not ancient
enough for veneration. For that reason alone it should be treated
cautiously.

Significantly it arose out of academic and philanthropic concern –
gaining currency after Alfred Marshall introduced it into the language
of political economists in 1888. Today, 'unemployment' still holds us
in its thrall: there remains no other word ('joblessness', and 'worklessness' are merely cumbersome synonyms, used in an identical sense).
Yet unemployment today and unemployment in the Great Depression
of the 1880s have little common ground.

We are not today directly affected by the sentiments of the 1880s,
apart from the weight of the idea of unemployment itself. Instead, the
legacy is almost entirely from between the two World Wars, and
especially from the 1930s. In addition to Marxist and liberal theoreti-
cians (John Strachey, John Maynard Keynes, Friedrich Hayek), whose
pre-war concepts continue to dominate the language of social and
economic science, the principal source of received wisdom about the
present depression is probably George Orwell. But if Orwell wrote
the music, there are others who provided the lyrics: Walter Greenwood, Wal Hannington, Ellen Wilkinson.

Once again we are in a 'slump' in which industries are 'killed' and towns 'murdered', their inhabitants 'joining the dole queue', which consequently 'lengthens', helping to swell 'the army of the unemployed'. Some of these terms pre-date the last depression. All, however, owe their place in political language to it. Thus, towns may have been 'murdered' before Ellen Wilkinson wrote about Jarrow, but it was *The Town That Was Murdered* (Left Book Club, 1938) that attached the metaphor to industrial closures.

'Slump' in the sense of stock market crash first appeared in the last century, but its use (more expressive, with its sense of physical droop, than recession or depression) to denote the wider experience of economic collapse and hardship dates only from between the wars: Carey Street, site of the Bankruptcy Court, became 'Slump Alley' in the London argot around 1930.

It is hard to fix a date for the overtly political 'army of the unemployed'. Yet, the phrase, with its implication of latent strength as well as massed ranks, undoubtedly gained substance from the inter-war National Unemployed Workers' Movement, a crusading body which led hunger marches and civil disobedience campaigns, claimed 100,000 members, and once held a demonstration attended by a third of a million.

'Dole', in the sense of state handout, has the clearest origin between the wars. Eric Partridge's *Dictionary of Slang* has 'to be on the dole' established in 1919, but colloquial only by 1930, three years before the title of Greenwood's novel gave it a permanent niche. From 'dole' comes 'dole queue', another 1930s coinage, and one of the most powerful inheritances. 'Dole queue' arguably helped Mrs Thatcher ('Labour Isn't Working,' said the slogan, beneath a snaking queue of film extras), even though the usual experience at employment offices is to sit and wait to be called, and queues are longer at the bank.

The diction of a half a century ago supports a universal theme: the present depression is like, or somewhat like, or not yet as bad as, the last one. Since the Conservatives came to power, this theme has obvious attractions for the Left, for whom in any case recollections of the devil's decade are not wholly bleak: there are folk memories of angry poetry, comradeship, clear objectives and heroic defeat. Nevertheless, the theme has been of greatest political value to the Right.

This is partly because of the moral example. Contrary to legend, there were prosperous parts of Britain as well as impoverished ones. It was possible for enterprising members of the unemployed, like

Tebbit *père*, to find work if they showed determination – therefore, goes the argument, the same must be true today.

However, the Right mainly benefits from the connection because of the contrast in material conditions. So distant from most contemporary experience is the traditional imagery of 1930s unemployment – dole queue, hunger march, pawnshop, soup kitchen, sullen silent men, bread-and-marge, barefoot to school, bailiffs, tuberculosis – that it provides a perfect camouflage. The syllogism runs as follows: really serious unemployment means terrible conditions; conditions are far from terrible; hence unemployment in its present form (except where race or religion complicates the picture) cannot be seen as really serious.

Thus, while the Left uses the language of the 1930s to show how bad the depression has become, the Right shows how bearable by comparison with the 1930s are the present conditions, by using the same language. For both, as indeed for much neutral but concerned opinion in between, the pre-war period is the reference point. That, we all take for granted, was true unemployment.

A moment's reflection will show this assumption to be absurdly false. It is not a matter of conditions getting better. It is a matter of social consequences that are fundamentally different. Much of the confusion lies in the word, now hazy in its meaning. The simple negative implies precision, yet precision is precisely lacking. Thus: is it necessary to be 'genuinely seeking work' to be genuinely unemployed? What if you have genuinely and understandably given up?

Are housewives unemployed? Are the early retired, the disabled, the mentally ill, full-time mothers, students on vacation, vagrants, young people on training schemes, participants in the black economy? Is a writer unemployed who sometimes but seldom gets published, or an actor who sometimes but seldom gets parts? Can unemployment ever be voluntary? What of somebody who refuses (or accepts) worse-paid, less skilled work?

On few of these points is there agreement. It will be seen that, no less than with poverty, the use of the word 'unemployment' is heavily laden with values, the balance of which varies according to the speaker. It should also be apparent that what was called unemployment before the war and what is called by the same name today are quite separate social phenomena.

Pre-war unemployment was a bitter storm: concentrated, intense, rising sharply to historic levels, but falling rapidly away, even before the Second World War brought it abruptly to an end. Modern unemployment by contrast is chronic. In the early 1980s, Michael Foot spoke of the new recession as an 'economic blizzard'. Arctic winter would have been more appropriate.

During the lifetime of those now leaving school, fluctuations in the total number out of work have been on an upward ratchet. Not for a generation has the level fallen in three successive years. Hence the steepest graph is that of the long-term unemployed, already almost double the figure for the later 1930s as a proportion of all those on the register, and bound to continue upwards even if total numbers remain static.

There is another aspect. Attention has rightly been paid to inner cities, where unemployment takes its toll in physical conflict, and where distress is visible, and deep. Handsworth and Tottenham, however, are by no means typical of British unemployment. Much of it is in the badly hit areas – West Midlands, South Wales, Scotland, the North-West and North-East – and is small-town, even semi-rural. Here especially, the conventional rhetoric, which lays patronizing stress on the supposed misery of unemployment, misconstrues the nature of the tragedy.

Whatever may have been true in the 1930s, many of the unemployed (it seems almost blasphemous to say it) are not particularly miserable. Go to some of the places where unemployment is highest, and you will find a better and more generous spirit than in the unneighbourly dormitories of the South. To be down on your luck is not necessarily to be unhappy, and poverty is a great leveller.

Nor (to use a related rhetoric) does it necessarily lead to wanton violence. In Toxteth there is arson, on the Broadwater Farm Estate, murder. But in Shotton, County Durham – where male unemployment is more than one in three – there is civic order, even a deceptive serenity. J. B. Priestley once called it the worst village in England: smoke and heat billowed from a coking plant at its very core. Today coke works and pits are closed, the centre has been bulldozed and tastefully landscaped, and a proud and active parish council has earned awards for the 'most improved' village in the county.

In the 1930s, in places like Shotton, being out of work carried a stigma (the pit was closed for only one year). Today, the distinction between in work and out of work is blurred by low pay, part-time work, and evidently pointless Manpower Services Commission schemes. For the young, a zig-zagging from unemployment to youth opportunity programme to unemployment, at roughly the same remuneration, has become the normal pattern.

On the poorer council estates in Northern Ireland, the most splendid building is generally the army barracks or the Catholic church. In north-east England it is the leisure centre, temple of the empty future. Populations live on memories of a harsh productive past. Once they had a purpose. Now workers and non-workers alike simply exist.

The language of unemployment ('army', 'queue') is about separation, but away from the big cities the population is not divided. Instead 'redundancy' (a new term) has come to define a society and a way of life.

The Times, 28 December 1985

UNEMPLOYMENT

II · THE NORTH-EAST: BACK TO THE 1930s?

UNEMPLOYMENT IS HIGHER in the Northern Region than in any other part of Great Britain.* This maintains a long tradition. In North-East England unemployment was massive between the wars, and markedly above average after 1945. As a result a knowledge if not an expectation of life on the dole is part of the working-class heritage. In areas like the West Midlands, where the job shortage is new, unemployment is seen as a bewildering aberration. In Newcastle and Middlesbrough, by contrast, there is a battening down of hatches with a weary sense of the return of a familiar adversary.

'The spectre of a return to the Thirties has become a frightening reality,' wrote the authors of a study of unemployment in Newcastle two years ago.[1] Today, the pre-war slump is in everybody's mind. Recalling the past, people view the future with an understandable foreboding. The prognosis for the region is certainly bad. However, despite surface similarities, a simple identification of this depression with the one of fifty years ago is misleading.

The North-East is still an area of old industries in decline. Shipbuilding, engineering, metal manufacture, whose contraction caused chronic unemployment before the war, have all been making workers redundant in the present slump. However, the proportion of the workforce in these industries had already shrunk dramatically before the 1970s,

---

* 11.7 per cent (excluding school-leavers) on 11 September 1980. The Northern Region (as defined by the Department of Employment) is composed of 22 Travel-to-Work Areas bounded by Berwick (in the North), Teesside (in the South-East) and Whitehaven (in the West). When I refer to the 'North-East' I mean the 14 – largely industrial – Areas in the East of this region, where seven-eighths of the population lives, and where unemployment is generally higher than in the other more sparsely inhabited Areas.

as part of a major revolution in the economy of the region. The biggest changes in the post-war period were a sharp decline in coal-mining, a fast growth of light industry, and a rapid increase in employment in the public services sector. Pit closures in the 1930s produced unemployment figures of 80 per cent or more in many Durham villages. By the 1970s, few communities remained that were solely or even largely dependent on coal. Transport, communications, metal manufacture, shipbuilding, distributive trades, agriculture and fishing all shed workers in the decade 1965–75. Yet the combined total of jobs lost in all these industries was less than the number in the Northern Region who left mining and quarrying in the same period: 69,000 in all. Some ex-miners left the area, and others retired early. But many remained, making up a large pool of de-skilled surplus labour. Since the late 1930s, the prospect of employing cheap labour had attracted light industry to the region, and it was the aim of successive post-war regional policies to encourage this trend. The 1960s saw the final phase, with the introduction of plastics and rubber-based production, and the expansion of the hosiery and knitted goods industries and other types of light manufacture.

How successful were attempts by post-war governments to steer the growth generated by firms in the prosperous Midlands and south to the North-East? Many companies came, or established new branches. For a long time, however, the disparity between local and national unemployment rates remained remarkably stable. From the late 1960s the gap began gradually to narrow, suggesting that the problem of a North-Eastern regional pocket of unemployment was at last being brought under control. The narrowing was especially marked during the sharp 1975–6 recession, in which the North-East seemed to be less affected than the rest of the country. Thus, by the beginning of 1976, the difference between regional and national unemployment had become smaller than at any other time in the decade.[2] But this relative improvement was short-lived. During the last four years, unemployment in the North-East has grown faster than the national average, restoring the old differential. Was the relative improvement, or the subsequent deterioration, part of a long-term trend? It is likely that the factors which caused things to get better up to 1976 had little to do with the basic industrial health of the region. Thus increases in public sector services employment (accelerated by local government and health service reorganization) were important, and so was a growth in local spending power caused by a sharp increase in earnings among manual groups over-represented in the region. After 1976 such accidental advantages ceased to apply.

Moreover, in the new economic storm the light industry which had been attracted to the region in the 1960s and earlier – whether by relative factor costs or government incentives – was seriously affected as well. Many of the new factories were owned, or had been acquired, by large firms based outside the region, or by multi-national companies. 'Uncle Sam has a big stake in the North-East,' a local paper commented cheerfully when President Carter visited Newcastle in 1977: '30,000 Geordies are on his payroll.'[3] It was calculated in the same year that seventy-six companies in the region were American-owned, a symptom of a growing concentration of control of jobs among a decreasing number of large firms or consortia: Northern Engineering Industries, Dunlop, Ever Ready, Courtaulds, GEC, Thorn prominent among them. Involvement by large concerns, especially those with major interests abroad, now began to reveal its less attractive side. A tendency to switch investments to other low-wage areas overseas became apparent; so did a pattern in which big firms having bought up little firms used their new North-Eastern subsidiaries as marketing outlets rather than for production, or shut them down altogether. One calculation suggests that about two-thirds of closures involving more than thirty redundancies in 1979 in Tyne and Wear were of factories acquired, through purchase or merger, by a larger concern. Similarly, in the first seven months of 1980, over half the private employers laying off more than thirty workers were linked to 'multi-nationals', broadly defined.

Thus the decline of the new manufacturing sector has compounded the effects of the contraction of traditional industries, producing a sharply worsening position over the last four years in the South Tyneside, Wearside, Teesside and Hartlepool Areas in particular. There have been local crises. In Hartlepool, the high rate (15.9 per cent) is because of steel closures and severe cutbacks. On Teesside (13.7 per cent), a large number of redundancies in construction followed the completion of the huge blastfurnace at Redcar. In addition, capital-intensive investment by ICI has resulted in a thinning of the workforce – with an expectation of a further 25 per cent reduction over the next five years. The most devastating blow of all struck the steel town of Consett in September, when the decision by the British Steel Corporation to cease production created 3,700 redundancies and raised the unemployment level overnight to an estimated 40 per cent. More than any other event, the extinguishing of the furnaces in Consett brought back memories of the 1930s and of the closure of Palmer's Shipyard in 1933, which gave Jarrow a place in history as 'The Town that was Murdered' with two-thirds of its workers on the dole. There are fears that Consett is just the beginning. It is arguable, however, that if unemployment continues to grow it will tend to do so, not in concentrated lumps, but evenly across the region. Apart from Consett, where the long-term rate is not yet known, no Area is more than 4.2 per cent above the level for the region as a whole. This is partly because there are few one-industry towns. It is also because of the greater diversity of work even where industry is concentrated. Not only are there new, small factories producing a wide range of goods scattered through much of the region, there has also been a massive growth in public sector services employment (health, education, local and national government). For a generation, the expansion of this kind of work from a low base has masked the erosion of jobs elsewhere. Today, one worker in five is employed by a local or national authority – providing an important cushion against cyclical fluctuations. Even in Consett, more people worked for schools, hospitals or local government than for British Steel.

Public sector services are not, of course, invulnerable. Cash limits imposed by central government are likely to take their toll. So is modern technology. Communications has already been affected. Many white-collar jobs are now under threat. The huge DHSS 'clerical factory' at Longbenton in Newcastle is expected to shed a large part of its 12,000 – mainly female – workforce as a result of computerization. In general, however, public sector services employment provides a degree of security which the private sector can no longer offer. This is particularly true for women workers. The official figure for female unemployment in the Northern Region (9.7 per cent) is much more unreliable than the male statistic (13.0 per cent) because women often fail to register, or remove themselves from the job market. Nevertheless, the gap between regional and national levels of unemployment is greater for women than for men, suggesting that women are faring worse in comparison to men in the North-East than elsewhere. This is in itself a product of the changed economic structure of the region. Traditionally the North-East has been an area of low female activity. In the 1930s, when there was little work for men, paid employment for women outside the home barely existed. After the war, female activity rapidly increased and by the 1970s it had begun to approach the rate for the nation as a whole. In 1971, 40 per cent of women over 15 in the Northern Region were economically active, a rise of 8.7 per cent over the decade, compared with an increase of only 5.3 per cent nationally.[4]

The accusation is sometimes made that female employment has put men on the dole, and it is certainly true that if all unemployed men took over jobs done by women, there would still be more female employment than existed in the 1930s. However, such a calculation ignores the nature of the jobs available for women: usually unskilled, short-term and part-time, generally low paid, almost always poorly unionized, and with a high turnover. These features, which made female labour attractive to the new manufacturers of the 1960s, also place women on the vulnerable margin of employability in time of recession. Indeed, the 'feminization' of the workforce – the growing proportion of the labour market that is composed of women – is one sign of the declining demand for skills in an area where the percentage of skilled workers has traditionally been high. One effect of unemployment has been to de-skill the skilled, and repeated studies have shown how workers have been forced to seek jobs which do not make use of their qualifications or experience, gradually swelling the huge army of the unskilled, among whom competition for work is most fierce, and for whom jobs are worst paid and most casual. In some occupations, job loss almost inevitably means a change of trade, or the acceptance of less-skilled work. Thus, in March 1980, there were more than ninety unemployed platers and welders for each notified vacancy in the region.[5]

The ratio of men seeking work within the category officially described as 'general labourers' is so bad that a prolonged period of unemployment is almost certain for anybody made redundant who falls within it. Table 1 (which compares the Northern Region with the South-East) shows how false is the belief that unemployment is much the same problem everywhere, or that the variations around the country are less important than the common features.

Of course, these figures give no indication of the actual competition for jobs in each region or category. As many as two-thirds of all vacancies are never notified, and this proportion varies between groups.

Also, far more workers are listed in the bottom category than properly belong in it. What is interesting is the contrast between the two regions. Even allowing for scaling down and a wide margin of error, the table suggests that there are more than four times as many unemployed for each vacancy in the Northern Region as in the South-East. In both regions, there is the same concentration at the bottom. In the Northern Region, however, there are fiercely unfavourable ratios in all categories except the highest, whereas in the South-East, skilled and clerical workers are relatively immune. The incomprehension of the politically influential Southern professional – who may still find it hard to get a good secretary – is partly explained by these figures.

TABLE 1: *Ratios of Unemployed to Notified Vacancies (excluding school-leavers) August 1980*

	South-East Region	Northern Region
Managerial and Professional	3.8	6.0
Clerical	3.8	14.2
Other non-manual	2.0	10.9
Craft, foremen, etc.	2.5	12.9
Semi-skilled	2.8	10.2
General labourers	40.8	172.5
All	3·9	17·6

The table also reveals, once again, the danger of a simple analogy with the last great slump. A feature of the 1930s was a steady migration of younger men from Tyneside and the Durham coalfields to the South and Midlands. In 1934, when unemployment was 67.8 per cent in Jarrow, it was only 3.9 per cent in St Albans and 5.1 per cent in Oxford. Today, however, there are no boom towns to take on the surplus labour of other regions. Making workers go to the work is no good if there is no work to be had. For the worst affected category – the unskilled – the South-East offers little hope. One effect of unemployment has been not to increase movement away from the north-east, but to reduce it.

*   *   *

It is commonly believed among people whose lives are insulated from the realities of unemployment that joblessness is a problem only for those without work. This is quite untrue. Anxiety and frustration arising from insecurity and from an inability to change jobs affect a high proportion of those in work, and fear of redundancy determines the mood of the whole region to an extent that outsiders find hard to understand. As unemployment rises, those with jobs start looking over their shoulders. Older people are the most frightened, but younger people are affected too. 'The over-45s tend to hang on to their jobs like grim death – whatever the working conditions and pay,' comments one trade unionist. 'The under-30s have increasingly come to expect their work to be of limited duration.'

Those with work and those without it have more in common than is at first apparent. As the jobless total rises, so does the likelihood of a period of unemployment for those currently holding jobs. The unemployment statistic is like a transit camp, through which many more people pass than are at any one time residents – and which people will visit more frequently and occupy longer the more crowded it gets. Among the unskilled, frequent spells of unemployment have long been a normal experience in the North-East. A survey of economically active men in an area of North Shields where male unemployment was currently 16 per cent showed that almost half were either unemployed at the time of interview or had been in the recent past. In periods of relatively full employment, the decision to give up work for a short period may be a rational option. This choice ceases to be available for most people when jobs are scarce. As unemployment rises, so does the 'expectation of worklessness'. The North-East not only has more people on the dole than elsewhere but unemployment tends to last much longer. In April 1980, 48 per cent of the unemployed in the Northern Region have been out of work for more than six months, and 17 per cent for more than two years, compared with 37 per cent and 11 per cent in the South-East. Given the disparity in unemployment rates between the two regions, this means that almost three times as high a proportion of the total workforce had been unemployed for more than six months in the Northern Region (5.6 per cent) as in the South-East (2.0 per cent). Since long-term unemployment always goes on rising after the turning-point of aggregate unemployment, this feature is bound to get worse.

For many workers the problem does not end when a job is eventually found. A period of unemployment often precipitates a downward spiral.

Those affected often have to accept worse-paid and less-secure work than they had before, and are the most likely to be dropped in the next economic contraction. The North Shields study showed that two-thirds of the men currently unemployed had been in and out of work for years. A third had been among the low paid (as defined by the Low Pay Unit) when last in work, but their last job often did not reflect their highest skill in recent years. Experience in the North-East suggests that in a deepening recession the condition of being unemployed is like a disease, hard to shake off, and most likely to be contracted by the economically weak and marginal: the over-45s, school-leavers, the unskilled, the disabled.

Real poverty rapidly affected those put out of work and unable to find a new job. Fewer than half of the unemployed among the North Shields sample were receiving unemployment benefit, the rest having exhausted their entitlement. Seven out of ten were on supplementary benefit. The study did not lend support to the view that many people prefer unemployment because the financial advantages of working are so slight. Only a quarter of the unemployed men were within 20 per cent of their income from work when they were employed, without taking account of the means-tested benefits many could have claimed if they had been working. One effect of the 'poverty trap', however, was that wives often stopped work when their husbands became unemployed or when they started to collect supplementary benefit.[6]

Sometimes the pill of redundancy is sweetened with redundancy pay. Management and unions have both found that workers are often more than willing to take a large lump sum as the price for their job. The advantage even of a substantial redundancy payment, however, is often far less than its cash value suggests. The means testing of supplementary benefits cuts the real value sharply after the first few months. Moreover, redundancy pay can make a period of unemployment more likely. A study of workers made redundant after the closure of Adamsez Ltd, a sanitary-ware factory in Scotswood, Newcastle, suggested that fear of losing redundancy money reduced the incentive to look for alternative work in advance of the shutdown.[7]

Not all unemployment is recurrent, and most is not permanent. A year after the Tress Engineering Company in Newcastle closed in June 1978 only a third of the 350 workers made redundant were still without jobs.[8] Among former workers at Adamsez, 88 per cent had found work within two years, though many had taken jobs they liked less. Significantly, a high proportion had got work through family connections rather than through orthodox channels. Elsewhere, especially in smaller communities, family links are even more important, as are social contacts which cost money to maintain. The fishing and holiday town of Whitby[9] has a level of unemployment which has long been among the highest in the country (and will shortly be increased as a result of 650 redundancies at the nearby potash mine at Boulby). This is how a local postal worker describes the business of seeking work:

> There are tried and tested strategies available to our people when they lose their jobs. Some of our activities have always been on the fringe of the black economy or worse. Coastal fishing and taking fishing parties have always operated on a cash in hand basis, as has poaching. To make use of the opportunities here, you must belong to the appropriate family network or be acceptable to it. The traditional values of thrift and abstemiousness can actually be counter-productive if you lose your job. Most job information is available in pubs and this is particularly true of 'fringe' opportunities. I found when I was out of work that the place that had most rumours and chances was the Working Men's Club. This is at its most active between 2.30 and 4.0 p.m. when a fair bit of drinking is done and also some pretty heavy gambling. To be part of this you need some ready cash.

As unemployment grows, so the need to make use of such techniques increases, and the possibility of finding work without the right connections gets less. 'Employment is like a tide,' a government official has written: 'When full, it draws in almost all adult men and a high proportion of adult women. As it recedes, those least attractive to employers tend to get stranded first. If a recession deepens, others, many of whom will never have been unemployed before, become stranded also.'[10] The last ten years have seen a steady extension of the social territory in which unemployment is an expected state.

The young form the largest new group of those least attractive to employers. Between January 1971 and January 1978 unemployment among people under twenty rose in the Northern Region from 14 per cent to 20 per cent, declining slightly in the following year under the impact of the Youth Opportunities Programme, before rising again in 1979–80. The problem is exacerbated by the low proportion of children in the North-East who stay at school beyond the age of sixteen.

In towns like North Shields, Sunderland, Hartlepool and Consett, and also in the big urban centres of Tyneside and Teesside, most school-leavers expect to go on to the dole. Older children in Newcastle schools are taught how to sign on for social security, and everywhere there is a coffee-bar society of unemployed teenagers. Again, the distinction between the employed and unemployed is ill-defined, as much of the work available to the young is temporary, and so to be 'between jobs' is part of a normal pattern.

Thus unemployment in the North-East is having insidious long-term effects, which go beyond the breakdowns, suicide and divorce which highlight the tragedy in individual cases, or the poverty that affects those who are out of work for any length of time. The North-Eastern experience shows how false is the comfortable belief that while inflation hurts everybody, unemployment only affects the unfortunate minority who make up the statistics.

Unemployment causes bitterness and fear. But it would be wrong to assume from this that there will be a strong political or industrial backlash. On the contrary, few regions are likely to cause politicians less anxiety than the North-East, for several reasons.

Most of the North-East is safe for Labour. Of twenty-nine constituencies, twenty-five are Labour-held, one is Liberal and only three are Conservative. Labour has hopes of winning all three Tory seats, and in a landslide victory might conceivably do so – but only one, Newcastle North, is really marginal.[11] A big swing to the Right could give the Tories Darlington, and the solitary Liberal at Berwick is always vulnerable in a traditionally Conservative seat. Nothing else is likely to change hands without an electoral revolution. The political parties realize this, and during election campaigns it is extremely hard to get leading politicians to spend time in an area where so little is at stake.

Conservative hopes of making even minor inroads into this unpromising territory must be dampened by evidence of a continuing pro-Labour drift in voting behaviour. This has accelerated over the last generation, though it was perceptible by 1964.[12] It probably has little directly to do with unemployment. One of the biggest relative improvements in Labour's position occurred at the last election, when most North-Eastern seats under-swung to the Right, and one, Teesside Thornaby, actually swung the other way. Yet this was after a period of Labour government during which unemployment had grown even faster in the north-east than elsewhere – widening the gap between nation and region which had narrowed under Mr Heath. Arguably, the 'de-skilling' effect of recession and unemployment keeps a larger proportion of the electorate in the poorer manual groups where Labour voting is most common. Apart from this gradual strengthening of Labour's base, there is nothing in the voting record of the region to make any party hopeful or alarmed. The North-East has a much stronger sense of regional identity than most other industrial areas in England. But unlike in Scotland, Wales or Northern Ireland there is no third force or separatist movement that needs to be assuaged.

Thus, in Westminster and electoral terms, the North-East is a part of the country which the Conservatives can afford to ignore. Of the three Tory MPs in the region, only one, Geoffrey Rippon, carries any weight among his colleagues, and none have influence in the Government. On the Labour side, the North-Eastern MPs can sometimes have more power. Regional unemployment and resentment at the financial terms of the Scottish settlement were major factors in the successful opposition of a number of North-Eastern MPs to the proposed Scottish Assembly in 1979. In situations other than the hung Parliament of 1976–9, the Northern Group of Labour MPs is an important political phalanx within the PLP: a strong pressure for regional aid and (when Labour is in office) a powerful lobby for government contracts. But with Labour in opposition, no region has less parliamentary bargaining power.

According to one view, the deepening depression will force the working class to make its voice heard in radical, even non-constitutional ways. There is no evidence to support this in the North-East. Trade unions and the Labour Party in the region have been traditionally 'moderate', and MPs include several prominent members of the Manifesto Group: William Rodgers, Ian Wrigglesworth, John Horam, Giles Radice, Mike Thomas. 'Very recently', comments one, 'the young unemployed have strengthened the Militant Left and enabled their case to get a better hearing.' Yet no MP has had any serious trouble from his general management committee on political grounds. Despite a conviction in the media that CLP activists are usually extremists, many constituency parties do not really divide along a Left–Right axis at all. The far Left (Trotskyist or communist) is weaker in the North-East than elsewhere, and weaker now than it was even ten years ago, when memories of the 1930s were fresher.

There is no sign of an industrial reaction to unemployment either.

'Unfortunately, unemployment has not stimulated any shop floor activity,' observes the regional organizer of one of the largest unions. 'Actually, quite the reverse. What we find is that when companies declare redundancies and we encourage some resistance then we find that members are prepared to accept redundancy pay and make a quick exit.' When the Transport and General Workers' Union in Newcastle offered to make a stand over the Consett closure, by bringing transport in the region to a halt and closing the Tyne Docks, the plan was dropped because the response from the steelworkers was lukewarm. Similarly, the workforce at NEI Reyrolle in Newcastle rejected a recommendation from shop stewards to resist 800 redundancies.

So far from causing resistance to employers, unemployment has had the effect of reducing wage demands and discouraging industrial action. Willingness to compromise at levels lower than the inflation rate has become the pattern. It was symptomatic that a seven-week official strike at the Ronson plant at Cramlington in Co. Durham in the summer of 1980 ended when the workers went back to work on the employers' terms. As one trade unionist put it: 'The whole gloom story is getting through to the workers.' For the first time since the war, the fear of forcing or providing an excuse for closures has begun seriously to inhibit wage bargaining.

Unions themselves have been hard hit by redundancies, which cut their membership and their income. Very few workers remain union members, even at a much-reduced rate, when they go on the dole. The TGWU has lost 7,000 members and £180,000 in dues because of lay-offs in the Northern Region over the twelve months to October 1980. Others have suffered similar losses, and there is concern lest falling membership should cause friction between unions in the future because of competition in recruitment.

There is little sign of organization or militancy among the unemployed themselves – no recrudescence of Wal Hannington's pre-war National Unemployed Workers' Movement, the communist-led association which campaigned against the Means Test and helped to bring about the Jarrow March. In April 1979 a group of young trade unionists in Newcastle set up an Unemployed Workers' Union. With the aid of grants from trade unions and the Priority Area Team (funded by the local authority and the Department of the Environment), this now has an enthusiastic paid organizer, a crumbling office on the quayside, and fifty-two paid-up members. Similar unions for the unemployed have been set up in Durham, Darlington, Spennymoor and Middlesbrough, and there is an unemployed centre in Stockton. The Newcastle union sees itself as an information centre and as a pressure group – giving advice to those on the dole, and making their case heard in the city. A recent minor victory was to persuade local cinemas to offer one free afternoon to unemployed teenagers. It was pointed out that the normal cost of a ticket is a fifth of a sixteen-year-old's weekly social security. Local activists were gratified: but it is scarcely the start of a social upheaval.

In sum, unemployment is having a colossal economic, social and psychological impact on the whole of the North-East, and in time this will take a political form. But it is wishful thinking to imagine that there will be repercussions for any government that neglects the region, or that North-Easterners will somehow force a change for the better. This did not happen before the war, and it is even less likely to happen now. Compared with fifty years ago unemployment in the North-East is less concentrated, less dramatic and as yet much less severe, and the unemployed are usually better off. The 1980s will not be like the 1930s, when most people in the North-East were almost unimaginably poor, and some were close to starvation. The tragedy of the next decade may well be, instead, that a chronically high and growing rate of unemployment with all its evil consequences gradually becomes something which everybody takes for granted.

Political Quarterly, vol. 52, no. 2, January–March 1981

NOTES

The author thanks Keith Hodgson, Andrew Gillespie, Joe Mills, John March, Nick Anderson, Gary Craig, Chris Edwards, Martin Upham and John Griffiths, among others, for help in preparing this article. The views expressed are, however, entirely his own.

1. Benwell Community Project, *Permanent Unemployment* (1978).
2. A. Gillespie and D. Owen, 'The Relationship between National and Local Unemployment Rates: A Case Study of the Northern Region 1971–80' (SSRC Paper, 1980).
3. Benwell and North Tyneside CDP, *Multinationals in Tyne and Wear* (1979).
4. M. J. Moseley and Jane Darby, 'The Importance of FAR', *Regional Studies* (1978).
5. *Regional Employment Market Intelligence Trends* (MSC Northern Region), Spring 1980.
6. North Tyneside CDP, *In and Out of Work* (1978).
7. Benwell Community Project, *Adamsez: The Story of a Factory Closure* (1980), p. 53.
8. City of Newcastle upon Tyne Policy Service Department, *Redundancy in Newcastle upon Tyne: a case study* (1980)

9. Whitby is just outside the Northern Region as defined by the Department of Employment, but has many links with County Cleveland and Teesside.

10. R. Harrison, 'The Demoralizing Effects of Long-term Unemployment', *Employment Gazette* (April 1976).

11. The boundaries of Newcastle North are likely to be radically changed before the next election.

12. D. E. Butler and D. Stokes, *Political Change in Britain* (1969), p. 136.

UNEMPLOYMENT

III · ONE NATION

THE PAST IS A FOREIGN COUNTRY: they do things differently there. In politics, however, the things they say are often identical. Discussion on unemployment is a case in point.[1]

In 1958, Transport House published a booklet called *The Future Labour offers YOU* which declared:

> Tory ministers have now admitted publicly that they deliberately caused the sharp increase in unemployment. In the Tory view, unemployment is *the* remedy for soaring prices.
>
> The first objective of the Labour government will be to *restore* full employment and to *preserve* full employment. This is the prime purpose of our plan for controlled expansion.
>
> Where local pockets of unemployment persist, we shall steer jobs to the workers . . .

Twenty-six years later, the Labour Party issued another booklet, this time entitled *A Future that Works*, which announced:

> The next Labour government will be faced with an historic task: to put Britain back to work and build an economy for the 1990s out of the industrial wasteland left by a decade of short-sighted and dogmatic Tory rule . . . The Conservative Government will not act against high unemployment because they have a vested interest in high unemployment. The reduction in inflation is their only economic 'success'. But this has been achieved only by using mass unemployment to weaken trade unions and force down wage demands.

So not much changes. Except that in 1958 unemployment never rose above 536,000, whereas in 1984, by a more cautious method of counting, the lowest official figure was 3,005,100.[2] Unofficially but not unrealistically, estimates of the 'true' total ranged from four to five million, or even higher.

New problems, old vocabularies. In retrospect, the 1958 'unemployment' which the Labour Party saw as its mission to eradicate constituted a level of full employment which few people today imagine even as a possibility for the rest of the century. Yet the political language used to lash the Tories in the 1950s, and still used, in the hungry 1980s, is of course much more than three decades old. In 1958, Labour was playing on not-far-distant memories of the 1930s, with a rhetoric to match.

The inter-war crisis gave rise to a view of the unemployed as an organizable force, an 'army', and to Wal Hannington's National Unemployed Workers' Movement, which attempted to turn aspiration into reality. 'By far the best work for the unemployed is being done by the NUWM,' wrote Orwell in *The Road to Wigan Pier*. 'This is a revolutionary organization intended to hold the unemployed together . . . It is a movement that has been built out of nothing by the pennies and efforts of the unemployed themselves.'[3] Hannington cultivated the idea of the unemployed as a sleeping leviathan. As early as 1922, he described one hunger march as 'the Greatest Organized Effort ever yet carried out in Great Britain by the unemployed', which had 'certainly made the ruling class apprehensive of the future development of the National Unemployed Workers' Committee Movement'.[4] At its peak in the 1930s, the NUWM claimed between 50,000 and 100,000 members, and could sometimes bring enormous crowds into the streets: in 1935, an estimated 300,000 people demonstrated in South Wales against Unemployment Assistance Board Regulations.[5]

Marching – often of a very disciplined, almost military kind, accompanied by bands and banners – was the movement's favourite form of demonstration. The most celebrated symbol of all was the Jarrow Crusade in 1936: two hundred men marched from the Tyne to the Thames in dignified protest at the dereliction caused by the closure of Palmer's shipyard. This demonstration was not 'militant' in the sense of aggressive or potentially violent, but it successfully conveyed an impression of unity, comradeship and proud determination in the face of adversity. There is yet another image of unemployment inherited from before the war: what Orwell called 'that frightful feeling of impotence and despair . . . far worse than any hardship, worse than the demoralization of enforced idleness'.[6] As one report put it, in general, unemployment was not an active state. Rather, 'its keynote is boredom – a continuous sense of boredom.'[7] Such characterizations, however, lay alongside – and did not contradict – a view of the unemployed as a *potentially mobilizable force*.

The public attitude to unemployment created in this period had an impact on policy. 'I am certain that the battles we fought on the streets [in South Wales] created a conviction that mass unemployment was a social condition to be avoided at all costs in the future,' claimed Will Paynter, a pit-head revolutionary who became President of the NUM.[8] It is hard to disagree. The movement to 'plan' the economy through the use of fiscal and monetary instruments, the agreement of all parties to the 1944 'Full Employment' White Paper, owed much to the belief that mass unemployment was a threat to the social order. 'Protest against unemployment, such as it was, did not on the whole seriously threaten the stability of British parliamentary democracy', concludes one historian of the inter-war period.[9] What it did do, though, was to arouse anxieties. Rightly or wrongly, these were reawakened in the 1980s in a series of riots in inner cities which were immediately attributed to unemployment. Today, the fear is less of the organized army than of the mob. Even before Toxteth and Brixton, it had become the conventional wisdom of the concerned, as of the punitive, middle classes that unemployment would lead, not to revolution, but to 'simple undirected violence and pointless destruction'.[10]

All this should make us pause. It has become commonplace for people to say that the 1980s are *not* like the 1930s, while showing, in their terms of reference, how far their minds are enslaved by the pre-war decade. Perhaps we should consider, when looking at the social and political effects of the recession, not only whether the problem has changed since the 1930s, but whether we are faced with a different problem. At the root of the conundrum is the concept of 'the unemployed'. The political significance of unemployment and the unemployed in the North-East, the region which has been worst affected both in the 1930s and today, will be the subject of the remainder of this article.

My personal starting point is an article I wrote nearly five years ago.* In it, I concluded unremarkably, 'The prognosis for the region is

* See p. 172, above.

certainly bleak.' In September 1980, the Northern Region,[11] already in the grips of a recession that was the worst since the Second World War, suffered an unemployment rate (excluding school-leavers) of 11.7 per cent. How much difference has five years made? Economically and socially, decline has become collapse. The seasonally adjusted figure for the first quarter of 1985 in the Northern Region was 17.9 per cent. In March, unadjusted, it stood at 18.5 per cent, compared with 13.3 per cent for Great Britain. Most unemployment is concentrated in the industrial or formerly industrial areas of high population in the east of the region (the 'North-East'). Thus while Travel to Work Areas (TWAs) in the West and North have comparatively low rates,[12] unusually high rates are to be found in South Tyneside (60,700 employees, 24.9 per cent unemployment), Hartlepool (42,000 and 24.7 per cent), Middlesbrough (131,100 and 23.3 per cent), Sunderland (172,600 and 21.6 per cent), Bishop Auckland (42,000 and 22 per cent), and Stockton (77,300 and 20 per cent). Newcastle, with 358,000 employees, has an unemployment rate of 18.1 per cent – slightly below the regional norm, but with many pockets that are much higher.[13]

There is no mystery about North-East unemployment. According to the Department of Trade and Industry, the North-East has in common with Scotland and Wales an industrial milieu less favourable to successful entrepreneurship than other regions, 'a somewhat unfavourable rate of production innovation; a relatively low level of employment in the business services sector; an occupational structure characterized by a low proportion of managerial and professional jobs; a high level of dependence for manufacturing employment on branch plants by national or international companies whose UK head offices are concentrated in the South-East'.[14] It is a truism that the North-East is a victim of its own past achievements. The very reasons that produced heavy concentrations of population around the mouths of the Tyne, Wear and Tees in the nineteenth century account for the severity of the region's recession in the twentieth. However different the form of unemployment in the 1980s, as compared with the 1930s, there is certainly a continuity in the cause: the contraction of shipbuilding, engineering, mining and metal manufacture, the traditional industries of the region.

In the coal industry, the biggest contraction took place before the present crisis. Between 1965 and 1975, nearly 70,000 jobs were shed by the Coal Board in the region, many ex-miners obtaining work in new light industries brought into the area with the aid of regional policy. Much of this new employment has since been lost, as national and international firms have drawn in their horns, closing marginal plants. The steel industry has been particularly hard hit by the recession. The biggest single blow to the region was the closure of the steel mill at Consett in 1980. Uncertainty now clouds steel production on Teesside, where a few years ago the future seemed assured. The decline of heavy engineering is symbolized by the reduction in the workforce of Vickers in West Newcastle, which had already shed two-thirds of its employees in the 1970s. In the long run, however, the most devastating impact has been on shipbuilding. A 1977 workforce of more than 30,000 in British Shipbuilders subsidiaries in the North-East had fallen to below 15,000 by 1984. In Newcastle, shipbuilding had been reduced to two yards, one marine engineering factory and a small number of associated firms. In Sunderland, one observer predicted just over a year ago that job loss in shipbuilding in the following twelve months would exceed the anticipated initial employment at the new car plant which was to be established, with a great fanfare of local self-congratulation, by Nissan.[15] This has proved accurate, and unemployment rates in the old shipbuilding areas of the Tyne and Wear remain at or close to the highest in the region.

The impact of the contraction of staple industries this time has not been the same as in the 1930s. There are several reasons. A huge post-war expansion of service employment, particularly public sector, and the diversification of industry as a result of pre-1970s decline and replacement, has meant that even when 'one industry' towns (Consett, Shildon) have been struck by disaster, the effects have been cushioned so that most of the local workforce has not been immediately affected. Though primary poverty is still common among those made unemployed, the extremes of deprivation experienced before the war have been less usual because of higher benefits, subsidized housing, better schooling, free health treatment and a lower incidence of poverty-related diseases such as tuberculosis. On the other hand, this depression seems destined to go on longer than the last one. The loss of world markets is likely to be permanent and it is hard to see a significant long-term future in the region for shipbuilding, or even steel, as major employers.

Compared with the late 1930s, there is already more long-term unemployment. In 1936, 21.2 per cent of insured workers were jobless[16] – higher than the figure for 1985. But in 1936 only 26 per cent of those without jobs had been thus afflicted for more than twelve months, whereas in 1985 the figure was 43.5 per cent and sharply rising.[17] In 1936, the year of the Jarrow March, the main feature of North-East unemployment was its acute concentration, locally and industrially. In the mid-1980s, by contrast, it is dispersed – not only geographically, but also within communities and occupational groups, among young and old, men and women. Some categories (the un-skilled, the over-45s, the disabled), on the margins of the labour market, are more affected than others, but there are few categories in which joblessness is the norm. 'So long as Bert Jones across the street is still at work, Alf Smith is bound to feel himself a failure,' wrote Orwell in *The Road to Wigan Pier*, adding, 'It is not only Alf Smith who is out of work now; Bert Jones is out of work as well, and both of them have been "out" for years. It makes a great deal of dif-ference when things are the same for everybody.'[18] In the 1980s, the Bert Joneses are doing nicely while the Alf Smiths feel beaten and isolated.

The main exceptions to this picture are the very young. 'Unemployed fitters or electricians may see themselves as fitters and electricians who happen to be out of work,' writes Beatrix Campbell, '– they don't necessarily identify themselves with the bald boys in Doc Marten boots who've never had a job, who have come to symbolize modern unemployment.'[19] The symbol, nonetheless, is significant: recent school-leavers are the only major category (unless 'women' are counted as one) in which unemployment is the normal state. Thus a recent study of 248 sixteen-year-olds in Gateshead reveals that for 90 per cent the immediate experience after school was being out of work, and for 42 per cent of those thus placed, unemployment lasted for more than 12 weeks. 'The predominant path (for both sexes)', concludes the author, 'was unemployment – YOP – unemployment.'[20] According to Newcastle Education Committee statistics, by the end of September 1974, 80 per cent of the City's school-leavers for that summer had found jobs; the comparable figure for the end of September 1983 was 16.6 per cent.[21] As many as one in three of all those unemployed in the North-East for more than one year in 1984 were under 25.[22] Many young people have indeed come to think of unemployment as natural, with cultural adjustments to fit: a survey of Newcastle unemployed youngsters found that much of their time was spent socializing, especially with friends who were also unemployed. In this one group, therefore, Bert Jones and Alf Smith – and their sisters and girlfriends – keep each other company.

But the overwhelming majority of young people eventually find work, even if short-term or dead-end. The same is not true of the middle aged for whom a redundancy notice often marks the end of a working life; nor is it true of those suffering from disabilities which, in better times, would not have excluded the possibility of self-sufficiency. One in six leavers from ordinary schools had found a job by the end of September 1983: the figure for leavers from schools for the educationally handicapped was zero out of 126.[23] Some found placements later, but for many the prospects remain non-existent.

Youth may thus have provided an image for unemployment, but it is a misleading one, accounting only for a proportion of those out of work and by no means the most grievously afflicted. North-East unemployment today has no profile: no proud and sombre working man in clogs and muffler to stand for a whole class. Even the heaviest concentrations are comparatively dilute, with the most suffering Travel-to-Work Areas only a few percentage points above the national average. Much modern unemployment is in any case hidden – women or older people who do not register, part-time workers, or people suffering the anxieties of unemployment (fear of redundancy, inability to change jobs) without the direct experience of being without work. Few metaphors could be less appropriate today than that which portrays the unemployed as an army. The attendant imagery of violence, militancy, anger and conflict – even the anarchic aggression that supposedly arises from alienation – could scarcely be further from the reality. It is hardly surprising, therefore, to find that the region of Great Britain that has suffered most disastrously in recent years from unemployment should also be the region of greatest political stability.

In the North-East, political rhetoric is all about unemployment. In 1945, 1955, 1965 – as in 1985 – the North-East saw itself as a have-not, hard-done-by region towards which central government had a duty to direct investment. Even when jobs were at their most plentiful, unemployment was treated by the politicians as the central, endemic, problem. And yet, as an issue, it is scarcely divisive or even controversial. The reason is evident. Those who suffer unemployment are not so much powerless as politically non-existent.

The purpose of political parties in a liberal democracy, so we were taught, is to aggregate demands, including the demands of minorities. The unemployed in the North-East have no demands. This is because they are not 'a minority', in the sense that blacks, or miners, are minorities. Ethnic or occupational groups seek common interests, set up organizations, elect leaders. People without work for relatively short periods are the most alone, and often the least inclined to organize. In areas of the Midlands and South, being unemployed is part of the experience of being black, and helps to fuel black consciousness. In the North-East, there are few blacks, and old-age pensioners have more group identity than 'the unemployed'.

Except where the arm of central government is to be felt, politics in the North-East is Labour Movement politics, and trade unions have a particularly strong influence. Like politicians, active trade unionists in the region talk about unemployment; but unions exist to serve members, almost all of whom have jobs. Industrial groups hardest hit by the recession – engineers, miners, boilermakers – have been losing ground to those better able to keep their members: the white collar unions, and among the lower paid, NUPE. It is the employed who set the tone, and the employed have not done badly out of the recession. Despite the disappearance of the industrial base of the region, GDP per head in the North-East in the early 1980s was higher in relation to the UK average than in the early 1970s,[24] and higher in real terms for those in employment than ever before in the region's history.

This helps to explain the virtual non-response of voters to unemployment at the last election. Whether or not most voters blamed the Government for the drastic increase in joblessness, one might have expected in the worst-hit region a somewhat different electoral result from elsewhere. In fact, the regional result replicated the Great Britain average: the Conservative vote fell by 1.6 per cent (GB 1.4 per cent), the Labour vote by 9.6 per cent (9.5), while support for the parties of the Alliance rose by 12.5 per cent (11.9).[25] The slightly higher-than-average increase in the Alliance poll may be explained by the defection to the SDP of four Labour MPs of whom one (Ian Wrigglesworth, Stockton South) succeeded in retaining his seat.

The Labour Party is probably more active in the region now than fifteen years ago, partly because of the participation of a larger number of middle-class professionals. But it is scarcely much more radical. None of the four defectors to the SDP had been in any danger from his local party. It is true that Sunderland, before and since the last election, has made hard Left selections (Rob Clay and Chris Mullin).

Elsewhere, however, traditional local establishments have held solid. In Gateshead East – a seat once held by the near-fellow-traveller, Konni Zilliacus – a Militant challenge was beaten off. Newcastle District Council continues to be ably led by Jeremy Beecham, a solicitor and one-time right-wing stalwart of the Oxford University Labour Club.

Most action on unemployment is bureaucratic rather than political, and hence non-controversial. Everybody in the region is in favour of regional aid. Regional aid continues to be available under Thatcher, as under Callaghan, though with a different emphasis. A 1983 White Paper stressed the need for greater cost-effectiveness by moving away from automatic subsidies towards more 'selectivity' and an increased emphasis on service industries. The North has recently done better than most regions out of both Regional Development Grant payments and Regional Selective Assistance.[26] This is partly because of the Nissan project, which gained the enthusiastic support of central and local government and even of the trade unions, who agreed to abrogate many of their rights.

The Nissan venture has been widely publicized. Usually, however, regional incentives attract little attention – an aspect of policy taken for granted. Far more visible is the Manpower Services Commission. Like undertakers in a famine, the industry of catering for the victims of unemployment has flourished during the recession. The MSC in the North-East now employs 340 staff. At the end of 1983, the Regional Director proudly boasted of a 'Year of Success', claiming that the new Youth Training Scheme, unlike the Youth Opportunities Programme, 'is essentially a scheme about training, not about youth unemployment'.[27] MSC officers exude a missionary zeal and their social importance can no longer be in doubt. For most young people they provide a transition from school to unemployment. At its most positive, the MSC gives employers a chance to give new workers a probationary year. There is evidence that young people value the schemes: many Newcastle youngsters claim to have enjoyed the experience, that the schemes are better than school and that 'attitudes of supervisors were ... better than that of teachers'.[28] 'The kids don't have a high level of cynicism,' comments one observer, who does. In fact, the MSC seems to evoke more resentment in rival organizations and bureaucracies – especially local government – than among its own clients. There are complaints about constantly changing rules, and remoteness from the world of politics. 'We have to justify whatever we do,' says one District Council official in Newcastle. 'They have to justify nothing.'

One reason for local authority resentment is that the powers of councils to create new employment are highly circumscribed. Section 137 of the 1972 Local Government Act, allowing councils to spend the equivalent of a two-penny rate on unspecified schemes, does not give much scope, and there has been no equivalent of the Greater London Enterprise Board. Councils concentrate as much on enticing as on subsidizing new investment. Despite restrictions on local authority spending, Newcastle has increased its Economic Development Budget, shifting the emphasis from general promotion to specific targets such as (for example) Northumbria tourism. The nearest approach to GLEB has been the Derwentside Industrial Employment Agency which created some 2000 jobs in the wake of the Consett closure, through investments in small factories and service industries. Since, however, other firms suffered from the new competition, and many created jobs did not go to redundant steel workers, the net effect has been more limited than the total suggests. On a smaller scale, Newcastle has set up three so-called Enterprise Workshops with a total of 82 units, generating about 200 jobs. The Council charges low rents, and gives cheap or free equipment and one year's subsidy and advice. It has been a successful scheme, but those helped have seldom been among the long-term unemployed, and as an approach to the problem it is scarcely more than spitting in the wind. There has also been what one officer calls the 'alleviating-the-effects side': subsidized prices for the out-of-work, and special facilities, including youth centres, day-time sports programmes, library arrangements. The take-up rate for all these, however, is low.

So far, the measures described have a common aspect: direct intervention by government, local or central, to help create employment or otherwise to assist those without jobs. There is, however, another kind of policy, on the margin of state activity, that relates to the notion of an 'army of the unemployed'. Mainly as a result of legislation towards the end of the last Labour Government, a number of agencies have been set up on the basis of 'partnership' between local and central government, with joint funding. The initial aim of these bodies was to tackle inner urban deprivation generally; increasingly, this has meant dealing with the consequences of recession. The interesting features of these (generally small) organizations are their semi-autonomous status; their origin outside the state system; their pressure group function; the crusading fervour of their leadership; the 'participatory' philosophy that pervades them and the general failure to give this practical meaning; and their ultimate dependence on those who pay their bills.

In the 1930s, local organizations for helping the unemployed were run by the unemployed themselves. Today, they are run by middle-class graduates, usually on the left in politics, who seek to combine, in varying doses, the roles of professional adviser and *agent provocateur*. One of the oldest and most effective is Benwell Law Centre, in Newcastle's rundown West End, which has four paid posts and an annual budget of approximately £50,000. Under the Urban Aid Programme, 75 per cent of its funding is from central government, which it loathes (Tory councillors, in return, complain about its activities), 25 per cent from the city. Much of its work concerns housing problems and supplementary benefit, and in particular delays in obtaining payments from the DHSS. At the same time, it sees itself as having a campaigning function: a thorn in the flesh of its own paymasters. One aim is to persuade local residents to fight for their rights. Tenants' associations, and a 'People's Elswick Riverside Campaign' against a proposed council-backed hypermarket along the river, have been set up. Support has also been given to shop stewards opposing closures, and to a campaign against social security 'snoopers'.

The Law Centre operates from rent-free, Council-owned accommodation. So does the Northern Region Co-operatives Development Agency, with offices in Newcastle's Westgate Road-NRCDA began as a part-time voluntary body in 1978; it obtained county and city funding, and three full-time workers, in 1982.[29] It sees itself as part of a movement: rescuing and building employment through the establishment of co-operatives. In Sunderland, the new co-operative movement (as distinct from the old, long-established societies) began in the mid-1970s with a housing agency called Banks of the Wear. In 1983 an application to the Urban Aid Programme led to the setting up of the grandly named Sunderland Common Ownership Enterprise Resource Centre Ltd, which has also obtained EEC funds. NRCDA and SCO-ERC belong to rival movements: the Sunderland body scorns the CDAs, and draws inspiration from the Leeds-based Industrial Common Ownership Movement. The issue is democracy. 'The CDAs are top down, argue the Sunderland people. 'ICOM is bottom up.'

SCOERC has two full-time workers, and claims credit for three small co-ops.

Another Sunderland body interested in co-operatives is the Wearside Disablement Centre Trust, with a specialized clientèle. This runs an Employment Resource Centre set up in 1983 'to combat the enormous problems facing disabled people seeking work'.[30] The Resource Centre owes much to the enthusiasm of its Enterprise Officer, Ed Cairns, a young Cambridge history graduate. The Trust and Resource Centre grew out of an active branch of the Disablement Income Group. An application was made for Urban Aid funding, which succeeded. One of the Employment Resource Centre's successes has been Pallion Business Services Ltd, a co-op run by disabled people. Single Homeless on Tyneside (SHOT) caters for another problem made worse by the recession: large numbers of young people leaving home because of tensions caused by unemployment. Like other agencies, SHOT's funding is through the Inner City Partnership. Like the others, it combines advice (on housing possibilities), services, including a walk-in Medical Centre for people without a GP, and a campaigning function. Like Benwell Law Centre, it actively seeks the involvement of its clients, while control remains, in practice, in full-time, funded, professional hands.

There is a pattern: voluntary or charitable work leading to an application for Inner City Partnership, EEC or direct local authority funds. Official funding provides the salaries and support services that make efficient operations possible. It also bestows legitimacy. 'Any group that starts up tries to get local authority money,' says a worker for Trade Films, a radical filmmaking company in Gateshead, funded by Tyne and Wear County Council and the British Film Institute ('to encourage innovative work out of London'). 'Once you get local government cash, you become proper. That constitutes the objective, amounts to success.' Talking to organizers in these groups, one is struck by the way that local government funding is worn like a badge of honour. Yet funds allocated can be increased, cut, or withdrawn. The problem with incorporation is the political price. 'There is a difficulty about being rude to people who pay your salary,' as one Sunderland organizer puts it.

One kind of agency is more aware of this potential conflict than most: the Unemployed Workers' Centres. The Newcastle Centre Against

Unemployment – which claims to be the first of its kind in the country
– was established in 1978, on the Quayside. The idea was for the
unemployed to organize themselves and 'fight for a better deal'. The
Centre remains sharply radical. For a time, it had an organizer from
Militant Tendency. Then there was a coup: now it has a communist.
Alone among agencies dealing with the effects of unemployment, the
Centre puts campaigning first, and its present rooms in the Jesmond
Road resemble the headquarters of a revolutionary group. There have
been many ventures, including fund-raising for miners' families during
the strike, and an effective battle (with help from the Benwell Law
Centre) against 'snoopers' – aided by clerical officer spies within the
DHSS, who made it possible for snooper victims to be warned of an
impending visit, and advised of their rights. The Centre also runs
courses for unemployed activists, and has issued a report: 'Educate –
Agitate – Organize'.

Since the founding of the Newcastle Centre, others have sprung up,
and in June 1984 the Tyne and Wear Association of Trades Councils
held a national conference of Unemployed Workers' Organizations.
There are now fourteen of these in the Northern Region. The process
of establishing them has been similar to that for other agencies.
Enthusiasts set up a 'centre' in cheap or free accommodation, an application for money is made, full-time workers are employed. The
unemployed centres, however, have encountered a problem which
other bodies have not faced: the suspicion of the trade union movement. In this respect, pre-war Labour Movement attitudes remain
unaltered. A 1981 TUC circular declared that 'it would not help the
unemployed . . . for them to be organized separately outside the structures of the Trade Union Movement . . . Separate unions for the
unemployed would make it easier for the Government to drive a wedge
between the unemployed and the employed.'[31] Exactly the same sentiment is contained in trade union directives of the 1930s.

The Newcastle Centre is funded by the city and county jointly, with
a total budget of £33,000, and controlled by a council consisting of
trades council, county councillors, city councillors and unemployed
members. What distinguishes it from most other centres is that it
rejects MSC funds on political grounds. At the Conference of
Unemployed Organizations, the subject of MSC funding was hotly
debated. The issue was seen as a choice between alternative roles.
'MSC-funded centres keep the unemployed occupied,' concluded one
group of delegates, 'whereas Unemployed Centres should be fighting

for a better deal for the unemployed, with campaigns like Anti-Snoopers, Benefit Campaigns, Support the Miners and all workers opposing redundancies and closures.' The far Left speaks of the TUC and the MSC in the same breath. '[W]ith the intervention of the TUC and the introduction of the MSC many of our centres operate under serious restraints as far as political campaigning work is concerned,' complained one speaker. 'To erase the scourge of unemployment from our midst ... will require the massive mobilization of much wider sections of the Labour Movement and beyond.'[32]

Unlike most funded agencies, the Newcastle Centre is working class both in leadership and in style, and members of the unemployed are directly involved, as volunteers, in its operations. 'Unless you have actually experienced the misery and poverty of unemployment', says Alec McFadden, the main paid worker, 'how can you work in the centre?' The centre and the national movement draw inspiration from pictures and accounts of Hannington's NUWM. Modern unemployed centres, however, cannot be compared with pre-war organizations. For one thing, even the Newcastle centre takes state money. For another, the centres remain leaders without followers. There has been no 'mobilization'. In 1980, the Newcastle centre had 52 members on its books. Today, it claims 182. Of these, only 25 or 30 are active, in the sense of making an appearance at least once a month. As there is no subscription, this is scarcely an impressive figure in the heart of a region with a quarter of a million people out of work.

At the height of the last great depression, the Marxist John Strachey wrote a book called *The Coming Struggle for Power* which appealed to those who imagined that industrial collapse would be followed by conflict between workers and capitalists. Today, nobody believes in the imminence of struggle, and yet there is a gathering sense of foreboding. There is a fear of *them*, the outsiders, the rabble ('Hark, Hark, the dogs do bark, The beggars are coming to town ...'), turning against their oppressors. There is fear of crime, alienation, and supposed totalitarian threats to democracy. There is the concept of two nations, and of a shadowy, dole-queuing, latently powerful army of the unemployed. If such an army were to be found, its sturdiest troops would certainly be in the North-East, not only the region with the longest and most severe experience of unemployment, but also a region with an unusually homogeneous, strongly organized working class. But in the

North-East, the army does not exist. Outside the main political parties, there is no significant organization even speaking for – let alone representing – the unemployed, that is not funded and hence in the end neutralized by the state. The reality of modern unemployment is not dole queues or marching men, but the scene that greets any visitor who steps off a train at Newcastle: a still-flourishing commercial and cosmopolitan city with boutiques and wine bars in every main street, a new underground system, a show-piece shopping centre, and a town hall like a modern cathedral. The unemployed are nowhere to be seen: scattered through a hundred council estates, sitting in clubs, or slumped in front of television sets. There are not two nations. There is one society, and one universal, creeping sickness.

Political Quarterly, vol. 56, no. 4, October–December 1986

NOTES

1. In addition to published sources and some other, unpublished, documentary material, this article is based on interviews with about two dozen people, mainly in Newcastle and Sunderland. I would like to express my thanks to all of them.

2. Seasonally adjusted (excluding school-leavers).

3. G. Orwell, *The Road to Wigan Pier* (Secker & Warburg, 1936), p. 87.

4. W. Hannington, *The Insurgents in London* (The Southwark Press, 1923), pp. 3, 28.

5. J. Stevenson, *British Society 1914–45* (Penguin, 1984), pp. 290–2.

6. Orwell, *Wigan Pier*, p. 77.

7. Cited in Stevenson, *British Society*, p. 292.

8. W. Paynter, *My Generation* (Allen & Unwin, 1972), p. 107.

9. Stevenson, *British Society*, p. 290.

10. F. F. Ridley, 'View from a Disaster Area: Unemployed Youth in Merseyside', *Political Quarterly*, vol. 52, no. 1, 1981, p. 26.

11. See p. 172 for definitions of 'Northern Region' and 'North-East'.

12. Kendal, Windermere, Penrith, Hexham, Barrow, Carlisle, Berwick.

13. *Regional Employment Market Intelligence Trends* (REMIT), published by MSC Northern Region, Spring 1985.

14. Cited in A. R. Prest and D. J. Coppock (eds.), *The UK Economy* (Weidenfeld & Nicolson, 1984), p. 256.

15. I. Stone, 'The Crisis in Shipbuilding in the North-East', *Northern Economic Review*, Summer 1984.

16. Stevenson, *British Society*, p. 273.

17. REMIT, Spring 1985.

18. Orwell, *Wigan Pier*, pp. 87–88.

19. B. Campbell, *Wigan Pier Revisited: Poverty and Politics in the 80s* (Virago, 1984), p. 209. See also Jean Seaton, 'The Media and the Politics of Unemployment', in S. Allen, A. Watson and S. Wood (eds.), *Unemployment* (Macmillan, 1985).

20. S. King, 'Entering the Labour Market: The Experiences of School-leavers in Gateshead', *Northern Economic Review*, Summer 1984, p. 15.

21. 'Unemployment of Young People Within the City', Report by the Director of Education, February 1984.
22. REMIT, Winter 1984.
23. 'Unemployment of Young People', *op. cit.*
24. *Northern Economic Review*, Autumn/Winter 1984, p. 43.
25. P. Dunleavy and C. T. Husbands, *British Democracy at the Crossroads: Voting and Party Competition in the 1980s* (Allen & Unwin, 1985), p. 224.
26. *Northern Economic Review*, Autumn/Winter 1984, p. 49.
27. REMIT, Winter 1983.
28. 'Unemployment of Young People', p. 3.
29. NRCDA, *Co-operatives and the Local Economy*, 1983, p. 1.
30. Wearside Disablement Centre Trust, Information sheet, September 1984.
31. Cited in Tyne & Wear Association of Trades Councils, *Unemployed Conference Report*, 1984, p. 11.
32. Ibid, pp. 19, 23.

NORTHERN IRELAND

I · ENNISKILLEN

IT IS IMPOSSIBLE to imagine a successful British policy in Northern Ireland, or at least one whose success could begin to be judged for at least a generation. But there can be symptoms of obvious failure, and the Enniskillen massacre was one.

A difficulty facing any British Government is deciding upon aims. So far the main conflicts have been within parties rather than between them: disputes between those hoping to edge towards a united Ireland, those wanting to integrate Ulster into the United Kingdom, and those who see no choice but to maintain the *status quo*. Uncertainty about the secret purpose of successive administrations has caused more political heat than any policy in itself. For all governments, however, the first objective has been to reduce the killing. Enniskillen shows how little progress has been made.

In strictly military terms, the opposite may also be true. It is clear that the bombing has opened up a deep fissure within the IRA. Did the Army Council know and approve? If so, there must be a pretty big split between them and Sinn Fein, whose denunciation of the bombing was as emphatic as it was unexpected. Did a Provo unit act on its own initiative, without the backing of the high command? If so, there are serious problems of indiscipline. Either way, the IRA is not doing well in its own terms. Meanwhile, there have been recent reports in West Belfast of effective police pressure through an increased use of informers.

British newspapers have seized on such evidence and have argued, with London logic, that this time the IRA has gone too far, and Sinn Fein will lose support as a result. Such a conclusion is wildly optimistic and sadly misinformed. The Provisionals are small in number – a hard core of between 300 and 600 according to different estimates – but their capacity to bounce back has repeatedly been shown. In addition, they have a bedrock of passive support which regards the conflict as a liberation struggle, and accepts casualties as a necessary by-product.

The fond belief that 'decent Catholic families' will share the Fleet Street sense of outrage misses this point.

There is a rhetoric of regret, anger and determination which always accompanies such events. It is appropriate but – as the next bombing will show – inadequate. Certainly, a get-tough policy at this stage must be what the Provisionals are praying for, to restore unity within their ranks. A show of restraint by the Government would do most to bring off the best security coup – the ratification of the extradition treaty in the Dáil on 1 December. At the same time, the only sensible long-term strategy is to work on that section of the Catholic population – around a third – that feels enough anger to go on voting for Sinn Fein.

The votes are not significant in themselves. It is the feelings behind them that are at the root of the problem facing any policy-maker in Northern Ireland. British observers, even concerned ones, have tended to regard the Sinn Fein support as ignorant or perverse. That is dangerous, as well as absurd. If the Provisionals are to be isolated within their own community – and they will continue to kill and maim until they are – the reasons why so many poor, working-class people condone what we call murder must be better understood.

Softening the attitudes of these people was, of course, a primary intention of the 1985 Anglo-Irish Agreement, which remains the cornerstone of British policy in the province. How does it now look? There are pluses and minuses. Abroad the Agreement has been seen as a serious attempt at conciliation, and this has helped reduce supplies of money and arms to the IRA. At the same time, the presence of Dublin in Belfast has not displeased the Catholic population on either side of the border: nor has the fury which it has aroused among the Unionists.

On the other hand, the practical impact of the Agreement in the Sinn Fein heartlands of West Belfast has been marginal or non-existent. If Unionists were suspicious because they saw the Agreement as a symbolic step towards a united Ireland, Catholics regarded it sceptically as a gesture without substance. So far the Catholics have been proved right. The supposed aim was to provide regular discussions about the government of the province. But what is the use of discussions that produce no result? Cynics have been saying that jaw-jaw has stimulated far less concrete reform than war-war. The Anglo-Irish Agreement can only be made to work if it is used to tackle the two continuing problems of the province: unemployment and discrimination.

Unemployment on its own is not the only cause of the conflict. When the present troubles started, the rate of joblessness in the province was lower than in much of south-east England today. Nevertheless, absolute and relative deprivation – lack of money, jobs, skills and prospects – has become the biggest factor in preventing this suppurating sore from healing. In Northern Ireland as a whole, unemployment is now around 20 per cent. Among the Catholic population, according to the Fair Employment Agency, it is more than twice as high. And in the urban wilderness of West Belfast – Ballymurphy, Turf Lodge, Whiterock, Lower Falls – male unemployment is reckoned to be 50 or 60 per cent.

More than in any other part of the United Kingdom, West Belfast has unemployment as a way of life, dominating its culture, humour, attitudes and values. Whether or not the inhabitants have grounds to feel bitter towards those they regard as their enemies is a matter for argument. That they do feel bitter is a political fact, and it is bitterness, fuelled by lack of hope, that produces sympathy for Sinn Fein and a seedbed for the IRA.

But attachment to the militant republican cause also has another aspect. There is a simple formula which holds good in most parts of the world: economic grievance plus separate national identity equals rejection of legal authority and support for violent protest. The Thatcher Government has approached the dual identity problem by seeking, through the Anglo-Irish Agreement, to massage the Catholics. What the Government has not done is attempt to turn the Agreement into a vehicle for the promotion of civil rights, which might reduce the Catholic scorn for Protestant and British justice.

Whatever view might have been taken at the outset, the Agreement should not now be scrapped. The Unionists can live with it and the Catholics can still gain from it. What is needed instead is for it to be adapted. Reform *is* possible in Ulster – since 1968, electoral abuses have been curtailed, and the Protestants have been deprived of much of their political power. Much of the reform was insufficient and too late, which strengthens the case for speeding up the pace. The aim must be to fight discrimination, principally in employment, and provide jobs in the areas that need them most.

A recent glossy statement of intent on how to change labour recruitment practices has to be followed through. There must also be a proper regional policy. Ideally, tackling the Ulster economy should be part of a UK expansionary programme. Alas, the wrong side won the general election. Nevertheless, given a more pragmatic approach to economic matters of late, the Government should be able to see the argument for making Ulster a special case. Throwing large sums of money at the problem has, so far, failed to solve it. But Ulster is a small province, and within it the key populations are heavily concentrated. Throwing, or sensibly investing, even more at a time when the national economy can stand it, may pay political dividends in the future. Labour gave big financial gifts to any plausible millionaire (such as De Lorean) who came along. There is a need not to repeat the same mistake. One positive step would be to use the Agreement to develop economic links with the South.

Within Belfast, Sinn Fein enjoys three kinds of support. There are those who have personal experience of British imprisonment, or are the relatives or friends of present or former inmates. This ever-growing group is unpersuadable. There are those who, in desperation, see Sinn Fein as the only party with the determination to get things done. And there are the young – often aimless and nihilistic – who regard the IRA with a combination of fear and fascination. Both the second and third groups contain people who, in different conditions, might be detached.

Enniskillen will quickly be forgotten, except by the injured and the bereaved. Anybody who imagines that such an event might prove a catalyst for some kind of change lives in a world of make-believe. On the other hand, the latest tragedy could encourage the British (as well as the Irish) to re-think their approach. The Anglo-Irish Agreement is due for review next year. There is still time for London and Dublin to consider carefully the opportunity it provides.

New Statesman, 13 November 1987

NORTHERN IRELAND

II · MILLTOWN

WILL THE AUTHORITIES be speaking in the same terms about Northern Ireland in 2008 as they are today? Certainly the past two decades, since the present troubles began, have produced little change in the language of official response. The main element – after every miserable tragedy – is *moral condemnation* linked to the notion that those who commit acts of violence are abnormal, exceptional, even social outcasts.

The aftermath of the Milltown lynchings provides characteristic examples of the genre. Within minutes of receiving the news, those expected to make observations made the observations that were expected of them. 'There seem to be no depths to which these people will not sink,' said the Prime Minister. 'People who stoop to such barbarous and evil savagery,' said the Northern Ireland Secretary, 'have no place in civilized society.' A spokesman for the RUC called the murders 'an obscenity' committed by 'depraved and perverted people'.

How often have we heard such remarks before and how many times will they be heard again? A cynic might estimate the degree of official dismay by the number of key words that occur in the same sentence. A sick game would be to contrast appropriate reactions. A bomb in a crowded church, for instance, might rate: 'There are no evil limits to which these depraved and perverted savages would not obscenely sink,' and so on.

And all of it, of course, misses the point. For the sad truth about Northern Ireland is not the existence of evil, depravity or savagery in the province – though as in all troubled lands, war loosens the inhibitions of the aggressive and the amoral. It is that violence, both spontaneous and calculated, reflects the misery and hatred in whole communities. Hence the inevitable response to Milltown – police swoops, interrogations, arrests and convictions – will provide a measure of retributive justice but will do nothing to reduce the problem.

Exemplary punishment only works in the context of social disapproval, or as a deterrent. In West Belfast, neither applies.

Nor did they apply when the recent kaleidoscope of events began. The shootings of the IRA suspects in Gibraltar are precisely a demonstration that rooting out perpetrators, however necessary it may be, is at best a peripheral aspect of policy and one which can easily bring fresh disasters. Whatever went wrong in Gibraltar – whether the order to fire if there was not an immediate surrender came from above, or whether the British forces involved were simply not instructed to take every precaution to capture the bombers alive – the episode will be remembered as one of the biggest blunders in the long, sorry tale of attempts to reduce killings in the province. Yet that catastrophe was itself a product of the illusion that this is a war against a numerically finite enemy, and the first task is to eliminate its members one by one.

The same illusion lay behind the 1985 Anglo-Irish Agreement. Ostensibly, the Agreement was political: aimed at massaging the national identity of Catholics on both sides of the border, and isolating Sinn Fein who, it was believed, would lose support if there was a symbolic Dublin presence in Belfast. It also seemed to make international sense, by showing previously sceptical foreigners that the British Government was prepared to be flexible. But the major underlying aim was improved security. The Agreement was supposed to produce better cross-border co-operation on policing. Above all, the Agreement was intended to produce extradition. The British hope was that Dublin's thank-you present would be a flow of wanted men from Irish to British gaols and courts, thereby undermining the Provisionals' military strength. It hasn't happened. But – and this is a critical point – even if the unexpected occurred and Charles Haughey delivered extradition on a plate, in the present climate it might actually cause more trouble in terms of nationalist emotion than it would be worth. As Sinn Fein has shown so often before, the martyrdom card, skilfully played, can be a trump.

The biggest political masterstroke of the Agreement appeared to be that it infuriated the Unionists even more than it annoyed Sinn Fein. Hence it could be sold to the majority of moderate or uncertain Catholics as a concession. But the difficulty about masterstrokes is that they raise expectations. This one so far has mainly produced disappointment.

The British have been disappointed because, despite some recent successes in penetrating the IRA command structure and in the uncovering of arms hauls, the hoped-for co-operation with the southern Irish has not been forthcoming. Dublin has been disappointed because its involvement in Northern Ireland affairs has been no more than token, while British handling of the Birmingham Six, Stalker and Gibraltar affairs has been tactless, in terms of Irish public opinion, to say the least. The Northern Catholics have been disappointed because those who supported the Agreement thought that their lives might improve as a result of it. Everybody involved is disappointed because the SDLP, who were supposed to be the main beneficiaries, have singularly failed to dent the rock-solid Sinn Fein ghettoes of West Belfast.

Meanwhile the level of violence does not lessen. This was true even before Gibraltar and the funeral killings. Indeed, the death rate since 1985 has shown an increase. In 1984, the toll for the province was forty-four; in 1987 it was ninety-seven. In the five years up to the Agreement, Belfast itself had become almost incident free, with most attacks occurring in the country districts, and close to the border.

The Anglo-Irish Agreement cannot now be wished away. It provides a framework for discussion which must be used, and work is needed to calm understandable Southern suspicions of British arrogance and high-handedness, if not of indifference to Catholic grievances. But what recent weeks and months do conclusively demonstrate is that the Agreement can never again be regarded as a solution.

There are no solutions to the Northern Ireland problem, but there are remedies which, determinedly applied, can have an impact upon it. During the nineteenth-century potato famine, British economic doctrines of *laissez-faire* did more to kill the Irish people than centuries of military incursion. In the 1980s economic Thatcherism is to blame for much of what has happened. The manufacturing base of Belfast has collapsed since 1979. Catholics in Northern Ireland are two-and-a-half times more likely to be unemployed than Protestants. The present Government's policies have helped to create a culture of unemployment on the Catholic council estates and Sinn Fein has adopted that culture, identified with it, spoken for it, based itself upon it. The only way to start to undermine the culture is by providing jobs.

Mrs Thatcher's trumpeted 'inner cities' campaign is supposedly based on private enterprise. No capitalist in his or her right mind, however, would set up shop in West Belfast today. That, of course, is how Sinn Fein likes it. The other possibility is for this Government to swallow its pride and do more of what it refuses to do on the mainland: provide employment through public investment. Many Catholics are would-be building workers. A massive housing programme would help. Last week there was a province-wide protest about NHS cuts. The health service is labour intensive. Spending more on health care would be a productive start.

Politically, there are no rabbits to be pulled out of hats. The proposal, increasingly advanced in middle-class (and especially socialist) circles, in favour of British political parties organizing on a constituency basis in the province, reflects a widespread resentment at Northern Ireland's alienation from mainstream political life.

Such a view deserves a hearing and may eventually provide the best hope. Immediately, however, the nihilism of the IRA has to be met by the opposite, in terms of direct economic intervention. There is a need to understand and reduce – fast – the anger that turns killers into heroes. 'We must restore a clear ethic of personal responsibility,' Mrs Thatcher said last weekend in a speech directed at the United Kingdom as a whole. 'We need to establish that the main person to blame for each crime is the criminal himself.' Quite so. And Milltown shows how much we need also to make politicians see their own responsibility for the corrupting consequences of social inaction.

New Statesman, 25 March 1988

A ROAD DEATH

THIS REMEMBRANCE WEEKEND I went to a funeral which nobody present is ever likely to forget. It had been a dramatic, tragic death. But it did not hit the headlines. It was much too common.

The wooden box contained a boy, just seventeen, son of a friend and colleague. Eight days ago he was a healthy, happy, active youth, founder-chairman of a local scooter club – the leader of the pack. A very safe, careful rider, everybody said.

On Sunday November 2, he set out on an errand in quiet, suburban Finchley and never came back. The police are still working out what happened. Two cars and a concrete lamp-post were involved. An ambulance came in record time. The doctors who spent several hours trying to put together the bits were weeping at the finish.

So were mourners at the cemetery. He must have been a popular lad. There were as many standing as sitting in the crematorium, with every age, class, race and hairstyle represented.

The occasion was secular and not too sombre. He had been a free spirit. His brother likened him to a shooting star, seen coursing across the clear north London sky the night after the accident. After the orations, the boy's girlfriend played tapes of his favourite pop songs. It seemed fitting. We were celebrating a good life: light-hearted, affectionate, sensible, funny, generous, whimsical, full of hope and love and promise. He was a pupil at a sixth-form college, and wanted to join the Royal Marines. He lived at home with his mother.

There were many emotions, as the blue curtains closed – shock, sympathy, anger at the pointless pity of it, even perhaps a frightful feeling that the fates had been propitiated: *at least it wasn't my child*. But for the men in black top hats it was all part of the day's work. There's nothing unusual, after all, about the death of a teenager on two wheels.

Perhaps it is because road killings are so ordinary, when they happen to strangers, that we take them for granted. Perhaps we just don't like to be reminded. Big, comfortably remote, mega-death disasters – such as last week's Chinook helicopter catastrophe – get the attention. But it is the mundane, domestic motor smash that takes the most lives.

Terrorism, murder, drug abuse, sexually transmitted disease – each has its tally of familial grief. Bombs and guns and dirty needles, however, do not begin to compare with the deadliest weapon of all wielded so casually by the majority of adults. How odd it is that a means of transport, a mere object of consumer convenience, should produce violent death on a scale only exceeded by the slaughter of war.

In 1985, a staggering 5,789 fatalities were recorded: twenty times as many as were killed in boats, trains and aircraft. Of these, 1,292 people were killed riding motor or pedal bikes. In the same year only 425 people were murdered. From the discovery of the virus up to the end of October, a mere 278 people had died of Aids. By contrast, in the fifteen-to-nineteen age group, road accidents in 1985 accounted for more deaths (925) than every other cause, including illness, put together (880).

Drink is the biggest killer. One in four road deaths are linked to this socially acceptable poison. Excessive speed, faulty brakes or steering, can also be deadly. A split second's inattention, a signal not given, can cause a sacrifice as empty as any at Auschwitz or Verdun. And, as in the lunatic casino of modern warfare, the victim's only offence is usually to have been, by bad luck, in the wrong place at the wrong time.

'He will be remembered,' it was said at the funeral, as at a thousand cenotaphs throughout the land. Yet what will never have been known, or remembered, are the things which those who are lost might have said, or done, or been.

Like wars, accidents are events which need not happen. 'If only' – the meaningless past conditional – gives birth to a thousand regrets. Unpredictable and unmotivated, accidents shatter faith in an ordered world and destroy belief in reason and endeavour. Sickness has a cause. An accident is sheer stupidity. Yet which of us can say that we have never – behind a wheel – gambled with the lives of others?

Accidents provide no explanation, no comfort for the bereaved. If, however, a moment's reflection on their absurdity may lead a single driver to drink one glass less, or check the mirror before turning, a mother or brother or lover may be luckier than they will ever know.

Today, 10 November 1986

1 · THE HOLOCAUST

AT MINSK, IN AUGUST 1941, German soldiers broke into the ghetto three times, rounding up thousands of people and taking them to nearby pits for execution. On one occasion, Heinrich Himmler asked if he could watch a shooting operation. SS General Karl Wolff ordered the selection of a hundred prisoners for 'a demonstration'. Wolff later described how the victims were forced to lie face downwards in an open grave to be shot. Others were made to lie on top of them, and were killed in turn.

Himmler had never seen dead bodies before. Curiosity aroused, he stood at the edge of the triangular hole. 'While he was looking in', Wolff recounted, 'Himmler had the deserved bad luck that from one or other of the people who had been shot in the head he got a splash of brains on his coat, and I think it also splashed into his face, and he was very green and pale; he wasn't actually sick, but he was heaving and turned round and swayed and then I had to jump forward and hold him steady and then I led him away from the grave.'

It is hard to know what to do with such a book, so awesome is its tale, so profound its importance. At times, it fades into a dreamlike, Dante-esque allegory. Yet the events took place, and it is the monumental achievement of this chillingly brilliant, non-sensational and dignified work that it shows with precision how they occurred, when, where and to how many. What it does not and cannot do is answer the question why.

The approach is chronological. Event follows event in a march of doom. The tone is coldly accusatory, almost muted, with comment restrained. The indictment, based on impeccable eye-witness and documentary sources, is allowed to build up for itself. After a brief background account of East European anti-Semitism and the rise of the Nazis in Germany, the main story begins with Hitler's seizure of

The Holocaust: The Jewish Tragedy, Martin Gilbert (Collins, 1986)

power in 1933. We are made to realize that from that single, political incident all else followed.

In the same year, Dachau concentration camp was established, and the Gestapo were placed above and outside the law. In 1934, a German newspaper was already prophesying that the day would soon dawn 'when throughout the whole of Germany there will no longer be a single Jew'. Persecutions became authorized, official, encouraged. The most immediate cause was National Socialism. But as Gilbert makes clear, the new ideology was not the only factor.

The Nazis repeatedly described Jews and Jewishness as a 'bacillus' or 'virus' that needed to be 'cauterized'. Gilbert borrows the metaphor and presents anti-Semitism as a contagion, long endemic throughout east Europe, which became a plague as a result of the Hitlerite incubus. Polish anti-Semitism had reached such a pitch that 10 per cent of Polish Jewry had emigrated by 1937. Spreading outward from Germany, victimization of Jews infected Rumania, Hungary and the Ukraine, preparing the way for wartime collaboration. 'Gradually entire populations became immune to feelings of outrage,' writes the author, 'and learned to shun compassion.'

Knowledge of what was happening, though always incomplete, was widespread in the West and among local populations before as well as after the death camps had been set up. Abroad, stories filtered through from escapers, and appeared as minor items in the press. In Germany and the occupied territories, there were the unavoidable sounds and smells of slaughter. Gilbert's accusation, however, is of something much worse than passive awareness: it is of satisfaction, even collusion.

We read of mobs cheering and jeering, of betrayals and lynchings not only in Germany but in the invaded countries as well. There were also individual acts of gentile – very occasionally, Christian-inspired – self-sacrifice, even of public outspokenness. But these were as remarkable for their extreme rarity in the regions where the butchery was most intense, as for their courage. They were, in addition, far less common than expressions of popular enthusiasm.

Collusion was a necessary background to mass murder. But the most crucial element was organization. Adolf Eichmann appears in the story early on, as a minor, almost innocent-seeming character: head of the Central Office of Jewish Emigration. Expansion of the murder programme revealed his talents, accelerated his rise, and instilled him with a missionary zeal. In January 1942, SS General Reinhard Heydrich arranged a secret conference at Wansee, near Berlin. 'In the course of the practical implementation of the final solution', he explained, 'Europe will be combed from west to east.' At his trial, Eichmann recalled how, after the conference, 'we all sat together like comrades. Not to talk shop, but to rest after hours of effort.'

The effort had only begun. Wansee became the basis of a demonic structure that existed until six million Jews were dead, mainly after the most brutal torture and ill-treatment. For this to happen, Gilbert writes simply, it was necessary 'to rely upon the tacit, unspoken, unrecorded connivance of thousands of people: administrators and bureaucrats who would do their duty, organize round-ups, supervise detention centres, co-ordinate schedules, and send local Jews on their way to a distant "unknown destination", to "work camps", in "Poland", to "resettlement" in "the East".' Who were they, these administrators and bureaucrats? How many survived the war and were never caught? How many are still living? How many have children or grandchildren, happily unknowing and guilt-free, living in Europe, Britain, the United States? One finds one's mind straying to such irrelevancies.

Many of the administrators were physically removed from the direct consequences of their acts. The same was not true of the guards and SS men, the agents – usually ignorant, ill-educated and young – of the political religion. Statistics, on the whole, do not touch the imagination. It is the details of wickedness, sometimes playful or even whimsical, that have the greatest effect. Some, one absorbs with a sort of grim fascination. Others are very hard to read at all. Often, one is filled with wonder that such things could even be conceived.

What is revealed is not sadism, or pleasure seeking, but a frenzied addiction to the infliction of suffering in which the immediacy of horror is blotted out by the perpetration of another horror, even more terrible. And behind the horror, fear. 'They rightly hate us,' said Hitler in 1942, 'just as much as we hate them.'

Why did the Jews not resist? Gilbert answers, emphatically: they did, wherever and whenever they could. In the camps, there were riots, killings of guards, mass break-outs. In the Warsaw ghetto, there was an uprising, bloodily suppressed. At Babi Yar, 325 escaped, of whom fourteen evaded their pursuers. Others made it to the forests, setting up guerrilla bands or joining the resistance. The odds against them, however, were always overwhelming. Apart from German military might, there was the certainty of reprisals, and – frequently – the hostility and treachery of the local non-Jewish population.

'My arms are long,' declared Eichmann. They reached into every part of the German empire, until the very end. Even the liberation of the camps did not immediately stop the carnage. During the first forty-eight hours of nominal British control at Belsen, the Hungarian SS shot seventy-two Jews and eleven non-Jews for such offences as taking potato peel from the kitchen.

Gilbert's book takes us beyond the language of morality or even of psychology. Time and again, one is struck by the average, ordinariness of the oppressors. What seems to have occurred – a description, not an explanation – is that the Nazis succeeded, through much of Europe, in redefining normality and acceptability. Under the intense pressure of the powerful German state and propaganda machine, basic values changed and inhibitions were removed. Through a combination of authority and incitement, latent feelings were inflamed and human sympathy became the aberration. The warning provided by this study for our own epoch – with its constant danger of another holocaust, even more horrendous – is terrifyingly apparent.

New Society, 21 February 1986

11 · THE NAZI HUNT

NOW THAT ANSCHLUSS WEEKEND is over, Kurt Waldheim is enjoying a respite from the world's front pages. For the time being, accidental tragedy in Austria (the avalanches) has displaced the deliberate variety. But the issues surrounding Europe's most embarrassing post-war head of state remain unresolved.

There is no doubt that Waldheim should resign. More to the point, the Austrians and their leaders owe it to themselves to kick him out. There is not just the need for a bloodstained nation to proclaim the moral distance it wishes to keep between its modern identity and its past. There is also the matter of the cover-up. You are not guilty just because you know about something, Waldheim told a British television interviewer last week. Perhaps. But, even if knowledge of murder was the only accusation, no country can preserve its self-respect and retain in office a president whose publicly distributed curriculum vitae has been shown up as a tissue of lies.

Nevertheless there is a huge element of hypocrisy about the international hue-and-cry against the Austrian reptile. The righteous indignation of reactionary foreign governments – the USA and Britain in particular – is neither an edifying nor a convincing sight. A cynic would discern two motives: the acquisition of Brownie points, especially among war veteran and Jewish voters, at zero cost; and an opportunity to stress once again what has been the West's most plausible defence, from Vietnam to Nicaragua: only the Nazis committed *real* atrocities.

So much has been said, written, filmed about the Nazis that it is time somebody looked for a change at the perverse nostalgia industry to which they have given rise. The continuing universal fascination with Adolf Hitler is partly because his régime was qualitatively worse than anything else in modern times. But it also has something to do with cultural proximity. When we peer into the blank, expressionless eyes and contemplate the neatly parted hair of members of an *Einzatz-*

gruppe murder squad, we know that every one of us furtively contains a potential stormtrooper.

Heaping calumny on Waldheim removes the need to consider too closely the conditions, in any society, that permit bureaucratized and officially-sanctioned outrages to occur. One role of the latter-day Nazi hunt has thus been to help to cloak Allied errors of judgement or of morality; another has been to obscure military and civil obscenities that still go on. In the Second World War there were the famous holocausts of enemy civilians, readily justified on strategic grounds at the time – Dresden, Hamburg, Berlin, Tokyo, Hiroshima, Nagasaki. There were also the nasty, unnoticed little decisions, some of which are only now beginning to emerge and many of which never will. The playwright William Douglas-Home recently drew attention to one significant incident, at Le Havre in 1944. Ordered to take part in an attack which he believed would cause unnecessary civilian deaths, he refused to do so. 'We frequently told German officers to disobey illegal orders,' he says. 'I thought it was time some of us did what we were telling them to do.' Douglas-Home not only resisted an order: he wrote to the press explaining why. In Germany (or Russia) a firing squad would have been the inevitable result. In Britain, the penalty was a year's hard labour. Yet, the interesting thing is how very, very seldom such protests were made.

Here is a point that applies almost as much in peace as in war. For the Nazi atrocity was not simply the product of military conflict. There is the uncomfortable historical problem of the non-Nazi public service. Why, in the early 1930s, did so many decent, ordinary, dutiful bureaucrats not only do what they were told, but do it with enthusiasm? The key to the catastrophe is to be found as much in the behaviour of career civil servants, teachers, lawyers, academics and churchmen as in the doctrines of anti-Semitism. Dr Waldheim excuses himself today by rejecting the idea of collective guilt. Yet the accusation against him, as against many other minor cogs in peace and war, is of *individual* responsibility. Each faced a personal moral choice. Almost all ducked it.

To sustain such an indictment we need also to apply the argument to our own times. As Douglas-Home has pointed out, we cannot demand of others – under much greater extremity of pressure – that they should show moral (and physical) courage without imposing at least as high standards on ourselves. It will be objected that contemporary Britain offers no comparison with Nazi Germany and that it is naïve, even bad taste, to imply otherwise. Yet that is precisely why the Waldheim dissection is so insidious. Every time freedom of expression is suppressed in our courts, every time a member of the IRA is shot without trial, or an honest copper is drummed out of the police force, we absolve ourselves by booting an elderly war criminal, and feel a lot better.

It is not necessary to be a conspiracy theorist, or to present (mainland) Britain as a police state, in order to be concerned at growing abuses of state power. It is not necessary to accuse Mrs Thatcher of Hitlerism to wonder why, so far, John Stalker has been the only individual to leave the government employ, on principle, over the shoot-to-kill affair. It is not necessary to place whoever gave the orders to execute unarmed suspects in Gibraltar alongside the Gestapo, in order to feel patriotically ashamed at Britain's declining moral authority in Ireland and the world.

The truth is that the preservation of democracy entails constant vigilance in small things. Obsession with historic transgressions is not particularly helpful. A realization that there is no clear dividing line between an everyday condonable abuse of authority and one that requires protest and sacrifice, is. As confrontation, discrimination, selfishness, outright oppression become government-approved virtues, so the unhappy choices facing public employees increase. It is impossible to know how often civil servants, in recent years, have stayed at their posts only because of a family to feed and an unpaid mortgage: but the incidence must have increased. For every Sarah Tisdall and Clive Ponting, who actually took action against behaviour they found to be repugnant, it is reasonable to imagine that there were dozens who wished they had the fortitude, but lacked it.

At any rate, it would be nice to think so. Alas, though civil service morale has notoriously plummeted under Mrs Thatcher, evidence of conscientious doubts is scarce. And that is another reason why pillorying morally defective central Europeans misses the point. For the reality is not, in such situations, that state servants suffer torments of secret regret. It is rather that they readily and unimaginatively accept the values of the dominant power. Hitler united his people in murderous hostility to the Jews. Mrs Thatcher has done an impressive job of uniting prosperous, modernizing, mainly-southern Britain into a self-interested coalition against the poor, the marginal, and the disadvantaged. Straight-talking callousness has become a point of pride: we live in a social Darwinian economic culture.

The historian Martin Gilbert has described how, after the Anschluss with Germany which many Austrians welcomed, the rights of Austrian Jews were swept away 'and in their place the Jews suffered all the humiliations of a puerile and sadistic imagination'. Nothing like that, of course, can be expected here. Yet history, as this century shows, moves at a cracking pace. The unemployed already have fewer rights than seemed conceivable a decade ago; there have been two elections at which the Government benefited directly from its proudly-proclaimed negative redistribution. This administration, whose economic 'success' was celebrated once again on Budget Day, and which remains so resoundingly popular, has drastically altered the parameters of the socially acceptable. When I was a child, beggars were people in nursery rhymes and story books. Today I step over them on my doorstep and dodge them daily in the Hogarthian city streets. Perhaps the next subject for investigation by an international commission should be the brutalizing slippage of values which has accompanied this Government's political triumph – and which, one day, will puzzle historians quite as much as Kurt Waldheim's conscience.

New Statesman, 18 March 1988

ROYALTY

1 · GRANNY'S REGAL REMARK

NOW THAT 'WE' ARE APPROACHING our tenth anniversary of taking power, who are 'we' coming most to resemble? For longevity as prime minister, Lord Liverpool and William Gladstone. In other respects, the closest parallel is with the short-serving Neville Chamberlain.

The conventional view, of course, places the Man of Munich and the Woman of Goose Green at opposite ends of the political personality spectrum. Margaret Thatcher is more frequently (if ludicrously) compared with Winston Churchill. Yet in almost every respect apart from her relative international bellicosity, the present Prime Minister grows more like Chamberlain by the day.

'We have become a grandmother.' It is that delightful absurdity – so innocent, genuine, joyful and redolent of *folie de grandeur* – which brings the old umbrella man sharply into focus.

That it is funny is interesting in itself. A Douglas-Home or a Wilson uttering the male equivalent would scarcely have raised a smile. Yet from Mrs Thatcher's lips it provided, in an ozone-obsessive and water-depressive week, some good-natured comic relief. It was significant that she should have been disoriented by it during Neil Kinnock's questioning on Tuesday about the future of Nicholas Ridley.

> *Mrs Thatcher*: May I advise him to listen to the interview I did on Channel 4 which pointed out that our Secretary of State for the Environment (*Labour MPs*: Our? We are a grandmother) . . . Ours, on our side . . .
> *Neil Kinnock*: Obviously we are not amused (laughter) . . .
> *Mrs Thatcher*: May I say it is we (*Labour MPs*: We?) . . . We on this side . . . This Government has poured money into investment in water.

The point about the granny remark is that it awakens memories of other one-liners that acquired a life of their own. The most celebrated example during the last Labour administration was 'Crisis? What Crisis?' attributed (falsely) by the *Sun* to James Callaghan, the then prime minister, in January 1979 at the height of the winter of discontent. The three words apparently triggered a slump in support for the Government from which it never recovered.

It was Chamberlain who was hoist with the most notorious verbal petard of the century. 'One thing is certain,' declared the Prime Minister on 4 April 1940, 'Hitler has missed the bus.' Poor Chamberlain. As the Nazis swept through Norway, and British forces at Namsos and Andalsnes collapsed, 'missed the bus' turned into an Opposition chant. Like 'Crisis, What Crisis?', it became a symbol of misjudgement and – that most terminal of political disorders – hubris.

As yet the pregnant 'we' in Mrs Thatcher's Downing Street declaration does not have the same resonance: the moment was scarcely as historic. But the regal presumption of the pronoun, and the circumstances of its delivery (did Lord Liverpool summon the nation's press for such a private announcement? Did Gladstone?) provided a salutary reminder of an earlier Tory prime minister who took too much for granted.

There is some slight parallel in the political setting – Chamberlain and Mrs Thatcher both presided over governments with huge majorities, against a background of Labour Movement weakness and high unemployment. But it is the similarity of character and style that is most striking.

True, Chamberlain wore a moustache, came from a famous family and did not go to Oxbridge; he also did not become premier until he was four years older than Mrs Thatcher is now, and he never led his party in a general election. Yet both conducted themselves like elective dictators. Both were single-minded (and tunnel-visioned) iconoclasts and reformers – intervening in ministerial affairs, running their own foreign policies, and treating critics as unpatriotic, as well as disloyal.

Neither was an orthodox Conservative. Both were urban, business-oriented Tories, with a philistine rotary club mentality. Both were suspicious of the old upper classes, whose easy-going manners they contrasted with their own ramrod self-discipline. Both terrified their ministers and were adored by some of their civil servants. Both inspired feelings of worship, sometimes amounting to masochistic love, among the majority of Tory backbenchers, and bitter detestation, amounting to a devil-may-care vendetta, among a rebellious minority. Neither had a sense of humour.

Both quarrelled with the ablest of their ministers (Eden, Heseltine), and turned to dependent flatterers instead (Sir John Simon, Parkinson). Both, in consequence, gave their Cabinets an air of work-a-day dullness which the public seemed to like, and themselves a reputation for toughness. Both were impressive in Parliament in the limited sense that they did their homework and could remember facts. Both were (usually) adept at media management, and were fawned upon by newspaper proprietors and editors. Both were well regarded among Conservatives partly because they were ruder towards the Labour Party than any other premiers of the century.

That Chamberlain was a would-be conciliator, while Mrs Thatcher is a sabre-rattler, is a less important difference than it appears. Arguably, if Chamberlain ought to have been bolder internationally, Mrs Thatcher needs to be more conciliatory.

More significant, in terms of political psychology, is the similarity in their use of doctrine. Both have had bees in their bonnet. Each seized on a fashionable theory (appeasement, market economics) and turned it into a state religion. Both became zealots, ignoring the warning signs of a changing world, scorning U-turns, denouncing pragmatism and losing touch with what ordinary people were thinking.

It took a war to budge Chamberlain, and that lever is mercifully not available now. Yet there are other instruments today that also played a part half a century ago. In the late 1930s, right-wing domination of the British political scene led to a 'popular front' movement of the left and centre. Although never officially adopted by parties of the Opposition, this scored a famous victory at one by-election, Bridgwater, and a near miss at another, Oxford, where the youthful Ted Heath joined Labour in fighting the Chamberlainite Tory, Quintin Hogg.

Eventually a parliamentary popular front of Labour, Liberals and dissident Tories toppled the Prime Minister in May 1940. Today a similar movement of opinion within all Opposition parties – towards a popular front of the mind – could similarly isolate the Prime Minister, especially if some Tory rebels could be persuaded to join.

An issue will be needed to make any such combination crystallize. The poll tax, which will hit marginal English voters a year from now? A Westland-type banana skin? If the centre parties were to give Labour (the main challenger) a clear run at the crucial Vale of Glamorgan by-election, that would help. Unfortunately, they won't. Nevertheless, as the recent discomfiting of Mrs Thatcher shows, the Opposition is cheering up.

Sunday Times, 12 March 1989

11 · WHEN A ROYAL ROMANCE
HAS A HOLLOW RING

LIKE THE PRIME MINISTER, we – everybody is using that pronoun nowadays – were overjoyed about Fergie. Who could be otherwise? In the very week that the Government, as usual, played Robin-Hood-in-reverse with the nation's resources, here was a ray of sunshine to gladden our hearts.

So three cheers for ITN, which devoted almost half of the *Ten O'Clock News* to a mixture of droolingly sycophantic and squirmingly impertinent questions directed at the happy pair, and much of the rest to deep investigative reporting of the innermost feelings of beer-swillers at the Fergie local. It was riveting, too, to have the views by satellite of Fergie's mum, flanked by the gaucho stepfather-in-law-to-be. Searching question: 'Do you have any special message?' Haughty upper-class glower: 'No.'

This was the British media at its democratic best: free, fearless, uninhibited, giving the news behind the news on a matter of vital national importance touching every one of us.

It is shameful, therefore, to have to own up to a sneaky, near-treasonable thought about that £25,000 engagement ring.

Probably it is just bourgeois guilt. The other night, opening our front door to some dinner guests, we found a grey-haired lady of around Mrs Thatcher's age curled up on our doorstep. She sat up at once, talked about Jesus, and showed no inclination to depart. Not especially surprised (such things are quite common in this part of Hackney, where unemployment is 38 per cent), we invited our visitors to step over her and into the house. When they left a few hours later, the lady was still there. We took out a blanket and some food, but she shook her head proudly and shuffled off into the night.

I rang agencies next day to ask how many people sleep rough in London. Nobody seemed to know. I did get some relevant figures though. In 1984, 24,050 families were officially homeless in the capital, compared with 14,410 in 1978. Some were housed temporarily in bed-and-breakfast establishments, short-life housing, or hostels. Hostel accommodation is now down to 6,000 beds, compared with an estimated 10,000 a decade ago.

Down-and-outs are in a different category from most of the 'respectable' homeless. Many are confused or distracted. The majority are male, but there is a growing band of 'bag ladies' like the one on our doorstep – women wandering aimlessly with rag-filled plastic bags.

'You'll find tramps in all the squares in the West End,' a social worker told me. 'Look in the shelter in the middle of Lincoln's Inn Fields, or under Waterloo Bridge. They sleep in cardboard boxes. There's a black cave on the Embankment, a tunnel with a grille across where they store sheets of cardboard in the daytime. People often die when there's a cold spell.'

The ruby and sparklers on Fergie's finger look brill; it would have been dog-in-the-mangerish for a journalist to have asked the radiant couple if they realized that the ring cost sixteen times a single person's supplementary benefit for a year. Still, I wonder how they might have answered, if one had.

Today, 25 March 1986

III · THE CUSTARD MONITOR

AS A CHILD, there was a confusion in my mind between King George VI and God. So when, one wintry day in February 1952, an apocalyptic rumour spread at the Rowans Nursery School in Wimbledon, my reaction was more of disbelief than horror.

I got the tale from a big girl called Mavis, the custard monitor. 'The King', she said in a portentous stage whisper, as she smothered my prunes, 'is Dead.' Rubbish! The King couldn't be dead! The teacher would soon tell Mavis off for making up stories, and ones in doubtful taste at that.

But the teacher's long face confirmed Mavis's whisper, and over the next few months we in the lower kindergarten slaved away with plastic scissors and flour-paste, filling scrapbooks with pictures of the King's coffin and then, when his mother died (a natural thing to do, we felt, in the circumstances) of Queen Mary's as well.

The period of mourning was finite. Suddenly at the beginning of 1953, the fashionable colour changed from black – redolent of the austere, drab, heavy-curtained 1940s – to red, white and blue, symbolic of the new Elizabethan age of affluence and abandon. Scrapbooks bulged with crowns and coaches, as well as family snaps of Charles and Anne, with whom every lower kindergarten tot vividly identified.

Coronation Day itself was a bit of a comedown. Billed as a sort of midsummer Christmas, it rained for most of the time, and the only excitement in Wimbledon was the desultory roasting of an ox on the Common. However, most of us got to watch a new-fangled kind of cinema in the living-room called 'television'. Flickering images of a solemn Archbishop lowering a huge and heavy crown onto the head of a beautiful young woman filled our infant imaginations, and have stayed there ever since.

The King was dead: long live the Queen! What was it all about? We did not know then, and I do not know now. I'm aware, though – as some flavour-of-the-month republicans seem not to be – of a lifelong relationship between us, the British people, and this woman and her averagely fallible family whom few of us have ever met.

Like most others in Britain (or at any rate in England) I have grown up and spent all my adult life taking for granted the psychic embrace of the strange institution embodied by the Royal Family, and can't quite envisage our nation without it.

Although I am no obsessive royal-watcher, the drip-feed of daily press coverage and bus-queue gossip means that I could easily fill in any visitor with the basic details of the Windsor dynasty for the past generation or so, and I could probably name, off the top of my head, more members of the Royal Family than of John Major's Cabinet.

So what is royalty all about? It is odd that we have only just begun to consider that question. Until a few years ago, there were stock answers to people who asked about the monarchy, though generally such people were regarded as naïve and tiresome, like children who will go on and on with questions about where babies come from.

Royalty was a wonderful pageant, it was said, and it was especially wonderful for the tourist trade. It also enabled us to have a flexible, unwritten Constitution, in contrast to those bits of paper excitable foreigners kept on writing and then tearing up.

Mainly, however, any questions about the monarchy were rather contemptuously treated as trivial. Politicians of the Right were sentimental about royalty; politicians of the Left affected indifference, except when they got their baubles. But both had more important things to discuss than a purely formal institution outside the political arena.

Yet, in retrospect, it seems that there was always an uneasy aspect to such insouciance. Maybe the monarchy was purely formal, but – throughout the long period in which it has been a no-go area for proper debate – it continued to fascinate the British public, not occasionally, but all the time.

If it was just a quaint alternative to a presidency, why should it be such a delicate topic in polite society? Above all, why did we care? Could it be, as a Freudian might suggest, that the subjects we find difficult or embarrassing are those that matter to us most?

Of course, many of the taboos surrounding royalty have long since been broken. At a modest estimate, there are 150 books about the Queen and her children, and the number is growing all the time. Moreover, the latest crop spares nobody's blushes.

You might think, therefore, that – so far from not being talked about

– the subject has been flogged to death. In fact, nearly all these books are deeply conventional, including those that follow the current fad for kiss-and-tell. Most shamelessly plagiarize each other, shamelessly make things up, or are exclusively concerned with the politics of the bedchamber.

If you are interested in sex, dukes and horses, there is certainly lots to get your teeth into. But scan the shelves for anything about our head of state's dealings with the nine premiers who have served her, her relationship with the fading British Commonwealth (or post-Maastricht Europe), her hierarchical role as the pinnacle of an outmoded aristocracy, her constitutional importance in relation to Parliament, Government and Law, her religious status as head of the Church, her inherited hold over the collective imagination of her 'subjects', who continue to regard her with honour – and you find little.

If you look for a proper discussion of the change in media and public treatment of royalty from the days when the historian John Grigg was publicly slapped for saying that the words put in the Queen's mouth by courtiers were 'schoolgirlish' to the age of Camilla's tampon and Fergie's boobs – you find virtually nothing.

Whatever the republicans may say, we in Britain are riveted by our monarchy. We peer at it through wide-angled lenses, we mock it, we identify with it, we scorn it, we love it, we even worry about it. But we never think about it, perhaps because we prefer not to think about aspects of ourselves.

Maybe for a change we should try conceiving of the monarch not only as a human being, but – for good or ill – as a vital and subtly influential part of our polity, and of our way of life.

Daily Mail, 4 September 1993

THE MYTH OF CONSENSUS

POLITICS CONTAINS FASHIONABLE words and phrases that are soon on everybody's lips, acquiring the status of instant explanation. Some quickly vanish: others linger, become universally absorbed, and gain a permanent niche in our vocabulary – shaping and perhaps distorting the way in which we view our world.

'Consensus' is one such word. It is a long-established term, but one which has gained an important place in British political parlance only during the last decade. Especially since Mrs Thatcher took office in 1979 and began to introduce major changes, the view has gained wide acceptance that British politics used to be characterized by a consensus, but that this nation-uniting mood no longer exists.

The alleged consensus has been regarded in different ways. For some, particularly on the political Right, it was disastrously mis-conceived: an ostrich-like refusal to accept hard economic facts, a wrongheaded conventional wisdom that led to the crises of the 1970s. For others, especially in the centre and centre-left of the political spectrum, the supposed consensus was the cause of much that has been good, a fertile source of progressive social and economic policy, and the basis for a more harmonious and less divided society. Whether the consensus has been villain or hero – whether its passing is celebrated or mourned – few of the writers, journalists and politicians who need to give contemporary politics a reference point doubt that it once existed.

The proper instinct of any critical observer of affairs, when con-fronted with near unanimity, is to query its assumptions. I want to consider the assumptions behind this notion of a consensus and look at the way in which the proposition that it once existed but does so no more has shaped our perceptions of political events in the twentieth century.

Consensus is Latin for agreement, and like many Latin terms, its first use in English was scientific. Physiologists spoke of a *consensus* to describe an agreement or harmony of organs of the body which had a specific purpose. In the middle of the last century, the term began to be used to refer to the body politic, but with the anatomical usage still in mind.

In the present century the physiological origin has been forgotten, and the link consciously discarded. Nevertheless, the organic metaphor remains embedded in our modern understanding of the term. 'Consensus' in political language is certainly a more powerful and emotive term than mere agreement. Consensus is said to exist not when people merely agree, but when they are happy agreeing, are not constrained to agree, and leave few of their number outside the broad parameters of their agreement. Thus in the modern – as in the old-fashioned – sense of the term, a consensus is a harmony. Further, those who are a part of it frequently share a purpose, in a way that is analogous to the common purpose of bodily organs.

Consensus generally carries with it a value element. The idea of a consensus is a positive thing – better again than mere acceptance or agreement. People seek to 'embrace', 'capture' and 'influence' the consensus, and are proud to claim possession of it. Yet it also implies freedom of choice. It would be odd to talk of consensus under a Hitler or a Stalin. Normally consensus is regarded as the product of the free flow of ideas in a liberal society where the shared attitudes of men and women may have some influence over events. Consensus is to a free country what fear is to an unfree one.

Harmony, purpose, freedom. There is no rigid definition, but there is certainly both a history and an appropriate context. The question now arises: can we pinpoint a particular, historic British consensus, cast in such terms, that goes beyond shared values about constitutional rules, and represents a temporary yet substantial unity of opinion on how major policy should proceed?

Those who have outlined such a consensus have presented a tale of narrative simplicity with a beginning, a middle and an end. It runs as follows, and we should consider its contours closely.

The origins of this consensus, according to the accepted version, are to be found in an earlier period of disunity and political strife, when agreement existed only on some basic national arrangements, such as the rule of law and the sovereignty of Crown and Parliament. Even on these, there had frequently been bitter disagreement. Up to 1914 fierce and irreconcilable divisions – over the status of Ireland, the rights of trade unions, free trade, the extension of the suffrage –

had threatened social stability. The First World War, so far from healing rifts, exacerbated them, and in the 1920s conflict over Ireland reached its bloody climax, while an angry Labour Movement challenged the power of the state. Even when a 'National' coalition was formed in 1931, it was National in little more than name, serving mainly to emphasize the depth of division. In the 1930s, political opinion was fiercely split on all major issues, and Britain remained a divided and antagonistic society, kept apart by differences of wealth, class, education, occupation and region.

Nevertheless – according to the argument I am describing – it is precisely in this period that the seeds of later agreement are to be found. The very clash of ideas provided fertile ground for conciliatory proposals aimed at bridging the gap between opposed social forces. Such, in particular, was the purpose of Maynard Keynes's *General Theory*, which advocated an expansionist solution to the rigours of the slump. Such, too, was the objective of parallel suggestions, receiving cross-party support, for measures of state planning.

From these beginnings, so it is maintained, a mighty oak soon grew. The official birthday of the 'post-war consensus' – according to true believers – was May 1940, when Winston Churchill took office at the head of a genuine coalition (in contrast to that of 1931), the most broad-based government this country has ever known. Paul Addison, author of a classic book about wartime domestic policy, *The Road to 1945*, and a leading evangelist of the consensus thesis, writes that 'in the course of time, the Coalition proved to be the greatest reforming administration since the Liberal Government of 1905–14.'[1]

Great emphasis is placed on the war years by the consensus theorists – both enthusiasts like Addison, and critics like Corelli Barnett[2] – because it is on this key period of emergency-created co-operation that their whole case rests. And there is no doubt that this *was* a remarkably innovative episode, in which politicians of all parties – as well as permanent and temporary civil servants – played a part.

The need to streamline the economy to meet the requirements of total war, the need to maintain civilian morale and give people something to work for, the red-tape-cutting dynamism which Churchill's own personality engendered: all these led to a string of reforms, on which there was undoubtedly wide agreement. During the period 1940–3, universal social security, family allowances, a root-and-branch educational reform, the main features of a national health service, a revolutionary new approach to budgetary policy, had all been placed on the agenda. At the same time, the policy goal of full employment, together with ideas about town and country planning and government intervention in industry, gained acceptance.

It is here, according to its proponents, that the British consensus theory takes off. Four events, practical and symbolic, are presented as foundation stones. The first – arguably the most important – was the pioneering 'Keynesian' Budget of Sir Kingsley Wood in 1941, the result of Maynard Keynes's direct influence in the Treasury, as economic adviser. The second was the famous Beveridge Report on Social Insurance and Allied Services in 1942 – blueprint for the welfare state. The other two both occurred in 1944, and were directed towards a post-war world already in sight. One was R. A. Butler's Education Act which raised the school-leaving age and provided free secondary education for all children, including grammar school places for a lucky minority; the other was an Employment Policy White Paper, whose full-employment goal was accepted by all three political parties.

On each of these measures, reports and statements there was some disagreement but on none (the 'consensus' historians point out) was disagreement fundamental. 'All three parties went to the polls in 1945 committed to principles of social and economic reconstruction,' writes Addison. '. . . The new consensus of the war years', he sums up, 'was positive and purposeful.'[3]

And so, according to the consensus argument, it remained. A Labour government, elected in July 1945 with Clement Attlee as Prime Minister, inherited the 'positive and purposeful' wartime consensus and proceeded to carry out many of the reforms which had been developed in principle during the coalition years, some of which were already in the administrative pipeline. Eventually defeated in the election of 1951, Labour passed on the mantle to a new look Tory Party, which quietly endorsed and even embraced them. Meanwhile, economic reconstruction and the Cold War forced both major parties to tie Britain's fate closely to that of the United States, bringing Labour and Tory foreign policies into agreement.

Here, then, we have the widely proclaimed British consensus – alternatively billed as a golden age of rising living standards, domestic and European peace, full employment and social improvement; or as locust years of spendthrift state socialism leading to national decline. The high priest of this era is often presented as Harold Macmillan, Vicky's 'Supermac', who combined in his chameleon personality old and new, ancient and modern, right and left. A crofter's grandson who married a duke's daughter, his manners were those of a grandee, but his background belonged to the progressive publishing world of Bloomsbury: Maynard Keynes had been a childhood friend, and Macmillan's pre-war book, *The Middle Way*,[4] scriptural text for the consensus-minded, helped to inject Keynesian thought into British politics.

Macmillan resigned in 1963, but – so it is generally maintained – the consensus which he led and epitomized survived him. There are different opinions about when it is supposed finally to have come to an end. Some believe that a deepening divide was already visible by the time of the 1970 election, when Edward Heath's 'Selsdon Man' proposals seemed to mark a Conservative shift to the right. For others, the turning-point was the 1973–4 miners' strike. The most decisive moment, however, is frequently seen as the 1979 election, after which Mrs Thatcher inaugurated a new kind of radical Conservatism, consciously distancing herself, not only from Labour policy, but also from past Tory practice. This allegedly consensus-breaking tilt by the Government was soon to be paralleled by Labour's tilt to the left, leading to the fissure that saw the launching of the SDP, and an enlarged centre-grouping between the (now far-apart) major party blocks.

So much for the 'consensus thesis': an inspirational union, once apparently blessed, but – in the last act – cruelly betrayed. Now we need to look at what lies behind it. The first thing to note is that, as with most historical theories, it is actually a way of commenting on the present. Thus the account of a past golden age of harmony is a way of underlining a sense of insecurity about the political debate today. Talk about the 'post-war consensus' generally crops up in the context of the argument that what we now have is a much broader spectrum of opinion, characterized by an authoritarian, anti-bureaucratic, privatizing and nationalistic Conservatism at one extreme, and a directive, union-orientated, neutralist socialism at the other.

Of course, there are aspects of the narrative that are perfectly valid. Few would deny, for instance, that 1940 was a major turning-point in domestic policy, or that a sea-change occurred in British politics during the 1970s.

It is not necessary, however, to leap from an observation of important changes in opinion and practice, to a belief in the Shangri La of a lost 'consensus': you can acknowledge the past as different, without assuming that it was less argumentative. Neither should we take for granted a lack of acrimony just because – with the passage of time – the things people *did* get heated about seem to matter less. It is certainly arguable – against the popular theory of the consensus – that genuine consensus in politics is very rare; and that, further, the so-called post-war consensus is actually a mirage, fading the more closely one tries to inspect it.

The problem is partly one of human psychology, partly of historical imagination. Any controversy in politics is bound to arouse fiercer passions while the debate is on: once it is over, even people with good memories are likely to wonder what the fuss was about, and the historian – if insufficiently alert – may be less impressed by the quarrel than by the lack of distance between rival points of view. It could be that both nostalgic and rejectionist historians – when viewing the post-war era – have fallen into this trap: in short, that they have committed the error of anachronism.

True, politicians of all parties, as well as civil servants and academic writers, were profoundly influenced by the giant figures of William Beveridge and Maynard Keynes. It is also true that the Right in British politics is less deferential towards the ideas of these thinkers than was true of many leading Conservatives twenty or thirty years ago. But this scarcely proves the previous existence of a 'consensus'.

One reason for increased criticism of Beveridge and Keynes is simply that they spoke to a different age: their remedies were offered as solutions to problems that no longer present themselves in the same way. Such criticism comes, of course, from Left as well as Right, as people of all kinds try to come to terms with a world in which old principles – for example those which used to provide full employment – no longer seem to operate. As modern practitioners and thinkers distance themselves from earlier approaches, there is a tendency to think in terms of a past unity. Yet this is incorrect.

Neither Beveridge, nor Keynes, nor any of the other leading theorists and policy-makers of their time offered anything that could be regarded as a gospel. There was never a body of literature that constituted a sacred text, never an orthodoxy towards which dutiful political leaders or officials could guide the ship of state. Neither Beveridge nor Keynes was a Marx or a Lenin, their suggestions were only gradually accepted, and never in their entirety.

The old Treasury, wedded to classical economics and the 'saving of candle-ends' philosophy of William Gladstone, fought a staunch rearguard action against the radical monetary and fiscal plans of Keynes, who continued to arouse deep suspicion, both on the left of the Labour Party, which rightly saw Keynesianism as an alternative to socialism, and on the Tory Right. 'Butskellism' was the sardonic term coined by *The Economist* to describe the alleged continuity between the economic policies of Labour's Hugh Gaitskell and his Tory successor at the Treasury, R. A. Butler. The use of the word, however, certainly did not indicate a consensus. Rather, it was a term of abuse, a sign of a widespread disapproval which was harmful to the reputations of both men.

Like Keynes, Beveridge was a Liberal whose ideas married well with Fabian socialist thought. Not every socialist supported Beveridge: one fierce critic of the 1942 Beveridge Report was Ernest Bevin, the trade union leader and wartime Minister of Labour. Nevertheless, the 1945 Labour Government took up the Report as its own, and implemented or adapted many of its proposals, which embodied the principle of universality in the provision of state benefits. Conservatives subsequently accepted what Labour had done, and no government (not even the present one) has ever ventured to advocate the abolition of the welfare state. Yet the notion that Tory paternalists had as much to do with extending the social role of the state as Labour welfarists, is folklore of the kind disseminated by Conservative Central Office at election time, or by Marxists keen to discredit the 'bourgeois' Labour Party. Few political battles have been as bitter as Nye Bevan's fight with the Tory-backed doctors over the creation of the Health Service. Few ideological strands have been as consistent as the Tories' hostility towards treating the 'undeserving poor' – latterly renamed 'welfare scroungers' – with generosity. Conservative opposition to the principles of universality, always latent, became increasingly vocal from the mid 1960s – almost a quarter of a century before Mrs Thatcher came to power.[5]

It is easy to take for granted hard-won reforms, and to forget how bitterly they were contested at the time. When one policy triumphs over another, it is tempting to regard the change as inevitable, and as part of a progressive, consensual evolution. Yet the reality of radical reform is that it has seldom come without a fight.

Take, for instance, the wartime coalition, that great reforming administration whose spirit of co-operation supposedly gave rise to the post-war consensus. We need not dispute the importance for domestic policy of the initiatives of the 1940–5 period in order to observe that the public amity of Churchill's Government masked deep ideological conflicts. Few proposals were the subject of more bitter inter-party disputes than those of Sir William Beveridge – proposals that were regarded by some Tory leaders as a perilous hostage to fortune, and by most of the Labour Party as a banner to fight under. For a time, there was a serious possibility that the coalition might break up.

Tensions that had existed between wartime ministerial partners, yet had been hushed up because of the political truce, surfaced as soon as Labour withdrew from the Government following the defeat of Hitler. No election has been fought more ferociously, or with more immoderate language, than that of 1945 – in which Churchill accused Labour of plotting to set up a 'gestapo', as serious an allegation, within weeks of the opening of the death camps, as it is possible to imagine.

'Thank God for the civil service,' King George VI is supposed to have said, when the result of the poll was known. Labour's assumption of power was marked by continuity, not by upheaval, and this has encouraged a later belief that the important measures which followed were the product of a 'consensus' rather than of socialism. A reading of the press at the time will swiftly banish such a notion. Tory opposition in Parliament was initially weak, partly because of the surprising scale of Labour's victory. Yet Labour's programme was fiercely resisted and furiously resented. The progressive and egalitarian taxation policies and low interest rate policy of the Labour Chancellor, for example, particularly outraged the City of London.

Take, too, the allegedly Butskellite 1950s, when Conservative Chancellors continued some of the policies established by their Labour predecessors. Here there was agreement of a kind between the two front benches and the Treasury, though scarcely amounting to a 'consensus'. Huge differences between the parties remained. There was certainly no element of me-tooism about Anthony Crosland's impassioned plea for greater social equality, *The Future of Socialism*, which was published in 1956 and conceived, not as a statement for the middle-of-the-road and the consensus-minded, but as a radical alternative to prevailing Tory attitudes.

What about followers, as distinct from leaders? Did they at least share a 'consensus'? The American scholar, Samuel Beer, in his book *Britain Against Itself*, argues that consensus existed in the 1950s and 1960s because 'party government had given rise to an agreement on the common good which, to be sure, fell far short of unanimity, but which did accomplish the aggregation of the preferences of a large majority of the electorate.'[6] Yet even this is far from clear. Indeed we may go further. Whatever lines of continuity or discontinuity may have existed at the top, ordinary voters appear to have been *more* divided during the period of the so-called consensus than since its supposed termination.

In an age of agreement, even of agreement that fell short of unanimity, it would be reasonable to expect the electorate to care little which party held office. Consensus-mindedness might also seem conducive to the growth of a centre party, which could best express the shared values, and lack of partisanship, of much of the nation. In fact, throughout the key years of the supposed consensus, rigid loyalty to one major party or the other was the norm, and switching the exception, while the third (and most consensus-minded) party was at its most insignificant. Opinion shifted little from one general election to the next. From 1950 to 1970 the Conservative vote was never outside the range 43.5– 49.5 per cent, or the Labour vote outside 43–49. This tranquillity – in contrast to the volatility of voting behaviour before the war, or of the last decade and a half – has been offered as evidence of consensus. A moment's thought will show that it is the reverse. Sandbagged in their electoral trenches, the early post-war voters can be seen as the anonymous infantry of two implacably opposed armies in an era of adversarial politics, with the middle-way Liberals floundering in no man's land.

It may of course be argued that the electoral preferences of citizens reflect culture and class rather than discriminating policy choices and hence the refusal of voters to vary their allegiances is quite compatible with a basic agreement, across party lines, on the issues of the day. This is a difficult case to sustain, however. On the one hand, it is surely contradictory to claim voters for the consensus, while discounting their behaviour at the ballot box. On the other hand, social and cultural loyalties (identification with a class, in particular) were just as important before the Second World War, when voters were much more fickle in their loyalties, as after it.

But the greatest problem for the consensus theory is in defining the essence of the consensus itself, that ghostly cloak which, we are assured, encompassed our national life through happy or wastrel years. I began by discussing the origins and usage of the term 'consensus', and then examined the topography of the supposed British one. Yet what, even notionally, does the terrain amount to? The British post-war consensus could be defined, not entirely flippantly, as the product of a consensus among historians about those political ideas that should be regarded as important, and hence to be used as touchstones of the consensus. Neither is it irrelevant to consider the political orientation of those historians from whom the consensus thesis is derived. Some – the rejectionists – bolster their sympathy for modern Conservatism by contrasting it with the alleged compromises of the past. Others, probably the majority, display towards the kind of policy package they choose to label 'consensus' a shamelessly sentimental yearning.

According to both groups of writers, we now live in a post-consensus age, in which a 'monetarist' Conservative Party is confronted by the 'collectivist' forces of Labour. Many instances of division are cited to illustrate the recent 'breakdown of consensus'. Yet we may wonder whether in future, when the dust has settled, division will appear so much sharper than before. To take the most obvious comparison: if it was a Tory Chancellor, Kingsley Wood, who opened the first Keynesian Budget in 1941, it was a Labour Chancellor, Denis Healey, who was responsible for the first monetarist Budget in 1976, three years before Mrs Thatcher took office. The monetarist/collectivist distinction possibly made some sense at the beginning of the 1980s, after Labour's lurch to the left. With contemporary Labour leaders seeking to outdo each other in their eagerness to abandon public ownership and to minimize central economic direction, the distinction can scarcely be given much credence today. It would be surprising if all of the new principles and practices established at the Treasury in the years of Howe and Lawson were to be abandoned when a non-Conservative administration eventually comes to power.

What will the consensus-hunters of the future find to say about the late 1980s? Much more, I would wager, than it is yet easy to perceive. Distance makes it possible to look beyond the emotion and the invective, and see prevailing attitudes which, because shared and uncontentious, do not hit the headlines and may not even be noticed at the time. But this is not to say that the visible differences – some of which are harsh and desperate – are not real.

The same may be true of the period after the Second World War. Then, as now, events were as much determined by dispute as by co-operation. In short, 'consensus' is a handy piece of jargon, with a pleasant ring, to describe a time when we were all younger, more eager or more foolish. But whether it will survive as a term for a discrete episode in British history – instead of joining other phrases in the dustbin of historiography – is to be doubted.

> This essay, based on a Channel Four television lecture, was first published in *The Making of Britain: Echoes of Greatness*, ed. Lesley M. Smith (Macmillan, 1988)

NOTES

1. P. Addison, *The Road to 1945: British Politics and the Second World War* (Jonathan Cape, 1977), p. 14.
2. See C. Barnett, *The Audit of War* (Papermac, 1987).
3. Addison, op. cit., p. 14.
4. H. Macmillan, *The Middle Way: A Study of the Problem of Economic and Social Progress in a Free and Democratic Society* (E.P. Publishing, 1938).
5. D. Kavanagh, *Thatcherism and British Politics: The End of Consensus?* (Oxford University Press, 1987), p. 46.
6. S. H. Beer, *Britain Against Itself: The Political Contradictions of Collectivism* (Faber & Faber, 1982), p. 9.

PART IV

The Last Party of Karl Marx

A JOURNAL OF THE
PORTUGUESE REVOLUTION

THE PORTUGUESE REVOLUTION of 1974–6 was the last spontaneous upheaval in Europe – perhaps in the world – that drew
inspiration from Marx, Engels and the Bolsheviks. At the time, it
felt like the start of something new, not an ending. This was not
wholly an illusion, for the fall of the *ancien régime* in Lisbon had
an undoubted world importance. The upheaval in metropolitan
Portugal rapidly terminated long-running colonial wars in Guinea-
Bissau, Angola and Mozambique. From then on, the days of white
minority rule in Rhodesia and South Africa were numbered.

In Portugal itself, the revolution paved the way for a European
destiny, as a signatory to the Rome Treaty. Such an outcome,
however, was far from apparent during the carnival months that
followed the collapse of the old dictatorship. There was no easy
transition to democracy: as one provisional government followed
another, each more radical than its predecessor, the possibility
that Portugal might become a kind of west European Cuba looked
real – not least to the United States and its allies, including Britain,
which exerted what influence they could to back the anti-
communist Socialist Party (PS) led by Mario Soares.

The revolution began on 25 April 1974, when a group of military officers carried out a successful 'captains' revolt', toppling the
government of Marcello Caetano and ending almost half a century
of right-wing authoritarian rule. There followed the 'revolution
of flowers', as freedom exploded on the streets of Lisbon and
other cities, and hundreds of thousands of refugees (*retornados*)
from Angola and Mozambique poured into a country ill-equipped
to cope with them. Remarkably, there was almost no bloodshed.
Until the end of 1975, however, Portugal seemed close to civil
war. In March of that year, an attempt to stem the leftward tide
with a counter-coup backfired, and the shift to the left accelerated:
banks were nationalized, and much of the media came under the
control of the communist-leaning régime.

In reality, the Communist Party (PCP) never acquired full

control even of the shaky administrations that tried to maintain a semblance of order during the 'hot summer' of 1975, and in August and September the tide began to recede. The Socialist Party now began to gain some ground. Yet there remained a gap between leadership and base, and confusion became intense.

In the sixth provisional government, led by Admiral Pinheiro de Azevedo, the Socialists had a bigger role than in the fourth or fifth. But the Government itself seemed to be losing the last shreds of legitimacy, as Lisbon fell prey to the rival claims of different sections of the armed forces and their commanders, and of the innumerable factions of the revolutionary Left. Meanwhile, there was a constant danger of a coup from the anti-democratic Right, in the name of discipline and order. It was a time of daily marches, organized by a plethora of political parties and involving industrial workers, peasants, tenants from the slums, soldiers who had formed their own committees (the so-called 'SUVs' – 'Soldiers United will Win'); also of leaflets, pamphlets, slogans, graffiti, people camping in hotels, revolutionary murals, music, gaiety and fear.

Portugal became a mecca for media people, political activists and revolutionary groupies from all over the world. Possibly I fell into all these categories. I spent several months in Lisbon in 1975–6, with the help of some university leave, and the indulgent editors of two or three progressive publications in Britain, who took my articles. Mainly I lived in Hotel Universo, a cheap, well-placed *pensão* overlooking Rossio Square, where the biggest demonstrations took place. It was here that foreign television crews lay in a state of vulture-like readiness for any scuffle or argument that threatened to get out of hand, in order to satisfy the demands of their employers for evidence that a left-wing upheaval must be violent. I was fascinated and exhilarated by the atmosphere in an ancient city newly liberated and apparently discovering itself. I kept a diary during a seven-week stay in October and November 1975 – the revolution's most anarchic phase, before the final crunch came.

Sunday 5 October 1975: My plane is only two hours late. The hotel is full of bewildered and anxious Angolan refugees, billeted by the Government. The cost of a room is up 60 per cent since July.

Monday 6 October: Get press credentials at the Ministry of Social Communications. A large Texan in a strange check suit declaims: 'Call this a credential?' He says that when the Spanish Embassy was burnt down last week, a soldier ignored his pass and poked a sub-machine gun in his belly. I learn of a Copcon (left-wing military police) move to prevent radio and television broadcasting 'inflammatory' statements and supporting ultra-left-aligned *deficientes* (disabled army veterans) who had occupied key positions in Lisbon – including bridges, and the National Assembly – as a protest.

Tuesday 7 October: Go to the President's Palace to talk to members of the Angolan Office about refugees, and interview a melancholy colonel who has an impressive grasp of marxist theory. 300,000 people have come back from Africa, he says, most of them in the last two months. Now many want to return, but the Government won't let them. I am given a lift by an elegant bearded official who I met briefly in July, who speaks good English with a cavalry accent, and claims to be a member of ex-MES (an intellectual leftist splinter group). He believes the next government will be right-wing. Where did he learn his English? I ask. 'I was at school in England,' he says, adding with a smile, 'but I keep quiet about that now.' Which school? 'Charterhouse,' he replies.

In the afternoon, I visit a 'moderate' friend – Alfredo Duarte Costa – at the Ministry of Foreign Affairs. When I last saw him in July, there had been rumours that Melo Antunes (a pro-Socialist-Party member of the powerful Revolutionary Council of the Armed Forces Movement (MFA)) was about to be arrested. Now Antunes is Foreign Minister, and Alfredo is much more relaxed. But the situation is very tense, he says, with everybody in the Government very jumpy about the extreme Left. He strongly supports the Government controls on the media. 'It is necessary to have some discipline, and sadly, some repression may be needed,' he says.

Wednesday 8 October: Talk to somebody at the Socialist Party headquarters who describes his own party's rise from almost nothing before the coup to 38 per cent in the April elections and more than 50 per cent now, according to some polls. He argues that communist tactics backfired: after the coup, the communists were the most popular party but they overplayed their hand, using their power in the economic sector of government to gain posts at local level, and in the banks, where their level of support did not justify it. Hence there was a reaction against them, made worse by shortages, and now they are fighting to survive.

Later, I visit IARN (an agency for Angolan refugees), but I can't get past the crowd of clients in the outer office, and so go to the headquarters of the Popular Democrats (PPD – a centre-right party) instead. Here a young, quiet, highly intelligent aide to the Party Leader, Sá Carneiro, claims a contrast between the 'social democratic' policies of the PPD, and its electoral base, which is essentially Catholic and conservative. While we are talking, he is called out of the office, there is much agitated talk next door, and he returns saying that a rally of Intersindical (the communist-run trade union federation) is to be used as an excuse for insurrectionary violence: extreme-left groups, with tacit communist support, are bringing large numbers of people up from Alentejo in the south, armed with shotguns. They fear an attack on PPD headquarters, and they are alerting their own 'militants' to ward off such an attack.

I go to the Intersindical rally at Campino Grande (Lisbon's bull-ring) half-expecting to see a wild mob. Instead, there are peasants in traditional costume, transported in tractor-drawn carts. Many are very old, and most (from their clothes) seem very poor. They chant their way into the arena, to loud applause. There are lengthy speeches. Banners say things like 'Workers of Philipe for the Socialist Revolution', 'The Vasco Goncalves farm-workers co-operative of Monte-moro-o-Novo', and 'Workers of Standard Electric – present'. There are songs, and some cheerful, spontaneous dancing. The peasants pile back into their carts and roll off into the night, and the urban workers peacefully stream out towards the tube.

Tuesday 14 October: While waiting to talk to an amiable PCP leader at the communist headquarters in Rua Serpa, I eavesdropped a group of middle-aged English ladies talking about hotels, the weather, what was in the shops. They were from the British CP.

I also talked (too briefly) to a stunningly pretty, beautifully dressed, girl of 18 or so – a kind of delicate blossom – who spoke English almost without an accent and had done A Levels at Eastbourne College. On politics, she was humourlessly rigid, talking the usual stuff about 'the reactionaries' and making me feel as if I was obviously one of them. She took me to a couple of more relaxed communist students, both in Lisbon University's Law Faculty, now in the possession of the MRPP (Movement for the Reorganization of the Party of the Proletariat – a fundamentalist Maoist sect). They claimed that the MRPP was CIA-funded and 'fascist'. One of them, a young woman in her third year, described the state of chaos in the Faculty, with far more students being awarded degrees than had actually studied there.

Tonight I wrote to a left-wing friend in London, fed up with the Labour Party, saying why she should not become a communist. The strongest argument (and today's experiences confirm it) is that to join a party like that involves deciding to educate yourself into not having an open mind.

The young girl haunts me in a way. It is partly the pretty face: but somehow it seemed very sad, especially in such a male-dominated organization – the amiable communist leader, so charming and helpfully efficient towards me, was brusque and commanding (in my presence) towards her. I wondered why, from her evidently very bourgeois background (and with no attempt to change out of very bourgeois clothes), she chose the PCP. An interesting aspect of the situation here. I must get round the left-wing groups.

Wednesday 15 October: Lunch with Fritz Caspari, the German ambassador, and his American wife Elita, in their suburban residence. I met him at the embassy, and as we drove, I remarked that when I had been at the British Embassy recently there were builders hard at work making it look like a sheriff's lock-up in a Western. 'We are doing the same,' he said. 'We are concerned about our own anarchists more than anything.' As we passed the quayside, we saw mountainous piles of luggage, which he said came from Luanda.

Fritz's view is that unless discipline is restored in the army, there will be civil war. He is very much in the 'What it's all about is keeping the communists at bay' camp, as befits his position. On Alvaro Cunhal (the PCP general secretary), he says that he seems to be seeking contacts with social democratic parties and countries. Fritz shares my view that the Soviet attitude is very ambivalent – they don't want to be embarrassed by the PCP being too successful. Fritz is himself very engaged and knowledgeable, though less so (perhaps not surprisingly) about the complex politics of the ultra Left.

I finally made contact with the famous Jane Bergerol (Lisbon correspondent of the *Financial Times*) this evening. She confirmed my expectations that she would be snooty and offhand, but softened a bit when I mentioned Steven Lukes (Politics Fellow at Balliol, who had recently visited Lisbon and written an article about it in the *New Statesman*). She suggested lunch next Tuesday, and would I ring to confirm as she was very busy, etc.

Coming back to the hotel, I ran into a march – very working class, and apparently PCP-inspired. They chanted 'Viva Classa Operaria' and 'Vittoria', both of which are pretty all-purpose and it wasn't clear what their aim was. I think they were from Setubal (a major industrial district).

Thursday 16 October: It occurs to me that the further right you go in Portuguese politics, the more people are inclined to accept the standard *Time* magazine line that all the parties of the extreme Left are in league with the communists, and being used by them. But the further left you go, the more you discover that this is utterly untrue, and that the far Left's tragedy in Portugal (as elsewhere) is its tendency to splinter into factions which regard their quarrels with each other as more important than their joint quarrel with the Right. The FUR (United Revolutionary Front) – with which, however, the PCP swiftly broke off relations – has been one attempt to provide left-wing unity, and so far it has held together. Outside FUR, however, are the Maoists: and they are quite as concerned with their own internecine warfare as with anything else. Of course, all the Maoist groups are hostile to the PCP, which they jointly consider 'social fascist'. But there is also a deep quarrel between the two main Maoist bodies, the UDP (Popular Democratic Union) and the MRPP. Last week, the battle between them reached the stage of a shoot-out (much to the PCP's gratification), following an incident in which UDP militants pushed some MRPP militants, who they caught sticking up posters, into the river, and one drowned. This unfortunate has now joined the sainted company of MRPP martyrs – his photo is everywhere – and the MRPP is calling the UDP 'Hitlerite' and 'Pide-esque', i.e. equivalent to the hated secret police, the PIDE, under the old régime. Yet to the layman, the only political difference between the two groups is that UDP is less hostile to tactical alliances with the 'social fascist' communists, while the MRPP is prepared to make tactical alliances with the Socialists.

Meanwhile, the *retornados* have more serious things than the odd misadventure on their minds. I spoke to a leading member of one of the self-help refugee agencies who said bitterly: 'When a handful of Spanish anarchists are executed, the world holds up its hands in horror. Ambassadors are withdrawn, pressure is put on Franco's Government. Yet on the streets of Luanda, I have seen, with my own eyes, dozens of people killed, and I know of thousands who have been slaughtered. It is genocide. Yet the world says nothing. Why?' One answer is that 'Spain' is still internationally emotive because of fascism, while –

among liberal-minded people, at least – the problems of white-settler Angolans pluck few heart-strings. Yet they remain the wretched victims of events over which they have no control, and pose the biggest refugee problem Europe has had to face since the aftermath of the Second World War. Imagine the crisis if the entire Protestant population of Northern Ireland, plus all the whites in Rhodesia, were forced to flee to England, all arriving within the space of a few months? That is the scale of the difficulty here, and the Government has a revolution to cope with, to boot.

Friday 17 October: This morning I talked to one of the founders of another refugee organization, which operated from a back room. He was angrily racist: 'The blacks are not human. They are animals. They are like apes – the only difference is that apes can't talk,' and so on. He was a lawyer by training.

After lunch, I went to the Ministry of Social Affairs and asked a helpful woman if I could arrange to see the minister responsible for the *retornado* problem. She said that would be all right, but the Secretary of State for Refugees had only been appointed this morning, and he was rather busy: did I mind waiting ten minutes, when he would be free? This is typical Portugal – you can barge into anybody's office, and they have nothing better to do than to be interviewed. He turned out to be a young, good-looking, nervous PPD lawyer, who hadn't yet learnt the ropes. Afterwards, the helpful woman told me her own story, which had a familiar ring to it. She had been brought into the office in January by a previous minister: she had the useful credential of three days in prison (for joining a cultural co-operative) under the fascist régime. She said that in the ministry, only the heads of departments, on the whole, were kicked out after the coup – 'apart from PIDE'. On the communists, she said it had to be admitted that they had fought hardest against the fascists. 'But then they became so triumphalist, and people found this irritating and now nobody could stand them.'

Then to the Ministry of Foreign Affairs to see Alfredo, on the off chance that he might still arrange a trip to Luanda, and he says he will try this. He says things are deteriorating, but if the Government lasts four weeks, it will be all right. If not, there will be a right-wing dictatorship. 'I can't see a seventh government working,' he says. Where *are* the fascists? I asked. Everywhere, he says. He thinks the communists would not mind a right-wing takeover: they could go underground and start again. A right-wing coup might come from Coimbra troops, led by General Charais. He thinks a left-wing coup could only last a day or two.

In the evening, I went to the cinema – a sort of baroque temple of capitalism – in the Avenida de Liberdade, to watch Clint Eastwood being macho in some forgettable Hollywood trash. A large, mainly young, audience enjoyed it hugely.

Tuesday 21 October: A quaintly pompous little note arrives at the hotel from the Counsellor at the British Embassy, inviting me to drinks – very different style from Fritz's informality. Clearly, though, Fritz has put the British onto me, and I am not considered grand enough for the ambassador.

A fruitless afternoon trying to speak to Mario Soares at the Assembly. I bumped into the bearded Carthusian who said, 'You should be in for some light amusement in the next two or three days – things will be getting hotter,' and referred vaguely to a forthcoming extreme-left demo. Back at the hotel, the refugees in the lobby were talking ceaselessly about politics.

Wednesday 22 October: At the instigation of the helpful Ministry of Social Affairs lady, Ana Vicente, I met a women's magazine editor called Maria João, who helps out as a volunteer with one of the refugee agencies. Pretty, young, confident, perfect English. She says that many of the older *retornados* are virtually illiterate and their papers have been filled in by others. Many are very poor. She recalls her shock and surprise on visiting Luanda for the first time, when she saw that the shoeshine boys were white. She says she is touched by the number of men she deals with at the refugee centre who arrive with black or mixed-race women, who they have brought out of Angola with them. One said: 'a wife that's good enough in Africa is good enough for me here.' She says she was very non-political before the coup, but supports the Socialists now. Under the old régime, it was easy to get along if you accepted things: though you had to be careful about friends who *were* implicated in underground activities. She says people were much more hostile towards Caetano – an opportunist – than towards Salazar, who really believed in his self-created myths.

I have arranged to see the British Counsellor, called Ure, at 6.30 p.m. tomorrow which is a drag because of the extreme-left demo at 7.30.

Thursday 23 October: At the Assembly, in search of the elusive Soares, I am able to watch the new deputies (elected in the first free elections, in April) strolling around for all the world as if they had been there for twenty years, and with all the tricks: the false smiles, the darting eyes, the hail-fellows-well-met, the trying to talk to, and keep on the right side of, several people at the same time, the young ones in their dapper suits, the old ones with their looks of deep wisdom. A kind of caricature in miniature of the House of Commons. And such a magnificent building, for fifty years without a function, and now with very little.

Instead of lunch, I go with Maria João to her refugee centre, and talk to a youngish man who left Luanda last month. For him, he says, as for most others, Portugal is a foreign country: until September, he had never been there. He had been affiliated to the marxist MPLA in Angola, believing that they would be least racist of the Angolan revolutionary movements – but this turned out to be wrong. 'There is no future for whites in Africa,' he says. Maria says she doubts if there is much future for *her* in Portugal, and thinks she and her husband may go to Canada if things don't settle down. She longs for a normal life: 'Quite frankly, I don't mind too much what happens provided we get back to normality.' Clearly many, if not most, people feel the same. She says she is thoroughly bourgeois: 'I admit it. I think Portugal is a bourgeois country.' I say what about the need for elementary welfare services – there are more beggars in Lisbon than I have seen anywhere. She says: 'There are more now than ever there were before, and people are commenting on it.'

Off to the diplomat called Ure and his wife Caroline, who was 'brought up in Ireland' (i.e. English ascendancy Ireland) and looks and sounds it. They live in a kind of apartment-palace in Rua do Sacramenta a Lapa, with dozens and dozens of the most beautiful rooms. While we are talking, he suddenly says to Caroline: 'Darling, come and look at the sunset,' and out we all go onto the verandah ('We have parties here on Boxing Day') and there is indeed a fine sky, with a view of the river and ships, with ancient multi-coloured trees in the foreground.

They are both professionally charming and polite, and if I was writing a novel or casting for a film, exactly as I would imagine a British diplomat of middle rank and his wife to be like. Intelligent but firmly not intellectual, good at putting you at your ease, with just a glint of wariness: it only occurred to me afterwards that, actually, he wasn't the slightest bit interested in what I had to say, and that many of his questions were really designed to see whether I was some kind of communist, or had communist links (he became suddenly alert when I told him that I had had an exclusive interview with Alvaro Cunhal, *à deux*). There was a curious kind of game in which he affected left-wing attitudes to see if I'd bite. I am not very subtle about this kind of thing, and after a whisky and a half there wasn't much I was holding back and we got on pretty well. But all the time, pump, pump. His own views about people were cast in social, cocktail-party terms. Soares is 'terribly nice' and 'doesn't want to hurt people' and 'the best horse in the race', but he is also impressed by Cunhal, I think genuinely: though his illustration of this concerned Cunhal's alleged sense of humour, as displayed to Caroline at some party or other. He also told the story (which I first heard from Fritz, and so is going the diplomatic rounds) about Cunhal going to a South Korean rather than a North Korean reception by mistake, and only realizing his error once he got there. Apparently 'he behaved just as he ought', i.e. as if he were an English gentleman.

The Ures have been here three years, and didn't think Caetano too bad, the PIDE apart. They said he was quite popular, and when he came back from a foreign trip in the summer of 1973, a crowd of 200,000 turned up at the airport to cheer him. Caroline said she didn't see much poverty.

All in all a strangely seductive evening. I never know where I stand with that kind of person. Am I at heart with them or against them? There is a common language, but also huge areas of mutual non-comprehension. But it is interesting to see the sort of people the Labour Government picks to represent itself abroad . . .

On to the much-heralded demonstration, which was something of a douche. But it was also a bit anti-climactic – thirty or forty thousand people, but dwindling by the time it got to Rossio and the boring speeches started: there was a feeling of having seen it all before. It ended up as a disorganized rabble, chanting 'MPLA, MPLA' – a deliberate (and slightly disgusting) slight to the many *retornados* who hang around the square, many watching from hotel balconies. After a bit somebody in a passing car yelled out and there was a kind of gasp, and then a fat demonstrator with a loud hailer said through it, 'Don't react to provocation' and nobody did. Within five or ten minutes the last few hundred dispersed. It didn't seem like a great display of strength. Going towards the lorries and buses, the peasants and workers from out of town were much taken by the news-stands with their displays of porn. I noticed one mag with a cover showing ladies doing naughty things to each other, apparently illustrating a story called 'Fim de Semana em Yorkshire'.

Saturday 25 October: I was writing at my table this afternoon when I was disturbed by two shots from the square – apparently from some military police. I went down, and a great, disorderly throng appeared – no organized demo, this – composed of *retornados*. Some of them were holding up tatty MPLA posters, and a crude placard which read 'Morte a Coutinho' (a pro-communist member of the Revolutionary Council). Twice round Rossio they went, chanting 'Abaixo MPLA!' People standing or sitting in the cafés clapped and cheered. Then they made a bonfire out of the posters and burnt them. There was more cheering and shouting and the crowd (really a mob) turned to the group of mainly very young and nervous military police, physically pressing up against them. The soldiers (about twenty of them) flicked at the safety catches of their rifles. In the end, they climbed into armoured cars and drove off midst jeers and catcalls. A minor incident, but its spontaneity was frightening – these were refugees who had been standing round in sullen resentment and then some argument, or action, sparked it off. Watching crowd dynamics in Rossio is indeed an education: a shout, a wave, a tussle can bring people around in no time, and then the size of the group attracts more people, and more still run over. On this occasion, there was a sense of *everybody wanting something to happen* and following up, with a mixture of curiosity and involvement, the possibility that it might.

Thursday 30 October: On Monday I had lunch with Jane Bergerol of the *FT*, who greatly impressed me – her knowledge and understanding made me feel humble. A big, neurotic woman, both shy and aggressive, with fine features. She was friendly and we talked for two-and-a-half hours. She knows people all over the place and has a very detailed feeling of what is going on. She agrees that most of what is reported in the British press is bad. My only negative thought was that by concentrating too much on plots and plotters she has too conspiratorial a view. But she thinks the days of the extreme-left groups are over. Her own position is a sort of left PS (Socialist Party) – and very anti-PPD. She says that the kind of people PPD selected for its candidate lists was very different from that of PS, which explains their different constituencies. She has a sort of journalist's view of the Centre Social Democrats (CDS – the most right-wing major party) – 'people who sit round the pool in Estoril saying "Down with the communists"'. She says that the current joke about the PRP-BR (Revolutionary Brigades – a far-left, semi-anarchist group) is that everything it starts, the communists move in and take over, e.g. the SUVs.

Friday 31 October: I managed to get Soares today – he was so tired (or bored) during the interview that he fell asleep, which is what I am about to do.

Sunday 2 November: In the stair-well at the hotel today, what I knew in theory, but hadn't seen – a man reading aloud a letter to a comfortable-looking, middle-aged lady of mixed race. She clearly couldn't read it herself.

This afternoon I went to see Graham and Sonia Levett in the apartment in the suburb of Algès. They knew Jean (my girlfriend) at Essex University: she is Portuguese *haute bourgeoise*, teaches at the music academy and is a music critic for one of the new papers; he teaches English at Lisbon University. They think that the sixth government will last a long time, 'more than a year'. Graham repeats a joke I have already heard: that the reason *Diário de Noticias* (a leading Lisbon daily, once a bastion of the fascist régime) is more expensive than the other papers is that they have to pay for the translation from the Russian.

I asked about the rich and what has been happening to them: clearly Sonia's family falls roughly into this category. I got a curious speech about how the very rich were OK, it was the 'upper-middle' people – those worth half a million pounds or so – who had been really hit. Palaces, apparently, are going for a song. Sonia's music school has just bought one for two thousand contos (*c*. £30,000) – it has twenty rooms. Another one they considered is going for £100,000, a drop in value (Sonia reckons) from a pre-1974 value of £500,000. The reason, of course, is that the owners want to sell before they get either expropriated or occupied. They were also full of a tale about a gypsy they had just met who took them to his house which contained a large fortune in antiques – he had been buying up stuff from the rich who had gone abroad. Apparently (so they say) a major British auctioneers is tacitly involved in the trade. Meanwhile, the 'middle rich' are dispatching offspring to live in second homes, to prevent squats. The big rich are mainly in Rio, Paris, London.

I put to them that Portugal is the first real revolutionary offspring of 1968: it is possible to trace the links, from the international student upheaval of that year, which helped spark the revolutionary movements in Lisbon, which in turn influenced young army officers, leading to the coup and what has followed. One theme we pursued was the extent to which the revolution is fundamentally bourgeois – in the sense that the leaders of nearly all the key groups are, themselves, bourgeois. It is noteworthy that the top men in all four major parties, from the communists on the left to CDS on the right, are lawyers educated at Lisbon University's Law Faculty.

As I write this (around midnight) a bearded man looking rather like the hippie poet Ginsberg is keeping up a monotonic, megaphonic speech just outside in Rossio, where workers for *Seculo* (a newspaper) have occupied editorial offices in protest at PCP domination of the news: though apparently, as far as I can tell, their criticism comes from an ultra-left position.

Graham said he had been reading Orwell: 'Revolutions always fail. They just fail in different ways,' or words to that effect. He talked about Lisbon's version of Newspeak. He gave examples: apart from 'social fascism' and 'neo-revisionism' – (after a brief pause, Ginsberg has started up again) – he mentioned 'integrated into the revolutionary process', which everybody has to be. It is also amusing the way the sects always put 'C' for communist in inverted commas when referring to the other sects. Thus the Maoists never refer to the PCP but always to the P'C'P. Graham says a student in one of his literature classes asked if he could submit a paper on 'fascism and social fascism in twentieth-century Portuguese poetry'!

Tuesday 4 November: Things seem to be moving towards some kind of big clash on or around 11 November. There is a sense of polarization in the city. A couple of nights ago, another minor mob of 'Abaixo MPLA' people passed my window: tonight there has been a communist rally of pro-MPLA sympathy.

It is curious that everybody – even anti-leftists – acknowledges the dominance of Marxist thinking. Yesterday I spoke to a PPD International Committee man who was very keen to identify the Popular Democrats as a Left party (the Left, of course, thinks of it as semi-fascist). 'We have very good relations with the British Labour Party,' he said, and claimed that the PPD Youth Organization sees itself as Marxist. I pointed out that the nature of PPD voting support is incompatible with socialist pretensions – but it is an interesting feature that it does have these pretensions. 'We are with the revolutionary process,' says this bloke, solemnly.

A note on *beggars*. There are a lot, and their number seems to grow. When I have breakfast at a café in the square, they queue up. There are two or three women with kids – one is very pregnant. Another is very young, and bangs the table aggressively. There is also a horde of street arabs – little boys and girls, sometimes a small girl carrying an even smaller child. The pregnant woman hovers when you buy a newspaper, in the hope that you will donate the change. There is also a very gnarled old lady. There are people who pretend to sell, like the lottery-ticket salesmen, and the candle tout, who yells the same thing, in a curious hollow cry, ten thousand times a day. There is a blind beggar, and another young woman and child who squats on the pavement outside the hotel. Up the hill, a man is usually standing at the street corner with his withered leg exposed. Then there is the man in the invalid carriage with two fat, podgy, naked stumps. Finally, there is 'the neck' – a man who, from a distance, looks as if he has a huge, scarlet rubber tyre around him, but who turns out, as you approach, to be suffering from some ghastly glandular complaint or cancer which makes his neck, literally, trail to his knees. All these are within fifty or a hundred yards of this hotel, in central Lisbon. The notable thing is how quickly one gets used to it and takes it completely for granted. I practically never give anything to any of them.

Wednesday 5 November: Guy Fawkes Night – and the weather here is still like an English June, sunny all day, mild and windless, except for an occasional light breeze.

I got to see Rui Machete, the PPD Minister of Emigration, a thirty-eight-year-old professor of constitutional law 'with an interest in political science'. It was possible to talk properly with him, as it seldom is with politicians. He said that both PPD and PS claim to be mass parties, but they aren't really: they are parties of notables. There is still only one mass party, and that is the communists.

I saw Alfredo, too, looking very smart in a suit: perhaps the suit reflects the extent to which the sixth government has established itself (*cf*. Orwell on Barcelona and the significance of clothes). Alfredo has just unearthed a 1955 photo of the Coimbra civil governor, who is supposed to have been an anti-fascist since early youth and is now a communist, receiving a citation as a member of the fascist youth from a captain in the PIDE. He is very delighted and is going to publish it in *Jornal Novo* (a pro-PS daily) and get *Expresso* (a liberal weekly) to publish it too.

A. has been very busy with the Romanian party that has been visiting Portugal – four days non-stop Ceauşescu. He says C. brought his own tailor (for four days!) and two food analysts – who tested everything served to him before he ate it. The girl in charge of protocol spent her time furiously buying up western consumer goods – bras, everything.

Thursday 6 November: Around lunch-time today I passed a big crowd outside the Ministry of Social Communications, near the Restaurados metro station: angrily pushing and jeering at police at the entrance. I could see a baton being used vigorously, then there was a series of shots into the air. At this everybody (including me) ran for cover. After a minute or two, however, people began to push forward, and this time the police tossed tear-gas grenades into the crowd, a wholly counter-productive move which heightened the sense of a confrontation. People responded with stones and bricks, and threw the grenades back. A couple of windows broke. The tear gas mainly blew away from the crowd, or back at the police. After a bit the police shut themselves into the building and started throwing grenades out of the window.

When I came back in the evening at about 9.15 p.m. the crowd had grown, and there was a circle of troops: I was told that inside the Ministry the police had wounded some people (according to rumour, a man had been killed), and now about forty policemen were trapped inside together with staff who were occupying the building, and who the police had originally been sent to eject. The police couldn't get out for fear of the crowd, which was in sympathy with the staff. But the crowd was being kept at bay by the circle of troops, who were however – such are the subtleties of Portuguese street politics – in sympathy with the crowd, rather than the police: it was a SUV force, mainly PMs (military police), stiffened by a few sailors. I saw one airman. Meanwhile office staff watched the crowd from a balcony, and from time to time made speeches or read out communiqués explaining their case. The issue concerned the Minister of Information, Ferreira de Cunha, who was alleged to have been involved under the old régime with the PIDE. A big banner proclaimed 'Out with Fascists'. Apparently negotiations were going on with the President.

After midnight, I came back again: people were lighting fires in the street, and troops were playing elaborate games with ladders and ropes, hoisting food parcels in plastic bags up to the occupiers. The SUVs now made their own political contribution, unfurling a huge red banner which said: 'Reactionaries out of the barracks. Workers, Soldiers, Sailors United Will Win.' (What about airmen?) The crowd was about 1,000 strong, or less – mainly PCPish, but I also saw UDP, issuing literature. There were sporadic attempts to sing the 'Internationale'. Earlier in the evening, there was a moment of light relief when I came across a group of young men (who told me they were from Camden) selling the IS (International Socialist) pamphlet by Tony Cliff translated into Portuguese! They said proudly they had sold sixty copies ('at a demo in England we would have sold ten'). I talked to one for a bit – a nice chap who worked for Camden planning (the others were mainly in social services) – well-informed, proud of having found a cheap *pensão*.

Reflecting on the demo: it is certainly a big test for the Government. If they climb down and dismiss Cunha, it will be a humiliating defeat; giving in to the SUVs who are on the staff's side. On the other hand, what else can they do? They can't send in other troops (except perhaps at 4 a.m.?) without bloodshed, which they want to avoid. It comes back to my long-term point: the Government can only consolidate itself against the SUVs if it is prepared to shoot people – especially other soldiers – and this it fears to do.

I noticed that the SUVs seemed entirely unarmed. But almost all wore neckerchiefs round their faces, like the IRA or UVF, to prevent identification.

If I were the Government I would move in in the early hours and have a showdown. But mightn't that provoke a reaction?

There has been a big television debate between the leaders of the Socialist and Communist Parties, Mario Soares and Alvaro Cunhal. Soares said, in effect, the working class are not the exclusive property of the PCP and that people voted in larger numbers for other parties. Cunhal tried to get in some clever digs about Soares's Maoist allies. I watched it in the café/restaurant around the corner, packed out with a largely pro-Cunhal audience.

Friday 7 November: I seem to have been about an hour and a half out. This morning outside the Ministry of Social Communication there was an armoured vehicle with a mounted gun, where last night there had just been a peaceful SUV. The building was open. I went into the press room and talked to a nice witch-like girl who had helped me before. She told me that at 5.30 a.m., new troops, including marines, had arrived, sent by the Prime Minister, and after lengthy negotiations had broken down, they had entered the building and released Ferreira de Cunha who had been in his room all day and night. Then they released the police. Apparently the story about Cunha and the PIDE first appeared about a month ago.

I spoke to Alfredo later, and he was inclined to regard the whole thing as a communist ploy. 'All military men were implicated one way or another in the war,' he maintained.

I had a meeting today with Helena vaz de Sousa, of the quality weekly *Expresso* – she was nice and helpful, though distracted. She says *Expresso* is mainly left, despite having a PPD director and sub-director. It works all right, she says, because part of the editorial philosophy is liberalism – hence live and let live. The front page tends to be PPD, inside it is on the left.

I went to the PCP rally at the Pavilhão dos Desportos in the Edward VII Park this evening, arriving at about 10.30, in time for Cunhal. What a strange man he is. Wearing a jet black suit and black tie (to offset his white hair, I wonder?), he looks like a successful undertaker. His speech was read from an ostentatious sheaf of notes, like a lecture or perhaps a sermon. Only very briefly was there a touch of humour – a moment of sarcasm at the expense of PS and the PPD – when he departed from his notes. Otherwise it was solemn, serious and long. Periodically there would be breaks for applause and chants, and (as is the Marxist custom) he would clap along gently himself. Yet the Pavilion was packed, and – of all the Left groups – there is no doubt that the class and age range of the PCP is greatest. There were many middle-aged and elderly people. One little old lady stood on a chair and waved her fist and shouted her head off. There was also an elderly man blowing up balloons and tossing them, one by one, into the throng.

Sunday 9 November: Over lunch, I met a man from 'Big Flame', a British leftist group that has produced a rather handy pamphlet on Portugal, explaining all the factions. He is living in the PRP-BR head-quarters across the river. He felt it wasn't as active with 'mass activities' or whatever the phrase is, as it should be. I let him use my hotel room to wash his hair, and then we wandered down to the big pro-Government rally in Praca de Commercio – which PS motorists have been hooting about around Rossio for the last couple of days. Using my press pass, I got inside the building and had little trouble in getting to stand on the balcony (such is the casual lack of security in revolutionary Portugal) a few feet away from the Prime Minister. Also there were Alfredo and Norma Costa, two Canadians I had met called Jeremy and Bill, and a woman called Sue Ross from the BBC, who said she remembered me from Oxford. We had a grandstand view, in the clear November sunlight, of the crowd: fifty thousand or so, I should guess, about a third PPD, the rest PS.

Azevedo (the Prime Minister) arrived and stood on the balcony, flanked by Soares (who, standing just back from him, read his speech over his shoulder, visibly mouthing the words), Sá Carneiro (the PPD leader) and somebody described as 'an old anti-fascist who spent many years in exile in Brazil' who looked about a hundred. The crowd chanted, 'Socialism, Yes, Dictatorship, No', though the PPD section was less enthusiastic about the Socialism part. The favourite cry, taken up by PS with as much enthusiasm as by PPD, was 'Dis – cip – lin – a!' over and over again. You don't get that at the Winter Gardens in Blackpool.

The Prime Minister had been speaking for about half an hour (so it must have been about a quarter to six), when suddenly in the middle of the PPD section – to the right of where I was standing – a tear-gas grenade exploded. People immediately ran in all directions, and it looked as if there would be many injuries in the crush. In fact, only a few people fell, and the area soon cleared. A few seconds later, what looked like banners, but turned out to be an effigy of Cunhal brought by a tiny PCP–ML (i.e., Maoist) section, burst into flames, adding to the confusion.

Then some firing started – apparently from military police over by the river front. I was told later that they were shooting at a window which had been the source of the tear-gas grenade, but nothing ricocheted and they may have been shooting into the air to frighten people. This they succeeded in doing, and for a few seconds the view from the balcony looked like that famous picture of a street battle in Petrograd in 1917: people flattened themselves on the ground, or ran. For a ghastly moment, it looked as if the square was strewn with corpses.

On the balcony, the Prime Minister, Soares, Carneiro and the other man stood their ground. Azevedo called for calm, and then led some community chants. About half the crowd clearly had no idea what was going on, though they must have seen and felt the gas, and heard the shots. Yet there was no real panic. I was impressed by the politicians on the balcony, who only dabbed their eyes occasionally. Mine were running, and after a bit I had to go back inside. Soares's wife was clearly under great strain. 'Mario!' she shrieked at him, as he stayed on the balcony.

After the politicians had gone, I went downstairs and out with Norma Costa, Alfredo's English wife, and we walked towards Rossio, thinking that the day's events were over. They weren't quite. As we left the square, some more shooting started, we weren't sure where from. As it continued, and seemed to come from a line of soldiers directly facing us, we darted down a side-street and round the next corner. As we ran for cover, Norma called out in broad Lancashire: 'Bloody country!' It seemed the appropriate comment. It turned out later that the military police had been firing over people's heads as a way of answering back boos and jeers from the departing crowd. Who planted the gas (CS, according to an American journalist with experience of the Chicago Democratic Convention), nobody knows.

Norma says that the Soares–Cunhal television marathon lasted four hours, and Soares got the better of it.

Monday 10 November: The proofs of my Angola refugee article arrive. Lina Miranda, my Portuguese teacher, says that because everybody thinks there is going to be a coup or confrontation, there won't be one.

I arrive inexcusably late to see Rui Machete at his Ministry. He keeps me waiting for five minutes while he looks at newspaper cuttings just to show that government ministers are not instantly available. Then we talked for an hour. He was interesting (though pompous) and I liked him: but he was playing some funny politician's game called 'spread coup rumours'. His first words were, 'I think we are approaching an open conflict.' He thinks Otelo (Carvalho), Coutinho, Fabião (leading leftist members of the military Revolutionary Council) must move fast, or be moved against. He also thinks the Prime Minister has to deliver the goods quickly, or he will lose popularity.

Later I saw Rabello Marcello Sousa, also PPD but no buddy of Machete's – he described himself as extreme-left PPD whereas Machete is right-wing. He is only twenty-six. He is very bright and interesting. He says people in PPD would be Christian Democrats or Liberals in other countries. He agrees with me that PPD is really a conservative party, but says that the real difference between PPD and PS is religion, plus a masonic influence in PPD.

This evening, I followed a *retornado* march from Rossio for miles and miles to the UNITA headquarters. It was a very sad affair. There were never more than a few hundred people and they were hopelessly unorganized and ill-disciplined, not a patch on the extreme Left. Their slogan range was very narrow, just 'UNITA' and 'Abaixo MPLA', and 'Savimbi' over and over. Nearly all were white. When we got to the UNITA office, the staff came onto the balcony and tossed down leaflets, and a well-educated African made a speech and called for a minute's silence.

Where is the coup? Wait till tomorrow's papers.

Thursday 13 November: 1 a.m. I write this trapped in the National Assembly building. I am sitting in the lobby with nervous, tired, bewildered deputies padding past, a blonde American journalist asleep at the other end of the couch, with – a few yards away – a trade union militant making a speech to a huge crowd of construction workers outside.

Yesterday afternoon there took place the biggest march and demonstration I have yet seen, starting with a march from Praca de Commercio to the National Assembly, and composed of (mainly helmeted) construction workers – possibly 100,000 to 150,000 of them. When they got to the Parliament building, I went inside and talked to a couple of PS deputies. I asked them what they thought would happen. One shrugged and said: 'A right-wing dictatorship', and then – pointing to the crowd – 'in five months' time they will be shouting for Pinochet.' Both stressed the impossibility of meeting the workers' demands, that they were being manipulated by the Left, etc. I left and came back around 9.30, by which time it had become very clearly a siege. The total number of workers visible in the area in front of the Assembly was smaller, but they were settled, and there was much coming and going among them. On the balcony at the front of the building, members of the workers' committee, lit up by spotlights, were speaking to the crowd beneath.

Earlier, every time anyone touched the net curtains in the Socialist deputies' room, there had been howls and jeers and whistles. Now it was possible to lean right out and watch. You could see workers sitting, lying, standing – lighting fires – all over the square, the Parliament steps and the gardens, chanting from time to time, though now not very often.

I got to talk to Eugenio Mota, a PPD deputy from a Lisbon suburb, fiftyish, intelligent, said he was on the left of his party, and a socialist. He said, however, that he had been very suspicious of Mario Soares's demagoguery in the early days after the coup, when Soares had seemed to many an 'extremist'. Hence the need for the PPD. At this time, Soares had apparently thought that the Communist Party might be respectable like the Italian one, but it soon became clear that it was out for power by any means. Now he doesn't see much difference between PS and PPD – says they would be wings of the same party, but acknowledges some difference on the religious point, though he himself is non-Catholic. He reminds me that what is happening now happened in September (just before my return to Lisbon) with the *deficientes* – they arrived at the National Assembly at 4 p.m., and the commandos eventually rescued the imprisoned deputies at 3 a.m. But could commandos do it peacefully this time? And how often can military force be used to release deputies when they are besieged? He says the crowd isn't just under the sway of communists. The FUR groups are important too, and especially the UDP. If true, it really is bizarre that a party with just one deputy (the UDP) and 1.6 per cent of the vote in Lisbon should apparently count for more than all these scores of deputies sitting round.

About an hour ago, I tested the cordon by trying to get out. But the stewards looked at my press card, and politely refused.

The scene now is quite extraordinary. Deputies are sprawled around on chairs, sofas, floors (as I write these words there is a new outburst of catcalls and whistles from outside). They are looking bewildered, subdued – disbelieving – though also, perhaps, with a little excitement at the sense of being at the centre of a major Lisbon event. There is also a touch of hysteria. While I was talking to Mota, another PPD deputy nearby was talking on the telephone to Sá Carneiro (who isn't here) and saying, his voice rising, that 'if it goes on for one day, two days, three days, twenty days, there must be no surrender.'

At about 10 p.m., the Prime Minister – who is imprisoned with the rest of us – appeared on the balcony and told the workers he could give no answer to their demands (principally on wages) until 27 November. The crowd replied with cries of 'the strike continues' and then 'Unidade venceremos'.

Back to the situation now. There is a most peculiar sense of all being in the same boat – foreign journalists (a dozen or so, including photographers), deputies, varieties of civil police, guards, secretaries. Deputies who are awake huddle in corners, or stride around. Occasionally, the workers' committee – unhindered by anybody in the building – climbs up to the balcony to address the crowd, then sweeps back through and out. Perhaps significantly, no deputies apart from the Prime Minister have made any attempt to address the crowd.

There is indeed a sense of total impotence, of separateness, out-of-touchness. And of course there is a way in which the deputies – most of whom are PPD and PS – have no political experience, don't know how to deal with political situations, aren't workers and aren't leaders in any normal sense. Of course, if the workers give in, this is a big victory for the Government. If the Government gives in, it might as well resign now. My money is on the workers.

The building workers have been on strike for three days. They are mainly from greater Lisbon and Setubal. There are also some metal workers.

It is now after 2 a.m. It is a bit like a railway waiting room after the last train has gone. There are secretaries flitting round, and – mysteriously – a few children, including one blond-haired little boy who amuses himself by playing a private game of trains, propelling himself at speed along the corridor. The deputies seem to have nothing to *do*. They don't discuss properly in groups. There has been talk of a special session, but nothing has come of it. They don't read or work and when I asked the way to the library a guard looked at me in bewilderment. There is now a long-haired, bearded deputy asleep at the other end of the couch.

One irony is the magnificence of the building – late Edwardian classicism, high ceilings, pillars, mirrors and chandeliers. The balcony from which the workers' speeches are delivered opens out from a huge banqueting hall, with large murals in high noon (*c.* 1940) fascist realism – depicting Portuguese explorers subjugating and converting black natives.

I said to Mota that the MRPP is like a sixteenth-century Calvinist sect. He agreed, but said he had thought of it in terms of Savonarola. He speculated about it filling a gap where Catholicism once was.

Of course without the GNR (Republican Guard – civil police), the crowd would just break in. Apparently 200 did, but were pushed back.

At the other end of the corridor, a bleary deputy has just woken and is smoking dolefully, with his shoes off and displaying grey and white woolly socks. Poor chaps! They scarcely realized what they were taking on. I said to Mota that more and more people seem to be thinking a civil war might happen, and he agreed. He felt the lack of discipline in the army was key: 'it means the Government can't govern.'

3.25 a.m. Somebody in the crowd has just started up with 'Venceremos'.

About half an hour ago, a couple of lorries loaded with pears and vegetables arrived, warmly greeted by the crowd which remains noisy: stewards keep up the chants, and from time to time there is a chorus of catcalls. A short time ago, a worker announced that the Prime Minister was about to meet the Workers' Committee, which means he is negotiating. One of the main leaders of the committee is a boyishly good-looking bull of a man with bloodshot eyes and a friendly smile. A PS deputy from Braga told me an hour and a half ago that the President had ordered in Copcon (a special military unit). But they haven't arrived, so presumably aren't obeying orders. The deputy says: 'We think this may be the beginning of a communist attempt at revolution – there might be more strikes, and the communists would demand the dismissal of the Government.' He thinks that in any case this is the final crunch for the Government. Things have been getting steadily worse each day, and 'the army is decaying.' If the Government falls, there will be anarchy. 'But then, eventually, a right-wing government.'

5.35 a.m. About twenty minutes ago, a workers' delegate read a communiqué saying that the peasants in Alentejo will start moving at 7 a.m. if there is no positive answer from the Prime Minister – then that he had a proposal from Azevedo, who undertook to present the issue to his next Council of Ministers, but had no competence to do anything before then. (Cries of 'No'.) Then the delegate appealed to the crowd: should he suggest an immediate meeting of the Council of Ministers? (Cries of 'Yes'.) The presumption now is that the Council of Ministers *will* meet. But what can it decide? To climb down? Not to climb down?

A Portuguese journalist I have been talking to says the Assembly, with the Prime Minister's residence attached, would be a symbolic 'Winter's Palace' as a place to storm. He says a lot depends on Otelo. My feeling is that if the Alentejo peasants start to march, a real conflict would be hard to avoid. Indeed, it seems very hard to avoid in any case. And if that happens and the sixth government falls whatever would replace it would be so widely unacceptable that it wouldn't get off the ground. So civil war seems probable and difficult to avert.

While I was talking to the journalist, a man in a velvet suit and a diamond ring stopped for a word. I said, 'Like an English Tory MP and he must be a lawyer.' I was right about the second (many of them are lawyers). But he turned out to be left-wing PS.

5.55 a.m. There is no doubt about who are the élite. A couple of deputies attempted to say something from the balcony: they seemed to be aggravating the crowd, and were roundly sworn at by a member of the workers' committee, and they meekly retired, tails between their legs, while the committee member chanted, 'Don't respond to provocation.' The workers' committee has the run of the place, and struts around proudly and self-confidently and everybody jumps when they say so. But why are the deputies and the Assembly staff giving the committee all their facilities, the balcony, loudspeakers, lights? It greatly strengthens its sense of presence and authority.

An elderly, unshaven PPD deputy said to me an hour or so ago that in fact neither the Prime Minister nor the Council of Ministers have any power, and even the Revolutionary Council has lost power now that Otelo has decided to leave it. So everything rests with Otelo and Copcon. The same deputy also said he had heard that twenty-five truck-loads of peasants were on their way, and thought the situation would go on for days. He foresaw the storming of the building etc.

Earlier, there was an unseemly squabble over food. One deputy announced to a group of others that the workers had said that food should be sent in, but for PCP deputies only – at this, there was a roar of protest. (I saw some of the police laugh scornfully.) One elderly PPD deputy who looked at death's door was eventually brought food, and then taken away in an ambulance. I write this in the press gallery of the Chamber – deputies have begun to assemble, apparently for a special session.

Another PPD deputy says to me: 'What I want now is food and drink, you understand? Even if expensive.' A sentiment which, I think, everybody is beginning to share, especially as the smell of cooking – meat and chestnuts – is beginning to come from the fires outside.

11.15 a.m. I am thinking of going out – or trying to.

Friday 14 November: Well, the deputies were finally let out, at the request of marines and military police, at about 1 p.m. – with workers linking hands in a kind of gauntlet, and whistling them as they went. When I got back about 3 p.m. the building was almost empty. I returned the same evening to find a different situation: the Assembly now fully occupied by thirty or so workers' leaders, plus a few journal-ists and a handful of civil and military police, the latter closely fraternizing with the workers. The atmosphere was totally different from the night before – not so much the storming of the Winter Palace as the occupation of the Dumas. Nobody was in charge, and everybody had the run of the place. I was able to ring straight through to Jean in London, no problem or charge. But there was also an atmosphere of busy purposefulness, as the Committee went to and from the Prime Minister, the Revolutionary Council and the workers. The workers were obviously more radical than their leaders. At one point the committee asked them – still encamped outside – to allow the Prime Minister (who, unlike the deputies, had not left) to go to a meeting of the Revolutionary Council. The crowd shouted back: 'No – let him resolve the matter first, let the CR (Revolutionary Council) come to him.' So he remained fully under house arrest. I talked to a Portuguese journalist and a young French doctor who was the girlfriend of a photographer who had spent the night in the Assembly: she'd spoken to progressive priests in the north – and to *retornado* leaders, who were spoiling for a fight. She made the point that the *retornados* are strengthening the right-wingness of the north, where many of them come from.

The workers' committee (all very young, mainly in their twenties) were sitting around, sleeping, or chatting to the military police with whom fraternization was total. In the middle of the banqueting hall with the fascist murals there was a huge bag full of bread – offering a kind of symbolic simplicity. Most of the committee were obviously genuine workers, but there were a few intellectuals. Looking back, the whole operation was carried out with great professionalism – especially the way the crowd was kept out of the building, the road blocks (I was searched for weapons as I came through), and the constant, constant orchestrated chanting (no singing) – 'A Luta Continua!' over and over, and other slogans too. Also the political parties were kept well out of it.

At 5.30 a.m. – having got about 1½ hours' sleep in the central lobby – I woke up, just as everybody was crowding onto the balcony. There was a lot of hugging and congratulating as the announcement was made that the workers had won: the Revolutionary Council (or so it was said) had given in to their demands. Almost at once, the workers outside formed into a column and started to march back into the centre of town, chanting 'Vittoria!' and 'Venceremos!', to the applause of early morning cleaning ladies in office blocks along the route, some of whom seemed beside themselves with joy. Indeed, it was hard not to share in the collective pleasure and sense of triumph and solidarity.

One feature of the whole exercise was its excellent discipline and lack of any violence.

My feeling afterwards (apparently widely shared) is that there are now *no* options: this Government cannot survive, yet there is no alternative to it. After all this, I turned up for my regular Portuguese lesson with Lina Miranda: she said she had an awful 'constraining feeling' inside – of fear and insecurity about what is going to happen. She said, 'you can see it in people's faces' in the streets.

In the afternoon, I went to the MRPP headquarters – which is much as I imagine the Hare Krishna temple in Bloomsbury to be like – i.e. it is a temple. There are huge pictures of Arnaldo Matos, their leader; the walls are painted red and yellow, the cult's colours, and the place is draped with what amount to decorated altar cloths. A press committee man was found for me, who made me fill in a form, and then interviewed me, rather than the other way round.

On the way back, I bumped into the Carthusian who said that yesterday civil war seemed likely, but today he wasn't so sure. He thinks some new military grouping is still possible. I rang Norma and she said that the previous night she had been about to pack the children off to England.

Saturday 15 November: Wrote my article today. In the afternoon, *retornados* in Rossio attacked a car for reasons unknown – perhaps the driver was distributing leaflets for the big PCP rally on Sunday. An argument developed, and people started jumping on the bonnet and then they turned it over. Thereupon the driver – a bearded middle-aged man with glasses and a roll-neck sweater – beat a retreat. Later, PMs (military police) arrived and the car was righted, while *retornados* shouted abuse about Rosa Coutinho.

Sunday 16 November: Big extreme-left demo (PCP plus FUR, but not – according to Norma – UDP) from the Praca Marques de Pombal down Avenida da Liberdade and through to Praca de Commercio. Huge – probably twice as big as the pro-Government one last week: Norma said she was surprised (in an alarmed way) by how many well-dressed people there were, and that it wasn't just working-class; also that there were lots of peasants. True, there were many lorries containing peasants, but I would judge them a small proportion of the total. I asked Norma what the rumours were, and she said that today was the day for the civil war to start. Soares and Carneiro are both out of town, up north, where there is a big rival demo. Azevedo is ill (poor chap – enough to make anybody ill, the last few days). Norma says, 'this really is the crunch.' The papers are full of Costa Gomes (the President) saying that he is not trying to sack Otelo Carvalho as military governor of Lisbon, and that it is 'advisable' that the communists should be in the Government. The truth is that anything the Government now does which the extreme Left disapproves of, it can check through demos, etc. Yet there is no going back for the Left now: having whipped up its supporters to this extent, it can't afford to lose momentum.

At the end of the demo, there was a joyful little dance and singing. The song they like best is a jolly dance tune, and the one they know least is the 'Internationale'. 'Venceremos' comes up over and over. It is notable the way the Left hands out lists of approved slogans to marchers – the Right now does this too, of course. It has become one of the conventions of Portuguese politics.

Afterwards, the crowd spilling back into Rossio was looking for aggro. 'MPLA! MPLA!' they chanted. At Hotel Universo, a dark, sallow, 35-ish *retornado* woman, watching from the balcony, was pushed too far and spat something in impotent hatred. She was a silly lady: a vicious crowd quickly gathered, and if they'd known how to get in, it would have been very nasty: fortunately, the proprietor had locked the door. Inside, the *retornados* were discussing politics as usual, in hushed voices and with long faces. I spoke to an old man with stomach trouble and his pretty daughter, who had a baby on her arm. She said they'd been here a month, that her parents had been born in Angola, and so was she, and they had no family in Portugal. Her husband is a post office electrician and is still in Luanda. She hopes to go back. 'We were caught in the cross-fire between MPLA and FNLA,' she says. 'Not once but many times. We have lost everything, houses, cars, everything. I have been in South Africa, Paris, London. But I have never seen anything like what I have seen in Luanda.' What? 'Terrible things which they do to white people, and blacks too. I have seen terrible things. And they are putting boys like this' – pointing to a child of about twelve – 'into the army. And women too.' They are pro-FNLA – she says UNITA has been anti-white, and FNLA offers the best hope of a return. She says if MPLA had been good to the whites then it would be supported by them now. MPLA is just restricted to Luanda – all other big towns are UNITA and FNLA. Like all the *retornados*, all she really wanted to talk about is Angolan politics –

Angola is her country, not Portugal. I asked her about today's event and she said 'A bad scene – I think there must be a war, a civil war.' She doesn't like Portugal and her husband may go abroad if he can find work – there is no work here. 'The people here hate us, they think we are going to eat their food, take their jobs. Only in the north are people all right – there, there are no communists. In Lisbon the people are like animals. The way they chant MPLA! MPLA! It is a provocation.' She is twenty-one or twenty-two I would guess.

On telly, a Congress of the British Communist Party expressing solidarity with the PCP and MPLA is regarded as a major news item: evidence of TV's political leanings.

I spoke to Sonia on the telephone. She doesn't think the Government will necessarily fall, but agrees an armed conflict is more and more likely. The chestnut sellers, anyway, are doing well out of it all.

Monday 17 November: This morning the telex room was full of people from the British International Socialists having a noisy row about whether there had been 300,000 people or only 150,000 at the demo.

Tuesday 18 November: *Diário* and *Seculo* this morning both have big stories about a coup from the Right led by the Northern Regional Commander – which, as various people have said, means there won't be one. *Jornal Novo* in its evening edition has General Charais saying 'people with power don't have to make coups.' I spoke to Alfredo who said that when the fifth government was in power, the PS press had been full of stories about coups to scare them away, and now the left-wing is trying the same trick.

I had lunch with Sacontela (Lina's cousin, and a former trade union official in London) who was a bag of nerves – wondering whether to take her daughter right away, feeling that this is a bad atmosphere for a child. I said it was educational. However, she doesn't think there will be a civil war, or that the PCP wants one.

Wednesday 19 November: My last Portuguese lesson with Lina Miranda, before my return to London. We have had a strange kind of relationship. It has been very friendly, and she is a nice kind of very *bourgeois*, very Portuguese lady and extremely open – but at one level she never unbent. She told me little about her husband. She described herself as nervous, which she was in a way, yet very outgoing and sure of her attitudes which must be typical of her class: she is a semi-intellectual daughter of a colonial judge, and the wife of a pro-PPD army officer (engineer).

Lunch with Alfredo at the Ministry of Foreign Affairs canteen – after a communist trade unionist had objected to A.'s presence because he was using government subsidy money. A. was rude to him. Apparently this kind of personal politics is constant, though A. says there are only about ten communists at the Ministry.

A. says that he is sure of one thing – Portugal is not going to go communist. It nearly did in July, but not now. He is frightened of right-wing coups, though.

Thursday 20 November: What a time to be going home! This morning's news is that the Government has suspended itself in order to force the Revolutionary Council and the President to 'clarify their positions' and sack Otelo and Fabião.

At noon, I had an interview with the PPD leader Sá Carneiro in Avenida Duque de Loule. He is a funny little man, like a nattily dressed Italian waiter, and there is something slightly absurd about his seriousness. Yet he is clearly clever, tough and much more straightforward than Soares, who is all cunning and evasions. He told me he thought a military confrontation was probable if the Revolutionary Council (which was meeting this afternoon) didn't deliver the goods (it isn't quite clear whether these would include President Costa Gomes's head on a charger). He maintained that the military dominance of the Left is 'a myth' and he is obviously very keen to get foreign diplomatic backing.

While I was waiting to see him, I talked in the office to a nice PPD secretary I had met before, and who voiced the confusion and dilemma of many in this situation (as, presumably, in all such near-civil wars). She had a good friend, she said, in the MPLA and she cannot imagine that this girl would lend herself to anything that was bad or wrong, yet she found herself on the opposite side.

One feature of Sá Carneiro is his Cold War analysis: the whole thing is a communist plot to get a Russian base in southern Europe and the South Atlantic, to take Gibraltar and hence control the Mediterranean. (But anyone who has seen the demonstrations of the extreme Left *cannot* just leave it at that.)

This evening, after unsuccessful attempts to sell something to a snooty *Times* foreign editor, I went to the Presidential Palace at S. Belem where ten or fifteen thousand workers and peasants were assembled, singing, chanting and dancing – 'Venceremos', 'Avante Camponeses', 'O Povo Portugues', the Internationale, and, an especial favourite, the funny little dance tune. The PCP was quite strongly in evidence. Lorry loads of peasants kept arriving, indicating careful organization. One amusing thing is the way the peasant women segregate themselves from the men – sitting round in little groups and clapping together. There were plenty of camp fires – though the weather is still very mild and pleasant. As time went on, workers scaled the wall of the Palace and installed speakers etc. on the parapet, watched by the police. Eventually the President appeared and made a rather hoarse speech which was well received ('Costa Gomes', they kept chanting). CG seems to have become a left-wing hero overnight.

An Orwellian touch: PRP–BR banners calling for 'Armed Insurrection Against Civil War'.

> When I left Lisbon for England on 23 November, anarchy in the city was almost complete: two days later, a confused radical *putsch* (an 'armed insurrection against civil war', aimed at forcing changes in the Revolutionary Council) was easily neutralized by commando units organized by a military cartel known as the Group of Nine. Otelo, Fabião and other radical officers were demoted, and Colonel Ramalho Eanes, a previously little-known officer, became chief of staff. Against expectations, the sixth government survived: discipline was restored to the army, and preparations were made for a new Constitution, and for a full restoration of civilian rule. Over succeeding months, the influence of the extreme Left waned – never to be restored. The fear of a military-imposed right-wing dictatorship also receded. So, eventually, did many of the socialist reforms, as Portugal joined other southern European states – Spain and Greece – which were preparing themselves, economically and politically, for membership of the European Community.

THE AFRICAN CONNECTION

IT MAY BE PREMATURE to place the 1974 Portuguese *coup d'état* alongside the Fall of the Bastille or the assassination of Archduke Ferdinand, as a key turning-point in world history. Perhaps in ten years' time such an idea will not seem so fanciful. The collapse of the old imperialist order in Portugal has implications for the world which we are only beginning to grasp. The most immediately tangible result, with knock-on consequences for the whole African continent, has been the rapid success of pro-Marxist movements in the former Portuguese territories.

Less noticed than the effect of Portuguese events on Africa, is the recent African impact on Portugal. European influence on the Third World is something we take for granted; tropical Africa returning the compliment is not so expected. Nothing has been as important for Portugal as the process of colonial disengagement. Above all, the end of the Portuguese empire has caused a mass migration of former settlers to the home country which makes the return of the French from Algeria in the 1960s seem almost insignificant. There is indeed an epic symmetry to the final stage of Portugal's ancient relationship with Africa. It can be seen in the contrasting stories of two former colonials I talked to recently in Lisbon – Salome and João.

Salome is twenty-five, a tall, beautiful girl with swept-back crinkly hair, high cheek bones, taut pale skin, and a quiet composure. She grew up in the Portuguese Cape Verde Islands, off the West African coast, the sixth of eleven children of a Portuguese radio engineer and his locally born, part-African wife. Her childhood memories are of a household run by servants, perpetual sunshine, and huge family picnics. A change came in the mid-1960s, when her father's employer, a large international firm, moved him to Lisbon, and it was here that Salome completed school.

In 1972 she went to read literature at Lisbon University and encountered politics for the first time. Naturally shy, she associated with childhood friends from Cape Verde. Some of these were in touch with PAIGC, the guerrilla movement by now virtually controlling large areas of Portuguese Guinea. Salome is not sure why she became politically active. She thinks it was partly a rebellion against her father's stiff, old-fashioned, Portuguese authoritarianism. But it was also normal for students to be involved with one or another of the many ultra-left groups, whose main impetus was a bitter opposition to conscription and military service in an unpopular colonial war. She recalls, too, that most of the key people on the Lisbon University far left at this time were students, like herself, with colonial roots.

Salome's own activity was limited to attending surreptitious meetings and helping to print and distribute illicit leaflets. Her political consciousness was, however, sharpened by the imprisonment of two close friends who had worked with PAIGC. There was also a steady interchange with young soldiers in the African war – officers returning to their studies, talking about guerrilla activities and ideas; students drafted into the army already committed on the side of the enemy they had been conscripted to fight.

When the Armed Forces Movement, led by radical young officers, ended the forty-eight year dictatorship in April 1974, Salome joined the vast, festive crowds in Lisbon's Rossio Square, and was swept up in a ferment that was to last nineteen months. With lectures abandoned, exams abolished, and formal university life at a standstill, she threw herself into the revolution: organizing, discussing, demonstrating, picketing, splitting, re-grouping, with occasional heady forays into factories to offer skills to sometimes bemused, occasionally receptive, workers. Like many others of her generation, she was a part of the great 'popular power' upheaval which in 1975 paralysed government and helped to make possible the occupations which led to administrative collapse, expropriations and nationalizations, and increased the pace of decolonization.

Salome believed that it was vital to make the most of this time of instability and chaos. 'We knew that the period of revolutionary opportunity must end,' she says. 'We were amazed that it went on so long.' Drawing inspiration from the short-lived German revolution of 1919, she helped to start a political review, *Spartacus*, which regarded itself as a friendly critic of the Portuguese Communist Party's left-wing, and of the pro-Marxist African independence movements. When a section of the army intervened to restore order in November 1975, paving the way for the present 'bourgeois' democratic régime, she was disappointed, but not surprised. Nevertheless, for her and for her friends, it was a kind of ending: it was as if life could never again be so full and urgent. Now, more than two years later, 1974–5 seems like an important love affair, over but not yet dead.

Few of the old radical groups are still seriously in business, and Salome sees less and less of former student friends. *Spartacus* no longer appears. Exams are back, and degrees have begun to matter again in an employment market where ex-students are scarcely an automatic first choice. Salome is completing her studies part-time, while teaching in a poor neighbourhood in industrial Setúbal. Though thinking of herself now as 'a kind of anarchist' she has little time for politics these days, and finds the present squabbling among parliamentary parties dull and irrelevant. But she plans to stay in Lisbon. She likes the people and the city, and all her family, as well as most of the people her family knew in Cape Verde, are now in Portugal. She has heard that conditions on the islands since independence have been bad, and there are stories of people starving. She does not think there is any possibility of returning, even if she wanted to, except for a holiday.

Salome is one of those from Africa who helped to make the Portuguese revolution. João, from Luanda, has been spending three years fighting against it. A large, rugged man in his late thirties, with a heavy black beard and a vividly tattooed forearm, he is bitter, angry, determined. Born in northern Portugal, he comes from a family of small traders; his parents emigrated to Angola, where he grew up over his father's newspaper shop. João did his military service as a private soldier during the mid-1960s, and returned to Luanda to work as a reporter. He knew little, and cared less, about politics. Angola was less affected than other Portuguese territories by nationalist guerrillas, and as late as 1974 there was little sense of insecurity.

Then came the civil war and the massacres. João joined the western-backed FNLA, the movement which seemed most likely to salvage something for the whites. When the FNLA were pushed back by Agostino Neto's pro-Marxist MPLA, João's house was ransacked, his sister disappeared (and is still missing) and he was arrested. After ten days under guard he evaded his captors, and took the first available plane to Lisbon – one among hundreds of thousands of refugees airlifted from Luanda and Nova Lisboa in autumn 1975, without money, belongings or ultimate destination.

João found himself in a city he did not know, at the height of its own convulsions. With the 'Lisbon Commune' strongly pro-MPLA, and almost the entire Lisbon press controlled by the far Left, prospects of an orthodox reporting job were nil. João thought of trying to get to Brazil, or Canada. Then he met up with three other Angolan journalists, and together they decided on a gamble. Rossio Square, once the focal point for revolutionaries, was now swarming daily with thousands of *retornados nacionais* (returned nationals), huddled in groups and swapping vitally needed news and information that was not available in Portuguese newspapers. *Jornal O Retornado* was launched, on credit from the printers, to fill this gap, and the first issue sold out. The paper has been appearing weekly ever since, with a circulation now over 35,000 and a comfortable capital base.

The main reason for this success is that the refugee community has never stopped growing. After the panic evacuation of whites from Angola in 1975, there has been a remorselessly steady flow of *retornados* from Mozambique. Official statistics show that in the first eight months of 1977, net immigration averaged at 700 per week, over 90 per cent from Lourenço Marques. In October 1975, when João arrived, the Government did not expect the final total to be above 350,000. Now the official figure for those in Portugal is a staggering 600,000 (including about 100,000 non-whites), of whom nearly two thirds are from Angola. Most of the rest are from Mozambique, with a sprinkling from Timor, Guinea and Cape Verde. Before the influx, some eight million people lived in mainland Portugal. Now the population has increased by 7 per cent. It is as if all 3,800,000 white South Africans had just arrived penniless in Britain – with the difference that, unlike Britain, Portugal is backward and agrarian and has no welfare state.

There are few Portuguese left in Africa – 5,000 whites in Angola, perhaps twice as many in Mozambique. Yet the refugees keep coming – 362 in the second week in December, mostly Asian, mixed or black. What is surprising, as João acknowledges, is that the Portuguese authorities have been able to cope at all. João's anger is not against the High Commissioner for Refugees, an army officer who in eighteen months has created a remarkable degree of order out of chaos, but at what he regards as a Marxist-inspired administration which refuses to give the *retornados* their due. What the Government sees as a victory, like the reduction from 70,000 to 17,000 in the number of refugees in expensive, state-financed temporary accommodation (sometimes luxury hotels, more often overcrowded holiday camps), João sees as sweeping the problem under the carpet and placing an unfair burden on families and relatives.

Salome and her friends have lost their former political enthusiasm. João's fascination with politics is just beginning. The mainspring of his interest is a deep hatred and resentment of the communists, whose influence in Portugal and in the former Portuguese territories he sees as all pervading. Like many other *retornados*, he cherishes the hope that one day it will be possible to return to harmonious, multi-racial societies in Africa, where Europeans will be able to provide technical skills. For him, Angola is still home, and Lisbon a temporary exile. But first it will be necessary to defeat the communists in Portugal and in the former colonies. This is the purpose of a secret political refugee organization, soon to go public. It is also one of the jobs undertaken by *Jornal O Retornado*.

Another of *O Retornado*'s tasks is to tell the Portuguese what they would rather not know about the decolonization. This includes a great deal of detailed information about African atrocities. The paper has published a children's comic book graphically devoted to this topic. One drawing shows a mutilated corpse pegged to the ground in a jungle clearing. Nearby lies a severed head. A white soldier is saying: 'So this is how the terrorists are liberating the people of Angola!'

João lumps communists and terrorists together and says: 'We will never forget.' It will certainly be hard for the Portuguese to forget. The presence of the vast new population of refugees will be increasingly felt. This is not just because of the numbers of the immigrants, or the degree of their bitterness. It is because of the kind of people the *retornados* are: young (only 7 per cent are over sixty), and a high proportion with skills and qualifications. Portugal, notoriously lacking in medical and educational resources, is better off for doctors, nurses and teachers than ever before. The Portuguese economy may eventually benefit from the influx of engineers and technicians. Business initiative is also strong. A government scheme to make loans available to *retornados* on special terms for setting up small enterprises has received 7,500 applications, with 4,500 projects already approved.

According to the Government, only one active refugee in three is still unemployed, less than half as many as a year ago. The first stage of integration has passed remarkably smoothly. But as immediate physical necessities come to dominate the lives of the *retornados* less, their role in Portuguese life will increase.

The present condition of Portugal owes much to its historic links with Africa. Formal ties have now been broken, and the trend of Portuguese trade is away from the old empire and towards Europe. But Portugal will continue to live with the African connection; and João, not Salome, will be making the running.

New Society, 12 January 1978

POLITICAL POWER AND
THE PORTUGUESE MEDIA*

ARE THE MASS MEDIA the mere instrument of whatever class or group happens to gain control of them – or should they be seen as a thing apart, with an independent power to affect opinion? Recent (1974–6) experience in Portugal, where newspapers and broadcasting have acquired a very special role – as the arena of political conflict and also as the prize – provides a good testing ground for both theories.

The commonly held view has long been that the media are a vital political tool. Right-wing politicians have acted on it, doing their best to manipulate the press. Left-wingers, meanwhile, have been equally convinced that control of the media is the key to political power.

Thus the Belgian sociologist, Armand Mattelart, has recently dismissed the idea of mass communications as an autonomous entity, 'a sort of epiphenomenon' transcending society,[1] and abstracted from the real conditions which control its production.[2] People who blame the media for problems or crises, he maintains, are guilty of elevating a 'pseudo-cause to the status of actual cause of social occurrences and processes in an undifferentiated way', thereby hiding 'both the identity of the manipulators and the function of the ideas which move in the direction of the social system favoured by the ruling class'.[3] According to this argument, attempts to present the communications media as a dynamizing element in society simply mask their true role as the instrument of the ruling class.

At first glance, Mattelart's case seems to apply very neatly to Portugal, where the media have played a colossal part in the revolution, and where, since the early days of the old dictatorship, political leaders and activists have behaved as if the press have great persuasive power

---

* This essay was written collaboratively with Jean Seaton, and presented as a paper at the June 1979 meeting of the International Conference Group on Modern Portugal, at Durham, New Hampshire.

that can be put at the disposal of whoever pulls the puppet strings. Belief, however, is not the same as reality: and a closer look at Portuguese history and politics suggests a collective illusion, in which the political élite has accorded more direct influence to the media than they have ever actually possessed.

If the 'persuasive power' of the media is largely illusory, this does not necessarily make them less important. However, it changes the way in which they need to be interpreted. Thus it is arguable that at least in Portugal – and possibly elsewhere as well – newspapers and broadcasting have never been a very effective 'instrument' of anybody; that they mattered less for their direct effect on public opinion than for the *symbolic* role they acquired in Portugal's factional struggles; and that, in consequence, they had a certain kind of 'autonomy' after all.

The media and the arts acquired a peculiar significance in Portugal during the Salazarist dictatorship. This grew during the subsequent régime of Marcello Caetano, partly because censorship was the most immediate aspect of the repressive nature of the régime. Portuguese fascism under either Salazar or Caetano displayed few of the totalitarian features of the systems it took as models: it was never dynamic or mobilizing in the German or even the Italian sense. Instead it was traditional, paternalist, and conservative, using corporatist institutions not to promote but to minimize change, and to maximize stability. The régime was far from being non-ideological. But the stock of political concepts by which it was guided (characterized by Herminio Martins as 'Luso Maurrassism')[4] was more concerned with the preservation of old values than with the inculcation of new ones. Even at its height, the União Nacional (National Union) was never a mass movement. Popular education was more often regarded as a threat than as a weapon. That the régime should have been so suspicious of innovation and should have considered ignorance the best guarantor of civil order owed much to the dependence of the governing élite on the Church, the army, and the great landowners, and also to the absence, until the 1960s, of any important technologically advanced or modernizing sector.

Government involved restraint more than direction, and the censorship was an extremely important part of the restraining apparatus of the state. As Martins and others have argued, the highly effective Portuguese strategy was to use terror as economically as possible:

something to be brought into play only when other techniques had failed.[5] Salazar was able to rule securely without the blood-baths of the *caudillo*. The amount of actual violence and physical force employed by the régime in Portugal varied between 1926 and 1974. But there was less official murder, imprisonment, and torture in proportion to population than is usual in countries where basic civil liberties are denied. Increasing urban prosperity from the 1960s, moreover, was accompanied by a decreasing level of physical repression. Some groups (working-class communists in particular) suffered more than others. Nevertheless, a foreign investigation conducted in 1963 found that the total number of people in prison for political offences amounted to the comparatively low figure of 353,[6] while an estimate made in 1970 (perhaps an unduly optimistic one) gave a total of only 100.[7]

Portuguese authoritarianism functioned on the basis of limits. A degree of freedom from official interference was possible, provided a threshold of tolerance was not passed. This 'negativism' applied most of all to publishing and the media, which (like schools and universities) were seen not so much as means for indoctrination as potential sources of opposition and resistance. The régime did not seek to own or to direct the press (though it was happy when its supporters did so). Instead, it depended on the censor to maintain standards of 'dignity' and 'decorum' and to act as a bulwark against the forces of chaos and revolution. As Salazar told a journalist shortly before the Second World War, the objective of the Government's policy toward journalism and writing was defensive:

It may seem a paradox, but censorship is today the legitimate means of defence that free, independent states have against the prevailing anarchy of thought, against the international confusion of mind. I am not afraid of the criticism of a true journalist provided he is a Portuguese and acts like one. But I am afraid of the minor journalist who, without knowing it, has become denationalized, possibly because his mind is not strong enough to resist the allure of certain facile theories. I must remind you that there is no such thing as Portuguese, French or British communism, but international communism, which strives to impair and destroy national independence. Against this ideological imperialism – as dangerous as any other form – the Censorship is surely a lawful means of defence.[8]

The New State was built on memories of the upheavals and disorder of the Republic, and the nightmare of a new collapse, sustained by the reality of a highly organized, clandestine Communist Party (the PCP), haunted the régime until its end – the censor remaining ever sensitive to 'the prevailing anarchy of thought', which, if allowed to enter journalism and the arts unchecked, would lead inexorably to revolution in the streets. However, except in the darkest periods, the censorship was not always so rigid, or efficient, as to exclude the possibility of evasion. With the introduction of periodic elections, a considerable amount of criticism was allowed for the duration of election campaigns.

These 'semi-free' elections, which inevitably resulted in complete victory for government lists, reflected the concern of the régime to assuage international opinion, and also the need for domestic 'tension-release mechanisms', which (as Martins has argued) 'use up, but do not create or regenerate, the opposition's political capital'.[9] Yet on at least two occasions – 1949 and 1958 – the degree of opposition revealed or created during the campaign was a major embarrassment to the Government. Elections were thus rather more than mere exercises in public relations. They were regarded with keen interest even when the Opposition decided to withdraw its own lists, and especially when a contest actually took place. For opponents of the régime, the elections were 'episodes of latent political communication whereby the Opposition seeks to disclose the scale, extent, and intensity of dissent to the effective electors, viz. the armed forces, the Church, and the business oligarchy',[10] of which only the army was actually capable of effecting changes. As important as the relaxation of prohibitions on freedom of speech and assembly was the partial lifting of the censorship during the campaign period.

There were still major and frustrating limitations. When, in 1969, the censor refused *Diário de Lisboa* permission to publish an interview with Mário Soares, the newspaper, in retaliation, refused to publish a statement by the chairman of the National Union, José Guilherme Melo e Castro; as a result, Soares's statement, in which he declared that the 'institutionalization of freedom' was the prerequisite for solving all other problems, was duly printed.[11] However, more subtle methods of checking the voice of the Opposition were also employed. Soares himself has recorded the explanation of the governor of a commercial radio station for the latter's refusal to sell time for political broadcasting, despite official assurances: 'For a long time I have been trying to get a permit for shortwave broadcasting. Before this statement about election stuff on commercial stations came out, the Government warned me I could say goodbye to it if I let the Opposition have any time at all. There is a fortune at stake, you understand.'[12]

It was this give-and-take aspect of the régime's relationship with the media that critics found particularly irksome, and which increasingly characterized non-election periods as well. Where in the past the rules had been clear, in the 1960s and 1970s their operation seemed more arbitrary and unpredictable. Censorship and the régime's developing indecision about the press became central to the controversy between Caetano and his liberal opponents as other aspects of tyranny and the fear of punishment diminished. At the same time, the censorship became sufficiently lax, or unsure, and opponents sufficiently confident and determined, to provide scope through sections of the press for a steady, nagging, half-hidden opposition. By 1974 the media (especially newspapers) were the vehicles for a very muted criticism, and a central cause of resentment directed at the regime as well.

An important essay by José Cardoso Pires,[13] published abroad two years before the 1974 coup, is of interest for two reasons: first, because of its description of the bizarre ritualism of the battle involving censor and editor, writer, or publisher – a kind of animal dance in which both sides snapped and pecked with strangely predictable movements, but in which teeth and blood were seldom seen; second, because what Pires actually shows, in spite of himself, is the extent to which the régime was already morally and physically in full retreat. Ostensibly, the author was protesting at the dishonesty or cowardice of the authorities who had reneged on a promise to institute a major liberalization, and was seeking to demonstrate the enervating effect of the Portuguese form of censorship on serious writing. Thus Pires describes the impact of economic pressures similar to those used against Soares:

A series of measures frequently put into effect clearly shows, by its gradation, that the final stage is prepared for by creating in the publisher a conditioned doubt and uncertainty. The first move is to alarm him by issuing an unexpected demand that certain books, selected apparently at random from his list, must be submitted to the censor for appraisal. The verdict is then delayed interminably while the books continue to circulate freely. The suspense inevitably leads the publisher to hold up any further activities in relation to the books under scrutiny. Finally, any reference to a particular book ceases to appear in the press. There is no warning and no justification. There is simply a total blank: reviews and advertisements of the doomed book are banned in all newspapers. The book may still be on sale but it is annihilated by the wave of silence imposed by the censor.[14]

Such pressures were frustrating and depressing, but in fact they were scarcely emasculating, and they became less and less effective. There is ample evidence – the writings of Pires himself are an example – that Portuguese literature, so far from being destroyed by censorship, was actually given added purpose by it.

Pires maintains, however, that the effect on journalism was 'much more serious' than it was on literature, and it is certainly true that most Portuguese newspapers retained the characteristics of official gazettes by publishing government announcements undigested, avoiding comment, providing no investigative reporting, and using a writing style marked by the worst of bureaucratic clichés and circumlocutions. Under Caetano the main function of the press remained what it had been under Salazar – to communicate official attitudes. Journalism was a semi-clerical subprofession, and it would be absurd to present the pre-1974 press as other than tame and quiescent. Nevertheless, the conflict which Pires describes in Portuguese literature existed on a daily basis in many newspaper offices as well; and precisely because the battle was so constant and repetitive, it came to be seen as the essential political struggle, the trench warfare in the fight against the régime.

In his essay, Pires describes the underground metaphors stimulated by the censorship which had given poignancy to much of Portuguese literature since the 1940s: 'dawn' or 'daybreak' for socialism; 'spring' for revolution; 'poppy' for popular victory, and so on.[15] So pervasive were these images that by the 1960s they had formed the basis for a culture that was not so much alternative as dominant. The intellectual revolution, indeed, was largely complete before the political revolution had even begun.

In this process, newspaper and periodical journalism had been playing a crucial part. As in poetry and novels, so too in part of the press, a whole vocabulary of dissent came into play, a shifting code of hint and innuendo and *double entendre*, designed as much to make the censor look foolish as to engage in oppositional debate, but by its very success reinforcing the increasing contempt that was felt for the authorities, especially among the urban middle classes. There were many devices.

The juxtaposing of photographs and copy was a common method. In the last eighteen months before the coup, *Expresso* made use of cross-word clues, and even included hidden political meanings in children's stories, which the initiated could read as parables.[16] It was an invigorating game, with damaging economic penalties – in terms of presses stopped and issues seized – for arousing the censor's suspicions or disapproval. But the more adventurous dailies, such as *Diário de Lisboa* (with a number of clandestine communists on its staff) as well as the traditionally oppositional *República* and (from 1973) *Expresso*, were continually pushing and testing, as a handful of intellectual journals like *Seara Nova* and *Tempo e Modo* had done for a generation or more. It is certainly no exaggeration to say that the underground language and conventions, created and spread by writers and journalists, fostered the climate of opinion which not only made the 1974 *coup d'état* against the Caetano régime possible, but also made quite clear what it was going to be about.

> Grandola vila morena,
> Terra da Fraternidade,
> O povo é quem mais ordena
> Dentro de ti, o cidade.

This old song about the town of Grandola where the people rule, which was used as a signal for the coup, was a code in more senses than one. Other images of the revolution – taking place at dawn, on a spring morning, with a red flower as an emblem – grew out of a long and bitter cultural tradition, given potency by official persecution. It was not by chance that some of the most critical domestic battles of the Caetano period should have been concerned with press and literary freedoms. The failure of the régime to liberalize the press law had precipitated the resignation from the National Assembly of Francisco Sá Carneiro and others on the progressive wing of the ANP (Popular National Action, Caetano's successor organization to Salazar's National Union), a split that separated the Caetanists from a powerful section of *haut bourgeois* Portuguese society, and dealt a crippling blow to the régime's attempt to present a modernizing image.

A number of literary battles (in particular over the 'Three Marias')[17] in the last months of the dying régime served to demonstrate a growing enfeeblement and lack of confidence. Finally, it was a literary sensation, the appearance of Spínola's *Portugal e o Futuro*, which provoked the military crisis that gave the MFA (the Armed Forces Movement) its opportunity. In one of the most significant sentences in his published recollections, Caetano stated that two months before the coup he had read Spínola's book and immediately understood 'that the military coup, which I could sense had been coming, was now inevitable'.[18] There has seldom been a clearer declaration of the political power of the written word. 25 April 1974 was thus in every sense a culmination, an intellectual and cultural event as much as a military and political one. For a long time there had been a growing awareness of a middle-class intelligentsia – expansive, outward-looking, and essentially liberal – steadily gaining confidence in an offensive against an anachronistic and traditional oligarchy whose institutional and corporate supporters were increasingly distracted and unsure, and which was moving toward its last stand.

The MFA, though initially concerned with the privileges of the officer corps, was already the champion of essentially civilian, liberal grievances by the time of the coup, as the original MFA programme clearly shows. If any doubt remained, the crowds that assembled in Lisbon on 25 April and 1 May determined that, from the start, the coup was to be more than a praetorian revolt. What was it about? In a word, freedom. The early decisions after 25 April were liberal in nature, of a kind that reflected almost universal desires within the urban bourgeoisie and caused a minimum of offence: the release of political prisoners, the incarceration of the secret police, the legalization of freedom of assembly and of association, the promise of free elections based on universal suffrage, and above all the abolition of censorship and the guarantee of free speech.

The symbolic significance of the ending of the hated censorship was emphasized in a spontaneous move by Socialist Party cadres who took over the vacated censor's office in Lisbon, where they established for a time their national headquarters. Indeed, for all the powerful ideological shifts of 1974 and 1975, the Portuguese revolution began as it ended, as essentially a 'bourgeois' revolution, asserting the coming of age of a newly expanded and newly prosperous middle class, concerned to establish for itself the freedoms possessed by most of western Europe. The other major causes of the upheaval, and their manifestations in the former colonies, in factories, in the army, and on the land, threatened but never annihilated the 'bourgeois' programme.

The strength of the demand for liberal freedoms in the class which (despite shifting labels and alliances) always provided a majority of the ministers and administrators, seemed to ensure a remarkable democratic survival, in spite of continuing predictions of imminent destruction and threats from both Left and Right. Why were first Spínola and then Vasco Gonçalves unable to impose a new authoritarianism, with press controls or restrictions on freedom of expression in a new form? Neither Spínola's Junta of National Salvation nor the Fourth Provisional Government led by Gonçalves were made up of men who had previously shown much interest in liberal democratic principles, and both made some attempts to restrain the activities of the media, and even to direct them. The failure to capitalize on temporary political advantages and silence critical voices may be attributed, in part at least, to a fear of alienating sympathizers inside and outside the Government who regarded freedom of expression as a value worth maintaining.

It is not easy to disentangle cause and effect in the rapid evolution of the media after April 1974, and especially between September 1974 and the summer of 1975.[19] Did radicalization of the press, radio, and television lead the revolutionary upheavals, or merely reflect them? The media were certainly swept along by the mood of the times. The 'flood-gates' theory, expounded by Caetano as a reason for opposing any sudden relaxation of the censorship, was in one sense vindicated: there was a dramatic increase in the volume of newsprint, and the media responded almost immediately to an unquenchable public demand for discussion of the social and political issues that had previously been taboo. Undoubtedly a kind of competitive political hysteria, in media previously characterized by caution and sobriety, contributed to a mood of unrest; and this provided the background to occupations, demonstrations, strikes, and workers' control. Yet the behaviour of the media, and of editors, producers, and journalists cannot really be isolated, and should be seen as part of an organic process.

If the media had a catalytic effect, alongside and not separable from that of parties, groups, unions, and so on, it is important to stress the limitations to the persuasive power over mass opinion which they were generally assumed to exercise. Portuguese newspapers catered to a comparatively small, largely urban, élite. Indeed the press, in contrast to broadcasting, was barely a 'mass' medium at all. A poll conducted on behalf of the Ministry of Social Communications at the end of 1976 found that fewer than one Portuguese adult in three claimed to have read or skimmed *any* daily paper during the preceding month; outside greater Lisbon and greater Porto, the proportion was scarcely one in five.[20] The amount of *regular* newspaper reading in the country-side was much lower, partly because of high rural illiteracy and semi-literacy rates, and partly because of poor distribution. There were no mass circulation newspapers, and no paper mainly depended on sales to the poorest people. Indeed, the Portuguese press was among the most élitist in Europe, its readers most commonly skilled workers or members of the middle class, young and urban.[21]

But in any case, the conventions of the Portuguese press, essentially unchanged since before the revolution, were not geared to a wide or uneducated reading public. There were no Portuguese tabloids. The heavy prose style that had characterized the Salazarist press was main-tained, with few concessions to modernity. The subtleties and devices used in some papers to get past the censor had been aimed only at the highly sophisticated. Portuguese journalists had no experience of directing political news and copy toward people who had a low level of political understanding and a limited political vocabulary. As the Lisbon press became increasingly Marxist in its orientation, there was little attempt to make the shades of difference between groups and factions intelligible. Indeed, virtually the whole of the Portuguese press throughout the revolution seemed to be addressed to a readership of *cognoscenti* far smaller even than the number of those who bought and read newspapers. The proportion of people, even among the Lisbon middle class, who were able to follow from the press the rapid move-ment of events during the spring and summer of 1975 was probably small.

The proportion that depended on newspapers as a source of reliable information about political developments was even smaller. In a country with a long history of censorship, there was a universal sus-picion of all public media. This suspicion was not diminished in the months that followed April 1974 – there was little enough reason to rely on reporting and comment produced by a profession which found it possible to switch from fascist to communist copy with so little difficulty. There is ample evidence – for example, the enormous increase in the audience of the Portuguese section of the BBC – that alternative sources of information became more important, not less, during the period that followed the coup, and most of all during the 'hot summer' of 1975. Pires reported a popular Portuguese joke of 1972 vintage: ' "What's the latest local news?" asks an immigrant on a visit to Lisbon. "Haven't the faintest idea," replies his friend, "I haven't seen today's *Le Monde*."[22] In 1975, French, British, and American papers were still being eagerly read – even by politicians – as the most reliable sources on domestic events.

What of radio and television? Radio reached the vast majority of the population. The penetration of television was less complete, and in some rural areas reception was poor and the ownership of sets unusual. However, far more people saw television than saw newspapers. A 1972 poll showed that 67 per cent of the population had seen television in the preceding week.[23] During the revolution the percentage may have been considerably higher. Moreover, television could be understood by illiterates as well as literates (though poorer people may have had access to television sets less often than others). The broadcasting media were thus clearly 'mass', and might be expected to have had a much bigger role as political persuaders than newspapers – especially during the months of intense political interest among the general public, when parties could repeatedly attract crowds of a hundred thousand or more to their rallies in the big cities.

Undoubtedly the novelty of open discussion aroused great interest, and political news and discussion were keenly listened to and watched. But, once again, the actual effect on the public is difficult to gauge. It was certainly not as great as many people took for granted. Politicians tended to assume that television was a weapon of immense power: that whoever controlled the networks came close to controlling the public response to political events. Yet such a view – derived in part, as we have seen, from a traditional obsession with media influence and control, and in part from international conventional wisdom about the role of the media everywhere – was clearly quite false. Televised propaganda had no more magical, hypnotic effect on its audience after the *coup d'état* than before. Indeed, there is strong evidence that control of, or influence over, radio and television did the far Left remarkably little good in 1975.

There was never a monopoly of control over the media by any one group after April 1974, but by the time of the April 1975 election the media were overwhelmingly dominated by the far Left. By the election of April 1976 the situation had been neatly reversed: Lisbon's press and broadcasting had become largely liberal-democratic. If the media, particularly radio and television, had indeed been as of persuasive as has been claimed there would presumably have been a dramatic falling off of support for the far Left between the two elections. In fact, no such trend is visible, and the main contours of the electoral map remained remarkably stable.[24]

The evidence of the elections certainly does not bear out the exaggerated hopes or fears of politicians that control of the media would confer great power to sway mass opinion. It is even arguable that, just as the censorship became the focus of bitter criticism under the old régime – cause for opposition in itself – so the appearance of a left-wing media monopoly in 1975 (and the somewhat crude propagandist uses to which influence over the media was often put) alienated people, creating fears of a new authoritarianism. What is probably true is that the ascendancy of pro-communists in the media – seen by the Left as a key to political power – gave an impression of actual power over policies and events where very little power really existed. Consequently, the Portuguese Communist Party was widely blamed (especially in the north) for disruption and economic collapse which it was wholly unable to prevent.

The media may have had little manipulative or persuasive power over public opinion. Nevertheless, they were crucial to the Portuguese revolution in a number of ways.

First, they were a means of communicating instructions or exhortations from leaders to followers, when instant reaction to a new political situation was required. Thus most of the huge demonstrations were announced and publicized through the media (though Soares succeeded in holding one of the biggest and most effective demonstrations – over the *República* affair – despite the fact that most of the media were against him).[25] The press became the vehicle for warnings against real or imaginary plots, in order to forestall any possible *putschist* plans within the officer corps, especially during the anarchic autumn of 1975. Broadcasting was sometimes used to inflame crises by urging militants to participate. The burning of the Spanish Embassy was provoked by a television broadcast which urged people to join demonstrators who were protesting against the execution of Spanish anarchists. The media also raised temperatures by bringing the revolution into the family living room; most dramatic of all was the live television coverage of the confusion and discussions among troops participating in the failed counter-coup of 11 March 1975. Thus – while not persuading or convincing the masses – the media had an agitational effect, whipping up feelings among the activist minority.

Second, in the confusing battlefield of an anarchic struggle, the media acquired an important symbolic role. In all *coups d'état*, broadcasting stations and newspaper offices are early targets; during the critical hours in which those with the power to affect the outcome make up their minds, the media can establish a sense of authority. In Portugal, where legitimacy and authority of a conventional kind disintegrated and virtually disappeared for a period of months, the media were in a strategic position for a very long time, partly because political actors believed that people and institutions would be guided by the media in their choice of whom to obey.

There is little evidence that this perception was correct – that the public did in fact equate the press and broadcasting with a legitimate source of power. What mattered, however, was that a legacy of concern about the media had created within the political élite an unshakeable faith in their importance. Before the revolution many of the most important battles had concerned literary and press freedom. During it, the same tradition was maintained. The *República* affair (when the pro-communist government threatened to close a socialist newspaper) was the turning-point for the Gonçalvists not because of the actual importance of the paper itself, but because it was seen as a hill that had to be taken. Though Soares lost the skirmish, he won the battle by demonstrating the huge popular anxiety that existed about a far-left media monopoly. In a different way, the radio station *Renascença* was able to rock the Sixth Provisional Government by symbolizing the uncontrollable features of Lisbon society in the autumn of 1975. *Renascença's* defiance mattered because of a general acceptance among political and military leaders of the importance of the media. Thus, the inability of the Government to deal effectively with radio and television was seen as a symptom of a general lack of control.

Indeed, the rules in 1975 were not so very different from those in 1958 or 1969, when the Opposition sought, through the temporary freedoms provided at election time, to convince the army of the strength of dissent. In 1975 political players were still performing before a military audience – Soares seeking to prove the extent of disaffection with the Gonçalves Government, and the far Left concerned to show the lack of popular backing for Azevedo. As in the past, it was always assumed that the military would be the final arbiter.

In this competition the media played a central part, though less as an instrument than as a prize. The media were seen as a means to the end: decades of struggle against the censorship had invested the media with powers they did not possess. In fact, though the media were sometimes a lubricant, they could not be crudely used as an ideological tool. The media in Portugal obeyed their own laws and were beholden in their influence to nobody. Indeed, there were many features of the Portuguese revolution which could be 'blamed on the media' in the sense derided by Mattelart, rather than on the groups or classes that attempted to exploit the press and broadcasting for their own advantage.

First published in Lawrence S. Graham and Douglas L. Wheeler (eds.), *In Search of Modern Portugal: The Revolution and Its Consequences* (University of Wisconsin Press, 1983)

NOTES

1. Armand Mattelart, 'The Nature of Bourgeois and Imperialist Communication', in John Caughie, ed., *Television: Ideology and Exchange* (British Film Institute, 1978), pp. 4–5.
2. Karl Marx, *A Contribution to the Critique of Political Economy*, cited in Mattelart, 'Nature of Communication', p. 5.
3. Mattelart, 'Nature of Communication', p. 6.
4. Herminio Martins, 'Opposition in Portugal', *Government and Opposition*, 4 (1969), p. 257. Charles Maurras was a political writer and founder of *Action Française*, an extreme right-wing movement that espoused direct action, rejected elections, defended the role of the Church, and made an ideology out of the hereditary principle.
5. Martins, 'Opposition in Portugal', p. 263.
6. Lord Russell of Liverpool, *Prisons and Prisoners in Portugal: An Independent Investigation*, cited in Hugh Kay, *Salazar and Modern Portugal* (Eyre & Spottiswoode, 1970), p. 339.
7. Kay, *Salazar and Modern Portugal*, p. 339.
8. António Ferro, *Salazar – Portugal and Her Leader* (London, 1939), pp. 26–7.
9. Martins, 'Opposition in Portugal', p. 253.
10. Ibid., p. 263.
11. L. A. Sobel, ed., *The Portuguese Revolution 1974–76* (New York, 1976), p. 17.
12. Mário Soares, *Portugal's Struggle for Liberty* (Allen & Unwin, 1970), p. 247.
13. José Cardoso Pires, 'Changing a Nation's Way of Thinking', *Index on Censorship*, no. 1 (Spring 1972), pp. 47–63.
14. Pires, 'Changing Thinking', p. 103.
15. Ibid., p. 95.
16. Ben Pimlott interview with Marcello de Sousa, Lisbon, July 1978.
17. Maria Velho da Costa, Maria Isabel Barreno, and Maria Teresa Horta, three professional writers, were arrested for offending public morals three weeks after their joint book, *The New Portuguese Letters*, was published in April 1972. Court proceedings began in October, and the trial dragged on for many months. Meanwhile, the cause of the 'Three Marias' was taken up by women's organizations and others abroad who protested against a new Portuguese law which made writers,

publishers, printers, and distributors legally responsible for the morality of their works. In April 1974, immediately after the coup, the trial ended abruptly and the judge proclaimed the book a work of literary merit.

18. Marcello Caetano, *Depoimento*, cited in António de Figueiredo, *Portugal: Fifty Years of Dictatorship* (Penguin, 1975), p. 232.

19. See Jean Seaton and Ben Pimlott, 'The Role of the Media in the Portuguese Revolution' in Anthony Smith, ed., *Newspapers and Democracy: International Essays on a Changing Medium* (Massachusetts Institute of Technology Press, 1980), pp. 176–99.

20. Taking the sample for the nation as a whole, the percentage claiming to have read or skimmed a daily paper in the preceding month was 30. Regional percentages were as follows: greater Lisbon 53, greater Porto 63, Littoral 20, interior north 16, interior south 26 (Source: Ministry of Social Communications [Lisbon, 1976]).

21. See Seaton and Pimlott, 'Role of the Media' for a development of these points.

22. Pires, 'Changing Thinking', p. 98.

23. Ministry of Social Communications, *Informação popular e turismo*, vol. 1 (Lisbon, 1972).

24. See J. Gaspar and N. Vitorino, *As Eleições de 25 de Abril: Geografia e Imagem dos Partidos* (Lisbon, 1975); Ben Pimlott, 'Parties and Voters in the Portuguese Revolution', *Parliamentary Affairs*, vol. 30, no. 1 (Winter 1977), pp. 38–58; and Seaton and Pimlott, 'Role of the Media'.

25. In the spring of 1975 the workers' committee of the pro-Socialist Party (PS) newspaper *República* demanded the removal of PS members of the editorial staff. The Socialist leader, Mário Soares, succeeded in attracting international attention to what was presented as a further example of the suppression of press freedoms by the communists and their allies. Within Portugal, Soares was able to use the *República* affair as a reason for pulling the Socialist Party out of the Government, and for holding the biggest demonstration of opposition to the Gonçalves régime that Lisbon had yet seen. Thus Soares adroitly turned a minor, but symbolically important, dispute about editorial control (in which the communists were probably not involved in any direct way) into a challenge to the whole direction of the revolution. The Fourth Provisional Government fell, and with it disappeared any chance that Portugal would become an outpost of the Soviet bloc.

DIETZGEN AND
THE AUTODIDACTS

IS THERE — CAN THERE BE — an independent working-class culture that is truly intellectual? As Professor Joad might have said, it depends on what you mean by intellectual. But the question also concerns the nature of speculative thinking, and the extent to which it can be self-serving.

In his pioneering *A Proletarian Science* (1980) Stuart Macintyre drew attention to an important tradition of British working-class 'autodidacts', self-taught scholars who developed a brand of 'proletarian' Marxism that reached a peak of influence in the early 1920s, before it was killed off by the sterile dogmas of middle-class stalinists. Examining the decline of this essentially pre-leninist vernacular, Macintyre felt that much of value had been lost. Jonathan Rée, retreading some of the same ground, is less sure. In this elegant and energetic essay, Rée suggests that quackery and self-justification were the main ingredients of autodidactic Marxist theory. At the same time he points to a central, and continuing, proletarian dilemma. How can the working-class escape the political and economic domination of other classes, while accepting the domination of their ideas?

It was this conundrum that led Victorian self-improvers to the study of philosophy, conceived as an all-embracing attempt to explain an oppressive world. 'Philosophy finds its *material* weapons in the Proletariat,' wrote the young Marx, 'just as the Proletariat finds its *spiritual* weapons in Philosophy.' For the autodidacts, however, philosophy was less a spiritual weapon than a form of spiritual expression. Marx was admired, in some cases even read, by self-taught working men who did not seek to emulate or join the middle classes. Yet it was precisely the most defiantly class-conscious who faced the cruellest dilemma.

Proletarian Philosophers: Problems in Socialist Culture in Britain 1900–1940, Jonathan Rée (Oxford University Press, 1984)

On the one hand, according to Rée, the acquisition of literary culture against the odds filled them with 'a somewhat acrid feeling of proletarian righteousness' at their ability to equal or surpass the leisured classes in the middle-class cultural game. On the other hand, there was an uncomfortable awareness that the rules of the game, providing the framework and much of the content of their learning, had been set by their exploiters. What made the dilemma more acute was the link that existed between self-teaching, self-help, self-denial and nineteenth-century religious nonconformity. 'In 1900 we got converted to socialism,' wrote Tommy Jackson, whose autodidacticism began with a sixpenny junkshop copy of G. H. Lewes's *Biographical History of Philosophy*, 'almost literally in the same way that we became converted from sin to "Salvation".' Such conversions increased the appetite for knowledge, and hence for books written by representatives of the class enemy.

Jackson and his friends, believing (as Rée puts it) in 'a certain rather majestic kind of Marxism', hoped that education would open the workers' eyes to the tricks played by the capitalist class. The aim was to discover the human potential for happiness, but also to change, in the words of the Socialist Labour Party (a Marxist forerunner of the British CP), the working man's 'crude and untutored discontent into intelligent and educated revolutionary thought and action'. Reaching up into the citadels of middle-class learning for what it could give, the radical autodidacts encountered bourgeois progressives coming the other way: high-minded disciples of the 'Oxford Hegelian' T. H. Green, seeking to bestow upon their less fortunate brethren the benefits of civilized culture.

Though more successful among aspirant members of the lower middle class than among the working class, the University Extension Movement nevertheless offered the proletarian autodidacts both an opportunity and a challenge. When Ruskin Hall was established in Oxford, the aim, according to the founders, was to enable working-class scholars to 'lead a life worthy of a citizen and a man', while not disturbing the social order. 'It is not intended', they declared, 'that a man should rise out of his class to swell the already-crowded professional classes.' Here, as it happened, was a real problem. For if the function of a liberal education was to train men to become lawyers, clergymen and civil servants; and if the number of positions for lawyers, clergymen and civil servants remained small; what was the purpose of a liberal education for the large and growing numbers who wanted it but were surplus to requirements?

Rejecting the view that Ruskin should help workers to take up culture 'in much the same way that a professional man might take up gardening', a dissident group of students within the college (as it had become), presented their alternative: working-class education that was of, as well as for, the working classes. The result was the Plebs League, set up in opposition to 'the permeation of University ideas in the minds of the young blood of labour'. By the early 1920s, the 'Independent Working-Class Education' movement, with its Central Labour College and its residential and correspondence courses, had 30,000 part-time enrolments.

The 'Plebs' considered proletarian philosophy an indispensable part of revolutionary socialist education. Yet what was 'proletarian philosophy', and what were the features that made it distinctively proletarian? For members of the IWCE movement, one 'proletarian' philosopher, almost unknown in the university world, was pre-eminent: Joseph Dietzgen ('Ditchkin' as the miners called him), a former tanner, a contemporary, disciple and interpreter of Marx, and the author of many opaque Germanic tomes. Rée is interested, not in the thoughts of Dietzgen, which he finds anodyne, but in the phenomenon. Why, he wonders, did generations of knowledge-seeking workers treat Dietzgen's ponderous and often incomprehensible works as holy writ?

The reason appears to have been the compelling appeal of Dietzgen's central idea. The proletariat, Dietzgen contended, was the progenitor and true inheritor of philosophy. Dietzgen's heavy foreign jargon seemed, paradoxically, to justify a message which the working-class radicals wanted to believe: that university wisdom reflected the assumptions of the university-attending classes, and that true understanding resided elsewhere. 'When he was not tanning hides in his tannery in the little Rhineland town of Sieburg', wrote a typical admirer, 'he was in his leisure hours tanning the hides of the decadent philosophers.'

In the end, university-trained marxists rumbled Dietzgen, asking the embarrassing question 'Is Dietzgen and all Dietzgen stands for worth studying at all?', and the labour college movement was persuaded to put the old charlatan on the shelf: but not before he had gained a place in the autodidacts' pantheon alongside Marx and Engels. Few British workers made much progress with Dietzgen undilute. Vernacular textbooks on 'Dietzgenism', however, turning gobbledy-gook into homespun proverbs, continued to circulate among working-class radicals long after the British Communist Party had officially proscribed them.

Did Marxism have a 'philosophy' at all? Lenin, who apparently held Dietzgen in high regard, followed him in thinking so. Not all of Lenin's supporters agreed, and there were some in Russia who campaigned under the banner: 'Science to the bridge – Philosophy overboard!', seeing philosophy *per se* as a prop to the bourgeoisie. It was after Lenin's death that 'philosophy', redefined, came into its own as part of the Comintern's global strategy. Pro-Stalin red guards seized control of the Soviet academies, seeking to codify 'dialectical laws' and demanding 'the unity of theory and practice'. According to Rée, it became absolutely indiscernible whether the new, 'proletarian' professors 'supposed that party policy was to be determined by philosophical argument, or whether it was the opposite way round'.

Thus, in Britain, one kind of opiate replaced another. Here was a strange twist. The new 'dialectical materialism' had been invented in Russia to beat down the Russian bourgeois professors. It was imposed on British comrades in the early 1930s to replace the vulgar Marxism of Dietzgen and its locally adapted forms. Yet dialectical materialism was, if anything, even more impenetrable than Dietzgenism, and only the bourgeois professors could claim to understand it. As a result, British working-class communists, while accepting the correctness of dialectical materialism, left its interpretation to the intellectuals – the very group whose influence it had originally been devised to undermine.

Oddly enough, while the appeal of Dietzgenism had been almost entirely restricted to working-class socialists, dialectical materialism for a time enjoyed a vogue in some sections of the intelligentsia. Little interest was aroused among professional philosophers, who saw it as a throwback to the bad old days of Platonism and Hegelianism, which had been overtaken by advances in the discipline. Natural scientists, however, were attracted by its apparently 'scientific' view of society, and by the light it seemed to shed on the history of science. In the hungry and war-threatened 1930s, it also appealed to many writers, poets and artists, encouraged by its alternative certainties.

There was widespread agreement with the biologist Lancelot Hogben, who saw as a virtue of the new doctrine that it had 'laid quietly to rest the ghost of Joseph Dietzgen'. Unlike the Dietzgenists, however, those who professed to see meaning in dialectical materialism generally stood outside the culture and routines of most socialist and

Marxist activists. The communist hierarchy was happy to keep them there. Where the old autodidacts of the Plebs League had regarded orthodox academic distinction with contempt, the Communist Party of Harry Pollitt revered it. There were many stories of eager young communist students being told to assist the class struggle by working for a first. British Marxism had, indeed, come full circle.

Often, in this stimulating book, one is struck by the inappropriateness of terms. The issue was theological, not – as the disputants believed – philosophical. The search was not for knowledge but for a politically serviceable religion. Perhaps, therefore, it is as unfair to set Dietzgen or his stalinist supplanters intellectual tests as it would be in the case of Joseph Smith and the Book of Mormon. Nevertheless, the dissatisfaction of the proletarian autodidacts – the reason for their search – is important. Questions fundamental to all education (where should it come from, what is it for, what values should it adopt, whose interests should it serve?) are no closer to resolution. With witty, lucid openmindedness, Jonathan Rée provides an imaginative and unusual contribution to the debate.

Times Higher Education Supplement, 6 July 1984

THE STRANGE LIFE OF
BRITISH STALINISM

COMMUNISM IS NOW SO DEAD and discredited in most parts of the world that it is hard to recall that it was once regarded by many free, intelligent, well-informed and honourable people in the West as the only hope for humanity. Why did they allow themselves to be duped? The question is as interesting as the still unsolved mystery of the Eastern version's cardiac arrest.

At the height of the Stalin era, Britain's best-known communists were Harry Pollitt and Rajani Palme Dutt – two powerful characters who reflected in their contrasting backgrounds and approaches the twin facets of the Party's appeal, to the proletarian and to the intellectual. Pollitt, a former shop steward, led the Communist Party of Great Britain as its general secretary (with one short interlude) from 1929 to 1956; Dutt was the British Party's chief theologian from the 1920s until the 1960s, editing its key theoretical journal, *Labour Monthly*, for fifty years. Both men gave inspiration to thousands of adherents. These excellent, scholarly and thoughtful books scrutinize the forces that shaped them, and provide fascinating insights into the workings of the CPGB in its proudest years.

Pollitt and Dutt were a double-act – the one offering working-class authenticity, the other sinews of analysis. But Pollitt was always the more considerable political figure. He was also the more attractive, with a vivid personality that belied the stereotypical image of the communist as an ice-cold manipulator. Morgan's study of him is one of the best Labour Movement biographies I have ever read. Admirably succinct, tightly written and politically sensitive, it deftly sorts out the historical wheat from the marxian chaff. Biographies of working-class heroes are hard to write: unlike Bloomsbury aesthetes, people who leave school at twelve do not usually leave trails of diaries and letters. Pollitt was an exception: Morgan has made use of a treasure trove of letters, generally written in a sturdy, cheeky vernacular, which enables him to paint a convincing portrait of Pollitt as a warm, vital, angry and charismatic tribune, without ignoring his self-deceptions.

Pollitt was born into Lancashire poverty in 1890. His father was a drunkard, his mother a fierce matriarch who worked her fingers to the bone and instilled in her son a lifelong hatred of her oppressors. Harry was an autodidact in the best Edwardian tradition: a graduate of trade union meetings, socialist rallies and picket lines. By the time of the Communist Party's foundation in 1920, he was already a battle-hardened militant. He was never much interested in marxian theory, and was hazy about whether communism existed to make the trade unions a revolutionary force, or the other way round. But (like most communists of his generation) he was unswervingly clear that the tide of history was towards a bloody civil war, and that it was the job of true socialists to prepare for it.

It was as a practical man of common sense that Pollitt was talent-spotted by the Comintern, and elevated to general secretary – in effect Stalin's instrument in Britain. He was, suggests Morgan, an unlikely agent of dictatorship; for a start he had a sense of humour. As his letters attest, he felt deeply about the working men and women he championed, but he was frequently ruthless and cynical. He was also a renowned diplomat and negotiator. When he was not 'cooing to the Independent Labour Party like a sucking-dove', he was often sucking up to Labour politicians, such as the gullible Sir Stafford Cripps. But he, too, was a gullible tool. After his former girlfriend disappeared in Moscow during the Great Terror, he made such vigorous representations on her behalf as to jeopardize his own position; yet when these failed, he did not draw the obvious conclusion that his Soviet masters were a bunch of paranoid murderers, but closed his mind to the subject, and never criticized the purges publicly or privately.

Pollitt's value to the Soviet Union lay partly in his rootedness. He was, as Dutt wryly put it, 'as English as a Lancashire rose or an oak', a part of the Labour Movement mainstream. He was an ardent supporter of links with the Labour Party, especially in the heady years of the would-be Popular Front following the Comintern's call in 1935 for a united stand against fascism. His efforts probably contributed to the mood on the left that made Churchill's 1940 'Popular Front' coalition possible. By then Pollitt was in the doghouse as far as Moscow was concerned, for temporarily refusing to toe the line on opposing the war. He almost immediately recanted. But it is fair to regard this wartime wobble as evidence that he was more than just a programmed robot.

It is hard to say the same of Rajani Palme Dutt, whose life story – skilfully told by Professor Callaghan – reinforces the impression of him as the aesthetic emissary of a foreign inquisition. Dutt's revolutionary fervour seems to have begun as a reaction to racial prejudice. Though born in Cambridge, he was the son of an immigrant Indian doctor. His mother came from a good Swedish family: his relations in the next generation included two Scandinavian prime ministers, Olaf Palme of Sweden and Sulo Woulijoki of Finland. Rajani owed much to a British establishment education, obtaining (after a period of imprisonment for conscientious objection and expulsion from the university) a brilliant First in Classics at Oxford. Perceiving the world at the end of the First World War to be 'rotten-ripe for radical change', he was drawn by a system that substituted order for chaos. Here we enter dark realms of psychopathology: why should an intensely rational man opt for a mental strait-jacket? How could a trained philosopher declare that 'there is only one correct answer for every specific situation,' an answer discoverable by 'the right method'?

One factor was his wife, the mysterious Salme Murrick, who deserves a biography of her own. A veteran of tsarist exile and of the Finnish civil war, Salme was an Estonian Bolshevik who had petitioned Lenin in 1920 to be 'sent to where the struggle was toughest'. Lenin obliged by despatching her to Britain to help found the Communist Party. Almost immediately not only Dutt, but also Pollitt, fell under her spell – she became a constant source of advice and admonition to both men, the oracle with a direct line to Kremlin thinking. Before setting out, Salme had been given 'four large diamonds': Callaghan speculates that these helped provide the capital for *Labour Monthly*.

In 1924, Rajani and Salme departed on a self-imposed exile to the Continent that lasted most of twelve years – ostensibly on health grounds, but more probably to be closer to the Comintern bureaucracy. It was in this period that Dutt established himself as the most ingenious and prolific interpreter of the Soviet gospel in the English-speaking world. Today, he is one of the least readable: indeed, the remarkable thing is that he was ever read at all, so stilted is his style and so obviously derived from Soviet sources. Unlike Pollitt, Dutt had no difficulty in arguing one proposition one day and the opposite the next. Like O'Brien in *Nineteen Eighty-Four* or Rasimov in *Darkness at Noon*, he saw no objective reality, but only ends that justified any conceivable means.

Such an approach made the truth impossible to accept, even when it became inescapable. Neither Pollitt nor Dutt ever came to terms with Stalin's villainy, but Pollitt had the good sense to die in 1960, while the evidence was still disputable. Dutt lived into the 1970s, pooh-poohing the Sino–Soviet split (although he was an expert on the Far East) and accusing Khrushchev of 'spitefulness' in launching his revisionist attacks on the old era.

Yet – and here is the irony contained within these two books – though one may scorn such self-delusions, one cannot dismiss the phenomenon of which they were part: an important and influential British culture which, for all its folly on big issues, was profoundly moral in its outlook. If the global evil that came out of international communism evokes horror, it is a curious fact that such accounts of earnest endeavour, selfless comradeship and misdirected purpose arouse in the reader not revulsion, but wonderment, grudging respect, for at least part of the time, and unease.

Independent on Sunday, 15 August 1993

FORWARD MARCH,
LEFT WHEEL

TWO QUITE SEPARATE questions are considered in this important and timely collection. First, why has the Labour Party declined in membership and votes since its early post-war peak? Second, how far has decline, stagnation and relative impotence come to affect not just the Labour Party, but the whole Labour Movement? Some contributors succeed in keeping these questions apart. Others, erroneously, regard them as inextricably linked.

The book contains three short essays by Eric Hobsbawm, seventeen by other contributors, and an interview with Tony Benn: all originally published in the theoretical journal, *Marxism Today*. The starting point is the 1978 Marx memorial lecture, in which Hobsbawm surveyed developments in working-class history over the past century. He points, in particular, to the changing occupational and class structure and the decline of the manual working class within it; to the reduced specialization of labour; to the growth of a large female workforce; to the disturbing development of anti-immigrant feeling within the working class; and to 'a growing division of workers into sections and groups each pursuing its economic interest irrespective of the rest.'

Finally – and most dramatically – he comes to the shrinking Labour vote (and here there is a prophetic element, because Hobsbawm was writing before the humiliation of the 1979 Labour defeat, let alone the local and by-election disasters that have followed it). Between 1900 and 1951, apart from the temporary setback of 1931, the Labour vote increased without interruption, reaching a peak of almost 14 million or just under 49 per cent. Since 1951, by contrast, there has been a persistent decline, both in numbers and percentages, apart from a short-lived upturn in the mid-1960s.

The Forward March of Labour Halted?, ed. M. Jacques and F. Mulhern (Verso, 1981)

Hence, Hobsbawm concludes, we can see that the Labour Movement which expanded for seventy years has in the last thirty 'got stuck' in every respect except one – the growth and unionization of a new labour aristocracy of white collar technical and professional workers, and the radicalization of the students and intellectuals of which this stratum is composed. As a result, at precisely the moment of a crisis in world capitalism, the Labour Movement appears tragically incapable of providing leadership to the working class.

Other essays respond to this thesis, often in a highly critical way. Writers come from a wide range of backgrounds: industrial, academic, parliamentary. All are Marxist, or at least militant left, in outlook. Almost all take for granted that the most hopeful political development of recent years has been the emergence of the movement with which Tony Benn has become associated. Many, if not most, agree with Ken Gill that, far from getting stuck, the Left has been advancing fast in recent years. The growing influence of militant shop stewards, the development of a powerful women's movement, the radicalization of Labour policy, Gill suggests, are all of greater significance than the superficial criterion of electoral success.

Kevin Halpin points to the achievement of the miners in challenging the Government on the picket lines. Digby Jacks draws a contrast between Baldwin who took on the miners in 1926 and won, and Heath who took them on in 1973–74 and lost. Royden Harrison argues that, since the war, even when the Tories have been in power, they have not been in power in the old kind of way. 'They either respected the new social settlement or else the workers rose against them and chucked them out.' Surveying events since the 1979 general election, Robin Blackburn suggests that 'the advances of the Left within the Labour Party, the growth in the activity and numbers of party members, and the encouraging results of the local elections of May 1981' all point to a reversal of the trends which culminated in the 1979 Thatcher victory.

Replying in a concluding essay, Hobsbawm declares that 'nobody can seriously deny that the British Labour Movement today is in a considerable mess', or that Labour is probably less of a mass party at the moment than the Conservatives. Indeed for the first time since 1923 the national Labour electorate is today actually smaller than the number of unionists affiliated to the TUC.

Taken together, the contributions make a fertile brew, the more so for reflecting the attitudes of radical unionists and shop stewards as well as professional brain-workers. Yet in a sense Hobsbawm's appeal to fellow Marxists 'to recognize the novel situation in which we find ourselves, to analyse it realistically and concretely, to analyse the reasons, historical and otherwise, for the failures as well as the successes of the Labour Movement, and to formulate not only what we would want to do, but what can be done' – is inadequately answered.

Though some writers consider the electoral aspect, none gives it the serious attention it deserves. This is a pity. For it is quite possible that the Labour Movement has been (as many of the writers claim) more radical and militant in recent years than in earlier stages of its history; and yet that, at the same time, Labour's electoral base has been so dangerously eroded that there may never be an opportunity to implement the new policies which this radicalism has helped to produce.

Indeed, by conducting the debate wholly within the temple of Marxism, empirical evidence has been sadly neglected. Though there is some examination of union and Labour Party membership figures, there is almost none (except in a single paragraph by Hobsbawm) of the opinion poll data on which SDP calculations have been so professionally based. If (as is clearly the case) a large and growing section of the electorate has detached itself from automatic loyalty to Left or Right, this is a subject which should be given first priority in any discussion of the prospects for a socialist policy.

Industrial militancy alone cannot improve education, revolutionize social services, or reduce unemployment. At the level of policy-making, the Forward March of Labour may be halted for a very long time unless the Labour Party can discover, and discover fast, why with three million people on the dole and a Conservative government in power, the electorate so dislikes it.

New Society, 3 December 1981

THE HARSH WEST WIND
OF FREEDOM

BY MANY CRITERIA, Hungary is already a democracy. It certainly has freedom. True, 85 per cent of the non-agrarian economy is state-owned, which doesn't give newly-exalted entrepreneurs much room for manoeuvre. But there has been effective liberty of speech on all but a few delicate matters (such as the Soviet occupation) for years, and there is now full press and literary freedom. Until recently, a handful of writers whose books had once offended Moscow were kept on the index – Orwell, and the Hungarian-born Koestler in particular. Now even that degree of censorship has gone.

Three hundred new publishing houses have sprung up in the last twelve months alone – pretty good in a country of ten million people. The less wonderful news is that most of what they produce is pulp fiction. Freedom of dramatic expression, meanwhile, has meant a dropping of inhibitions that is a characteristic feature of post-authoritarian societies. Mrs Whitehouse should avoid Budapest in her travels: at my skyscraper hotel every room was thoughtfully equipped with its own hard-core porn video, available at the press of a button.

More important is the absence of fear. Hungary had a pretty unpleasant first two-thirds of the twentieth century even by east European standards. But since the late and unlamented Janos Kádár – the traitor of 1956 – began his pioneering liberalization two decades ago, relatively civilized values have prevailed. The Iron Curtain stereotype has long since lost its relevance: contempt and irritation with a puppet régime replaced the last remnants of terror even before the Gorbachev era.

But it is not just that Soviet *perestroika*, when it came, kicked at a swinging door in Hungary as in Poland; nor that in recent years Hungary has had fewer political prisoners than Britain (no Guildford Four or Birmingham Six here). It is that the remaining dangers have been melting away. Nobody now imagines that the Soviet Union would be mad enough to intervene again militarily in Hungarian affairs, what-ever happens in the Kremlin. In contrast to the Russians (who have some grounds for fearing their own generals), Hungarians see little physical threat from their compatriots, if only because everybody – even the military top brass – knows that the kind of economic relation-ship their country desperately needs with the West could not be achieved under any kind of restored dictatorship.

There isn't even, any longer, a serious fear of German revanchism – the old bogey which the Soviets once employed to keep their satellites in line. On the contrary, there is mainly eager anticipation at the prospect – which comes daily closer – of a greater Germany penetrat-ing and dominating the economies of its eastern neighbours with its investments and vast spending power. Much of the talk here is about possibilities of joining the Community or, as a consolation prize, EFTA.

Yet, by the most critical test, Hungary is *not* a democracy: its govern-ment is not elected. That is the next stage – and when it comes the departure of all but a token Soviet force must surely follow. A Russian withdrawal is bound to become a popular demand, and the Kremlin will be looking for ways to achieve it to minimize its own embarrassment.

After a referendum which will almost certainly legitimize the trans-formation from a party to a democratic state will come (if the schedule is maintained) the presidential election in January and parliamentary elections in the spring. What happens then is anybody's guess. There have never been properly free elections in normal times, unless you count those that took place in the immediate aftermath of the Second World War, when voters and politicians stared nervously up the barrel of a Soviet gun. Hungarian parties have no recent background, no social or cultural constituencies to refer to. Hungary has the proudest post-war history of struggle against oppression in east Europe: 20,000 killed in the 1956 Uprising, ten times that number forced into exile. But – unlike in Poland – end-of-century concessions have not come through working-class or religious pressure. This is a top-down revol-ution, exciting to bureaucrats (who want a market-orientated economy) and the intelligentsia, but viewed quizzically by the populace. When Portugal held its first free election after half a century of dictatorship, turnout exceeded 90 per cent. In Hungary there is a buzz among the chattering classes, but also talk of public apathy and even cynicism.

Within the élite, the most active fauna are chameleons and leopards changing spots. Everybody believes in liberalism and denounces the command economy. Yet scratch many of the older officials and you find a Stalinist underneath: there has been no systematic purge of rotten elements. One sexegenarian economist, who argued eloquently about the need for an immediate Hungarian application to the EC, told me in the same conversation that he had been a minister in the 1950s, forced out of office during the uprising, and reinstated once it was safely over. But who is to say such conversions are not genuine? Snake-like would be one way to describe the behaviour of the old Hungarian Communist Party, as it shed its old nomenclature like a skin. Yet there are plenty of members of the Hungarian Socialist Party – as the former, now divided, Communist Party's advanced wing now calls itself – who are genuine reformers.

One of these, Imre Posgay, Hungary's closest approximation to a western-style charismatic politician, may or may not become its first democratic president. Whoever wins in January, however, the Democratic Forum – a loose grouping of wettish Tories, allegedly backed by the respectable, the middle class, church-goers, small businessmen and agrarians – should top the poll in the spring, if it holds together that long. The smallholders' party, legatee of a 1940s formation, will receive (in a country with few smallholders) mainly urban support; so will the intellectual Free Democrats, against whom, however, there exists a degree of anti-Semitic hostility.

The outcome – desired as well as expected – is a coalition or national government able to share out among its various elements not only portfolios but also blame for the harsh economic measures which will have to be taken. Hungary's political turmoil may be less important to average Hungarians than the economic crisis which has helped to precipitate it. Nineteen per cent inflation and an accelerating debt crisis could lead to a collapse within two or three years, without the kind of tough policies democratic governments are reluctant to enforce, or a generous foreign bale-out, or both.

Hence – in a country poised between East and West, political hope and economic alarm – there is a manic-depressive air. As the bush-fire spreads through middle Europe (hardline Czechoslovakia is confidently expected to ignite within months), the Hungarian arsonists are flushed with elation, but also with the heat of the flames: what if the Soviet economy cracks under multiple strains? With street markets, vivid shop fronts, packed theatres, English-speaking cab drivers and double parking, Budapest feels like a relaxed western city. But for how long?

'Europeanization is Hungary's best hope,' cry the economists. Yet what Hungary needs in the short run is the smack of firm government, after an uncertain interregnum: tight money, wage restraint and the rest. Strikes, sit-ins, mass demonstrations – of which, so far, there have been few – will then begin to teach this peaceable nation the painful lesson of what democracy is really like.

Samizdat, No. 7, November–December 1989

A MARSHALL PLAN FOR
EASTERN EUROPE

THE OPPORTUNITY FACING EC leaders at their Paris summit on Saturday is plain: to launch a grand, over-arching recovery scheme, similar in conception to the great Marshall Plan which pumped dollar aid into western Europe between 1948 and 1952. Its purpose should be to underwrite *perestroika* and democratization across all those parts of east Europe now seriously engaged in reform, and especially the Soviet Union. The economic nature of such a programme should be subject to careful negotiation; but the political conditions should be kept to a minimum.

The Marshall Plan was forged out of a combination of imaginative vision and crude national self-interest. The US wished to alleviate European hardship and rehabilitate the defeated nations. But it also wanted to halt communism and to build a market for American goods. Both the generosity and the selfishness worked. A new scheme – also addressed at a time of precarious imbalance between nations – should be similarly hard-headed and open-handed. East European liberaliz-ation is not only good in itself: its survival is greatly to our advantage and we should be eager to pay whatever it costs to sustain it.

Every east European country is threatened by debt problems, in-flation, shortages or even bankruptcy. Whatever happens in Moscow, the former Soviet satellites are probably safe now from re-invasion, but disturbances in the Soviet Union's own republics, coupled with a central economic disintegration, may eventually lead to a military solution and restored dictatorship, with a possible domino effect on neighbouring states.

If that tragedy occurred, all eastern Europe could be thrown back into a new, frighteningly unstable, dark age. Hence the West has an overwhelming interest in depriving any would-be authoritarian group of the excuse or opportunity to intervene. It needs to show that liberalization pays economic dividends, much as the Americans demonstrated to western Europe after the war the economic benefit of democracy.

But there is also, as in the 1940s, a wider historical aspect. While the success of the Marshall Plan lay partly in the rapid recovery of west European countries, its most remarkable achievement was the reconciliation, after three bitter wars, of France and Germany.

No such reconciliation has yet been achieved in the East, and, indeed, fear of a revived Germany was a major reason for the durability of the Cold War. If a greater Germany is now virtually inevitable, an ambitious Marshall-type scheme could go far towards alleviating the suspicions which it will arouse. It could smother traditional fears with its munificence and start to reintegrate not only the present GDR, but also the Soviet Union, into a wider European economy.

There is a danger, of course, of over-optimism: the literature of 'aid' economics is full of tales of the woeful effects on recipients of ill-considered handouts. Moreover, in critical respects the analogy with 1948−52 is a false one. The Marshall Plan successfully removed one major constraint on European economic pent-up strength: the lack of foreign exchange. With their storehouse of entrepreneurial skills, their advanced technologies and their appropriate infrastructures, the west European countries were ready for a fast expansion. By contrast, east Europe suffers from multiple constraints. Recent western experience shows how low can be the efficiency of investment in east Europe: the loans of the late 1970s led directly to the debt crises of the '80s. Whatever else, western economic assistance must avoid the danger of merely financing (even indirectly) increases in east European consumption.

Yet to appreciate such a difficulty is not to regard it as insuperable. The West has won Khrushchev's battle of peaceful co-existence: instead of burying us, we seem to have buried them. It is now up to us, for our own sakes, to dig them up. The Marshall Plan was not a simple infusion of cash. It was a skilfully administered, multi-faceted programme filtered through the offices of the Organization for European Economic Co-operation (OEEC). After General Marshall's Harvard speech in June 1947 there were plenty of doubting Thomases – including Denis Healey, who dismissed Marshall's remarks as 'not much more than waffling aloud'. It took Ernest Bevin to bring Americans and Europeans to the conference table, to hammer Marshall's words into deeds.

It may be unreasonable to ask Douglas Hurd to play the part of

Bevin: Britain no longer cuts the same figure in the world. Yet, as an offshore island little affected by historic anxieties, we are best placed to act as broker. The moment is certainly right for a new version of the OEEC, this time pan-European in membership, to act as intermediary and organizer for a great Community venture, towards which West Germany would be able, and would probably wish, to make the largest contribution.

Such an initiative would meet a willing response. So far from fearing German economic domination, most east Europeans are eager to link their destinies to the strongest economy in the continent. This in itself should provide a mutual incentive. Indeed the possibility begins to emerge of turning the rubble from the Berlin Wall into the foundation of a Europe that may eventually stretch from Siberia to Portugal.

The Times, 15 November 1989

PART V

Confound their Politics

NEW POLITICS

DISASTER CREATES ITS OWN SIMPLICITIES. Before we could enjoy, or thought we could enjoy, the luxury of theological disputation. Today there are two primary questions. How can the Labour Party be saved? How can an unpleasant government be displaced?

There used to be validity to the dictum: Oppositions do not win elections, governments lose them. It was never a formula for dynamism but it provided occasional spells in office. Twice after the great Attlee administration, it gave Labour a bare sufficiency of seats. In three-party Britain, the principle no longer holds. The Conservatives 'lost' the 1983 election, obtaining their fourth lowest proportion of the vote since 1945, and suffering a drop in support in every region. Yet they gained a larger total of seats than at any election for almost half a century. Waiting for ministers to discredit themselves has ceased to be enough. For Labour to win again, there must be a new element.

This necessity is underlined by the collapse in Labour's own vote: the Tories were able to increase their majority because the electors who rejected them – the overwhelming majority – were divided almost evenly between two alternative Oppositions. The litany of catastrophe is now familiar, but needs repeating. Labour's performance was worse than at any election since 1918. Labour remains the most working-class party; the majority of working-class people, however, are not Labour. Labour is still the party preferred by most council tenants; the Conservatives, on the other hand, are now the leading party among skilled workers. Geographically, Labour has been driven back into two separate, traditional redoubts, both in economic decline: the old regional heartlands of Scotland, Wales and the North of England; and the inner areas of big cities. In most constituencies elsewhere, it has been pushed into third place.[1]

For Labour to win, records have to be broken. The biggest swing in a general election since 1945 is 5.2 per cent. Labour needs 5.3 per cent even to deprive the Tories of their overall majority, and 10.5 per cent to obtain an overall majority itself. Such a colossal movement of opinion would be in the opposite direction to long-term trends. Except in October 1974, Labour's proportion of the vote has dropped at every election since 1966. This decline has been associated with social changes which are likely to continue: the spread of home-ownership, the contraction of the public sector, the decline in blue-collar trade unionism, the expansion of white collar and 'white blouse' work and the ageing of the electorate.[2] A drift back to two-party normalcy therefore seems exceedingly unlikely; especially when it is remembered that the old 'normalcy' was an historical freak, like full employment, and confined to the same period.

So much for the odds against us. They should not, however, be regarded as insuperable. If a Labour victory in such circumstances would be without statistical precedent, we should bear in mind that many precedents have recently been set aside and that we live in an age of electoral discontinuities. Over the past twenty years, the oscillations of public opinion have resembled the rocking of a boat in a gathering storm. Until the 1979 election it was the Conservative Party that seemed in the most serious trouble, having obtained in October 1974 the lowest percentage of the vote of any major party since 1931, and there was talk of the 'Scandinavianization' of British Conservatism. We should not forget that a projection from the Crosby by-election, just before the Falklands War, virtually eliminated the Tories from the House of Commons. 'Volatility', which pitched hard against Labour in 1983, need not always do so, as Ian McAllister and Richard Rose point out in a recent study:

> Turbulence offers both promise and threat to party leaders. It offers the promise of big shifts to the advantage of any party that can take positions and adopt a style of campaigning that is most attuned to the electorate at the moment. In a turbulent environment, voters are far readier to move than in the 'trench-warfare' elections between the big battalions of Labour Party and Conservative Party in the 1950s.[3]

Nor should we assume too easily that Labour is doomed by the erosion of its social base. The decline of traditional kinds of manual occupation, widely regarded as disastrous for Labour, need not necessarily be so. The class solidarity of British workers has been written off by social scientists once before, only to be rediscovered. At present it is again out of favour; we should not be amazed if it survived for an encore. If it is possible for the Conservatives to make inroads into social territory hitherto identified with Labour, it is by no means impossible for Labour to reverse the process (as happened in 1945) and draw in groups from outside its traditional base. The spread of trade unionism to white collar and even professional groups, and the consequent 'proletarianization' of the industrial behaviour of people whose assumptions had previously been individualistic, may be helpful to Labour in the long run.

Hence, defeatism is premature. But the imperative is clear. Given the existence of a rival of equal, if not greater, potential interest to disaffected Conservative supporters, Labour cannot expect to be the main beneficiary when the inevitable collapse of Thatcherism occurs unless it acquires the power to *attract* votes.

Where and how is the new ingredient, the philosopher's stone, to be found? For some, the answer is straightforward. Before the last election, opinion polls showed that in most areas of policy the electorate preferred Tory attitudes to Labour ones. Other research, meanwhile, indicates that policy preferences may have a more direct impact on voting than had hitherto been believed.[4] It is evident, therefore, that Labour lost votes because it failed to match its objectives to electoral demand. Labour can regain popularity (so it is contended) by jettisoning policies which the polls show to be unpopular, and by aiming to achieve a broader market appeal.

It is interesting to note that this argument, which caused a major split in the Labour Party when it was advanced by Hugh Gaitskell and his supporters after the 1959 election, is no longer divisive in the same way. After the much greater shock of June 1983, there was a feeling across the spectrum that changes of a fundamental nature had become necessary. At a conference of the Labour Co-ordinating Committee a few weeks after the defeat, heresy was in the air, and condemnation of those who preferred martyrdom to compromise received wide support.[5] At Brighton in October the new Party Leader, chosen by a 71 per cent vote in the electoral college, commended as 'the common sense of socialism, the realism of socialism', and as a maxim for the whole Labour Movement, Aneurin Bevan's words on political leadership: 'He who would lead must articulate the wants, the frustrations and the aspirations of the majority.' These words, Neil Kinnock seemed to suggest, had a new significance in the aftermath of 9 June.[6]

A different expression of the new revisionism has come from what might be termed the old traditional Left. Professor Eric Hobsbawm, whose distinguished works on labour history will be familiar to readers, has written extensively about the fortunes of the Labour Party since delivering a Marx Memorial Lecture in 1978 with the prophetic title: 'The Forward March of Labour Halted?'[7] Hobsbawm can claim to have seen it all coming. It is therefore in the spirit of 'I told you so' that he wags an admonishing finger at the Party of which he has never been a member. Labour, Hobsbawm asserts, must once again become the party of all who want democracy and a better and fairer society. To talk of 'opportunistic' concessions is inappropriate. 'It is not . . . opportunistic to take account of quite reasonable demands of bodies of people who are not satisfied that at present they are adequately met by Labour,' he writes, 'of home-owners, people who are dissatisfied with their children's schooling, or worried about law and order.'

Such remarks, like those of Mr Kinnock, will be widely endorsed throughout the Labour Movement. So will the sensible argument that Labour must avoid the folly of promising too much: such as a miracle cure to unemployment, which electors find unbelievable. It is where Professor Hobsbawm begins to throw the baby out with the bath water that we need to pause. There is a danger, he warns, that Labour activists may cease to care about their isolation from average demands, and choose their supporters to fit their convictions: 'For instance, they may see their most congenial constituency as "the dispossessed" in "the centre of the big decaying city", cosmopolitan and racially mixed, and look for a parliamentary seat in preference in such a place.'[8] Thus, it is implied, we should carefully weigh the electoral value of home-owners against that of inner city dwellers before deciding our programme.

The logic is tempting, but dangerous. One obvious objection is that for many of us concern about the dispossessed in the centre of the big city is the most compelling reason for working within the Labour Party. If the price of electoral victory is to give poverty and inequality as low, or even lower, a priority than in 1964–70 and 1974–9, we might become finally disillusioned. There is, however, a more fundamental objection. The implicit model of voting behaviour accepted by Hobsbawm derives, perhaps unconsciously, from American 'pluralist' redefinitions of democracy in the 1950s, in which the political arena is presented as a marketplace, where politicians bid for the votes of citizens (the stockholders). Policy becomes a currency, and votes go to the highest bidder. This model, reflecting American capitalist assumptions of the early Cold War era, in fact misrepresents the way in which voters actually behave. The alternatives for a party seeking power are not rigidity and defeat *versus* concession and victory. The dichotomy is a false one.

It is of course evident that policies influence votes. The dynamics of the relationship, and the extent to which particular commitments may affect the preferences of specific groups at various times, however, remain mysterious. Opinion polls, which provide remarkably accurate short-term predictions of voting behaviour, offer little enlightenment. Skimming the surface of instant responses, surveys are unable to trawl the deeper waters of political emotion. If the calculus of politics was based on a simple interchange between spoken desires and their satisfaction, how easy the task of politicians would become! Long before opinion polls were invented, Graham Wallas, an early Fabian thinker, stated the problem facing the would-be political persuader:

> [M]ost of the political opinions of most men are the result, not of reasoning tested by experience, but of unconscious or half-conscious inference fixed by habit . . .
>
> Some men even seem to reverence most those of their opinions whose origin has least to do with deliberate reasoning. When Mr Barrie's Bowie Haggart said: 'I am of opeenion that the works of Burns is of an immortal tendency. I have not read them myself, but such is my opeenion,' he was comparing the merely rational conclusion which might have resulted from a reading of Burns's works with the conviction about them which he found ready-made in his mind, and which was the more sacred to him and more intimately his own, because he did not know how it was produced.[9]

It is not that electors are irrational: on the contrary. It is just that their reason does not operate in easily accessible ways. We should not assume that by striking out some paragraphs from our programme and adding others on the basis of a dissection of opinion poll data we will have any more success with the electorate than Burns encountered with Mr Haggart.

Labour's historic strength as a party has derived from its interest in power and its ability to gain support across the regions and, to a degree, across classes. Since 1918 it has not been a sectional party. But it has not been a catch-all or 'voter-orientated' party either.[10] Many of its best policies have been implemented despite, rather than because of, majority opinion. It was not populism which induced Labour to carry out, or permit, reforms in the law on hanging, divorce, abortion and homosexuality in the 1960s.[11] In each case Labour sought, with some success, to lead rather than to follow public opinion. Equally, the Labour Party's political charisma has not been based on consumerism, or on the lowest common denominator of individual wants. If the Conservatives have been the greedy party, Labour has sought – with considerable electoral success in the past – to be the compassionate party. It is no coincidence that it has won most votes when feelings of community and altruism have been at their highest. 'What matters is not that the party should offer a glittering programme, with promises for everyone', wrote R. H. Tawney in a Fabian essay early in 1945, 'but that it should put the nation on its mettle.'[12] It was on this basis, rather than by consulting auguries of public opinion, that Labour surprised itself and the world at the polls a few months later.

Labour in 1945 did not, of course, set itself arrogantly against the popular will. What it did do – and the lesson is a crucial one – was to place itself at the forefront of a tide of progressive feeling, partly of its own making. 'Labour was uniquely identified with a sweeping change of mood during the war years,' writes a leading historian of the period, 'and with the new social agenda that emerged.'[13] But it was the public which caught up with Labour rather than the other way around.

The recent experience of the Tories is also instructive. There is no doubt that the modern Conservative Party pays close attention to opinion polls. Mrs Thatcher's electoral success, however, owes little to them. Indeed, the Thatcher Government may well be remembered as the one which exploded the myth that to win elections it is necessary to embrace the consensus. It has been the Prime Minister's perverse achievement to turn savage deflation into an electoral asset: something which no pollster anticipated when she embarked on her policy, and something which nobody imagined possible when she was elected to office in 1979 having fought a campaign based on Labour's failure to deal with unemployment. What Mrs Thatcher correctly sensed was that, in bad times more than in good, it is not just votes that are volatile: opinions may change rapidly as well. Desperate conditions call out for radical solutions. By this argument, Labour lost votes, not because of its supposedly left-wing programme, but because its solutions and its leaders appeared the most backward-looking and least radical. Radicalism involves the knowledge, confidence and will to bring about great changes. It was these which Labour, for all its airy sloganizing, seemed to lack.

Should we, therefore, cling defiantly to our 1983 Manifesto until the voters accept it or forget what it contains? Quite the reverse. Rigidity and pragmatic trimming are equally to be deplored. What is required is a bonfire of commitments, and a new beginning.

The basis for Thatcher's right-wing radicalism has been the sophistry of monetarism. The rapid transformation of this doctrine from fringe medicine to new orthodoxy has been one of the wonders of our age. Neither Mrs Thatcher, nor her leading ministers, began as monetarists. If, therefore, we conclude that it is new ideas, not mere adjustment, that Labour most desperately needs, it is important to note how the monetarist revolution came about.

As a collection of essays marking the twenty-fifth anniversary (in 1981) of the Institute of Economic Affairs makes fascinatingly clear, the Thatcherite experiment is by no means the work of a fanatical clique, briefly in control of the citadel.[14] *Fas est ab hoste doceri* wrote Colin Clark, the (ex-Fabian) market economist – it is legitimate to learn from the enemy.[15] It was the Fabian Society, more or less, which provided the model for the free-market Institute and other equivalent bodies in their attempt to win over the Establishment by gentle propaganda. Alfred (now Sir Alfred) Sherman, chairman of the innocuously named Centre for Policy Studies, wrote in the preface of CPS pamphlets: 'Our object is to re-shape the climate of opinion.'[16] Inspired by the work of Milton Friedman, Friedrich von Hayek and Lionel Robbins, the evangelists of the New Right extended their influence, commissioning Hobart papers, holding informal seminars and encouraging private discussions.

Suddenly the moment came. Hyper-inflation found the Keynesians in disarray. 'Into the vacuum of economic policy', as Robin Murray aptly puts it, 'monetarism marched with the confidence of a zealot.' Ideas hitherto regarded as eccentric became respectable; and the new Conservative Party, with its own record of shamefaced U-turns and inconsistency, gained a faith to live by. With justice Arthur Seldon, IEA Founding Father, could endorse the comments of David Hume on the primacy of opinion in the affairs of men. 'Above all', wrote Seldon, 'the IEA was not deterred by the tired defences of established practices – "politically impossible", "administratively impracticable", "socially unacceptable".' Such hurdles could be surmounted through the power of ideas.[17]

There are three points. The first is that it has been *ideas*, not (as many apparently believe) marketing cosmetics, which stimulated the Tory revival. Second, the ideas emerged, not instantly in response to a demand to replenish the stock, or update the Party's image, but over a long period and on the basis of wide research, argument and thought. Third, they came from outside, creating a groundswell of sympathetic opinion, before their adoption by the Conservative Party leadership.

Is a similar process possible on the left? As Clark indicated, it has certainly happened before. The same approach led to the adoption of many aspects of Labour's 1945 programme, and to the advocacy by Labour of Keynesian principles. Fabians, moreover, need no lessons on entryism. 'We permeated the party organizations and pulled all the wires we could lay our hands on with our utmost adroitness and energy,' Bernard Shaw boasted in a famous tract, 'and we succeeded so far that in 1888 we gained the solid advantage of a Progressive majority, full of ideas that would never have come into their heads had not the Fabian put them there, on the first London County Council.'[18] In such matters, Fabians leave the IEA standing.

The problem is not disseminating, or gaining a hearing, for new ideas. It is having them. When a tide of opinion (not just party opinion) sweeps in one direction, it is hard to think clearly in the other. In the present climate, serious economists have to struggle to escape the dominance of the new conventional wisdom.

Yet if, as one newspaper put it recently, 'in all the places where opinion is formed and influenced and packaged and marketed, to be on the right now is not merely respectable: it is fashionable,'[19] this will not always remain so. For the New Right, birds are coming home to roost. When false prospectuses are no longer buoyed by the illusions of electoral arithmetic, we may expect confusion and dismay.

There is unlikely to be a stampede back to socialism – or not at once. Labour, however, has its own intellectual resources, insufficiently exploited. This is a point overlooked by socialist writers, especially those with roots outside the Party. Nor is it the case that in intellectual terms Labour has never had, as Stuart Hall claims, 'a proper legitimacy'.[20] From the 1930s to the 1960s, British cultural and intellectual life was virtually dominated by Labour sympathizers. For British intellectuals of the 1930s, in the words of Stephen Spender, politics 'were almost exclusively on the left'.[21] By the mid-1940s the socialist mood, defined in Labour terms, encompassed much of the civil service (to be non-political in 1945, wrote Maurice Edelman, 'was to be Labourish').[22] In the late 1950s, the confident tones of Anthony Crosland's *The Future of Socialism* conveyed the mood of an intellectual class for whom socialism, in one form or another, was still the natural creed.

It is a mark of our time that this is no longer the case. Yet it is by no means true that Labour has become the stupid party. If left-wing phrases have ceased to give Bloomsbury its patois, they are increasingly used today by a new breed of intellectual for whom they have a greater meaning. Even more than the working class, the contemporary middle class has splintered, and worships at many temples. Gareth Stedman Jones (for whom the 1945–51 reforms were the product of a 'new alliance between the organized working-class and professional middle-class progressivism') has argued that by the late 1960s it had ceased to be possible to speak even of the professional class as a unitary group. 'Differentiation' had occurred because of the post-war expansion of the state and service sector: 'The traditional professions were joined by social workers, polytechnic lecturers and whole new grades of state and municipal employees ... New forms of radicalism appeared among students, social workers, lecturers, school teachers and, to a lesser extent, among doctors and lawyers ...'[23]

In Stedman Jones's view the old class 'alliance' in the Labour Movement, so productive in the past, has broken down; yet Labour remains unhappily constructed on the assumption of its continued existence. Whatever may be said of this hypothesis ('alliance' was always an inappropriate metaphor, implying unity of purpose or interest on each side) Stedman Jones does well to draw attention to the importance of Labour's middle-class and intellectual following, and to crucial changes that have occurred within it.

It is certainly arguable that in the last fifteen years Labour's brain-workers have increased in importance, actual and potential. 'Polytechnic lecturers and social workers', agitating among the *sans culottes*, have become a newspaper cliché, lampooned in *Private Eye*'s composite Dave Spart, a trotskyist with a limitless capacity for Marxist jargon. Stedman Jones perpetuates the myth. It is significant nonetheless that in the 1980s polytechnics should occupy the place in the demonology of the Right which the London School of Economics filled in the days of Laski, Tawney and Dalton. More significant, however, than those who teach at polytechnics are those who learn at them, especially in the arts and social sciences: public sector employees, workers possessing or acquiring new skills, bright school-leavers from poorer areas, including, in particular, future members of the expanding black and brown middle class. This new higher education 'under class' provides a better and tougher recruiting ground for the Left than the campuses of the 1960s.

'Polyocracy' and 'lumpen polytechnic' (encompassing all socially-minded students and graduates of proletarian origin, not just those at or of polys) are terms which have been coined by right-wing journalists to indicate their snobbish disdain, based on a deep unease, at the sharply articulate tone of the new radicalism. The rise of the polyocracy has been made scapegoat for Labour's crisis. As one writer puts it, the archetypal infiltrator is supposed to have entered the Labour Party in the late 1960s and 'by a mixture of unpleasantness and stamina for long boring meetings, [driven] away its "salt-of-the-earth" working-class members, pushed through "extremist" policy resolutions and condemned Labour to a generation of electoral unpopularity'.[24]

In reality, Labour's 'lurch to the left', for good or ill, had little to do with changes in party membership. Constituency Labour Parties had been intermittently in revolt, demanding left-wing policies and more power, since they were first set up in 1918. The crucial factor after 1979 was a change of attitude in the trade unions which decided, for complex reasons, to punish the parliamentary leadership and increase their own influence in Labour Party affairs.[25] A similar decision, following a more emphatic betrayal, was taken by the unions in 1931–2.[26] Equally, the argument that the *embourgeoisement* of local parties in the big cities has lost Labour working-class votes is not supported by statistics. The exceptional case of Bermondsey apart, the Labour vote stood up no worse, and possibly better, in the inner urban areas. There continues to be little direct relationship between the nature of party organization and the size of the local Labour vote. It is sobering to note, however, that new, unknown Labour candidates performed significantly better on average than sitting Labour MPs.[27]

In many constituencies, indeed, the supposed polarization between Left and Right has been less important than a division between young and old, active and passive, young turk and party establishment. One does not have to side with the far Left, or ignore the damage caused in a handful of constituencies, to acknowledge that the old Labour Party structure, based on pre-war working-class social networks, had long been in decay. The present writer, as it happens, was one of those who joined an inner city party in the late 1960s. The memory is scarcely golden. It was not just the evidence of membership decline, or the lack of youth.[28] It was the weary cynicism, the lack of collective ambition, the indifference to political issues. Each new recruit had a different story: the difficulty of joining, ward parties which never met, the corruption of local councillors, agents exclusively concerned with raising their own salaries, GMCs which could not raise a quorum, and, above all, keenness treated as evidence of subversion. Perhaps Newcastle upon Tyne at the end of the T. Dan Smith/Andy Cunningham era was not typical. But there, at any rate, in traditional Labour country, the Labour Party seemed a shell. Part at least of the 'decline of working-class politics' thesis seemed valid: there was an inverse relationship between the size of the working-class vote in a ward, and Labour Party activity.[29]

During the 1970s there was a perceptible recovery. This is difficult to quantify. There is evidence that the number of 'true' members may have increased after a low point reached in the previous decade.[30] Whether or not this is correct, anybody with a wide experience of constituency parties nationwide will have observed a revival of activity. Meetings are now better attended, politics is back on the agenda, newsletters, outside speakers, campaigns have become routine; so have branch discussions informed by direct knowledge of local affairs, and by a greatly expanded and improved socialist periodical literature. There are still corrupt councillors and wards that never meet. But they are fewer.

We should consider the possibility that local parties which are less 'representative' of the electors than in the past are nevertheless better able to represent them. Where the change in constituency parties has worked its way through to councils, there have been blunders as well as achievements. But there has also been evidence of a greater willingness to lead rather than to be led, and to think clearly about objectives. One of the most stimulating Fabian pamphlets of recent years, *Building from the Bottom: The Sheffield Experience* by David Blunkett and Geoff Green, captures the flavour of the new municipal socialism: iconoclastic, experimental, irreverent towards established methods, seeking to show how 'the concept of community can form an alternative to that of greed and self-interest,' with – no doubt – a tendency to be over-optimistic about human nature.[31] Such bursts of energy may not last. Yet few would dispute that the influence of the new reformers on the way that socialists think about administrative problems has been profound.

Hampstead and the university professoriate may have moved to parties of the Centre and Right. In a sense, however, they no longer matter. 'MacDonald's act of treachery has, in fact, served as a drastic emetic,' Beatrice Webb wrote in 1932.[32] It is permissible to feel the same about the Gang of Four. There has been a shake-out of the establishment-minded; if the history of ideas tells us anything, we may expect the values and illusions of the young *enragés*, championing the dispossessed in the big decaying city, to have the deepest impact on political assumptions. A recovery of Labour confidence and sense of mission may well begin in the most afflicted urban areas – where poverty, bad housing, unemployment, ethnic tension are most severe – partly because economic factors have pushed better off people into areas which hitherto they had been inclined to forget.

Here is a reservoir to be tapped. Evidence of the intellectual fertility of the Left is in every bookshop: not since the 1930s has so much been written by socialist authors, much of it of a high standard, as in the last five years. Few writers, however, have related their thoughts or experience in a direct way to the problem of implementation. Even the most important work has placed greater emphasis on the failures of past Labour governments than on methods of avoiding them in the future. It is significant that only one Fabian pamphlet (although a notably good one) has examined the machinery of government.[33]

If, as has been argued, Labour has the capacity for renewal, it is the Fabian tradition, which may help to give it form, by channelling the enthusiasm and thirst for experimentation that is to be found in every branch of the Movement. There is, as Mrs Webb might have remarked, no substitute for hard work. There is also no substitute for open-mindedness. Both will be necessary for Labour to convince itself, as a prelude to convincing the electorate. And in so doing it will need to draw on the experience and imagination of many people who, hitherto, have barely been consulted.

There are two models of Labour Party policy-making in Opposition. Both are equally unsatisfactory.

The first assumes that policy must be, in the end, what ministers in office decide is best. In Opposition, the Labour Party should indicate in general terms what it intends, arm itself with debating points to back up its intentions, and make some – but not too many – specific commitments. This model was implicit in the behaviour and attitudes of Labour's parliamentary leadership from about 1967, and gave rise to justifiable complaint. According to Geoff Bish, Labour Party Research Department Secretary, in 1979:

> Despite all our efforts to prepare careful and detailed proposals, the status of the NEC *vis-à-vis* the Labour Government was, in practice, that of a mere pressure group, just one among many . . . the Government displayed little serious interest in the policy-making effort of the NEC and the Party – except, that is, on occasion, to repudiate publicly certain of the proposals put forward.[34]

The second model arose largely in reaction to the first. According to the second view, Labour governments are not to be trusted. Hence the Party's programme is to be regarded as an architect's blueprint. Success or failure should be judged by the extent to which the programme is carried out to the letter.

If the trouble with the first model was that it was politically vacuous, allowing ministers to become super-civil servants, the trouble with the second is that it is dangerously simplistic, seeking – almost certainly in vain – to turn ministers into puppets. There can be few more certain recipes for disappointment than a Cabinet bound by a textbook in which it at best only half-believes, and which, under the influence of events, it rapidly concludes cannot be followed. Nor is the 1983 Manifesto, combining vagueness, detail and internal contradiction, a good advertisement for this approach.

In fact, both models put the emphasis in the wrong place: on the *directive* aspect of policy-making. The first hopes to evade it, the second to impose it. There is, however, a third model which – without undermining the ability of the Movement to make firm and binding commitments – moves the problem of implementation onto another plane. According to this model, policy-making is a dynamic process, with no finished product. Detailed suggestions will emerge, but without any expectation that they will be strictly followed. The aim will be to inquire, expose, inform and educate; to inspire rather than to instruct; above all to give confidence by indicating the extent of possible achievement. Such a process will be informed by shared socialist values, and it will naturally take account of political realities. But it will not be restrained by tradition or symbolism. Its success will be judged not by the capacity of its supporters to push it through the Party's committees, but by its ability to make people outside as well as inside the Movement think deeply about its conclusions.

The first task will be herculean: shifting the detritus of generations. There is no single area of Labour policy that is not corroded by ritual adhesions, the result of recent or long-forgotten battles, or included to placate some intra-party pressure. The second task will be a sober extremism, confronting the present catastrophe with as much contempt for procrastination as for slogans. Such extremism will be in the tradition of the Webbs, Shaw, Cole, Laski, Tawney, Dalton and other Fabian and non-Fabian socialist thinkers who helped to change British society in the mid-twentieth century.

Above all – and this mundane point cannot be over-stressed – we need to show ourselves *how*, practically, financially, administratively, our aims are to be achieved. Peter Townsend concluded his trenchant criticisms of the 1974–9 Labour Government with the comment that socialists had wholly under-estimated the power of senior civil servants and especially Treasury officials to initiate policies. 'More important than the mobilization of opinion within the Labour Movement on behalf of new policies', he wrote, 'is the analysis of establishment organization and methods linked with proposals to control and reduce that power.'[35] This should be our starting point.

There are many other problems to be examined and conflicts to be resolved. The greatest area of difficulty is not the ground disputed between janissaries of right and left, who from their labours rest. Far more serious is the tension that exists within accepted Labour and socialist thought between a wish to extend the powers of the state and a desire to put power in the hands of the people.[36] If we do not have to accept that greater equality entails sacrifices of liberty; or that greater liberty involves a loss of efficiency; we do need to show, more clearly than we have, how the reconciliation is to be brought about. Centralism versus localism; planning versus workers' control and democratic participation; management versus co-operation; help to the low paid versus free collective bargaining; even, perhaps, international-ism versus socialism-in-one-country: never have these apparent incom-patibles been more shrouded in contradictory rhetoric and never in greater need of review.

Introductory essay in *Fabian Essays in Socialist Thought*,
(Heinemann, 1984)

NOTES

1. D. Massey, 'The contours of victory ... dimensions of defeat', *Marxism Today*, Vol. 27, no. 7, July 1983.

2. I. Crewe, 'How to link up and pick up vital seats', *Guardian*, 23 March 1984.

3. I. McAllister and R. Rose, *The Nationwide Competition for Votes: The 1983 British Election* (Pinter, 1984), p. 218. See also 'The Psephology of Discontinuities', pp. 213, *et seq.*

4. See H. T. Himmelweit, P. Humphreys, M. Jaeger and M. Katz, *How Voters Decide* (Academic Press, 1981).

5. This was my impression, attending sessions as a guest speaker. I do not refer to any particular vote or resolution.

6. *Report of the Annual Conference of the Labour Party 1983* (Labour Party, 1984), p. 30.

7. Reprinted in *Marxism Today*, and in M. Jacques and F. Mulhern (eds.), *The Forward March of Labour Halted?* (Verso, 1981), pp. 1–19.

8. E. Hobsbawm, 'Labour's lost millions' in *Marxism Today*, Vol. 27, no. 10, October 1983.

9. G. Wallas, *Human Nature in Politics* (2nd edn.) (Constable, 1910), pp. 103–6.

10. 'Voter-orientated' is used by Jean Charlot to describe the French Gaullist Party at the time when the social profile of its support was virtually identical to that of the nation as a whole. See J. Charlot, *The Gaullist Phenomenon* (Allen & Unwin, 1970).

11. Richard Crossman made this point when describing the Labour Party to an American audience in his famous lecture, 'The Battering Ram of Change', at Harvard in 1970 reprinted in R. Crossman, *Inside View* (Jonathan Cape, 1972), p. 110.

12. R. H. Tawney, 'We mean freedom', in J. Parker (ed.), *What Labour Could Do: Six Essays based on Lectures prepared for the Fabian Society* (The Labour Book Service, 1945), p. 103.

13. K. O. Morgan, *Labour in Power 1945–1951* (Oxford University Press, 1984), p. 44.

14. A. Seldon (ed.), *The Emerging Consensus ... ?, Essays on the interplay between ideas, interests and circumstances in the first 25 years of the IEA* (Institute of Economic Affairs, 1981).

15. C. Clark, 'The IEA and the Fabians: comparison and contrast' in *ibid.*, p. 204.

16. W. Keegan, *Mrs Thatcher's Economic Experiment* (Allen Lane, 1984), p. 47.

17. A. Seldon, 'Preamble' in A. Seldon (ed.), *op.cit.*, p. xxxiv.

18. G. B. Shaw, *The Fabian Society: What it has done; and how it has done it* (The Fabian Society, 1892).

19. *Sunday Times*, February 1984.

20. S. Hall, *New Socialist*, March–April 1983.

21. S. Spender, *The Thirties and After: Poetry, Politics, People 1933–1975* (Fontana, 1978), p. 13.

22. *New Statesman*, 11 March 1950, cited in Morgan, *op. cit.*, p. 317.

23. G. Stedman Jones, *Language of Class: Studies in English working class history 1832–1982* (Cambridge University Press, 1984); pp. 248–9.

24. J. Carvel, *Citizen Ken* (Chatto, London, 1984), p. 177. Carvel rejects the archetype.

25. See my 'Trade unions and the second coming of CND', in B. Pimlott and C. Cook (eds.), *Trade Unions in British Politics* (Longman, 1982), pp. 230–1.

26. See B. Pimlott, *Labour and the Left in the 1930s*, (Cambridge University Press, 1977), pp. 18–19.

27. McAllister and Rose, *op. cit.*, p. 175.

28. See B. Pimlott, 'Are CLPs necessary?', in I. Bing (ed.), *The Labour Party: an organisational study*, Fabian Tract 407, 1971.

29. See B. Hindess, *The Decline of Working Class Politics* (MacGibbon and Kee, 1971). Hindess based his observations on a study of ward Labour parties in Liverpool.

30. P. Seyd and L. Minkin, 'The Labour Party and its members', *New Society*, 1979, Vol. 49, no. 885 (discussed in P. Whitely, *The Labour Party in Crisis*, Methuen, 1983, p. 57).

31. Fabian Tract 491, 1983, p. 28.

32. B. Webb: unpublished diary, 19 March 1932.

33. D. Lipsey (ed.), *Making Government Work*, Fabian Tract 480, 1982.

34. G. Bish, 'Working relations between government and party', in K. Coates (ed.), *What Went Wrong* (Spokesman, 1979), p. 164.

35. P. Townsend, 'Social planning and the Treasury', in N. Bosanquet and P. Townsend (eds.), *Labour and Equality: A Fabian Study of Labour in Power, 1974–79* (Heinemann, 1980), p. 21.

36. The problem is not a new one. See K. O. Morgan, 'The high and low politics of Labour: Keir Hardie to Michael Foot', in M. Bentley and J. Stevenson (eds.), *High and Low Politics in Modern Britain* (Oxford University Press, 1983), pp. 285–312.

A POPULAR FRONT OF THE MIND

DISCUSSION ABOUT HOW the Labour Party might maximize its chances at the next election, and even stop the Conservatives from winning a fourth term, starts from two premises: first, that Labour is not already inexorably doomed; second, that it is possible within its amorphous structure for any person or group to follow through a rational course of remedial action. Neither is necessarily true.

The belief that Labour can be rescued may be an act of faith. Simple arithmetic certainly points to the opposite conclusion. The 1987 result is scarcely a deviation from the dismal downward trend in Labour support that started after the 1951 peak. Labour's brilliant, streamlined, professional, almost faultless election campaign this June – few superlatives were absent from the patronizing praise of the leader-writers once the Tories had victory firmly in the bag – restored Labour to a level of popular support approximately equal to that of 1931, the election that produced the most unbalanced Parliament and the biggest right-wing majority ever.

However, faith is not necessarily a poor mistress in politics. Labour emerges from this election with something of the mood of June 1940: it was a bad defeat, but the fact that it might have been worse and that honour was salvaged, paradoxically inspires hope. Moreover, by widening the gap between itself and the Alliance[1], Labour has removed the question mark over its status as the main Opposition party, and much may flow from that.

The second assumption, that Labour is capable of responding to rational leadership, is more difficult. In the past, attempts to push the party forward have generally failed. Indeed, its relationship to history has often seemed more passive than active: events have occasionally made popular the attitudes and values it represents, but even its most successful periods have not been characterized by strong central direction. Hence there is no point in getting annoyed with it, or in regarding it as an obstinate mule. People who think in these terms – who become infuriated by what they see as its conservatism or incompetence – tend to forget that it is not a definable body of individuals. There is a famous diplomat who, when asked the Foreign Office attitude on this or that, dismisses the question irritably: 'the Foreign Office is an abstraction.' So too is the Labour Party – with its creaking federal structure, two-tier membership, and disparate industrial parts: and, unlike a government department, it has no undisputed sovereign or fixed chain of command.

There may also be little point in suggesting future changes of direction. Yet Labour's rootedness – which leaves a thousand trip-wires for the would-be innovator – is also a source of strength. It is worth comparing the fissiparous Labour Party, kept together by the loyalty of its members and supporters to habit and tradition, with the zappily impatient, anchorless, SDP. Nor is the Labour Party wholly unable to adapt: note the recent, and remarkable, reorganizations at Walworth Road. Nobody can shift the Party on their own, or when the different sections of the Movement are in conflict. The present broad unity of outlook, however, between NEC, Shadow Cabinet and the executives of key unions, offers an exceptional opportunity. Labour's chances of recovery, and of progress, seem better now than at any time since the beginning of the decade. A sudden advance is unlikely. But the possibility of cautious movement is there.

Much will depend on the Prime Minister, the Government and the economy. Arguably, Tory good luck should not have much longer to run. Since the introduction of universal suffrage, no party has held office continuously for more than the thirteen years achieved under four prime ministers, between 1951 and 1964. On this basis we are due for a change of régime by 1992 – especially as Thatcherism has been built on a much smaller proportion of the popular vote than the paternalist Toryism of the 1950s and '60s.

On the other hand, if Labour hopes to win merely by default it may have to wait a long time. There are several democratic countries in which the pendulum is stuck or seldom swings; this is one possible future for Britain. Another possibility is that if and when the Tory collapse takes place, Labour may appear insufficiently attractive to disillusioned Conservative voters. Is it too soon to calculate the long-term damage to the Alliance of the SDP disintegration, but it is reasonable to suppose that the new, Liberal-based formation will continue to offer a strong challenge.

At this point it may seem that the obvious solution is an electoral pact between Left and Centre, in order to maximize the representation of non-Conservative parties and reduce the danger that a divided Opposition vote will enable the Tories to stay in power on the basis of a shrinking minority vote within the electorate. In fact, it is precisely the unavoidable competition between Labour and the Alliance that makes any kind of pact involving mutual stand-offs in key seats unwise for Labour, even if it should prove politically possible.

If Labour had come third in 1987, and had obviously been displaced as an alternative government, than a pact might have made sense as a last ditch defence. There might also be a case if the Alliance had taken a serious beating, and if Labour were close to outright victory. The present stalemate, however, which leaves the Labour–Alliance rivalry still unresolved, makes a pact, from Labour's point of view, a dangerous and profitless folly.

The simple argument in favour of a pact is based on a crude interpretation of the arithmetic. In 1987, advocates point out, 53 per cent of voters backed Labour or the Alliance and only 42 per cent the Government; *ergo* a combination of Left and Centre would have sent Mrs Thatcher packing. If electors were soldiers in an army, the logic of this case would be indisputable. Once leaders had agreed a programme, they would merely have to order their troops to the ballot box in order to produce the desired result. Alas for the theory, British voters are independent and cussed individuals who do not do what they are told, or even behave in easily predictable ways. At best, a pact – however skilfully devised – would not be even-handed in its favours. At worst, it could help directly those it was designed to hurt.

In a few seats, the Alliance would probably gain from the withdrawal of the Labour candidate. It is a reasonable supposition that many normal Labour supporters who did not choose to abstain or vote for another minor party or independent candidate would prefer an Alliance MP to a Tory one. But there is little evidence that Alliance voters, lacking a candidate of their first choice, would return the compliment: indeed, depending on the candidates, the region, and the political mood at the time, they might be expected to split fairly evenly between Right and Left. Nor, given the fluidity of Alliance support, would entreaties by their parliamentary leaders have much effect. Indeed, it is arguable that in some seats Labour may even benefit from an Alliance presence, enticing Tory waverers who might, in the absence of an Alliance candidate, be frightened back into their previous allegiance.

Proponents of a pact point out that, even if it did not help Labour directly in terms of seats, it might deprive the Tories of their overall majority and hence bring in an anti-Conservative government. This is the main practical argument in favour of an electoral arrangement. The possibility of such an outcome, however, which would only occur if the levels of support of the main parties were fairly close, needs to be balanced against the cost to Labour of boosting the Alliance, even of providing it with the kind of launch pad which the Liberals unwisely gave Labour in an identical arrangement in 1903. Of course, if Labour formed a government the cost would at first be hidden, just as it was for the Liberals in 1906. But it would be hard to reject such an arrangement later, and the Alliance would have been given, through increased representation, a new and threatening credibility.

For Labour there would also be the psychological cost of admitting that for the first time since the First World War it had ceased to regard itself as a fully national party, able to meet the Tories on equal terms. Such frank self-awareness might do it credit, but would not encourage voters. There would be other dangers too: of alienating traditional supporters, sacrificing fragile party unity and demoralizing party workers in seats where candidates had been ordered to stand down, yet where Labour's prospects in local or European elections were better.

Finally, in media and campaigning terms, would an alliance between the Labour Party and the Alliance be any more successful than the Alliance between the Liberals and the SDP? Or would it be even more vulnerable? In 1987 the press did not find it hard to exploit real or supposed differences between David Steel and David Owen. The possibility of a disciplined united front of Alliance and Labour, with unhappy elements preserving a stoical silence right up to polling day, defies the imagination. In short, what might from the Alliance's point of view be a shrewd investment would be impossibly expensive and risky for Labour, with only the most speculative gain.

To dismiss this option does not, however, mean that the only remaining one is total war. The arguments against an electoral pact do, at least, serve to emphasize one point: that Labour and the Alliance increasingly share the central aim of getting the Tories out of office.

The common ground now goes far beyond a joint desire to beat Mrs Thatcher. As an inspection of the manifestos of the two parties shows, there is little distance between them on many domestic issues – especially those related to poverty, unemployment and social policy, which both regard as key concerns. On foreign policy and defence they stand further apart, though even here there is shared territory, particularly between Labour and the newly-dominant Liberals. Hence, though a pact may be ruled out as impractical, the mood of the Left and Centre may now be sufficiently in harmony to make other kinds of initiative desirable.

The case for improving Labour–Alliance relations is that the best chance for each must now rest on a hung Parliament, in which the Alliance either supports a minority Labour government or joins Labour in a coalition – after the two parties have fought each other at the polls. The need for post-electoral co-operation makes the pursuit of a better pre-electoral relationship obviously sensible.

We have dealt with the Jacobins, who want to leap immediately into a pact: it is now necessary to dispose of the reactionaries, who consider a hung Parliament too modest an ambition, and who eschew all dealings with the Alliance. As much as the first group, the second needs to take account of some unpalatable facts.

Since 1918 Labour has only twice ejected the Tories from office and immediately formed a government based on an overall majority of its own. The first time was in 1945, when Labour had recently left the wartime coalition and its leaders were well known to the voters in their ministerial roles. The second occasion was in 1964, when Labour turned a Tory majority of 100 into a Labour majority of 4: a margin which required a second election less than two years later. Labour's other outright victories (1950, 1966, October 1974) occurred at elections held while Labour was already in office. Labour's remaining three victories were all minority ones (1923, 1929 and February 1974), producing Labour governments dependent on Liberal tolerance or support. Labour has only twice (1945 and 1966) won a working majority in the House of Commons, in the sense of a majority that could be expected to sustain it for a full Parliament. It has only once, in the unique conditions of 1945, done so from scratch.

Given Labour's recent voting performance, it is scarcely conceivable that it will suddenly outperform all previous periods of Opposition since the Second World War. (Only in 1945 was Labour further from power, statistically, before winning an election.) Thus – while an overall majority should remain a long-term aspiration – the time has surely come for Labour leaders to abandon the traditional rhetoric which refuses to contemplate less than complete victory and which avoids the public presentation of any contingency plan.

If Labour were to declare officially that its primary aim is to remove the Tory majority, without necessarily achieving one of its own, then a serious overture to the Alliance would be a natural next step. No agreed programme would be needed, but the two parties might undertake to restrict the area of their mutual criticism. They might also agree to regular meetings and open discussions between whips, shadow ministers, research teams, even party leaders. Such meetings might be informal, relaxed, unforced, but publicly acknowledged, with the explicit aim of co-ordinating attacks on the Government in Parliament and outside it on any issue where there might seem to be a common point of view. To some extent this goes on already: it should be built upon and developed. From here, it would be sensible to move as quickly as possible towards the establishment of a liaison body – though too much should not be expected too fast of contacts which would not be intended to remove all differences between Left and Centre, or to produce a new party formation.

Mutual hostility in sections of both parties would stay strong – especially among those closest to the electoral battlefront, in constituency organizations and on local councils where the fight has often been most personalized and bitter. The ritual of mutual abuse at election time would not be lightly abandoned, though party leaders might find that they sacrificed little by reserving their most virulent insults for the Government. Candidates in the field, however, would not be expected to mince their words. Hence, to avoid embarrassment, a suspension of contacts in the run-up to mid-term elections might be necessary. Against a background of unpredictable stops and starts, the courtship would be bumpy: but the difficulty facing such a strategy of fraternization would be incomparably less than one based on a formal pact. The underlying aim would be to build – out of the anti-Conservative popular majority – a new mood, a fashion, a consensus in favour of change. In addition, each party could expect to benefit directly.

The direct advantage to Labour would be in its public image as a party which, while contesting every seat, had prepared itself for government by forging a link with its likely partner. The increased possibility of a non-Conservative government would encourage journalists and commentators to take Mr Kinnock more seriously as a potential prime minister; while voters who had been alarmed –

rationally or not – by the prospect of Labour governing on its own would be reassured by the new Labour–Alliance amity. At the same time, the danger that the Alliance might do what Dr Owen threatened to do in 1987 and bargain with the Tories, rather than with Labour, in the event of a hung Parliament, would be reduced. Labour and the Alliance, despite their competition for votes, would be firmly in the same camp. None of this would prevent Labour carrying out its full programme if, by luck or good management, it should do well enough to govern on its own.

The main advantage for the Alliance would be to reduce its isolation at national level, and to enable it to concentrate on fighting one party, rather than two powerful parties at the same time. Such an arrangement requires the Alliance to make as big a mental adjustment as Labour – lowering the level of its short-term ambition. If the Alliance still judges that it can overhaul the Labour Party, that is one thing: it may do better to battle on alone. But if it reckons that the chance to move into second place has for the moment passed, then much is to be gained from a link-up that gives it a clearer sense of purpose, and reduces the impact of the damaging 'wasted vote' argument.

The Alliance is in no position, after 11 June and the implosion of the SDP, to dictate terms: it cannot insist, for example, that Labour drops its defence policy or takes up proportional representation. There is no reason, however, why such matters should not be discussed to help both sides work out how they might be handled after an election victory. In all this, the self-destruction of Dr Owen may be seen as a piece of luck, making it possible for the Alliance to change from a fantasy government of the progressive professional middle classes, into a distinctive and independent element within an anti-Tory crusade. The Alliance, moreover, might hope to influence or even to participate in a government which it had indirectly helped to create.

Finally, there are uncharted areas of possibility, about which little can be said except that the opening of lines of communication between the frequently inward-looking ghettos of Left and Centre could turn out to be a stimulating experiment for both. Clearly no progress could be made if the new relationship became a smokescreen for attempts by Labour Right and Alliance Left to strengthen their positions. But there is no reason to believe that this would be the case. It may even be that the old, wretched, Left–Right spectrum within the Labour Party is losing its meaning: members of Labour's 'soft' Left (now more or less the Party's mainstream) – including the formerly Bennite

Labour Co-ordinating Committee – have been among the most ecumenical. There remain no-go areas: sacred spheres of socialism or liberalism in which values are distinct and debate pointless. But there are others where the pooling of interests and expertise could produce exciting results.

Unlike a mere marriage of convenience based on cold figures, a relationship that resulted in joint working parties and even joint policy documents could develop a mutual respect, with benefits both before and after an election. Such a strategy would require keen support from leaders on both sides, and this may be hard to come by. Too easily, caution may prevail until the chance has passed. Yet there is, in fact, nothing for either party to fear: the worst that can be said of the non-treaty formula is that it might dissolve into normal conditions of inter-party acrimony. Positively, there is an opportunity for each party to widen its horizons, without sacrificing principles. Such a loose anti-government combination cannot be called a 'solution' to the problems of either party. As part of a process of consolidation and mending fences, however, it could do much to strengthen the challenge against a narrowly based régime whose claim to speak for the nation urgently needs to be exposed.

Political Quarterly, Vol. 58, No. 45, October–December 1987

NOTES

1. The term is used for convenience. When this essay was written, the 'Alliance' had technically ceased to exist, but the 'Liberal Democrats' had not yet come into being.

Opposition Citizens Unite

DOES THE TORIES' recent theft of 'citizenship' leave the Whigs stark naked? The glib response of many commentators after the Conservative conference was that Mrs Thatcher had trumped again – as always, she was one step ahead of her opponents. On closer inspection, however, the Tory move looks more like a symptom than a policy. What is interesting is that the Prime Minister has precisely identified her own most vulnerable point.

In recent months disquiet has been growing – at least among the chattering classes – over the Government's contempt for personal as opposed to market freedom and its impatience with the idea of social obligation. Alarmingly from the Government's point of view, the disquiet has not been confined to any one group or party. Hence Mrs Thatcher's swift move to expropriate a word which might eventually engulf her.

But there is little reason for thinking that Tory 'citizenship' will amount to anything more than the imprecations ministers were uttering at Brighton.

What of non-Tory citizenship? That Conservatives should have discovered the word's appeal does not destroy its usefulness. Yet there is the danger that it becomes, in the hands of the divided Opposition, a vacuous aspiration. If all that can be offered against the Tory version is a variety of conflicting brands, the Government may well pull off its propaganda coup – shifting the fence (as it has, notoriously, with freedom) in an individualistic, or law-and-order, direction.

On the other hand, the progressive 'citizenship' campaign could advance if those that now oppose not only the Government but one another acknowledge that here – on constitutional liberty and social responsibility – their views are similar and sharply different from the Government's. In short (and one trembles to write anything so outrageously shocking), this is a field in which the Opposition parties need to make common cause.

Such a suggestion is likely to evoke hideous visions of unworkable compromises and pacts that further fragment rival parties. Yet there is no need for a useful combination to involve disaster.

The strongest argument for such a combination is the cold, unglamorous fact that Labour's statistical chance of winning an overall majority at the next election is very small indeed. For Neil Kinnock even to equal Mrs Thatcher in percentage terms in 1991 or 1992 requires a swing twice as large as Harold Wilson achieved against the faltering Tories in the victory year of 1964 – and if such an exceptional swing were to happen, Labour would still have to depend on smaller parties to stay in office.

Labour's 1964 triumph, moreover, happened against a background of a long period of left-wing electoral dominance, in which the previous result in 1959 (and its aftermath) can be seen as an aberration. By contrast, in the late '80s Labour looks back at a bleak decade of subordination, with no sign that the system is about to right itself.

It remains possible that an epoch-making movement of opinion might occur of sufficient magnitude to give Mr Kinnock an overall win. For the moment, however, it is surely impossible not to agree with Robin Cook's remark that a 'leap in one bound' is unlikely. Indeed, what was interesting about Mr Cook's statement last summer was not just that he should have had his knuckles rapped for making it, but that anyone should have regarded it as a news item.

Tradition and ritual require anointed leaders to hold fast to the legend of unconditional, massive victory for their own party. Yet all of them know, and most privately admit, that such a victory is unobtainable.

It is time to bring an end to this meaningless litany. It is not a question of Left or Right, of extremism or moderation, of steadfastness or sell-out. For anybody to the right of Militant it is a question of building a policy and a strategy that takes the actual and likely arrangement of political forces and makes the most of them. If depriving the Conservatives of their majority is a realistically dramatic aim, while a leap in one bound is close to fantasy, it is common sense for almost any opponent of the Conservatives to adjust to the first.

Part of such an adjustment must be to take account of those parties whose support would be needed after an election for any non-Conservative government to be formed.

What is needed, first, is a franker admission of the alpine climb ahead and, second, a loose and largely informal partnership based on those values that are shared and on the common belief in the need for a change of administration to give expression to them. If the aim of the leading Opposition parties *is* to replace Mrs Thatcher, the argument for creating a joint momentum is overwhelming.

Such a partnership is quite compatible with continued competition at the polls. It does not mean sacrificing principles or dropping policies – though it might eventually lead to the adoption of joint ones. What it could mean is a co-ordinated assault – in Parliament and outside – in order to demolish the myth of a pro-Tory consensus, by drawing together the threads of the consensus that actually exists: 57 per cent of the electorate, after all, at the last election voted against an administration that now rules. Such a partnership would start by abolishing the foolish and outmoded taboo against inter-party dialogue on the non-Right.

Perhaps it is over-optimistic to believe that such rationalism is possible; perhaps not. There are already, as a matter of fact, a few straws in the wind. As well as individual voices in the centre, there are several groups on the left (most recently Common Voice) that favour a broad-based approach, which is also implicit in the constitution of the new left-leaning think-tank, the Institute of Public Policy Research, deliberately not linked to any party. *Marxism Today*, and latterly the *New Statesman and Society*, have adopted an increasingly pluralist stance. This week sees a further step in the same direction with the launching of the newsletter, *Samizdat*, involving people from all the main Opposition parties, which is dedicated to exploring the common ground among them and calls for a popular front of the mind.

What characterizes all these ventures is a sense of frustration at the apparently permanent rule of a tiny club of un-representative people and a fear that waiting for another 1945 may be like waiting for Godot. There is also a belief that, despite the grim opinion polls, the growing despotism of the present régime – its trampling on citizens' rights in matters as varied as the suppression of local democracy and the destruction of state education – could produce a change of fashion.

The fear of sea-change may explain the Prime Minister's linguistic marauding. It is certainly in this area that the Government is weakest – and the Opposition's opportunity is greatest. The chance will be lost if politicians shelter in their exclusive redoubts. Is there a leader brave enough to make the first move into no man's land?

Guardian, 24 October 1988

LET SLEEPING DOGS
CRY FREEDOM

WILL KINNOCKISM BE to the 1990s what Thatcherism was to the 1980s? In the switchback ride of politics anything can still happen: yesterday's gleeful celebrations in Walworth Road over Cabinet back-stabbing could turn out to be premature. Nevertheless, the spectacle of a premier sticking to office like a leech on a corpse (to borrow a phrase used about Neville Chamberlain in 1940) has certainly caused irreparable damage to the Tories' image and, worse, self-confidence.

Michael Heseltine's letter said it all: it is now Labour, not the Conservatives, which occupies the mainstream. Narrow, immoderate, hysterical, isolated, divided – adjectives that once belonged to Mr Kinnock's party, today fit the Tories. So – despite a possible Heseltine (or Hurd or Major) effect – does unpopular. In such conditions, Labour's best strategy may simply be to lie low and quietly allow office to fall into its lap. Yet that leaves open the issue of what happens afterwards and also the very fundamental question of what the normally ebullient party over which Mr Kinnock presides may become. Up until this week, Labour benefited from the Government's crisis by keeping mum. Still waters, however, run deep.

Optimistically, the present, almost eerie, passivity of the Labour Party is partly a product of a fingers-crossed appetite for office: a deliberate and calculated self-denying ordinance. Less optimistically, however, it may also reflect a malaise that Labour's present standing in the polls dangerously obscures – namely an uncertainty bordering on total bewilderment, at every level of the Movement, about ideology and fundamental principle.

Labour used to suffer because it was a two-faction party, tribally split between the dedicated supporters of rival philosophies. Ironically, it is now at risk of becoming a no-faction, no-philosophy party, increasingly distanced from the trades unions which, for good and ill, once provided the reason for its existence.

Labour will be very effective over the next few months at campaigning *against* the remnants of Thatcherism – and against Heseltinism (or Hurdism or Majorism) which, for the most part, may not look very different. What it is campaigning *for* is the problem. A massive programme of public expenditure on education, health and social welfare? That would be financially irresponsible. A policy of break-neck European integration of a kind to make even Lord Jenkins of Hillhead say 'Whoa!' – or the opposite? Neither. Socialism in our time? Well, not exactly. A magpie collection of good causes? That could be closer.

It would be wrong to blame the Labour Leader, or even the Party's former publicity officer, Peter Mandelson. The causes lie deeper than recent, generally shrewd tactical manoeuvres. Labour's present lack of coherence results from a disorientation at both ends of the socialist spectrum.

At one end, there has been the unexpectedly sudden collapse of the communist version of socialism – a trauma that democratic socialists have been reluctant to acknowledge as something affecting them. The impact of that collapse on the Left worldwide, which includes the Labour Party, is massive. Until a year ago, it was possible to believe that *perestroika* offered a kind of socialist rebirth. Now that straw of comfort has been snatched away and it is clear that communism – the great, historic rival of democratic socialism – is finished, kaput, dead as a doornail. The British Communist Party is about to dissolve itself. In Moscow, communists vie with one another to denounce the '70-year nightmare' of Leninism.

In Britain, socialism is still part of the vocabulary of the Left but it has undoubtedly taken a battering. It is no use Labour Party speakers saying that our version is really socialist and theirs never was: the fact remains or is that Bolshevism and Menshevism had a common ancestry and shared many values and aspirations. Despite the long hate-love relations between the Labour Party and our own CP, there was also a real intimacy. There are still stalwart, middle-of-the-road socialists who were educated by the literature of the pre-war, Communist-front Left Book Club. In respectable Labour circles, there was far greater sympathy for disciplined communism than for the inchoate trotskyism that had infiltrated places like Bradford North: and a belief that there were socialist lessons to be learned from eastern Europe used to be widely held.

All of that, of course, affects the Labour Left – fascinated by different versions of Marxism since the 1920s – much more than the Labour Right. Yet the Right is scarcely in much better philosophical shape. In the old days, there were two Rights in a marriage of convenience: the Tammany Hall, trades-union, bruiser Right, which equated socialism with power and working-class prejudice and had as its mission the pulverizing of the Left – and the cerebral, high-minded Right, which carried a holy flame of Croslandite Keynesianism and Jenkinsite support for the European idea. The heirs of the first group are still to be seen, sometimes with a more intellectual veneer. The second group are scarcely to be found in the Palace of Westminster, except on the Liberal Democrat benches of the House of Lords. If Mr Gorbachev bears some responsibility for the listlessness of the Labour Left, the defection of the almost forgotten Gang of Four put their kind of ideals out of bounds in the Labour Party. Hence Labour today is firmly in the hands of the pragmatists.

That is certainly a better place to be than in the loony bin but it leaves a long-term problem of identity. One way of resolving it may be to take up, unashamedly, the principle of which Mrs Thatcher has made such a mockery – freedom.

To be fair, Labour has taken some steps in that direction. Its Aims and Values statement acknowledged that Labour's socialism needed to come to terms with a popular desire for ownership and choice. The step, however, remains tentative and has made parts of Labour's programme look like a watered-down version of the Thatcherite experiment, which is now itself discredited.

Having abandoned much of the state control, nationalization and planning that dominated Labour thought a decade ago, the Party has hesitated to go farther – accepting in practice Mrs Thatcher's right to hijack the word 'liberty'. The present opportunity, surely, is for Labour to go into the election not as the party in favour of freedom-with-qualifications but as the one that makes freedom – for all classes and groups – the absolute centrepiece of its intent. That would be significantly different from the Charter 88 demand for liberation based on constitutional reform alone.

Where Thatcherite freedom has meant the freedom of the corporation to make money at the taxpayers' expense (recently, and blatantly, the freedom of Mr Murdoch to monopolize artificial-satellite broadcasting), Kinnockite freedom might place liberty where it belongs: in the hands of the individual citizen. Freedom from excessive state interference, from racial and sexual discrimination, from environmental pollution, from police harassment would be included; so would the freedom not to suffer ill-health, the freedom for children to have a teacher, the freedom to earn a decent living, freedom of information, freedom of expression, and freedom to build up a business.

Some of these freedoms are socialist expressions for equality looked at another way. Others are openly and even provocatively *laissez-faire*. Both kinds would give the state the task of enabling people to do things, on every front. By adopting them, socialism could take a new and vital turn, uniting left-wing libertarians and socially responsible critics of the state.

They could also help Labour to maintain its present place in the mainstream: by joining forces with one strand of idealism that had previously been thought inimical to it.

Thatcherism has often been described as 'neo-liberalism'. In fact, from a liberal point of view, it left much to be desired – as Arthur Seldon, founding father of the Institute of Economic Affairs, has pointed out in his new book, *Capitalism*. Seldon recently used a Communist Party platform – of all places – to call for a 'concordat' between economic liberals and the Left. 'All societies require capitalism for productivity and socialism for collective services,' he told the bemused comrades. 'It is times for socialists and liberals to join in discovering the optimum combination.' Seldon's capitalism is not the Murdoch kind: it is a version in which the market can work with reasonable smoothness and fairness.

The idea of embracing capitalism while giving space to the needy and disadvantaged may see quaint. It could be, however, that western socialism will have to take philosophical leaps of that kind if it is to avoid the fate of its eastern cousin. It may also be that in a country like our own, exhausted by bureaucratic meddling under one label or another, the linking together of every kind of freedom makes sense.

It may not be entirely crazy to dream of an alliance of constitutional, market and – in the Marxian socialist sense – economic forms of liberty. Neither would 'set the people free' be an inappropriate banner for Labour to raise against the present repressive administration in the coming election. It would be a way of stealing all the best clothes from Labour's opponents.

'All men are naturally in a state of perfect freedom,' John Locke wrote exactly three centuries ago, in 1690. It would be exciting to evolve an anti-authoritarian, anti-Conservative socialism which really meant it.

Guardian, 23 November 1990

GIANTS OF POVERTY YET
TO BE SLAIN

FIFTY YEARS AGO THIS WEEK, the British Government brought out a blockbuster and bestseller. The queue to buy copies was reputedly a mile long, and sales reached a hundred thousand within a month of its publication.

Such a remarkable success was partly because of media hype followed by rave reviews, and partly because of the unusual subject matter – a fantasy about a patriotic war against five giants with funny names: Want, Disease, Ignorance, Squalor and Idleness. The author described how these monsters were to be banished, especially Want. The battle aim, he explained, was 'to make want under any circumstances unnecessary'.

The story combined elements of More's *Utopia*, Bunyan's *Pilgrim's Progress* and Swift's *Gulliver's Travels*, with a dash of *Star Trek* thrown in: it urged politicians to boldly go where none of their predecessors had dared venture before. The author's name was Sir William Beveridge, and the snazzy title of his creation was *Social Insurance and Allied Services: Report presented to Parliament by command of His Majesty*.

The Beveridge Report was talked about by nearly everybody. In those days, chattering was not confined to the professional classes: the word 'Beveridge' was soon on the lips of naval ratings and coal miners. 'From now on Beveridge is not the name of a man,' the author told his former research assistant, the young Harold Wilson, 'it is the name of a way of life, not only for Britain, but for the whole civilized world.'

It was an accurate prophecy. The Beveridge Report, with its pre-scription for cradle-to-grave social security, a free health service and policies for full employment, had a novelistic element. Nevertheless, its combination of soaring vision and a detailed ground plan has pro-vided the basis for all social policy discussion ever since – or at least until the arrival of a giant called Selfishness, against whom the Beveridge proposals were impotent.

Would there have been a welfare state without Beveridge – or without a Labour victory in 1945? The smart answer is that the report was part symptom and part cause, itself contributing to the political upheaval that made it possible to carry out its provisions. In retrospect, Labour's 1945 victory can be seen as a massive popular endorsement of Beveridge-style proposals – even though Beveridge himself, briefly a Liberal (not Labour) MP, lost his seat in the same election.

It is a truism that tidal changes in political affairs occur between elections, seldom at them. Denis Healey's 'monetarist' U-turn in 1976 was one such alteration of the flow, anticipating the advent of Thatcherism three years later, and the Beveridge Report and accompanying hoo-ha was another. The half-centenary of Beveridge occurs in a singularly bankrupt, barren and directionless year, and we may wonder whether another such symbolic moment is not overdue. Little can be expected from the Major–Lamont Ealing comedy. What of Labour?

After the 1987 election, Neil Kinnock made a brave attempt to update his party's creaking programme by setting up a 'policy review', with an open brief to slaughter sacred cattle. It was successful, possibly too much so. The result was a shiny document called *Meet the Challenge, Make the Change*, which was so inoffensive that only experts could distinguish it from what the Government was doing anyway.

During this year's post-defeat Labour leadership contest, John Smith pledged that he would set up a Beveridge-style investigation to take a fresh look at poverty. This scheme is now well advanced and a fifteen-person committee with a distinctly Beveridge-like remit will be announced early in the new year. It will be a kind of shadow Royal Commission, including expert and non-political inquirers well beyond the bounds of the Labour Party, and will report after eighteen months, leaving a Beveridge-length gap before the next election.

The Beveridge team was an interdepartmental civil service committee that acquired influence because of its access to Whitehall and because of the ferocious ambitions of its chairman. John Smith's enquiry will be different not least because it will be outside government. Still, the project of a new-style review that challenges not only traditional party shibboleths, but also party philosophy, has much to recommend it, especially if it is led by somebody as radical and as arrogant as Sir William. In the post-devaluation, post-US election era, in which state intervention has ceased to be a matter of apology, the new Beveridge must not be afraid to challenge the giants that the nation still faces, with the intention this time of finally exterminating them.

Here, Sir William sadly failed. If you take a walk, in 1992, from the glitter of London's Oxford Street to the shanty towns of Lincoln's Inn Fields, the giants of Squalor, Want and Idleness repeatedly confront you: in the faces of families huddled in doorways, young dossers scavenging in dustbins, respectable old gentlemen begging for ten-pences. Enter almost any underfunded, understaffed, inner city school and the giant of Ignorance will give an illiterate and ill-disciplined guffaw. Of course, for the majority, there is less hunger and disease than in the 1940s, but for the millions in the minority, there is much more.

What is required is not a dutiful re-examination of received wisdom or a weary recontemplation of values, but a grand, outrageous, over-arching and – yes – Utopian scheme, which ties the lot together: Europe, jobs, benefits, tax, incomes, hospitals, schools and training. It would not be the first time since 1942. In the mid-1960s there was such an undertaking, a well-meaning but ill-starred echo of Beveridge called the National Plan. That attempt foundered because the Wilson Government took it too seriously, without the wherewithal to carry it out.

The new Beveridge will need, of course, to think about practical constraints. But the aim should be to conceive of a new order, not to provide a politically acceptable blueprint.

The new Beveridge will be hard to find. He or she must be somebody who commands respect across the political spectrum, not just on the left and centre-left: an obsessional workaholic with the ability to write elevating prose. The members of the supporting team should, relatively speaking, be worker ants, able and experienced people who will per-form necessary but unglamorous tasks without expecting much of the glory. It must be one monomaniac's visionary scheme: the essence of the original Beveridge Report was precisely that it was the invention of a brilliant, overweening individual, not the product of committee compromises.

Such a report could turn out to be a flop, or even an embarrassment. It will certainly be a gamble. If it fails it can simply be shelved; that, more or less, was the intended destination for the Beveridge Report, whose author was widely regarded in Whitehall as a rogue elephant.

Yet the chance of success exists, perhaps as never before since the 1940s, and with it an opportunity to capture the imagination of the British people.

Independent, 1 December 1992

WINNING LINE

THATCHER'S LAW – the unexpected usually happens – was proved with a vengeance this week. The devastation of John Smith's death, which feels to so many people like a family loss, takes time to sink in. But for the rest of the political world, life goes on. What does the future hold, particularly for the Labour Party? Was John Smith such a titan that nobody can replace him? Or is it down hill all the way to a Labour government whoever picks up the baton?

On Thursday, many people compared Smith's death to Hugh Gaitskell's in 1963 – in some cases, perhaps, even hopefully. Gaitskell was succeeded by Harold Wilson who, as the world knows, turned a good political situation into an even better one. So is all set for Tony Blair, or Gordon Brown, or whoever it happens to be?

In some ways, any of them will be even better placed than Wilson in 1963. Not only is the Labour Party much further ahead in the polls than was true at the time of Gaitskell's death: the lead has continued for a good deal longer. Moreover, the Conservatives are in much more seriously bad shape. Criticism of Harold Macmillan within his own party does not begin to compare with the withering contempt in which John Major is held by many – probably most – of his colleagues. Moreover, Macmillan's problem was a plethora of plausible dauphins: if the Tories got rid of Major in an attempt to sharpen their image, they would be hard put to find any alternative to rally round.

Other differences also seem to make Labour appear stronger in 1994 than thirty-one years ago. The leadership contest that followed Gaitskell's death was bitter: Gaitskell had healed the wounds of the Left–Right split of the 1950s, but it was still there beneath the surface. When the vacancy occurred, Bevanites rallied to Wilson, Gaitskellites to George Brown. Those who felt that choosing between these alternatives was like deciding, as Tony Crosland put it, 'between a crook and a drunk' backed Jim Callaghan. Wilson won by cornering the Centre vote in the PLP, and by giving Brown enough rope to hang himself.

Afterwards, the Gaitskellites rallied glumly to Wilson, and unity was restored. But there was a sense on the Labour right of being robbed, which continued to damage the new leader for the rest of his career.

In the 1994 leadership election, by contrast, only a major upset would produce a leader who was not closely in tune with the essential views of John Smith, and – even if an upset happened – the disagreement would be political, not personal. Gaitskell was a 'love him or loathe him' sort of man; and many on the left hated his guts. Smith occasionally invited impatience, but seldom dislike. Amidst all the sometimes over-the-top tributes, one point often made is unquestionably true: his style of leadership made the comrades happier and more generous towards each other than had been the case for a very long time. That is an important part of his legacy.

United, ahead in the polls, competent, facing a government that is more deeply divided than ever before in the twentieth century – what more could an incoming Opposition leader wish for? It is, as the historian Peter Hennessy has put it, a peach of an inheritance.

Yet Labour would be making a serious mistake if it allowed the Smith eulogies to make it dewy-eyed. For there are also differences between the 1990s and the 1960s that are arguably are a lot less promising or healthy.

There is the voting problem, which the Tory collapse merely disguises. The problem of the decline in Labour's traditional voting support has not gone away. Since the Gaitskell–Wilson era – and especially since 1979 – there has been an erosion of the southern English working-class Labour vote which will make it much harder, if the Government begins to recover, for the Party to take seats in many of the constituencies where the Tories ought to be most vulnerable. The local elections results, though good, were less than brilliant everywhere, and Labour was often out-performed by the reviving Lib Dems. Nationally, the outcome came well within the range of what the Tories might yet bounce back from. Moreover, Major has twice as long in which to recover as the Conservative Government had at the beginning of 1963.

But there is also a more worrying problem for Labour, which has existed ever since Neil Kinnock's triumph against the dinosaur tendency within his party in the late 1980s. Labour may no longer be loony, fractious, or trade-union dominated – and may, in consequence, be 'electable'. But does it stand for anything worth fighting for? Can politicians of the Left really take office, and retain it, on a bank manager's manifesto, as the party of safe financial management?

To characterize the 1990s Labour Party in such terms is not entirely fair. Several key frontbenchers have been inventive in policy terms, especially since 1992. Tony Blair's approach to law and order, which has done much to adjust his party's image away from that of a society of bleeding-heart supporters of the criminal rather than the victim, has received a justifiably good press. Gordon Brown has extracted maximum political advantage out of the Tories' hypocrisy and failure on taxation, while flying a number of interesting kites, including a proposal for a 'University of Industry' (echoing Wilson's Open University). Meanwhile, Sir Gordon Borrie's Commission on Social Justice edges forward towards its eagerly awaited report on poverty and welfare in the autumn.

Yet there is no over-arching scheme. The jigsaw pieces, however interesting they may be, have so far failed to fit together into a design that is dye-stamped with Labour's trademark. In the early 1960s – in the wake of Tony Crosland's historic *The Future of Socialism*, published in 1956 – Labour forged an approach which, although possibly over-ambitious, had the virtues of coherence, combining the strength of Labour values with the authority of current economic wisdom.

After he became leader, Harold Wilson took the credit (and later the blame) for the 'white heat of the technological revolution' – a slogan which set the media alight with excitement, creating the atmosphere of eager anticipation that accompanied the 1964 election.

Wilson's winning line captured the imagination of a restive British public. Between February 1963 and October 1964, he was able to refine, simplify, and propagate this plausible package, and turn it into a revivalist hymn which even his own hard-bitten colleagues could sing with conviction.

In the Kinnock–Smith era, there has been no equivalent tune. Nor – and this is a matter that deserves attention – is there one in the process of composition. Neither former leader is wholly to blame for this. Both had their work cut out laying the ghosts of the past. John Smith – in particular – was a man who preferred to say nothing than to offer a hostage to fortune. In any case, the whole experience of the 1979 to 1992 period had taught him the bitter lesson that every policy idea must be backed up with hard data, every promise costed, and that voters are people who are regrettably much easier to scare than to seduce.

Some have suggested that the Kinnock period lobotomized Labour. That is too savage. However, there is a sense in which, since the late 1980s, the Labour Party has been like a patient in a state of convalescence following a breakdown. Sanity has been restored, but the price has been a loss of self-confidence or willingness to think for itself. Instead, it has sought to conform to the mainstream.

Part of the reason, of course, is that the world has moved on. Successive sterling crises in the mid-1960s all but destroyed the notion that state planning was a panacea for Britain's economic ills. When Labour returned to the idea in the late 1970s – briefly taking up an 'alternative economic strategy' or socialism-in-one-country approach – this had scarcely any economically-literate supporters. In the 1990s, the Maastricht Treaty and the globalization of markets have enormously reduced the scope for any kind of go-it-alone approach. Meanwhile, the unpredicted collapse of the command economies undermined any lurking belief that massive state intervention is a cure-all. Simultaneously, Thatcherite privatizations, deregulations and negative redistributions have meant that the scope even for what used loosely to be called 'social democracy' is tightly constrained.

Such points lie behind the dispute between so-called 'modernizers' and 'traditionalists' within the Labour Party, which – at first sight – re-labels the ancient battle between 'revisionists' and Bevanites. Actually, it is quite different: the former struggle was as much tribal as ideological, and had claims – at both ends of the spectrum – to radical thinking. One significant development in the modern Labour Party (in which the unions are weaker, and rapidly changing) is that the old political tribes have atomized and 'Left versus Right' has lost most of its former meaning. Europe – the issue which once split Labour down a left-right seam as emphatically as it now divides the Conservatives – no longer provides any kind of litmus test. Many of those who were on the left in the early 1980s and fervently anti-Europe are now born-again devotees of the Maastricht ideal.

The Gaitskellite 'revisionist' agenda – although tribally right-wing, and backed by the barons of the virulently anti-communist trade unions – had serious claims to radicalism. How far is the same true of the 'modernizers'? As yet, the label seems much more of a catch-all. At its best, it means a very necessary impatience with backward-looking Labour Movement prejudices often based on a romantic view of the working class; combined with a desire to speak the language of ordinary intelligent people, rather than (as happened, depressingly, in the early 1980s) the argot of a marginal clique.

But at it worst, it can mean excessive opinion-poll watching and a bastardized 'Clintonization' – equating the satisfaction of every popular demand or ugly mass preference with democracy and socialism.

Most people would rather be modern than traditional: whoever persuaded the media to apply the 'modern' label to Labour's new Establishment deserves a medal from Walworth Road. If, however, 'modernizer' is just a euphemism for 'moderate' or even 'passive' then it carries dangers for a party whose history has always been linked to the poorest section of the community. Labour needs to woo the C1s, and does not have to worry about losing the loyalty of DEs in the short term – but it needs to offer its firmest working-class and socially marginal supporters tangible benefits, or they will eventually drift away.

J. K. Galbraith has brilliantly argued – with regret, and even despair – that the poor are likely to suffer in America and other modern societies because they have been relegated to the borderlands of the political system. In the days when they formed a majority, he suggests, democratic politicians were forced to take notice of them. Today, however, the affluent are in the majority. The arithmetic of the ballot-box dictates that candidates for office attend first to the requirements of the 'contented'.

In cruder versions of 'modernizing', there is more than a hint that what Galbraith warns against is happening here, and not just on the right. There are, indeed, some Labour leaders who are arguing that the Party should get elected without worrying too much about programmes, and only think about applying principles afterwards.

Such an approach is not merely morally questionable. In Britain it is politically indefensible, if only because in any auction involving the more prosperous, Labour must surely be defeated in the long run, quite apart from losing its identity. Part of that identity – far more than has ever been true of the Democrats in the United States – is bound up with an appeal to the public's sense of community. In the past, British electors have voted for a decent welfare state and health service, not just for themselves, but out of a feeling that some kinds of deprivation are intolerable.

Is it starry-eyed to imagine that such sentiments are still there, waiting to be reawakened, even after fifteen years of state propaganda in favour of selfishness? Is it possible that a modernizing approach that does not hold cautiously back, but instead offers a new boldness in social policy, might actually win extra support? Is it not also arguable that one way to reduce Labour's ghetto mentality – and increase its confidence between now and the election – will be to open out the policy discussion so as to involve non-Labour people who also want a change of direction in Britain?

A leadership election is an occasion for reassessment. One of the virtues of a long drawn-out contest is that it offers time for a proper heart-searching on these and other issues. It is also a time for renewal. If the result is a leader of a new generation, then the possibilities for an inspirational assault on Britain's creaking social, economic and political system could be immense.

The present climate may call for a New Deal approach – identifying the problems and showing a determination to tackle them through state action. A leader who boldly declared his or her intention to provide a decent education system, to shake up the welfare state, and to offer a serious industrial strategy, and set experts to work to show how it could be done, would – at this stage in our history – receive a proper political reward.

This might include – who knows – not just a Labour victory, but the extraordinary, unexpected bonus of a period of office that transforms the lives of the British people.

Guardian, 14 May 1994

PART VI

Past Imperfect
and Future Conditional

NINETEEN EIGHTY-FOUR*

IT IS EASY TO SEE why George Orwell's last novel, published in June 1949 seven months before the author's death, was such an instant success. First, it is a wickedly disreputable yarn that takes adolescent fantasy – of lonely defiance, furtive sex and deadly terror – to a shockingly unacceptable extreme. Second, and more important, this singular tale was widely read as social comment, and even prophecy.

That it should have been so regarded is not, perhaps, surprising. Drabness, shortages, government red tape were a way of life not just in the novel but in the Britain where it was written. At the same time, totalitarianism was a stalking fear. Nazi Germany in the recent past, Russia and China in the present, framed the western political consciousness. There was a sense of grimly staring into a crystal ball at a just-imaginable near-distance.

Today it is impossible to think of the novel in quite the same way. It is a mark of the author's astonishing influence that, as the historical 1984 approached, the date on the calendar was discussed throughout the world almost with trepidation, as though it were a kind of millennium. But that is now over, and some may wonder whether the novel has exceeded its shelf life. For how long can a story about a future that is past continue to alarm its readers?

There are certainly aspects of the novel which tempt the modern critic to be condescending. Not only has the supposed warning been largely wrong within its time-span (there has, so far, been no third world war or western revolution, and totalitarian systems are not more but less common than forty years ago). The novel's literary weaknesses can now be seen in clearer focus. If *Nineteen Eighty-Four* is an accessible work, that is partly because of the lucidity of Orwell's writing. But it is also because of a lack of subtlety in his characterization, and a crude plot.

---

* This essay was written as the Introduction to the 1989 Penguin Twentieth-Century Classics edition of Orwell's *Nineteen Eighty-Four*.

The latter may be briefly summarized. The novel is set in the year 1984 in London ('Airstrip One') in Oceania, a superpower controlled by the restrictive 'Party' and led by its symbolic head, Big Brother. Within this state there is no law and only one rule: absolute obedience in deed and thought. Oceanian society is divided hierarchically between a privileged Inner Party, a subservient Outer Party, and a sunken mass of 'proles'. The hero, Winston Smith, is a member of the Outer Party and is employed at the Ministry of Truth (that is, of Lies) as a routine falsifier of records. Despite overwhelming pressure to conform to the system, Winston secretly reacts against it. He is approached by another minor official, Julia, who recognizes a kindred spirit. Emboldened by love, they ask a high-ranking Inner Party bureaucrat, O'Brien, to put them in touch with an opposition force called the Brotherhood, supposedly led by Big Brother's arch-enemy, the Trotsky-like Emmanuel Goldstein. The encouragement they receive from O'Brien, however, turns out to be a ploy. They are arrested and separated. Both are broken under interrogation and betray each other. Released before his final liquidation, Winston discovers that he has learnt to love Big Brother.

This works well, at one level, as entertainment. But it has limitations as art. The narrative lacks development, the dialogue is sometimes weak, and most of the people are two-dimensional, existing only to explain a political point or permit a side-swipe at a species in the real world. Among the novel's minor figures, a woman singing as she hangs out washing cheers us, and we are haunted by the mournful image of Winston's long-disappeared mother. But the hero's Outer Party acquaintances – the fatuously eager Parsons, for instance, or the zealot Syme – are merely caricature political activists; while most of the proles, with their dropped aitches and jumbled cockney clichés, seem to come from a pre-war copy of *Punch*. Mr Charrington, the junk-shop dealer who rents Winston a room as a love-nest and turns out to be a Thought Policeman wearing make-up, is plucked from a hundred cheap thrillers.

Of the three main characters, the sinister O'Brien is an intellectual construct: not a flesh-and-blood human being at all, but the ultimate, black image of totalitarianism. Winston and Julia are more substantial. Aspects of Winston have been encountered in Orwell's earlier novels. He is a loner and a loser, a prospectless member of the lower upper-middle class, filled with impotent rage at those who control his life. We are depressed by Winston's plight, and when he is elevated by love and political commitment we wish him well. Yet he never rises much above his own self-pity, and it is hard to feel the downfall of this unprepossessing fellow as a tragedy.

Julia is altogether a more sympathetic and pleasing creation. Perhaps she contains something of Orwell's first wife, Eileen, who died in 1945. Certainly Julia has a solidity and a touch of humour that are lacking elsewhere. The biggest relief is to discover, just as we are about to be suffocated in Oceania's slough of despond, that politics bores Julia stiff:

> 'I'm not interested in the next generation . . . I'm interested in *us*.'
> 'You're only a rebel from the waist downwards,' he told her.
> She thought this brilliantly witty and flung her arms round him in delight.

Yet Julia contains a contradiction. As well as the most engaging character in the book, she is also the least appropriate. Unlike the morose Winston, she is a free spirit. 'Life as she saw it was quite simple,' the author recounts. 'You wanted a good time; "they", meaning the Party, wanted to stop you having it; you broke the rules as best you could.'

We are grateful for Julia. But we are left wondering how this public school boy's fantasy ideal of uncomplicated, healthy, outdoors femininity could possibly have survived the mind-rotting propaganda of the Party. Or, if she could survive, why not others? Winston ('the last man in Europe') just about makes sense as an unreformed relic of the old era, but Julia looks like proof that the methods of the new age do not work. Yet a theme of the book is that they are inescapably effective. In the novel's own terms, Julia seems an anachronism: her clandestine affair belongs to a country under occupation, the land of Odette, rather than to one totally controlled.

Julia (for all this inconsistency) breathes life into the novel; but her presence alone would barely sustain a short story. If there were nothing to the novel apart from the characters and the narrative, it would scarcely be read today except as a curiosity. In fact, there is a great deal more. What makes it a masterpiece of political writing – the modern equivalent, as Bernard Crick has rightly claimed, of Thomas Hobbes's *Leviathan* – is the extraordinary texture of the backcloth. Disguised as horror–comic fiction, *Nineteen Eighty-Four* is really a non-fiction essay about the demon power. It works for us in the same way that Emmanuel Goldstein's heretical book, analysing and attacking the political system, works for Winston:

> In a sense it told him nothing that was new, but that was part of the attraction. It said what he would have said, if it had been possible to set his scattered thoughts in order . . . The best books, he perceived, are those that tell you what you know already.

As elsewhere in Orwell's writings, the deceptive, collusive amateurism of the author's style lulls us into the realization not only that he is right, but also that he is saying what we always thought but never managed to formulate into words.

As satire *Nineteen Eighty-Four* has been hard to place. Some have seen it as an attack on Stalinism, or on totalitarianism in general, or on the directive tendencies (at a time of Labour government) of British state socialism. Others have read it as an assault on the pretensions and illiberalism of western left-wing intellectuals. Others, again, have explained it as a feverish tubercular hallucination, as a lampoon of prep school life or (what might be the same thing) as a sado-masochistic reverie. Probably it contains elements of all these. Yet it is more than just a satirical attack, and much more than the product of febrile imagination. Though it contains a kind of warning, it is not prophecy (which Orwell knew, as well as anybody, to be impossible and meaning-less). Neither is it much concerned with contemporary events. It is a book about the continuing present: an update on the human condition. What matters most is that it reminds us of so many things we usually avoid.

The book shocks where it is most accurate. We are unmoved by embarrassing descriptions of Winston's encounters with the proles – which seem to say more about the author's own class difficulties than about social apartheid in a real or threatened world. But the account of a system based on ideological cant and psychological manipulation immediately affects us. The dream-like misappropriation of reason touches our rawest nerve. It is no accident, indeed, that of the many words and concepts from *Nineteen Eighty-Four* that are now in common use even by people who have never read the book – for example, *Newspeak, thought-crime, Big Brother, unperson, doublethink* – most relate to the power of the state to bend reality. At the core of the novelist's perception is *doublethink*, defined as 'the power of holding two contradictory beliefs in one's mind simultaneously, and accepting both of them'. Like many of Orwell's aphorisms, this seems at first absurd and then an aspect of everyday political life.

In Arthur Koestler's *Darkness at Noon*, an earlier novel which also explored the theoretical limits of totalitarianism, the author showed the moral annihilation produced by an ideology in which the end is allowed to justify any means. Orwell's innovation is to abolish the end. Where other ideologies have justified themselves in terms of a future goal, *Ingsoc*, the doctrine of the Party in Oceania, is aimless. As O'Brien explains to Winston, 'we are interested solely in power. Not wealth or luxury or long life or happiness: only power, pure power.' But power for what? O'Brien's answer tells us what we already know about oppression everywhere: 'The object of persecution is persecution. The object of torture is torture. The object of power is power.' Oceania is a static society running on an equilibrium of suffering. 'If you want a picture of the future,' says O'Brien, 'imagine a boot stamping on a human face – for ever.'

Nineteen Eighty-Four draws heavily on James Burnham's *Managerial Revolution*, whose image of a world divided into three large units, each ruled by a self-chosen élite, is reflected in Goldstein's 'Theory of Oligarchical Collectivism' and in the division of the world into the three superpowers of Oceania, Eurasia and Eastasia, continually at war with one another. But there is also much, indirectly, of Sigmund Freud. The furnace of Oceanian society, in which everything is done collectively yet everyone remains alone, is the denial of the erotic. It is this that fires the prevailing moods of 'fear, hatred, adulation and orgiastic triumph'. Sexual hysteria is used deliberately to ferment a sadistic loathing of imagined enemies and to stimulate a masochistic, depersonalized love of Big Brother.

Nobody, not even the sceptical Winston, is immune. Mass emotion, the author repeatedly reminds us, is almost irresistible. The 'Two Minutes Hate' is one of *Nineteen Eighty-Four*'s most notorious inventions. The author shows his hero, in the midst of this organized mania, unable to stop himself joining in. Winston manages to turn the 'hideous ecstasy of fear and vindictiveness' that 'seemed to flow through the whole group like an electric current' into hatred for the girl sitting behind him (who later turns out to be Julia). 'Vivid, beautiful hallucinations flashed through his mind. He would flog her to death with a rubber truncheon ... He would ravish her and cut her throat at the moment of climax.' Why? Because 'she was young and pretty and sexless, because he wanted to go to bed with her and would never do so . . .' Such private hatred, Orwell makes clear, is the purpose of Oceania's puritanism. Sexual happiness is the biggest threat to the system and Julia's code ('What you say or do doesn't matter; only feelings matter') is much more dangerous than Winston's intellectual doubts. 'We shall abolish the orgasm,' says O'Brien, with his usual knack of getting to the heart of things. 'Our neurologists are at work on it now.'

The psychic balance between private misery and the acceptance of official cruelty in *Nineteen Eighty-Four* did not so much anticipate the future as help to shape the way others – including survivors – would describe totalitarianism. Works by Alexander Solzhenitsyn (*A Day in the Life of Ivan Denisovich* and *The First Circle*, for example) show clearly the imprint of Orwell's notion of a stable, purposeless evil, into which victims and persecutors are mutually locked. It is *Nineteen Eighty-Four*'s account of the plasticity of reason, however, that has had the sharpest impact. The full horror of the book begins when it becomes plain that everybody in Oceania, even among members of the cynical-yet-fanatical Inner Party, is in flight from logic. Doubtless Orwell was thinking of Stalin's attempt to make the laws of genetics accord with Marxism–Leninism, when he presented Big Brother as master of the universe:

> 'What are the stars?' said O'Brien indifferently. 'They are bits of fire a few kilometres away. We could reach them if we wanted to. Or we could blot them out . . . For certain purposes, of course, that is not true. When we navigate the ocean, or when we predict an eclipse, we often find it convenient to assume that the earth goes round the sun and that the stars are millions upon millions of kilometres away. But what of it? Do you suppose it is beyond us to produce a dual system of astronomy? The stars can be near or distant, according as we need them. Do you suppose our mathematicians are unequal to that? Have you forgotten doublethink?'

This, of course, is madness. But who is to determine what is mad and what is sane in a society where all, including the thought controllers, learn to believe that two and two can equal five? Orwell reminds us how shaky is our hold on objective knowledge, and how uncertain our grip on the past.

Primo Levi – who lived through Auschwitz to become the finest writer on the Holocaust – has described in *The Drowned and the Saved* how Hitler contaminated the morality of his subjects by refusing them access to the truth. He concludes that 'the entire history of the brief "millennial Reich" can be reread as a war against memory, an Orwellian falsification of reality ...' Oceania's unceasing war on memory, in which every shred of evidence that conflicts with the latest official line is systematically destroyed and a false trail is laid in its place, is one of the novel's most ingenious and terrifying devices.

Another is the assassination of language. Accurate history is one essential vessel of liberty, perhaps the most essential, and *Nineteen Eighty-Four* can be seen as a charter for historical scholarship. A second is linguistic purity. Language is testimony: it contains geological strata of past events and out-of-fashion values. Orwell was making an observation that is as relevant to the behaviour of petty bureaucrats as of dictators, when he noted the eagerness with which truth-evaders shy away from well-known words and substitute their own. In Oceania the Party has created a sanitized language, *Newspeak*, to take the place of traditional English with its uncomfortable associations. This ideological Esperanto is composed of short, clipped words, 'which aroused the minimum of echoes in the speaker's mind', and which will eventually render the framing of heretical thoughts impossible. Orwell gives real-world examples of *Newspeak*: Nazi, Gestapo, Comintern, Agitprop. There are many others. Thus Levi notes how, in Hitler's Germany, phrases like 'final solution', 'special treatment', 'prompt employment unit' disguised a frightful reality. We could make our own additions from the age of nuclear terror: *overkill*, the verb to *nuke*, the semi-jocular *star wars*.

Doublethink, *Newspeak*, *crimestop* (the faculty of 'stopping short, as though by instinct, at the threshold of any dangerous thought ... In short ... protective stupidity') are hardy perennials in any authoritarian or totalitarian state, which helps explain why the novel, secretly distributed, has been so keenly appreciated in eastern Europe. At the same time, they also refer to aspects of any bureau, corporation or political party in a democracy, not to mention any jargon-ridden profession or orthodoxy-driven academic discipline. They are predictions only in the sense that any polemic predicts a dire consequence if its injunction is not heeded.

Nevertheless, *Nineteen Eighty-Four*, with its very specific date, does have an historical reference point. It is not by chance that Orwell calls the Party ideology *Ingsoc*, and presents it as a perversion of English socialism. Some have seen it as an indictment of the Labour Government of Clement Attlee. In fact Orwell, who continued to think of himself both as a democratic socialist and as a Labour Party supporter, was not greatly interested by the fast-moving politics of the mid-1940s, and much of the time during the gestation and writing of the novel (interrupted by a long spell in hospital with tuberculosis) he spent far from London political gossip at his farmhouse on the island of Jura.

Yet the novel can certainly be seen – like its predecessor *Animal Farm* – as a contribution to the debate within socialism. Like *Animal Farm* it does not look forward to future controversies but harks back to pre-war ones. The most important political experience in Orwell's life (described in *Homage to Catalonia*) was the Spanish Civil War, in which the author was wounded fighting for the revolutionary POUM (*Partido Obrero de Unificación Marxista*) militia. Orwell came back from Spain bitterly hostile towards Moscow-led communism, whose influence on the progressive British intelligentsia continued to be pervasive. He was less surprised than many on the left by the Nazi–Soviet pact in August 1939 (to be followed by the German invasion of Russia in 1941, which brought Stalin into the war on the side of the Allies, and then by the cooling of Allied–Soviet relations, which turned Russia back into a potential enemy of the West almost as soon as the war was over). The cynicism and impermanence of big power alliances is a feature of *Nineteen Eighty-Four*.

Oceania is not, in any sense, a socialist society. On the contrary. A cardinal example of *doublethink* is that 'the Party rejects and vilifies every principle for which the Socialist movement ever stood, and it chooses to do this in the name of Socialism.' Oceania cannot therefore be taken as an argument for socialism's failure. The point is not the achievement of socialist promises, but their rejection and distortion. Some may hear an echo of Friedrich von Hayek's *Road to Serfdom* in Goldstein's account of how 'in each variant of socialism that appeared from about 1900 onwards the aim of establishing liberty and equality was more and more openly abandoned'. Yet Orwell is no less critical of anti-socialists. By the 1940s, says Goldstein, 'all the main currents of political thought were authoritarian . . . Every new political theory, by whatever name it called itself, led back to hierarchy and regimentation.' If Airstrip One is a version of austerity London (as Michael Radford's interesting film of the novel suggests), then Labour socialism is scarcely singled out for particular criticism. Indeed, Goldstein also makes clear that the systems in the other superpowers, Eurasia and Eastasia, are practically identical.

Orwell's attack is not on socialism, but on credulous or self-serving people who call themselves socialists, and on some of their illusions. One illusion – still part of platform rhetoric – is that, whatever obstacles and setbacks may be encountered on the way, the working class will eventually and inevitably triumph. Orwell turns this on its head. In Oceania the relative freedom of working-class people is merely a symptom of the contempt in which they are held. 'From the proletarians', declares Goldstein, 'nothing is to be feared.' They can be granted intellectual liberty, he adds (with a kick in the groin for liberal, as well as socialist, assumptions), 'because they have no intellect'.

Yet the proles have an important place in the novel. If there is hope, Winston ruminates, it lies with them. Is there hope? The surface message of the novel seems to be that there is none. Oceania is a society *beyond* totalitarianism. Even in Auschwitz or the Gulag a community of sorts could continue to exist and heroism was possible. But in Oceania heroism is empty because there is nobody to save. Hope flickers briefly and then it is extinguished: Winston's attempt to preserve his identity is a mere spitting in the wind. Physical resistance to the Party's terrorism is self-defeating. Orwell underlines Koestler's argument in *Darkness at Noon* that to fight oppression with the oppressor's own methods is a moral capitulation. He uses O'Brien, while apparently testing Winston's resolve as a fellow-conspirator, to trap the hero into a monstrous pledge:

> 'If, for example, it would somehow serve out interests to throw sulphuric acid in a child's face – are you prepared to do that?'
> 'Yes.'

Later, O'Brien the interrogator asks Winston:

> 'And you consider yourself morally superior to us, with our lies and cruelty?'

He has only to turn on a tape of the earlier conversation to make his point.

For all this, however, *Nineteen Eighty-Four* is far from a despairing book. As an intellectual puzzle it is almost watertight: every facile answer or objection is cleverly anticipated and blocked off. But the grotesque world it portrays is imaginary. There is no reason to read into the blackness of Orwell's literary vision the denial of any real-life alternative. The novel, indeed, can be seen as an account of the forces that endanger liberty and of the need to resist them. Most of these forces can be summed up in a single word: lies. The author offers a political choice – between the protection of truth, and a slide into expedient falsehood for the benefit of rulers and the exploitation of the ruled, in whom genuine feeling and ultimate hope reside.

Thus the novel is above all subversive, a protest against the tricks played by governments. It is a volley against the authoritarian in every personality, a polemic against every orthodoxy, an anarchistic blast against every unquestioning conformist. 'It is intolerable to us', says the evil O'Brien, 'that an erroneous thought should exist anywhere in the world, however secret and powerless it may be.' *Nineteen Eighty-Four* is a great novel and a great tract because of the clarity of its call, and it will endure because its message is a permanent one: erroneous thought is the stuff of freedom.

SUEZ

THE MOST REVEALING MOMENT in the whole Gulf fiasco came at the end, when President Bush – having just wiped out 100,000 Iraqi conscripts at little human cost to his own side – announced during a triumphant press conference that, at last, the US had 'kicked the Vietnam syndrome'. So that, we realized in a flash, was what it was really all about.

Most wars are fought to kick some syndrome or other. Germany fought the Second World War to kick the syndrome, as the Nazis saw it, that produced the Treaties of Brest-Litovsk and Versailles. Since 1945, Britain's mini-wars have mainly been to kick the Munich syndrome. Thus, in both the Falklands and the Gulf conflicts, the anachronistic word 'appeasement' – coined in a different era to describe the ill-starred policy of seeking to integrate an unhappy country into the family of nations – was seldom off the lips of battle-hungry British politicians, as a thing to be avoided at any cost.

Undoubtedly, the Munich-kicking war *par excellence* was Suez. Today, the immediate causes of the 1956 Anglo–French adventure seem almost unimaginably remote. It is as hard to conjure up the short-term factors that led Sir Anthony Eden and Guy Mollet to gamble with world peace as it will be for our children, a third of a century hence, to understand the motives of Bush, Baker, Thatcher and Major in the Gulf. What is clear is that the ghosts at the mid-1950s feast were Hitler, Mussolini, and Chamberlain.

Keith Kyle's rich book unravels the tangled skein of events that produced the Suez landings. He is particularly good at showing the multitude of reasons that should have been apparent at the time (and mainly were) for resisting the angry impulse to go to war. Kyle is a journalist, documentary-maker and former politician-*manqué* who – quite far on in his career – has turned himself into a diplomatic

Suez, Keith Kyle (Weidenfeld & Nicolson, 1991)

historian. He has accomplished the transition with confident ease.

Under the thirty-year rule, those British state papers covering the Suez affair and its aftermath that do not embarrass the Establishment too much are now available and Kyle has done a magnificent job of digesting and making sense of them, together with a wide range of other European, US and Middle Eastern sources. There are no sensations: his conclusions broadly conform what most cool-headed people have known or surmised for decades. What he succeeds in doing, with a pointillism of meticulous detail, is in presenting the whole baroque edifice of Anglo–French frivolity in a way that is full of lessons for our own time.

Oddly enough, it is a tale without villains. Kyle is not exactly a fan of Anthony Eden, whose tragic misjudgements were the single greatest cause. But he is able to regard him with a degree of sympathetic understanding. The irony, as the author points out, is that nobody was better equipped to avoid a messy entanglement in the Middle East than the British Prime Minister. When Eden succeeded Churchill in April 1955, he had completed three and a half years of productive diplomacy – not counting two earlier spells as Foreign Secretary. Had illness forced him out of office a couple of years earlier than it did, he would be remembered as one of the great politician–diplomats of the century, instead of by one traumatic word, which, more than any other, encapsulates British decline, senescence and delusions of grandeur.

Eden is thought of as a ferocious hawk. Kyle shows that he was not so regarded until the summer of 1956 – and that was part of the trouble. His recent record had been one of calm arbitration, not sabre-rattling, to an extent that had evoked mutterings on the Tory Right. Not only was he perfectly aware (at a time when anti-Americanism was as prevalent among Conservative imperialists as on the left) of the need to be closely allied to the Americans; he was also much more pro-Arab than the 'Zionist' Churchill, sharing conventional patrician doubts about the Jewish nation. He might not quite have gone along with the British ambassador in Tel Aviv, who wrote in 1955 that the Israelis must be treated as sick people who could not be expected to have a mature foreign policy because their history had bequeathed a legacy of 'unsureness, over-confidence, emotional instability, fierce intolerance, superiority complex, inferiority complex, guilt complex'. But he was accurately suspected of sharing the Foreign Office's soft spot for Israeli enemies. He was proud, too, of his understanding of traditional Middle Eastern culture. Meeting President Nasser, in Cairo in February 1955, he surprised his host by addressing him in his own language.

'Grabber Nasser', shouted the *Daily Mail*, when the Egyptian nationalist seized the Canal. Eden had a difficulty, however, which President Bush and Mrs Thatcher would have appreciated if they knew any history. Just as Anglo–American *realpolitik* in the 1980s was bound up with a pretty cynical relationship with Saddam, so (as Kyle reminds us) in the 1950s 'Anthony Eden's public reputation had been bound up with the controversial policy of trusting Nasser.'

The author is probably right to attribute the change in Eden's outlook less to pique at being scorned than to the need to appease the right-wing Suez group, which had hitherto accused him of appeasement. Just as Bush and successive British premiers were tempted into a military escapade in the 1990s partly by a need to divert attention from dodgy domestic politics, so Eden's unease at No. 10, and his middle-of-the-road image, strengthened the need to present a tougher face to the outside world.

It is an established principle of modern war that nobody ever embarks on it without firmly believing that the whole world will benefit. This applied in 1956, no less than in 1990. The Suez operation was solemnly justified by the British Cabinet on the grounds that the Canal 'was not a piece of Egyptian property but an international asset of the highest importance which should be managed by an international trust'.

Another principle of modern warfare is that the stated aims are never the real ones, and the real ones are soon forgotten once the drama unfolds, producing unpredicted consequences. Military 'success' opens a Pandora's box, as surely as defeat. As in the Gulf, so over Suez.

There were, of course, critical differences. The real objection to Suez was not that big nations shouldn't play policemen in their own interests against little ones – the Americans did that all the time in their own continent. It was that the British and French went ahead in defiance of everybody: it was Eden's impatience with the UN and wilful misinterpretation of Eisenhower that did for him. Interestingly, Labour criticism may also have helped (by creating the impression of a bitterly divided nation) to put off the Americans. That is one contrast with the Falklands and the Gulf, when the Opposition sought to vie with the Government in patriotism.

The Suez group always believed that Eden's biggest mistake, having gone in, was in pulling out too soon. Kyle indicates that they may have been right: the spectacle of military *coitus interruptus* presented by the ceasefire did maximum damage to British standing. If so, the culprit was not Rab Butler, scapegoated by the Tories as Suez's Man of Munich, but the Chancellor of the Exchequer, Harold Macmillan, who was gung-ho at the start and panicky over sterling (Kyle thinks prematurely) at the finish.

The moral is that the British make very inefficient thugs. 'The Suez operation was crippled by the inability of British political leadership, having embarked on the cynicism business, to be sufficiently cynical about the follow-up,' Kyle thinks. A second moral is that in the Middle East it is usually best to leave well alone.

In the end, the Suez affair was more a farce than a disaster, hastening Britain's realization of its reduced status in the world. We were humiliated over Suez; the Gulf was a victory, yet we are only beginning to reap the whirlwind. If Britain is likely to escape most of the opprobrium this time, it is partly because Suez turned us from an ally of the Americans into a lackey. European integration could turn out to be the only way to kick that particular syndrome.

New Statesman & Society, 28 June 1991

MISSING THE BOAT AT
THE END OF EMPIRE

IT IS A GENERAL TRUTH about empires that they start to decline at the moment when their owners feel most secure. In the case of our own, serious disintegration began almost as soon as we had won a world war that was supposed to ensure its survival. What happened? Historians have devoted a lot of attention to the origins of a baroque adornment which, so far from making us happy and rich, caused a lot of bickering and brought us close to penury. They have been less interested in the bizarre finale. In his stimulating book about the anti-colonialist movement at home, Dr Stephen Howe of Ruskin College seeks to redress the balance.

This is a case study: the author is not primarily concerned with general reasons for imperial decline. Nevertheless, his account provides an important – and largely negative – piece in the jigsaw. Dr Howe is himself cautious in his conclusions. Yet the overwhelming impression conveyed by his account of left-wing opposition to the Empire is that efforts by domestic radicals to bring about decolonization were too late, too insubstantial, and aroused too little public interest to have any great impact on the eventual outcome. Since anti-colonialism is the one area in twentieth-century politics where the British Left has always claimed an indisputable triumph, that is a major indictment.

Part of the story is about what didn't happen, rather than what did. The comfortable liberal view of anti-colonial good gaining ground against pro-imperial evil appears simply to be false: the reality was much closer to a slowly changing consensus on imperial matters in which radical opinion was mostly a tiny, and not very dissonant, voice. There is a problem of historical imagination in reading such a book – it is now such a basic assumption of political debate that all races have

Anti-colonialism in British Politics: The Left and the End of the Empire 1918–1964, Stephen Howe (Clarendon Press, 1993)

equal rights that it is difficult to grasp how recently almost everybody in this country took for granted the exact opposite. In fact – as Howe reminds us – even as late as the 1940s it was not just the Colonel Blimps of David Low cartoons who believed in the superiority of whites over 'coloureds'. Many liberals and socialists, while paying lip-service to the brotherhood of man, were in practical terms crudely racist as well.

There were always exceptions. The seventeenth-century Levellers had offered the poser: 'How can the conquered be accounted rebels, if at any time they seek to free themselves and recover their own?' A few hundred years later, the Chartists applauded the Indian mutiny. Such attitudes, however, were rare. Double standards were the norm: at a time when the principles of Mill and Bentham were being hotly debated at home, nineteenth-century would-be democrats maintained a tactical (or oblivious) silence on the rights of recently subjugated peoples in Africa and Asia.

Even Karl Marx once declared that British rule in India was the 'unconscious tool of history', and hence to be regarded as a progressive force: a view shared by anti-Marxist Fabians, who believed that – however dubious the motives of the colonizers – the involuntary citizens of the British Empire were lucky to have such a benevolent country to look after them. In the first half of the present century, the Labour leadership took a similar line, treating the Empire much as the Opposition treats Northern Ireland today, as a sticky topic best kept out of inter-party controversy, and left to the civil service.

Nevertheless, from the time of the First World War, some people did begin to question the assumptions of the British Empire, largely on the basis of newly accepted principles of national self-determination that had been applied in Europe at the Treaty of Versailles. Campaigners in the inter-war period, however, were bitterly divided. On the one side, those who took instructions from the Communist International usually favoured anything that would destabilize imperial rule; on the other, moderate opponents of colonialism opposed both agitational 'sedition' and any notion of a precipitate rush to independence. Between these poles, there were many shades of sometimes romantic, sometimes cranky, and frequently warring, opinion.

That was one difficulty. Another was that if you happened to be a mother-country advocate of decolonization, it took two to tango.

Those who opposed the Empire on principle had little to offer nation-alist movements, until nationalist movements came into existence and were available to be helped. Communists tried to solve this problem, on Moscow's instructions, by sending out missionaries to establish revolutionary cells: but their initial success was slight.

In the case of Africa, there was little for British campaigners to latch onto until after 1945. Early gatherings of what Marxists called 'bourgeois nationalists' were primitive and unimpressive. Largely composed of 'wealthy, self-improving, constitutionalist, aspiringly faithful replicas of the English gentleman in their tastes, manners and aims', they were scarcely able to convince even the most favourably disposed of British sympathizers that they represented anybody but themselves. It was not surprising, therefore, that serious radicals stuck to anti-fascism and unemployment.

India was different: it is there that the real story of disengagement from our overseas Empire really begins. Yet one important revelation of Howe's book is the comparatively small amount of attention India received on the British left. True, Clement Attlee took a continuing interest in Indian problems. Yet there was never a pro-Gandhi equiva-lent of Winston Churchill, who thundered on behalf of the Tory diehards. The Left had a guilty conscience about the Raj, and wrote knocking novels about the public school prefect types who ran it. But for young idealists, the anti-fascist struggle in Spain had more resonance. Howe quotes the writer Edward Thompson (father of E. P.) on intellectual anti-imperialism in the 1930s: 'the mere mention of the word "India" is enough to empty the smallest hall in Oxford.'

After 1940 – partly because of Britain's military embarrassment and a consequent rise in nationalist excitement – British anti-colonialism began to advance. If, indeed, there was a period when British radicals *might* have had a major impact on colonial questions, it was during the decade of the Second World War, and of the first ever majority Labour Government, in which a founder of the Fabian Colonial Bureau, Arthur Creech Jones, served as Colonial Secretary. Yet the record does not suggest that the impact of socialist ideology on imperial issues was ever very profound.

A number of heroes do emerge: in particular, Fenner Brockway, Kingsley Martin and a few others who did a good deal to provide new African and Asian activists with friendship, encouragement and a pan-nationalist dating service which helped to build an Empire-wide nationalist network that was separate from the one created by the communists. Nevertheless, such things were relative drops in the ocean. By the mid-1940s, bigger factors than tea and sympathy at the home of a left-wing MP were making the rapid end of Empire an inevitability.

American capitalist misgivings about British colonialism probably counted for more, at this stage, than British socialist ones. When Churchill's War Cabinet declared that the call in the Atlantic Charter for the restoration of sovereign rights 'to those who have been forceably deprived of them' did not apply to British colonies – few people in Britain raised any objection. But in the United States – which did not have a territorial empire and did not see the need for one – the mood was different. Before and after Eisenhower's sabotage of Eden's Suez adventure in 1956, American 'imperialism' did much to pull the rug out from under the British version.

How much difference did the election of a Labour government in 1945 make? This major question deserves rather more than the single chapter Howe devotes to it. That it had some impact is beyond dispute. Thus there is no doubt that Attlee was personally impelled towards Indian independence, an event which might not have happened as quickly if Churchill had remained in office. Arguably, moreover, the granting of autonomy to the Indian subcontinent and adjoining territories was as much as could be expected from a single administration, especially as the idea of handing over power to a non-white régime was a novel one. Yet there is still a sense of an opportunity for socialist glory that was missed.

Labour *might* have taken the cause of colonial development a critical stage further. In fact, outside southern Asia and the Middle East, little happened. Partly, this was because Labour had made few commitments: its 1945 manifesto promised the Jews a bit of anti-Arab ethnic cleansing in Palestine, but otherwise gave few specific details on imperial questions. Chiefly, it was because Labour had no agenda. Attlee later claimed credit for the only case in history where, 'without external pressure or weariness at the burden of governing, the ruling people has voluntarily surrendered its hegemony over subject peoples and given them their freedom.' But there is no evidence that, India apart, the Labour premier ever had such a plan in mind, or that he saw India as a staging-post.

Preoccupied with other matters, the Government seems to have treated the Empire as though it was just another rundown nationalized industry. In 1946 Herbert Morrison fatuously remarked that Labour was 'great friends of the jolly old Empire' and three years later the party's *Speakers' Handbook* declared that 'imperialism is dead'. What it meant was that jingoistic imperialism was to be replaced by a Fabian model, in which the man from the Colonial Office was always right.

It also meant that no Labour minister seriously contemplated a general divestment of colonies. This remained true even of the second Attlee administration, which was desperately short of new ideas, and might have seized on the colonial issue as a good way to revive its juices. Instead, senior members of the Government regarded the Colonial Secretaryship as a poisoned chalice. It was left to the Conservative Governments of 1951–64, without need of prompting from the Left, to preside over the winding up of the British Empire.

Ironically, it was in this final phase that Labour interest in colonial questions sharply increased, earning the Party a new reputation as the champion of oppressed imperial peoples and of the nascent black Commonwealth. During the Attlee administration, the Labour Left had kept fairly quiet on the issue. Now it went on the warpath. There were two reasons: the rise of Bevanism, which made left-wingers less subservient to the whips, and the emergence of nationalist movements which, at long last, began to hit the headlines. Kenya, Cyprus, above all Suez, forced the Government onto the defensive.

According to Brockway in 1957, 'During the period in Opposition, Labour's policy in regard to the colonies has advanced more than on any other subject.' But the Tories' policy was advancing almost as fast. When the Left demanded firm dates for colonial independence, it found itself pushing at a swinging door. There was much in the small print of decolonization to quarrel with the Government about, but little in the substance: by the early 1960s, the Tories were passing independence bills almost as fast as they could find parliamentary time for them. After Harold Wilson became Prime Minister, there was little left to do, except to sort out Rhodesia – a problem which Labour approached in the bi-partisan spirit that had characterized its handling of colonial questions for most of the century.

Strangely, Howe – despite many of his own arguments – concludes by judging British left-wing anti-colonialism a success. Certainly, some left-wing objectives were achieved. Above all, the transition of power in India was a landmark of which Labour can be justly proud. There is also the importance of a heritage of British anti-colonialism, both in relation to Britain's own post-imperial ethnic minorities and for our dealings with the Third World. Yet the causal link between left-wing propaganda or action, and solid events in the saga of decolonization, is often missing; and the sad truth remains – as the author himself suggests – that the Empire and colonies were 'a remarkably marginal issue in British politics', almost as much on the left as on the right.

Guardian, 1 January 1994

LOOKING AT LEFTNESS

WILL THERE ALWAYS BE a 'Left'? Not since the 1930s have the prospects for the British Left seemed so bleak. Yet if pessimism is the normal state today among leftists, there is also a problem of identity and of definition. What does it mean in this country to be on or of the Left?

There is no objective standard: the answer depends partly on who you are talking to. For some, 'left' is a cabal of faction. For others, it is a blanket term to describe all opposition to the Centre and the Right. For still others, it can only be understood in terms of ideas and principles. There are obvious connections between the three usages, but they are not the same; and confusion arises because people often slip from one meaning to another, without a signpost.

Clearly in Britain there is no *essence* of leftism: no single reference point or standard against which all claims can be judged. The term 'left' is a quite modern immigrant, whose arrival and absorption into everyday language did little or nothing to change the political system within which it was applied. Its origins are French: supposedly it arose out of the seating arrangements of the Assembly of 1789. According to William Pickles, the word entered common parlance in Britain in the 1920s[1] – by which time the political spectrum to which it referred (including an officially socialist Labour Party) was already well established. It is significant that as late as 1933 the OED defined 'left' in its political sense only in terms of 'those holding relatively liberal or democratic opinions', with no mention of socialism.

In nineteenth-century France, left and right described attitudes to the revolution, with related domestic adhesions: not only change versus reaction, but also anti-clerical versus clerical and – later – state intervention versus non-interference. In Britain, there was no historic trauma to provide a dividing line, and the borrowing of often inappropriate Continental applications merely added to the imprecision. The

379

problem of Church and state is a particular illustration of this. In some European countries, the Church has been closely linked to the Right. In Britain, despite a (Protestant) Church closely linked to the Establishment, religion (including Anglicanism) is an important part of the socialist heritage.

The British usage of 'left' has been full of such contradictions, which owe much to its foreign roots. The main value of the term – and its most common purpose – is *positional*, as in its earliest days. Having no core philosophy, it exists primarily in relation to non-left parties and leaders. What constitutes non-left is, of course, itself a matter of debate. While for most people 'left' is a way of describing the Labour Party and its sympathizers, within the Labour Party itself – where 'left' is imbued with sacred significance – there are many who do not regard the dominant forces inside the Labour fold as truly left.

The importance of positioning cannot be over-emphasized. Since the aftermath of the First World War (if not before), the Labour Party has included a persistent tradition, often labelled 'Labour Left' to distinguish it from the mainstream, overall 'Left' of the Party as a whole. In the early 1980s, what had always previously been a minority grouping became the most powerful one – producing an immediate semantic crisis. On the one hand, to be 'left' involves struggle against an over-mighty enemy; on the other the Labour Left was itself divided. Hence journalists subdivided the Labour Left into consistencies, as of cheeses: 'soft' versus 'hard'. The changing identity of 'soft' left provides an interesting lesson in political psychology.

'Leftness' is an expression in political geography. But it also describes a mental attitude that can best be summed up as rebellion. Once power is acquired (in a party or the state), the momentum of rebellion is hard to sustain, especially as there are others who attack the new authority. So it has been with the soft Left. For most members of the Labour Party, and certainly for all supporters of the hard Left, Neil Kinnock – once an extremist and the triumphant leader of the soft Left – is to be identified with the (Labour) Right. In this, Mr Kinnock follows a long, almost unbroken, Labour leadership tradition. Of all leaders since Labour became the official Opposition in 1922, only three (Henderson, Gaitskell and Callaghan) were not seen at the time of their election as standing to the left; at the time of their departure only one (Lansbury) was not seen among active Labour Party members as standing to the right. MacDonald, Attlee, Wilson, Foot and now Kinnock

– whose combined régimes account for half a century of Labour Party history – have all lost the aura of leftness as their tenure of office progressed.

This may partly be a product of pragmatism or – as the 'true' Left would say – opportunism. But it is also an automatic consequence of authority. The Left's positioning is (almost always) in relation to existing leadership. Although it is not impossible for the Party hierarchy to be to the left of the active rank-and-file, such a state of affairs is very hard to imagine.

If left is to be seen both as topographical and as a state of mind, the role of specific beliefs and ideas may be less crucial. Nevertheless ideas have always been important to the Left, and (despite the OED) the dominant idea has been socialism.[2] This is not the only element: there have been other overlapping (and sometimes contrary) strands. The pacifist tradition within the Left has non-socialist roots, while the long-standing left-wing demand (derived from militant trade unionism) for free collective bargaining can have anti-egalitarian consequences. Early in this century, the division in the Labour Party was between the socialists – who in effect constituted the Left – and non-socialist trade unionists. However, after the adoption of the socialist Clause Four of the Party constitution, all active members of the Labour Party came to describe themselves as socialists, without necessarily altering their opinions. For many non-Labour people, left and socialist and Labour became synonymous; while within the Labour Party itself, there remained an intense consciousness of the difference between degrees of leftness, as between 'real' and counterfeit socialism.

In one sense, because of the Left's positional nature, there will always be a 'left' within the political system, and a 'left' within the Left. There is a tautological element here, as well as a psychological one. But in another sense of left – ideological and sociological – the Left is dependent for its survival on its roots, and for its political importance on its social and industrial base.

The collateral of British socialism and leftness has been trade unionism. Many unionists were slow in coming round even to a notional support of socialist doctrines, and socialist enthusiasts have always considered that within much of the trade union movement socialism does not go very deep. Nevertheless, what significance socialism possesses in British society has largely been derived from the sluggish, massive oppositional force which the organizations of the most proletarianized workforce in the world have, from time to time, been able to provide. That is the major difference between the British social-ist Left and, say, the beleaguered, marginal American equivalent.

The British Left may not have a future; or it may be unrecognizably different from its past. What is certain is that its fate is bound up with that of a Labour Movement of which the Labour Party is only a part. The key to understanding the British Left lies in an appreciation of the latent power, and above all the fundamental unity, of the single, union-based, class-conscious Movement. The history of this Move-ment is littered with quarrels, splits and expulsions. From the departure of the Marxian Social Democratic Federation from the original Labour Representation Committee in 1901 to the defection of the anti-Marxist SDP eighty years later, there have been those who have dreamt of an alternative formation drawing away the Labour Movement's electoral base or building a movement of their own. All have failed, and occasional trade union breakaways have always eventually returned to the fold.

Since the earliest days, there has been a tendency for outsiders – and some insiders – to exaggerate the industrial power and to under-estimate the underlying political strength of the Labour Movement, whose unity contrasts so sharply with the rival organizations of workers in some Continental countries. This strength derives from a relation-ship with a working-class constituency that is very deep. Like all politi-cal relationships, it is changing. But – despite the fondest hopes of some of Labour's critics – there is no sign that it is about to disappear.

Encouraged by journalists and market researchers, as well as by wishful-thinking politicians, a number of political scientists who ought to have a better sense of history have argued that support for political parties is today primarily determined by attitudes to 'policies' or 'issues'. Their case has been based partly on the increased fluidity of public opinion in the 1970s and 1980s, and partly on survey data which related answers to 'policy' questions to actual or intended voting behaviour. The argument, backed up by superficially impressive evi-dence, has had more than academic significance. The belief that the Labour Party was so out of tune with public opinion that a more poll-orientated rival could take over Labour's historic base encouraged the middle-ground optimism which precipitated the 1981 split. The SDP and Alliance adventure certainly showed how unstable electoral opinion had become. It also revealed a serious weakening of Labour support. But the most important demonstration was of the long run resilience of Labour, in contrast to the extreme fragility of its rationally-constructed, voter-friendly, progressive competitor.

There have been a number of reasons for Labour's survival. But the most important, paradoxically, has been its leftness. Labour has been protected by the polarized traditions of British politics which have continued to cast it as the most powerful alternative to the Right. Labour's position on the spectrum has never been usurped, largely because of its class profile, which offers a mirror image of popular perceptions of Conservatism, and because of a traditional, expected, set of attitudes. Various terms are applied to supporters of the political centre: for example, 'moderate' and 'sensible'. It is much harder to identify particular beliefs. By contrast, Labour and the Left immediately and vividly evoke a heritage. Labour is known to be against privilege, social hierarchy, capitalism, personal wealth, inequality, unregulated markets, the powerful, the Establishment, the upper classes, nationalistic fervour, military might; and in favour of equality, civil rights, state intervention, democracy, the working class, internationalism. Little in either list has changed in a hundred years, which is why the attitudes are so readily identifiable with the Left (and why Labour finds it so hard to disassociate itself from them). Many of them are supported by the Centre too – but without the same oppositional persistence. If one thing has underpinned the ethos of the British Left, it has been the spirit of confrontation: Us against Them. At times of national restlessness, that has been an advantage.

But behind this ideological mood lies the physical and mystical reality of the Labour Movement, which the progressive centre can never match. To many observers, the expression is no more than that – and an unreal one to boot. 'Lack of movement' might seem a more appropriate label. To insiders it provides a culture and a simple faith. It was said of Arthur Henderson, architect of the modern Labour Party, that when he spoke of the Labour Movement you could hear the capital 'M'.[3] Much has changed since Henderson's day. The Labour Movement no longer describes the complex network of unions, co-operatives, women's organizations and other groups that loosely tie together a large part of British proletarian life. Nevertheless, the notion of a wide fraternity of shared hopes and values still has the power to unite and enthuse, far beyond the narrow circles of the politically or industrially active.

The cartoonist David Low used to represent the TUC as a carthorse, symbolizing obstinacy and conservatism, but also decency and strength. There is another image of the Labour Movement in human form – also brilliantly caricatured by Low: Ernest Bevin. Bevin, the union leader turned politician, represented in his massive personage the characteristic features of the Labour Movement in its era of ascendancy: verbose, bullying, bad-tempered, and as solid as a rock. The link between politics and unions which Bevin embodied is still summed up by his own famously anatomical reminder to the politicians of their point of origin. The Labour Party, he declared, had grown 'from the bowels of the trade union movement'. As one writer has rightly remarked, Labour's 'bowel problem' – its historic link with the unions – is central to the Party's modern crisis.[4] It is equally impossible to understand Labour or consider the future of the Left without appreciating the past and continuing importance of the trade union connection for Labour's electoral strength.

The Labour Party was not only founded with the help of trade union money and trade union members; it was not only, from its earliest days, constitutionally in the hands of large union votes. In addition, the unions provided its class identity, and gave it legitimacy in the areas of industrial concentration. It was, from the early days, emphatically a 'labour' body. The myth that some process of evangelical conversion was involved in winning votes for Labour has been successfully dealt with by the historian Ross McKibbin.[5] Labour triumphed during the critical period of Liberal disarray and a widening franchise less as a result of successful propaganda than because of the organizing power of trades councils and the ability of an already established union movement to present Labour as a class party. Before 1945, Labour was able to offer voters little apart from vague aspirations which, during its brief periods of office, it proved singularly unable to meet. The increase in its support and its success in replacing the Liberals reflected the strong sense of communion between party, unions and a class.

Have policy commitments ever played much part in determining the long-term trajectory of Labour support? It seems unlikely, though an identification of Labour with the proposals of the Beveridge Report may have helped the Party during the 'sea-change' of opinion towards the end of the Second World War.[6] The original aim of the Labour Representation Committee – as its title implied – concerned class and representation, not policy.[7] Despite the inclusion of a socialist commitment in the constitution, Henderson's 1918 reorganization retained the same purpose. Nor was Labour unique in giving policy a low place in its priorities. The Conservatives were similarly indifferent. It was the Liberals, squeezed between the socially-based juggernauts of Left and Right, who turned in desperation to policy development as a life raft. Most working-class voters failed to notice. Labour support grew for reasons unconnected with its policies, of which there continued to be few of any substance. 'Deficient in brains and starved of money', wrote Beatrice Webb in 1927, 'it is a miracle that the Labour Party grows in voting power.' The basis for the miracle was the Labour Movement, and its octopus embrace with the working class.

Beatrice Webb spoke of a 'slow social upheaval moving independently of organization or leaders'.[8] Perhaps, recently, there has been an upheaval in the opposite direction. That was the claim made in the mid-1980s (as it had been made a quarter of a century before). Allegedly, the decline of class loyalty has produced a decline in class-based political attachment and an increase in issue-orientated voting.

Certainly, the huge changes in voting behaviour since the 1970 election, and especially since 1979, cannot be easily explained away. In 1983 and 1987 the Conservatives surpassed Labour in many areas as a party of the working class. In 1987 – despite Labour's partial recovery – the Conservatives obtained 36 per cent of the manual working-class vote nationally, only 6 per cent behind Labour with 42 per cent. Among skilled manual workers – the stratum from which the leaders of the Labour Movement had traditionally been drawn – the Conservatives did even better than in 1983, increasing their lead over Labour to 9 per cent. Even among the unemployed, the unskilled and the semi-skilled, the Conservatives obtained almost a third of the total vote, while Labour could barely muster a half. At the time of writing (and following the spectacular collapse of the Centre), Labour has recovered some lost ground. But even by the most hopeful interpretation it can no longer be regarded as 'the party of the working class' in the sense of the undisputed ruler of a particular social territory. After the last election, Professor Ivor Crewe sombrely concluded that his 1983 verdict that 'the working class was no longer largely Labour' and that Labour had become no more than a 'regional class party' had been amply confirmed. Furthermore, given the changing employment structure, demography and time were not on Labour's side. Yet

Crewe's analyses, and those of others, also confirm that the social character of Labour's vote retains its ancient features: Labour remains, for good or ill, overwhelmingly a working-class party. Peter Pulzer's classic dictum that 'class is the basis of British party politics' still holds for the Labour vote.

Obviously, if Labour cannot extend its social range and cannot even obtain the lion's share of the shrinking manual vote, it has no prospect of power. To be the party, as Crewe puts it, of 'a declining segment of the working class, the traditional working class of the council estates, the public sector, industrial Scotland and the North and the old industrial unions', and little else, is a position of stultifying weakness.[9] Yet there is also a positive side: there are circumstances in which a solid appeal to working-class voters in the traditionally working-class regions can have advantages.

Indeed – as the sorry fate of the SDP seems to demonstrate – the one thing worse than being a class party may be to be a national or classless one. Labour's governmental prospects depend on its ability to attract more support from the service-sector working class of the South and South-East, in particular. Yet there is something to be said for what Crewe calls Labour's 'old class fortresses'. Not only do they provide a vital concentration of support in hard times and hence (given our electoral system) a firmer parliamentary representation, so that Labour is better able to sustain a serious reverse than any other party. They also provide a moral base. The more Labour is pushed back into its ghetto, the clearer becomes it identity and – at least in theory – the clearer its purpose.

Behind that identity remains, as always, the trade union connection. Those who are concerned to widen Labour's appeal have wondered whether the link with the trade unions might not be weakened or even severed. The thought is scarcely new. After the 1959 election, a number of 'revisionist' leaders put forward a similar plan. It was even suggested that the Party might change its name – 'Labour', it was felt, might put off socially aspirant voters.[10] The argument in favour of such a move is that opinion polls have repeatedly shown public hostility to trade unions. The argument against breaking the link is that to separate Labour from its historic roots in order to increase its popularity among anti-union voters might in the end destroy the class consciousness and class loyalty that have been the Party's mainstay.

At the end of a decade of decline in power, rights and membership, trade unions are not fashionable. Bewildered, divided and under siege, unions in Britain have been less confident and more uncertain about their goals during the Thatcherite era than at any time since the Second World War. Yet their role as an intermediary between Labour politicians and their working-class supporters should never be underestimated. Unions are widely believed to *lose* the Labour Party votes. The extent to which Labour, in the long run, gains from the union-class association is less frequently considered.

What is most noticeable, of course, is the extent to which Labour behaviour is directly affected by changing union concerns. Just as Labour's post-1979 crisis reflected trade union attitudes (mainly in reaction to the Callaghan Government during the winter of discontent), so the recent mellowing of Labour is partly a product of the unions' urgent desire to displace the Thatcher régime, and consequent willingness to show flexibility in order to improve the Party's appeal. At the same time, the changing occupational structure – with white collar and service sector employment taking the place of manufacturing and mining – is affecting the shape of unionism, with a knock-on effect for Labour. White collar unionism does not necessarily mean less left-wing politics, as several recent union elections have demonstrated. But it is likely, in the long run, to entail a shift in the emphasis of the Labour Party's industrial interests – and in the nature of the 'working class' it seeks to represent. The days when the TUC – and hence the Labour Party – was overwhelmingly dominated by manufacturing, mining and other blue collar unions are past. In short, there is a trade union evolution in progress which will ensure a significantly different social image for Labour as well.

However, the pace of change is slow. Meanwhile, there is the question of whether Labour Party politicians and members can autonomously alter direction in order to perform better at elections – and in what direction they should seek to go.

The orthodox answer, the one supported by the psephological establishment and by the architects of Labour's own current policy review, is that the Party should pursue a better match between its policies and the preferences of voters, as expressed in opinion polls. There are a number of reasons for being sceptical of this view.

One is that there is no direct evidence of it working in the past. Many forces come into play during elections. It is hard, however, to think of a post-war contest in which party commitments determined the outcome. Labour's three victories against Conservatives in office – in 1945, 1964 and 1974 – seem either to have been reactive (against perceived Conservative failures) or to have reflected a wider shift in mood. A second reason is that public priorities on policy, and attitudes to policies themselves, change faster than it is possible even for a highly adaptible party to meet. A third reason is that the market model of voting behaviour – in which voters are presented as consumers and parties as sellers – is misleading. A general election is not a marketplace because no actual exchange is involved: voters pay no price and receive nothing directly in return. Hence it is unrealistic for a party to hope to 'buy' support by making pledges.

These are not arguments for insensitivity to public feeling, or for ignoring the need for policy development. Rather, they indicate that to concentrate on what voters say to the polling organizations may be to start at the wrong end, and that a party may do better to forget superficial expressions of opinion and consider instead what problems it wishes to solve and how to solve them.

In medicine, diagnosis has to precede the prescription of remedies. So, too, in politics. A policy review that is a serious intellectual enquiry makes much more sense than one whose purpose is image adjustment. Equally sensible is the proposal for a Labour Movement think-tank, which – properly staffed and funded – could provide a continuing source of ideas. 'Permanent policy review', instead of either permanent revolution or a once-and-for-all revision along supposedly popular lines, might well be the most promising approach.

Clearly, it also has its limits. If past election victories cannot obviously be attributed to policy bribes, they cannot be attributed to Fabian earnestness either. As Beatrice Webb observed, deeper and less accessible forces are involved in winning votes. Nevertheless, in looking for factors behind Labour's two most significant triumphs – in 1945 and 1964 – the role of practical ideas (as opposed to electoral window dressing) should not be discounted. The 1945 victory, in particular, was preceded by the most intensive period of backroom reflection and debate in the Party's history.

The discovery of Keynes and a coherent economic policy, linked to Labour's recent thinking on economic equality, did little directly to win the election. Yet it was not an accident that Labour's electoral peak came at the climax of what Professor Elizabeth Durbin has called British democratic socialism's 'rich tradition of designing realistic programmes'.[11] An enthusiasm for policy-making among socialist intellectuals and the sense they conveyed of being ahead of political rivals strengthened the confidence of the parliamentary leadership. A similar process occurred in the late 1950s, and early '60s, following the publication in 1956 of Anthony Crosland's *The Future of Socialism*.

'Most of the political opinions of most men are the result', wrote Graham Wallas, 'not of reasoning tested by experience, but of unconscious or half-conscious inference fixed by habit.'[12] Voting in Britain today remains as complex, and probably as ill-understood, as ever. Labour should be grateful for its union-linked social class ballast, and ought to avoid behaviour that risks losing it. It should also consider the possible role, among people outside Labour's normal supporters, of 'inference fixed by habit'. The point about genuine intellectual activity is not that it produces electorally tempting sweetmeats for the delectation of the voters, but that it gradually builds up an impression of a party of competence and conviction. The most convincing leaders are frequently those with the best understanding of what they are saying, and the firmest belief in their own prescriptions. After office has been obtained, the most effective ministers are often those who have been intellectually involved in serious policy formulation beforehand.

Labour is a working-class party, in terms of votes. Once upon a time, it was also the party of the progressive intelligentsia. As serious a disaster to the Left as the loss of votes and seats in the wake of the Party's civil war was the evaporation of committed intellectual support. From the 1930s until the 1970s, leftness and Labour voting was extremely common among liberal-minded journalists, lawyers, academics, and civil servants, while the cultural world was dominated by it. The foundation of the SDP in 1981 was the culmination of a long period of disaffection among such people. The importance of this numerically tiny layer of society is hard to overestimate – its influence on the media is immense, as it is also, directly, on the climate of opinion in and around government. Regaining the confidence of people who are the most susceptible to reasoned argument and the least available to bribery (because a Labour government would scarcely be to their personal advantage) is especially important. As the only alternative to illiberal Conservatism, Labour can play its positional, left card. But it will also need to make a case that is both more coherent than in the past, and more inspiring.

Among the same group, as well as within the wider electorate, Labour's best strategy may not be to hide its traditional base, but to celebrate it, and to show how a Labour government intends to help the working class's most deprived members. It should not discount either the altruism of many voters, or the benefit to the prosperous of a more united, less selfish, society.

For the Labour Party – as a trade union-based organization – a campaign on behalf of the poor is not the most natural crusade. Although Labour has always expressed concern about those at the bottom (who happen to be its most reliable supporters) it has done so piously: the main energies of the Movement have been fuelled by the interests of employed union members. The increase in unemployment since 1979, however, and the negative redistribution that has occurred in the same period, has widened the range of Labour Movement concerns. It has also (as survey evidence confirms) created a greater sense of unease among the voters.

In *The Next Left: The History of the Future*, the American socialist Michael Harrington comments on the existence in every western country of a 'sub-proletariat' of the unemployed, the precariously employed, immigrants and so on. 'Does one pension them off,' he asks, 'see to it that their material needs are met, but leave them floating and functionless? Or does one understand . . . that such an existence inevitably "marginalizes" human beings?' He concludes that full employment is a necessity; and also that 'one of the essential tasks of the next Left will be to re-establish, in imaginative ways, the historic fact that increases in social justice are the very best stimulus for increased production.'[13] The challenge in Britain for a proudly class-based party is not to target its appeal at the material desires of the better-off (who are unlikely to be convinced, in any case, that Labour can offer them more than the present Government) or to develop policy packages which will offend nobody. It is to provide imaginative proposals which link the requirements of social justice to those of economic efficiency, and call on every voter's sense of community and citizenship.

First published in *Thatcherism*,
ed. Robert Skidelsky (Chatto, 1988)

NOTES

1. In J. Gould and W. M. Kolb, eds., *A Dictionary of the Social Sciences* (Tavistock Publications, 1964), p. 383.

2. See my 'The Labour Left' in C. Cook and I. Taylor, eds., *The Labour Party: An Introduction to its History, Structure and Politics* (Longman, 1980), pp. 163–88.

3. See D. Carlton, *MacDonald versus Henderson: The Foreign Policy of the Second Labour Government* (Macmillan, 1970), p. 16.

4. A. Taylor, *The Trade Unions and the Labour Party* (Croom Helm, 1987), p. 1.

5. *The Evolution of the Labour Party 1910–1924* (Oxford University Press, 1974).

6. See P. Addison, *The Road to 1945: British Politics and the Second World War* (Jonathan Cape, 1977), p. 17.

7. According to the 1899 TUC decision that effectively launched the Labour Party: 'to ensure that working-class opinion should be represented in the House of Commons by men sympathetic with the aims and demands of the Labour Movement, and whose candidatures are promoted by one or other of the organized movements'. Cited in K. Coates and T. Topham, *Trade Unions in Britain*, 3rd edn. (Fontana Press, 1988), p. 334.

8. M. Cole, ed., *Beatrice Webb: Diaries 1924–32* (London, 1949), p. 138.

9. 'A new class of politics', *Guardian*, 15 June 1987.

10. P. Williams, *Hugh Gaitskell* (Jonathan Cape, 1979), pp. 538–9.

11. E. Durbin, *New Jerusalems: The Labour Party and the Economics of Democratic Socialism* (Routledge, 1985), p. 286.

12. *Human Nature in Politics*, 2nd edn. (Constable, 1910), pp. 103–6.

13. Michael Harrington, *The Next Left: the History of a Future* (IB Tauris, 1987), pp. 147–8, 166.

THE JIG IS UP

'THE ACTUAL PRIVATE OBJECT of the most skilled investment today', wrote a famous stock market gambler, 'is to "beat the gun", as the Americans so well express it, to outwit the crowd, and to pass the bad, or depreciating half-crown to the other fellow.' The gambler's name was Maynard Keynes. One happy by-product of the 1987 Global Village Crash could be to bring the Bloomsbury reprobate back into fashion.

There has been no shortage of explanations after, or even during, the event. The simplest is the 'bigger fool' theory, one writer's refinement of Keynes's 'beating the gun'. People go on buying shares greedily and foolishly for as long as they believe that there are others greedier and foolhardier than themselves. Then the fools run out.

Between January and August, Dow Jones rose 40 per cent in a country where the ratio of federal debt to GNP had increased from a third to a half in seven years. So what could you expect? The fact is that few people did expect it, otherwise it would never have happened. That is the point about stock market crashes. It is also something which should make us wary of the latest expert projections. Meanwhile commonsense indicates one thing. The fastest dissipation of financial vapour since the South Sea Bubble has blown away the centrepiece of the Tory programme as surely as forced devaluation did for Labour in 1967.

For the moment, the normal rituals surrounding stock exchange disasters will be observed. These may be summed up under the heading: Nothing Has Changed. This in itself, however, involves a dangerous contortion. On the one hand, business as usual is the order of the day. On the other, there is a flurry of activity aimed at limiting the damage.

Ministers who have been leading evangelists of the free market idea, and who have not been averse to the occasional flutter themselves, have suddenly become very pompous on the subject of the trade in equities. They share the view of the Director-General of the CBI, that much of it is 'candyfloss', without solid basis in the real world. According to the Chancellor, the behaviour of the stock exchanges has been 'rather absurd'. In a twinkling King Market has been dethroned. We are now advised to regard the ex-monarch as a untrustworthy fantasist, the purveyor of misleading gossip.

Officially, the economy is strong. Mr Lawson appeared on television the other night to tell us so. The growth rate is high (forget the abysmal early Thatcher years). Inflation is low (forget the unemployed). Manufacturing output has climbed back to where it was when Labour left office. 'There is nothing in the business situation to justify nervousness,' says Nigel Lawson. Oops, sorry. Actually the remark was made by the President of the Continental Illinois Bank at roughly the same stage in 1929. But never mind. The Chancellor's gist was much the same.

'Perhaps never before or since', wrote J. K. Galbraith of the interwar disaster, 'have so many people taken the measure of the economic prospects and found them so favourable.' *Plus ça change*. The trouble is that they can be right and wrong at the same time. Mr Lawson, who was happy enough to take some of the credit for the bull, dismisses the bear as not his responsibility. It is all the Americans' fault – for having a deficit, for having a President who cannot string together a coherent sentence, for confidence-destroying mishaps in the Middle East. Unfortunately, that won't help us if the American sneeze is big enough – whether or not the British economy has become tough as nails.

Which of course it hasn't. Though better in some respects, it remains perilously flawed in others. Edward Heath's question – 'What economic miracle?' – remains worryingly apt. It is not just that recovery has been bought at a terrible price to the former industrial heartlands. It is also that recovery remains extremely brittle. Roy Hattersley's Jeremiah warnings of balance of payments difficulties, delivered at election time and therefore universally disregarded, could still prove correct. The rise in British manufacturing output has not been matched by growth in exports. Oil prices peaked last year: this year, North Sea Oil's contribution to UK balance of payments will have dropped by a third. Despite Chesterfield euphoria, the crisis of capitalism is not at hand. But a second, homegrown London crash, followed by a serious economic downturn, has become a lot more likely.

Whether there is another, deeper slump or not, the crash is bound to become a political, as much as an economic, marker. October 1987 will be remembered as the month in which the Government had to give up buying electoral support with large sums of speculative money.

In retrospect, it was all so easy. The soaring of the index made successive privatizations wildly popular with an ever-growing army of prospering punters. Popularity encouraged the Government to print more bits of paper which doubled in value in the grateful voters' hands. In 1983 shareownership, concentrated among an exclusive 5 per cent, was not electorally significant; in 1987, distributed among 23 per cent (half of whom lived in the South-East and Midlands and two-thirds of whom were lower-middle- or working-class), it had emphatically become so. It was a clever wheeze but it won't work again. The happy game of national monopoly in which there were only winners has vanished. Whatever happens over BP, we need expect no U-turns in privatization policy. But it is unlikely that new issues will ever be launched with the same ideological razzamatazz, the naked appeal to avarice, as in the past.

Will some of the get-rich quick, something-for-nothing mood of the mid-1980s begin to shift? It is possible. Certainly the rest of Thatcherism had already been changing. Monetarism is the obvious example. It was the Government's loss of interest in M_3, floating exchange rates, strict adherence to spending targets, not its earlier obsession with them, that contributed to growth. Recently we have had currency devaluations, tax-cuts to stimulate the economy and old-style fine tuning. What Galbraith has said of the US ('we have had irresponsible Keynesianism in these last years from the Reagan administration') applies increasingly here. The reaction of both governments to the crash provides further evidence that monetarism survives only in the ivory tower of right-wing seminars. Monetarists would have imposed a squeeze – as happened in 1929, with catastrophic results. In 1987, both the Americans and British cut interest rates on a principle of which Keynes would have approved: if businesses are in trouble, let them borrow.

Monetarism is a handy doctrine for a dominant economy, like Britain in the nineteenth century, or for a yuppy one, like Japan today. In more mellow, problematic countries it rapidly proves unworkable, and the resulting contradictions in policy help to create international uncertainty. One American economist has argued that the world is economically happiest when it knows who's boss: before the First

World War, Britain was clearly in charge, and after the Second, America. Chaos arose between the wars because nobody was sure where economic power really lay. Arguably, we are back there now.

For Thatcherism, what is there left? Not much, except the radical right-wingery of union-bashing, school-disrupting and a refusal to spend money to create services and jobs. Previously, these fitted into a grand scheme, the Big Idea. Doubtless some domestic policies in the pipeline will still get popular support. But now that the Big Idea has popped, there will be plenty of people asking whether so-called gains in public 'freedom' are worth the sacrifices in health, schools, benefits and employment.

Tory hegemony is too strong a fortress to fall at one knock, especially when there are four years ahead in which to rebuild the ramparts. Nevertheless, for the first time since Labour bungled its Westland chances, it is possible to foresee a different landscape. 'The jig is up,' Max Gordon telephoned to Marx (Groucho) when prices tumbled in 1929. Keynes put it more suavely in *The General Theory*: 'Speculators may do no harm as bubbles on a steady stream of enterprise. But the position is serious when enterprise becomes the bubble on a whirlpool of speculation.' Millions of people, some with fingers badly singed, have suddenly had enough of speculation. It is a good week for Labour to begin its policy review.

New Statesman, 30 October 1987

THATCHERISM IN ITS
MAOIST PHASE

WHEN TORY CENTRAL OFFICE declares its preference for a 'moderate' candidate over a reactionary head-banger, as it did before the Young Conservative poll last week, we need to pay attention. Can the Government be going soft? The explanation, as you will have guessed, is not nearly so appealing. The hierarchy's cool-it call to the green-wellie brigade reflects the harsh new reality of Tory power struggles. Since last June, the centre of gravity has moved to the right. So, far from indicating a liberalization, the rise of the Tory loonies – and the need to resist them – is a symptom of the lack of effective opposition, of any kind, to the Government's recent campaigns.

Do not blame Neil Kinnock: there was never much scope for the *official* Opposition, in what Lord Hailsham once aptly called our elective dictatorship – at least at this stage in a parliament. In the past, however, there were a number of other restraints: the civil service, local government, the trade unions, even the media. All these have now been neutralized or reduced to a state of quivering sycophancy. As for the electorate, most ministers now believe that whatever the Government does, the Tories will always win.

There used to be two other limits to inner party, and especially prime ministerial, absolutism. One was Establishment ethos, a soporific substance, like old port, and good at cooling ideological ardour. The other, potentially most important, consisted of the Government's own backbenchers. Today, the ethos is no more, while the Tory backbenches offer little except knighthood hunters and ministerial hopefuls.

Gone are the days when the parliamentary party was a quagmire of patrician sentimentality about the deserving poor. Since the election, the hard (i.e. wet) Left has been reduced to a handful of embittered notables, whose sole Cabinet representative, Peter Walker, serves out time as manager of a Mongolian power-station. Apart from Edward Heath and Sir Ian Gilmour, there are the three Xes – Hugh Dykes,

David Knox and Robin Hicks – who glumly toast the memory of the late Lord Stockton. But these are gamblers who went on obstinately, and for too long, backing the wrong number. Though their constituency associations charitably tolerate them as eccentrics, they have few important friends at Westminster.

What used to be the mushy middle of the Tory Party is also greatly reduced. There are some with small majorities who get anxious about their marginal constituents. Doctrinal doubts, however, are becoming rarer. Keynesianism has become a shameful vice and clean-living members of the Prime Minister's team like Douglas Hurd, George Younger, Norman Fowler, Kenneths Baker and Clark, have long since disassociated themselves from it.

Typical of the rising generation is Christopher Patten, once errand-boy between the Prime Minister and Heath. At Overseas Development, he has risen to the challenge: in contrast to his dourly principled, old Etonian (ex-*New Society* editing) predecessor, Timothy Raison, he has shown that even so unpromising an outpost can be turned into a pulpit. Recently, in Africa, he was to be heard lecturing the inhabitants of some of the world's poorest states on the need to link aid to market economics. He should go far. Even the maverick Heseltine, who has nothing to fear from the Prime Minister because he has no hope of office until she goes, has found it prudent to trim to the right. Hence his curious little book, published last year, *Where There's a Will*, and some impressive television tub-thumping in support of the American slave-labour scheme, workfare.

The problem for the Tory soft Left, indeed, mirrors Labour's own dilemma. It is not just that would-be critics no longer see much point in stepping out of line. It is also that it is becoming exceedingly difficult to gain attention for old-fashioned tunes in the face of an innovative leadership that is so damned popular.

Much of what Mrs Thatcher is now doing is the sort of thing which estate agents, ten or twenty years ago, grumbled to barmaids at the Conservative Club *ought* to be done and bloody well *would* be done if they were ever in power. Now the estate-agent tendency rules, and the One Nation fellows are left buying the drinks if they are not – like eager Kenneth Baker – scribbling out lyrics in the new idiom.

There are a few of the old-timers who, in their cups, wonder hopefully whether she may not now be going over the top. The present, adrenalizing, ego-expanding crusade, they argue, goes much further than Thatcherism in the first two parliaments. The secret of the Prime Minister's success has been that, unlike the hapless Labour leadership, she doesn't stay awake at night totting up opinion poll statistics on her fingers. She acts and expects to take public opinion with her. Council house sales and privatization were ideological initiatives. The 'popular capitalism' slogan came later. Its impact, however, stoked the furnace of her messianism – perhaps dangerously.

This is a government, and above all a Prime Minister, that now believes it can break any convention, dispatch any sacred cow to the abattoir, with absolute impunity. In the present mood of exuberant iconoclasm, change and reform have become ends in themselves, and the rhetoric of dynamism has become the touchstone, not just of virility, but also of party patriotism.

Yet it may be, say some, that the very source of her apparent strength may become a fatal flaw. The removal of restraint has also meant the removal of protection. The contrast, once again, is with the Labour Party – and this time not entirely to Labour's disadvantage. Labour is a party of rules, majorities, electoral colleges, vested interests, holy scriptural texts. The Tories, on the other hand, have no constitution. Their conference is a rally, not a forum. They have no such thing as party policy, and they have no mechanism for the voicing of loyal (or disloyal) criticism. Tory loyalty has always meant obedience. Such a code worked satisfactorily when there was a presumption of consensus-seeking. From the Prime Minister's point of view, it continues to work in the charismatic, non-consensual present. But in the long run it is highly unstable.

It is not just that permanent revolutions are, in practice, impermanent. It is also that Thatcherism, in its maoist phase, has unleashed forces it may not be able to control. Among the estate agents, the Thatcher upheaval has opened a Pandora's box of unrealizable aspirations. Already (in health, for instance, where the Tories are proposing to smash up the structure they created) there is a sense of the Government meeting itself coming back. Will the Education Bill actually raise 'standards' in schools? Will the poll tax really solve the problem of local government finance? Will private enterprise tidy up the inner cities? There are too many chickens which, sooner or later, are liable to wing their way home to roost.

So argue the Conservative wishful-thinkers privately, and they may yet be right. For the time being, however, all that the Prime Minister confronts in her own party to the left of her is an ocean of silence. There is now, literally, no alternative. What would happen if she was run over by a bus? Once upon a time, a reversion of the crown to the wets seemed likely. Today it seems more probable that Thatcherism, like Gaullism in France, will outlive its creator.

It is even suggested that if the bus left her breathing, she would use her enormous authority (as Macmillan did in 1963) to influence the succession. The name that is frequently mentioned in this connection is the still-influential, and ambitious, Norman Tebbit. That is another reason why the most sensible tactic for Tory careerists, unless they take the very long view, is to do what they are told. It is also why as we have recently seen in the scuffle over the chair of what was once a non-ideological marriage bureau – the only significant pressure from within the Conservative Party comes from the bonkers, and exceedingly nasty, ultra Right.

New Statesman, 11 March 1988

THE END OF HISTORY

WHEN FRANCIS FUKUYAMA published an article called 'The End of History?' in the summer of 1989, he became a celebrity overnight, and the phrase 'end of history' tripped off the tongues of politicians and commentators around the globe. What caused the controversy was not so much what the article said but its timing. Appearing as the Berlin Wall bulged and teetered, Fukuyama's tentative prediction happened to coincide with a genuine ending: the moment of stunned realization in the West that the old certainties of the Cold War were over for good, and that a new world-view was required.

Since that time, the disappearance of the Soviet Empire has made Fukuyama's ideas even more relevant and may even be said to have vindicated them. At the least, this book, which fleshes out the original argument and bats off critics, shows that the fuss was not about nothing. Fukuyama is an ambitious thinker, whose limpid style and confident familiarity with every major political philosopher since Plato show him to be no computerizing futurologist. So beguiling, indeed, is the author's prose, and so dazzling are his intellectual fireworks, that the reader is half-persuaded, before putting down the book and realizing that the central contention is bunkum.

Now that Karl Marx and his communist utopia are dead, Fukuyama asks us to exhume Hegel. What interests him is the Hegelian concept of history as a series of types of human consciousness – value systems, religions, ideologies – leading up to a universal belief in principles of liberty, beyond which no further progress would occur. Such an 'end of history' – in the Hegelian projection – would not prevent people killing one another, composing symphonies or discovering new facts about the universe, but it would entail a certain worldwide stability; for liberalism lacks the 'contradictions' of earlier forms of social organization and would therefore bring the historical dialectic to a close.

The End of History and the Last Man, Francis Fukuyama (Hamish Hamilton, 1992)

The questions Fukuyama poses are these: assuming that modern democracies are made safe from external enemies, should we believe that successful democratic societies will stay that way indefinitely? And, if so, can the whole of human development be seen as a 'universal history' providing a pattern leading up to such a state of grace?

These questions are similar to those asked by mid-twentieth century 'modernization theorists' in the United States and elsewhere, who wondered whether industrial change followed a coherent pattern of growth, and would eventually produce uniform social and political structures across differing cultures: what the American sociologist Daniel Bell called 'the end of ideology'. A distinctive feature of Fukuyama's questions and affirmative answers, however, is the challenging suggestion of permanency. Against the 'relativist' opposition – those who believe that all political ideas are relative to their time and place – Fukuyama insists that, on the contrary, the principles of liberal democracy are not only lasting, but contain integral safety-valves and stabilizers.

Developing the Platonic idea of *thymos* (the human desire for recognition), he identifies in his own concept of *megalothymia* (the desire to be recognized as superior to other people) a potential 'contradiction' and threat to democracy. He argues, however, that advanced democracies have found ways of sublimating 'megalothymic', or aggressively competitive, tendencies into harmless risk-taking activities like making money on the bond market, or, as in California (the 'most post-historical part of the United States'), pursuing pointlessly dangerous pursuits like hang-gliding, sky-diving or marathon-running.

The problem with such reasoning is not that it lacks telling points, and certainly not that it lacks ingenuity, but that it requires a good deal more evidence to back it up. The author makes much of the breakneck speed with which the world is hurtling towards democracy, and even offers a quaint chart that shows how it all started with the American Declaration of Independence in 1776, since when there has been a steady growth in the number of liberal democracies, give or take the odd dip. He is quite right to direct our attention to the extraordinary late twentieth-century vogue for democracy, which has swept away right-wing authoritarianism in southern Europe and transformed Latin America, before getting to work on east Europe, and is now nibbling away at Africa and Asia.

Yet he does not dispose of the obvious objection that the success of liberal democracy may be more economic than political: a happy but ephemeral by-product of the contemporary success of capitalism, and of the desire of the poor to get in on the act. Meal tickets dispensed by the first world to the second and the third in the form of aid or better trading terms have generally had an ideological price-tag. The author does not fully perceive the importance for the spread of democracy of the association between full bellies and free ballots, or the likely effects when that turns out to be wishful thinking.

He does not seem to appreciate that capitalism itself is historically the least stable of economic systems and is evolving at a pace that makes it impossible to see what is happening now, let alone to anticipate the ever-changing political and social consequences. Nor does he notice that 'liberal democracy' – bureaucratized, internationalized, televised – is profoundly different from what it was like, not just in the days of Hegel, but before the Second World War, so different that it is doubtful whether one should use the same label.

Humanity lived in a kind of equilibrium with nature for millennia before recorded history began, and we may guess that unless self-extinction intercedes it will eventually attain some new balance. Eventually, however, may be a very long time. The present position is one of growing disequilibrium, which a proliferation of liberal states may actually exacerbate. There is certainly no more reason to see an end-point in liberal democracy than there would once have been to regard feudalism, absolute monarchy, or totalitarianism in the same way. And there is little reason not to treat 'the end of history' thesis as anything but a symptom of the worldwide need for reassurance.

Independent on Sunday, 1 March 1992

IF YOU CAN'T STAND THE HEAT

IT IS A DISTRESSING FACT about political decisions that there are people who make them. Distressing, that is, to the considerable number of other people who would like to, but don't.

Because distressing, partially hidden. One of the jobs of democracy and bureaucracy in a top-heavy modern state is to disguise the power of a few erratic individuals. For all our hostility to red tape, we feel happier with the notion of government by collective wisdom or folly, by due process or rule book, than with the reality of government by arbitrary whim. Even, or especially, on the left, there is an image of the office-holder as a faintly ridiculous puppet, blown about by impersonal interests and forces, and lacking independent will.

Harry Truman was supposed to have kept on his desk a notice with the words 'the buck stops here' to remind himself and others that in the end somebody had to decide. This truth about power is particularly disturbing to those who make their living out of knowing about politics as opposed to practising it.

Like book critics, and sports commentators, political writers frequently despise their subject matter. Contempt is the handmaiden of jealousy: but it may also, in this case, be a product of quite justifiable feelings of moral and intellectual superiority. For the power of the powerful has little to do with talent, still less with virtue. Often it is based on money, class, patronage, persistence, obsession and luck.

Powerful people are charming, egotistical, outgoing, paranoid, sentimental, subtle, lonely, sensitive, pompous, wary, sly and good at remembering names and faces. But they are seldom imaginative or well informed, and, indeed, there are obstacles (boredom, impatience, an ability to see beyond short-term expediency) to imaginative or well-informed people seeking and obtaining power.

Hence those who Arthur Koestler called the *demi-vierges* – the philosophers, historians, novelists and journalists who combine provocative words, snow-white principles and political inaction – tend to look down on contemporaries who have a practical importance. The business of politics and policy-making is seen as sterile and compromising, its practitioners ludicrous figures of fun. The bottom line, that powerful people are powerful, is comfortably and dangerously forgotten.

Harry Truman spoke also of the temperature in the kitchen. If you don't like it, he said, keep out: advice which most of those who write about politics have prudently obeyed, preferring the illusions of extra-parliamentary campaigning, or the higher altitudes of theory. Unfortunately, not everybody has been able to follow suit. There was no escaping the kitchen in Hiroshima or Nagasaki after the same mild, unobtrusive and generally derided President Truman had given the order; or, for that matter, the ovens of Auschwitz, product of the doss-house ravings of a media-manipulator laughed at by the intellectuals of Weimar. Certainly *homo sapiens* is the only species in which the little decisions of little unimpressive individuals can so directly shape or so swiftly end the lives of such large numbers of the rest.

'Beneath the rule of men entirely great', declared Lord Lytton to an appreciative audience of Victorian scribblers, 'the pen is mightier than the sword.' Alas, the history of our century suggests otherwise: the great contours of military and political organization in recent generations have been mapped, not by thinkers, but by desperate persons of action.

It was not Marx or Engels who invented the Gulag, but Stalin. It was not Nietzsche or Richard Wagner who gassed the Jews, but Hitler. More immediately, it has not been Friedrich von Hayek who has wrecked the British economy but Margaret Thatcher; and, should Labour win the next election, it will not be R. H. Tawney, Eric Hobsbawm or E. P. Thompson who tries to repair the damage, but Neil Kinnock. With each, tragically or absurdly, pens raised in spirited defence have been or will be almost wholly ineffective.

There is of course a difference between writing under or against dictatorship, and writing in the conditions of a parliamentary régime. In some countries, the mere act of unauthorized publication is a political defiance. In contemporary Britain, by contrast, it is usually self-indulgence.

Most political writing is either the system talking to itself (journalistic) or as arid and empty as the Sahara (academic), or a pornographic tickling of the fancies of the faithful (ideological). Most political writing in newspapers and journals passes through the body politic as casually as weak beer. Political writing between hard covers is shifted, pages uncut, from warehouse to institutional library shelf, unread except occasionally by a reviewer.

Political writings published by political presses, it is true, can provide quarry for parliamentary speeches. Recently it has become fashionable for politicians to quote the sayings of sainted elders. But this is a front. Serious politicians almost never read serious books.

Thus there are two quite separate worlds. In one, the brokerage of power is primitive, instinctive, usually private and unrecorded, involving intimate rivalries, terrors and memories. Here, instant reporting serves as a lubricant rather than an influence, a means of communicating coded messages and threats. In the other, there is a grinding of theoretical axes, the offering of prescription and rebuke. The two have almost no connection.

In the first, spades are called spades, judgements are commonsensical. In the second, political writers are original, bold, surprising, witty; they sort out the Labour Party and the GLC, give trade unions their marching orders, ban the Bomb, save the starving millions in Ethiopia. In the second, the reality of the first is hazy, a backcloth to argument and clear thinking. In the first, the second does not exist.

A cause of confusion is that political writers are sometimes famous long after death. The fame of powerful people burns like an August shooting star, or not at all: only a few (the Hitlers and Thatchers) are recalled by any but their contemporaries. By contrast, the works of lesser poets and novelists – without influence in their lifetime or, probably, after their death – become school textbooks.

Let us not overstate. A small number of authors *do* affect the climate of opinion, occasionally contributing to the stock of political language and idiom. Some works have been tributaries, flowing into the river of our times, or have helped provide a framework for the understanding of events. These are the exceptions: seized upon by less fertile writers who build ingenious and incomprehensible structures of ideas upon their backs, and promote a strange process of canonization. Yet fame and merit are to be distinguished from concrete effect. In the present century there has scarcely been a single British writer not directly involved in government who has had an immediate, major impact on the conduct of affairs or the progress of events.

Recently I have been editing for publication some political diaries of the Second World War – and acquiring thereby an encyclopaedic and entirely useless knowledge of the sometimes grubby, sometimes glittering careers of the great and semi-great of Westminster and Whitehall who now inhabit a kind of Hades: the footnotes.

What most merits fame is in silence hid. The vast majority of these characters – Cabinet ministers, union leaders, generals, press barons, civil servants, businessmen – are, however, justly forgotten. Few were noble, brilliant or even attractive. Most were vain, ambitious and normal. Many exerted great power over their contemporaries and (since we won the war and, without them, might have lost it) over the generations that have followed. Except in an official minute or Order of the Day, almost none gave a fig for the written word.

And so also in our own era. Political writing is part of the necessary froth of freedom: like decadent painting, a healthy sign of non-interference. But its direct influence is virtually as slight. At worst, it is a fatuous toadying to a closed-mind clientèle, or the present-day equivalent of angel-counting on the point of a needle; at best a branch of show business – even, perhaps, a very minor art form.

Guardian, 29 August 1985

Index

Harold Wilson

Ben Pimlott

'One of the great political biographies of the century.'
A. N. Wilson, *Evening Standard*

'The rehabilitation of Wilson has begun – and Ben Pimlott, the best British political biographer now writing, has made a hugely impressive job of it . . . His narrative of the young Wilson, from sickly boy scout to academic pupil of the formidable William Beveridge, and then to chirpy junior minister is quite outstanding – clear, thoughtful and gripping. This early part of the book is central to its larger achievement, since Pimlott shocks the reader out of basic anti-Wilson prejudice by demanding a human sympathy for him. The little, blinking, stubborn boy, hiding his hurt with cocky self-confidence, lives on as a permanent presence within the powerful politician . . . Some biographies enter the political discourse at once, thanks to their innate qualities and lucky timing. There are so many echoes of the Wilson years in the politics of today that this happy fate must surely belong to Pimlott's book. Wilson's soured relationship with the press (and the terrible problems it caused for him) – the conflict within him between national leadership and good party management – even the growing debate about national decline – are all suggestive and worth lingering over. As, indeed, are almost all of these 734 well-researched and finely written pages.'   Andrew Marr, *Independent*

'A masterly piece of political writing.'
Bernard Crick, *New Statesman*

'The narrative gallops along, sweeping the reader with it in a rush of excitement. A mass of complex detail is marshalled with the art that conceals art.'   David Marquand, *Times Literary Supplement*

'Fascinating . . . Pimlott the X-ray has produced another work of formidable penetration.'   Roy Jenkins, *Observer*

ISBN 0 00 637955 9